SECURE Act and the Further Consolidated Appropriations Act, 2020

Law, Explanation and Analysis

Editorial Staff Publication

This publication is designed to provide accurate and authoritative information in regard to the subject matter covered. It is sold with the understanding that the publisher is not engaged in rendering legal, accounting, or other professional service. If legal advice or other expert assistance is required, the services of a competent professional person should be sought.

ISBN 978-1-5438-2290-8

© 2020 CCH Incorporated and its affiliates. All rights reserved.

No claim is made to original government works; however, within this Product or Publication, the following are subject to CCH's copyright: (1) the gathering, compilation, and arrangement of such government materials; (2) the magnetic translation and digital conversion of data, if applicable; (3) the historical, statutory and other notes and references; and (4) the commentary and other materials.

Printed in the United States of America

Introduction

SECURE Act Implements Major Changes in Retirement Benefit Plan Rules

On December 20, 2019, President Trump signed into law a $1.4 trillion spending package that, while primarily designed to fund federal agencies through September 2020, includes provisions which substantially modify many of the rules governing retirement plans. The Setting Every Community Up for Retirement Enhancement Act (SECURE Act) (incorporated into the Further Consolidated Appropriations Act, 2020 (P.L. 116-94)) promises to have a major impact on the structure and administration of retirement plans. The impact will be greater given that the sweeping rule changes generally apply to tax years beginning after 2019.

Among the changes, the Act: authorizes a new "open" Multiple Employer Plan (MEP), called a Pooled Employer Plan (PEP); increases the automatic enrollment safe harbor contribution cap from 10 to 15 percent; extends the amendment deadline for nonelective safe harbor plans; increases the tax credit for small employer pension plan start-up costs; repeals the maximum age for traditional IRA contributions; authorizes penalty-free IRA withdrawals of up to $5,000 to cover birth or adoption expenses; enhances the portability of lifetime income options; extends plan eligibility to long-term, part-time employees; increases the age for taking required minimum distributions, from age $70^1/_2$ to age 72; allows employers to treat qualified plans adopted after the close of the tax year as having been adopted as of the last day of the tax year; requires benefit statements to include lifetime income disclosures; provides a fiduciary safe harbor covering the selection of lifetime income providers; expands the cross-testing nondiscrimination rules to provide relief to closed defined benefit plans; effectively eliminates the "stretch IRA" as a tool for managing retirement assets, by modifying the required distribution rules for designated beneficiaries; and increases the available uses for 529 plans. Other provisions of the Further Consolidated Appropriations Act authorize relief for the pension and welfare benefit funds of the mine workers; allow the use of retirement funds for qualified disaster distributions; and repeal the Cadillac Tax on high cost employer-sponsored health plans.

The stated goals of the SECURE Act are to expand retirement savings, improve plan administration, simplify existing rules, and preserve retirement income. Whether the Act will attain its stated goals remains to be seen, but it will afford plenty of opportunity for new planning strategies.

However, plan sponsors and administrators are cautioned that, while Congress sat on the bill for months, they are not afforded the luxury of delay, given the accelerated effective date of most of the Act's provisions. Accordingly, most qualified plans will need to adopt amendments implementing the Act, under the prescribed remedial amendment period, by the 2022 plan year. In the interim, all concerned parties may expect an abundance of regulatory guidance from the IRS, DOL, and PBGC.

Explanation and Analysis

SECURE Act Provisions of the Further Consolidated Appropriations Act, 2020: Law, Explanation and Analysis provides a thorough analysis of the SECURE Act and other provisions of the Further Consolidated Appropriations Act affecting retirement and health benefits. The detailed analysis will help plan sponsors, administrators, and service providers in navigating the multiple changes, the vast majority of which go into effect in 2020.

About This Work and Wolters Kluwer

Wolters Kluwer is providing practitioners with a single integrated law and explanation of the SECURE Act and other retirement and health related provisions of the Further Consolidated Appropriations Act. The *SECURE Act Provisions of the Further Consolidated Appropriations Act, 2020: Law, Explanation and Analysis* continues the Wolters Kluwer tradition of empowering pension, benefits, employment, and payroll professionals with the information and resources necessary to help them understand and work with new laws as they take effect. Other products related to the new legislation, including the Pension Plan Guide, Employee Benefits Management, and the Payroll Management Guide may be found at www.wolterskluwerlr.com

February 2020

Wolters Kluwer
EDITORIAL STAFF

Jan Gerstein, J.D., *Editorial Director*

Barbara S. O'Dell, J.D., *Managing Editor*

Explanation and Analysis

Glenn Sulzer, J.D., *Lead Author*

Lauren Bikoff, MLS	Georgia D. Koutouzos, J.D.	Elizabeth Pope, J.D.
Deirdre Kennedy, J.D.	Kerry McInerney, J.D.	John Strzelecki, J.D.
Kathleen Kennedy-Luczak, J.D.	Linda O'Brien, J.D., LL.M.	Tulay Turan, J.D.
Melanie King, J.D.	Linda Panszczyk, J.D.	

Print Production

Theresa J. Jensen
Manager, Production

Amy Styka
Production Coordinator

Kathleen E. Watts
Manager, Production

¶1 Features of This Publication

This publication is your complete guide to the retirement-related provisions of *The Setting Every Community Up for Retirement Enhancement Act (SECURE Act)* (incorporated into the Further Consolidated Appropriations Act, 2020 (2020 Appropriations Act) (P.L. 116-94)).

The core portion of this publication contains the Explanations of this Act. The explanations outline all of the retirement plan and employee benefits changes and what they mean for you and your clients. The explanations also feature practical guidance, examples, and expert commentary on the law changes.

The publication also contains numerous other features designed to help you locate and understand the changes made by this Act. These features include cross references to related materials, detailed effective dates, and numerous finding tables and a topical index. A more detailed description of these features appears below.

HIGHLIGHTS

Highlights are quick summaries of the major provisions of the *SECURE Act* (incorporated into the 2020 Appropriations Act). The Highlights are arranged in chapter and paragraph order. At the end of each summary is a paragraph reference to the more detailed Explanation on that topic, giving you an easy way to find the portions of the publication that are of most interest to you. *Highlights begin at ¶5.*

EXPLANATIONS

Explanations are designed to give you a complete, accessible understanding of the new law. Explanations are arranged by subject for ease of use. There are two main finding devices you can use to locate explanations on a given topic. These are:

- A detailed table of contents at the beginning of the publication listing all of the Explanations of the new law; and
- A table of contents preceding each chapter.

Each Explanation contains special features to aid in your complete understanding of the new law. These include:

- A summary at the beginning of each explanation providing a brief overview of the new law;
- A background or prior law discussion that puts the law changes into perspective;
- Editorial aids, including examples, comments, and compliance tips, that highlight the impact of the new law;
- Captions at the end of each explanation identifying the Internal Revenue Code and ERISA sections added, amended or repealed, as well as the Act sections containing the changes;
- Cross references to the law paragraphs related to the explanation; and
- A line highlighting the effective date of each law change, marked by an arrow symbol.

The Explanations begin at ¶100.

SECURE ACT

While the primary focus of this book is on the retirement-related provisions of the *SECURE Act* (incorporated into the 2020 Appropriations Act), other Divisions of the Further Consolidated Appropriations Act, 2020, are also part of the discussion. Divisions M through Q (including the SECURE Act) of the 2020 Appropriations Act have been reproduced in their entirety, *beginning at ¶5000.*

AMENDED LAW PROVISIONS

Changes to the Internal Revenue Code (Code) made by Divisions M through Q, including the *SECURE Act*, of the 2020 Appropriations Act appear under the heading "Internal Revenue Code Sections Added, Amended or Repealed" beginning at ¶6000. *Any changed or added law text is set out in italics.* Deleted Code text, or the Code provision prior to amendment, appears in the Amendment Notes following each reconstructed Code provision. An effective date for each Code change is also provided.

Changes to Employer Retirement Income Security Act (ERISA) made by Divisions M through Q, including the *SECURE Act*, of the 2020 Appropriations Act, appear under the heading "ERISA Sections Added, Amended or Repealed" beginning at ¶7000. *Any changed or added law text is set out in italics.* Deleted ERISA text, or the ERISA provision prior to amendment, appears in the Amendment Notes following each reconstructed ERISA provision. An effective date for each ERISA change is also provided.

SPECIAL TABLES

Other special tables and finding devices in this book include:

- A table cross-referencing Internal Revenue Code Sections to the Explanations (*see* ¶10,001);
- A table showing all Internal Revenue Code Sections added, amended or repealed (*see* ¶10,005);
- A table showing Act Sections Amending the Internal Revenue Code (*see* ¶10,010);
- A table cross-referencing ERISA Sections to the Explanations (*see* ¶10,015);
- A table showing all ERISA Sections added, amended or repealed (*see* ¶10,020); and
- A table showing Act Sections Amending ERISA (*see* ¶10,025).

¶2 Table of Contents

¶1   Features of this Publication

¶5   Highlights

EXPLANATION

¶100   Chapter 1   Expansion of Retirement Savings

¶200   Chapter 2   Administrative Improvements

¶300   Chapter 3   Revenue Provisions

¶400   Chapter 4   Bipartisan American Miners Act

¶500   Chapter 5   Health and Welfare Benefits

LAW

¶5000   Further Consolidated Appropriations Act, 2020 (P.L. 116-94, enacted December 20, 2019)

¶6000   Internal Revenue Code Sections Added, Amended or Repealed

¶7000   ERISA Sections Added, Amended Or Repealed

SPECIAL TABLES

¶10,001   Internal Revenue Code Section to Explanation Table

¶10,005   Internal Revenue Code Sections Added, Amended or Repealed

¶10,010   Act Sections Amending Internal Revenue Code Sections

¶10,015   ERISA Sections to Explanation Table

¶10,020   ERISA Sections Added, Amended or Repealed

¶10,025   Act Sections Amending ERISA Sections

TOPICAL INDEX

Page 309   Topical Index

¶3 Detailed Table of Contents

CHAPTER 1. EXPANSION OF RETIREMENT SAVINGS

¶100	Multiple Employer Plans: Pooled Employer Plans
¶110	Increase in Cap on Automatic Enrollment Safe Harbor Contributions
¶115	Notice Requirement for Nonelective Safe Harbor Plans Eliminated
¶120	Amendment Deadline for Nonelective Safe Harbor Plans Extended
¶125	Expansion of Plan Eligibility to Long-Term, Part-Time Employees
¶130	Increase in Tax Credit for Small Employer Pension Plan Start-Up Costs
¶135	Small Employer Automatic Enrollment Credits
¶140	Treatment of Taxable Non-Tuition Fellowship and Stipend Payments as Compensation for IRA Purposes
¶145	Repeal of Maximum Age for Traditional IRA Contributions
¶150	Difficulty of Care Payments Treated as Compensation in Applying Retirement Contribution Limits
¶155	Prohibition on Plan Loans Through Credit Cards
¶160	Penalty-Free Plan Withdrawals to Cover Birth or Adoption Expenses
¶165	Increased Age for Taking Required Minimum Distributions
¶170	Plan Amendments: Remedial Amendment Periods
¶175	Special Disaster-Related Rules for Use of Retirement Funds
¶180	Portability of Lifetime Income Options
¶185	Treatment of Custodial Accounts on Termination of 403(b) Plans
¶190	Clarification of Retirement Account Rules Related to Church-Controlled Organizations
¶195	Special Rules for Minimum Funding Standards for Frozen Community Newspaper Plans

CHAPTER 2. ADMINISTRATIVE IMPROVEMENTS

¶200	Treatment of Plans Adopted by Filing Due Date as in Effect as of Close of Year
¶205	Combined Annual Report for Group of Plans
¶210	Lifetime Income Disclosure
¶220	Fiduciary Safe Harbor for Selection of Lifetime Income Provider
¶225	Expansion of Nondiscrimination Cross-Testing Rules

¶230 Modification of PBGC Premiums for Cooperative and Small Employer Charity (CSEC) Plans

CHAPTER 3. REVENUE PROVISIONS

¶300 Modification of Required Distribution Rules for Designated Beneficiaries

¶305 Increase in Failure to File Return Penalty

¶310 Increased Plan Reporting Penalties

CHAPTER 4. BIPARTISAN AMERICAN MINERS ACT

¶400 Treasury Transfers to 1974 UMWA Pension Plan

¶405 Funding Multiemployer Health Benefit Plans

¶410 Reduction in Minimum Age for Allowable In-Service Distributions

CHAPTER 5. HEALTH AND WELFARE BENEFITS

¶500 Repeal of Medical Device Excise Tax

¶505 Repeal of Annual Fee on Health Insurance Providers

¶510 Repeal of Excise Tax on High Cost Employer-Sponsored Health Coverage

¶515 Pharmacy Benefit Services Exemption from Certain ERISA Requirements

¶520 Employer Credit for Paid Family and Medical Leave

¶525 Benefits Provided to Volunteer Firefighters and Emergency Responders

¶530 Repeal of Increase in Unrelated Business Taxable Income for Certain Fringe Benefit Expenses

¶540 Expansion of Section 529 Plans

¶545 Credit for Health Insurance Costs of Eligible Individuals

¶5 Highlights

EXPANSION OF RETIREMENT SAVINGS

¶100 **Multiple Employer Plans: Pooled Employer Plans.** A new "open" Multiple Employer Plan (MEP), called a Pooled Employer Plan (PEP), is authorized, effective for plan years beginning after December 31, 2020. A designated pooled plan provider would, as the named fiduciary, be responsible for plan administration. However, employers would be subject to fiduciary standards in the selection and monitoring of the pooled plan provider. The rules effectively eliminate the "one bad apple" restriction.

¶110 **Increase in Cap on Automatic Enrollment Safe Harbor Contributions.** The default maximum applicable to safe harbor qualified automatic contribution arrangements will increase, effective for plan years beginning after December 31, 2019, from 10 percent to 15 percent of an employee's compensation. The increase will apply in the year after an employee's deemed election first applies.

¶115 **Notice Requirement for Nonelective Safe Harbor Plans Eliminated.** The annual notice requirement applicable to nonelective safe harbor plans is eliminated, effective for plan years beginning after December 31, 2019.

¶120 **Amendment Deadline for Nonelective Safe Harbor Plans Extended.** Plan sponsors may, effective for plan years beginning after December 31, 2019, adopt an amendment implementing a nonelective safe harbor plan, including a Code Sec. 401(k)(13) automatic contribution arrangement, at any time before the 30th day before the close of the plan year. An amendment, however, may be adopted at any time before the last day allowed for the distribution of excess contributions for the plan year (i.e., by the close of the following year) if the amendment requires the employer to provide a nonelective contribution of at least 4 percent of compensation for all eligible employees for that plan year.

¶125 **Expansion of Plan Eligibility to Long-Term, Part-Time Employees.** 401(k) plans, effective for plan years beginning after December 31, 2020, must have a dual eligibility requirement under which an employee may complete either one year of service (not to exceed 1,000 hours) or three consecutive 12-month periods of service in which the employee completes at least 500 hours of service.

¶ 130 **Increase in Tax Credit for Small Employer Pension Plan Start-Up Costs.** The tax credit afforded small employers for starting a new retirement plan will increase, effective for tax years beginning after December 31, 2019, from 50 percent of the qualified start-up costs paid or incurred during the taxable year to the greater of: (1) $500, or (2) the lesser of (a) $250 for each nonhighly compensated employee eligible to participate in the plan, or (b) $5,000.

¶ 135 **Small Employer Automatic Enrollment Credits.** Small employers are provided, effective for tax years beginning after December 31, 2019, with a $500 tax credit to pay the start-up costs incurred in adopting a new 401(k) or SIMPLE plan that allows for automatic enrollment. The credit would be available for three years and would be provided in addition to the plan start up credit authorized under Code Sec. 45E.

¶ 140 **Treatment of Taxable Non-Tuition Fellowship and Stipend Payments as Compensation for IRA Purposes.** Stipends and non-tuition fellowship payments made to graduate and postdoctoral students will be treated, effective for tax years beginning after December 31, 2019, as compensation that may be used as the basis for IRA contributions.

¶ 145 **Repeal of Maximum Age for Traditional IRA Contributions.** The rule prohibiting contributions to a traditional IRA by a taxpayer who has attained age 70 is repealed, effective for tax years beginning after December 31, 2019.

¶ 150 **Difficulty of Care Payments Treated as Compensation in Applying Retirement Contribution Limits.** Difficulty of care payments will be treated as compensation for purposes of calculating applicable contribution limits, thereby allowing home health care workers to contribute to an IRA or defined contribution plan.

¶ 155 **Prohibition on Plan Loans Through Credit Cards.** Plan loans, effective on the December 20, 2019 date of enactment, may not be executed through credit cards or similar arrangements.

¶ 160 **Penalty-Free Plan Withdrawals to Cover Birth or Adoption Expenses.** Individuals are authorized to take penalty free "qualified birth or adoption distributions" of up to $5,000 from an eligible retirement plan (excluding defined benefit plans). Any portion of the distribution may also be recontributed to a retirement plan as an eligible rollover distribution.

¶165 **Increased Age for Taking Required Minimum Distributions.** The age at which required minimum distributions must begin to be made from qualified plans and IRAs is increased, effective for distributions required to be made after December 31, 2019, from 70 1/2 to 72.

¶170 **Plan Amendments: Remedial Amendment Periods.** A remedial plan amendment period, extending to the last day of the first plan year beginning on or after January 1, 2022, or such later date as Treasury may prescribe, is authorized for plan amendments required by the SECURE Act.

¶175 **Special Disaster-Related Rules for Use of Retirement Funds.** An exception to the Code Sec. 72(t) early distribution penalty is provided for qualified disaster distributions from retirement plans of up to $100,000. The qualified distribution will be included in income ratably over a three-year period and taxpayers are further authorized to recontribute the amount of the distribution to an eligible retirement plan. Finally, the Act increases the limits on plan loans made to individuals experiencing qualified disasters from $50,000 to $100,000 and extends applicable loan repayment periods.

¶180 **Portability of Lifetime Income Options.** Qualified defined contribution plans, 403(b) plans or governmental 457(b) plans are empowered, effective for plan years beginning after December 31, 2019, to make direct trustee-to-trustee transfers to another employer-sponsored retirement plan or IRA of lifetime income investments or distributions of a lifetime income investment in the form of a qualified plan distribution annuity, in the event the lifetime income investment is no longer authorized to be held as an investment option under the plan.

¶185 **Treatment of Custodial Accounts on Termination of 403(b) Plans.** Treasury is instructed to issue guidance under which the distribution needed to effectuate the termination of a 403(b) custodial account may be the distribution of an individual custodial account in kind to a participant or beneficiary. The Treasury guidance will be retroactively effective for tax years beginning after December 31, 2008.

¶190 **Clarification of Retirement Account Rules Related to Church-Controlled Organizations.** Individuals eligible to participate in a tax-favored retirement income account maintained by a church will include those participating in plans maintained by church-controlled organizations. Thus, effective for plan years beginning on or before December 20, 2019, individuals eligible to participate in the plan would include: duly ordained, commissioned, or licensed ministers, regardless of the source of their compensation; employees of a tax-exempt organization that is controlled by or associated with a church or a convention or association of churches; and certain employees who have separated from service with a church, a convention or association of churches.

¶195 **Special Rules for Minimum Funding Standards for Frozen Community Newspaper Plans.** The sponsors of community newspaper pension plans that have been frozen as of December 31, 2017, are provided relief from the governing funding requirements. Under the relief, the interest rate used to calculate funding obligations would increase to 8 percent and the applicable shortfall amortization period would be extended from 7 years to 30 years.

ADMINISTRATIVE IMPROVEMENTS

¶200 **Treatment of Plans Adopted by Filing Due Date as in Effect as of Close of Year.** Employers, effective for tax years beginning after December 31, 2019, will be allowed to treat qualified retirement plans adopted after the close of the tax year, but before the due date of their tax return for the year (including extensions), as having been adopted as of the last day of the tax year.

¶205 **Combined Annual Report for Group of Plans.** The IRS and DOL are directed to allow a group of similar defined contribution plans, effective for returns due for plan years after December 31, 2021, to file a consolidated Form 5500 annual report. The plans must have the same named fiduciary, the same administrator, use the same plan year, and provide the same investments or investment options to participants and beneficiaries.

¶210 **Lifetime Income Disclosure.** Benefit statements provided to defined contribution plan participants would need to include a lifetime income disclosure at least once during any 12-month period. The disclosure would illustrate the monthly payments the participant would receive if the total account balance were used to provide lifetime income streams, including a qualified joint and survivor annuity for the participant and the participant's surviving spouse and a single life annuity. The Secretary of Labor is directed to develop a model disclosure and applicable assumptions. Plan fiduciaries, plan sponsors, or other persons will not incur liability under ERISA to the extent that they provide lifetime income stream equivalents that are derived in accordance with the prescribed assumptions and include the explanations contained in the model disclosure.

¶220 **Fiduciary Safe Harbor for Selection of Lifetime Income Provider.** Plan fiduciaries are afforded an optional safe harbor to satisfy the prudence requirements of ERISA with respect to the selection of insurers for a guaranteed retirement income contract. In the event the fiduciary receives certain assurances from the insurer regarding its compliance with state insurance requirements, a fiduciary would be shielded from liability for any loss that may be incurred by a participant or beneficiary due to the insurer's failure to satisfy its financial obligations under the contract.

¶225 **Expansion of Nondiscrimination Cross-Testing Rules.** The governing nondiscrimination rules would be amended, effective upon the December 20, 2019 date of enactment of the SECURE Act, to allow expanded cross-testing between an employer's closed defined benefit plan and defined contribution plans. The modifications will help closed plans pass the applicable nondiscrimination tests and enable existing participants in such plans to continue to accrue benefits.

¶230 **Modification of PBGC Premiums for Cooperative and Small Employer Charity (CSEC) Plans.** Individualized rules are established for the calculation of PBGC premiums for Cooperative and Small Employer Charity (CSEC) plans. Such plans, effective for plan years beginning after December 31, 2018, are subject to a flat-rate premium of $19 per participant, and a variable rate premium of $9 for each $1,000 of unfunded vested benefits.

¶5

REVENUE PROVISIONS

¶300 **Modification of Required Distribution Rules for Designated Beneficiaries.** Under modified required minimum distribution rules, effective for distributions with respect to defined contribution plan participants and IRA owners who die after December 31, 2019, distributions to individuals other than the surviving spouse of the employee (or IRA owner), disabled or chronically ill individuals, individuals who are not more than 10 years younger than the employee (or IRA owner), or a child of the employee (or IRA owner) who has not reached the age of majority must generally be distributed by the end of the 10th calendar year following the year of the employee or IRA owner's death. Limited exceptions are authorized, but the provision will effectively limit if not eliminate the "stretch IRA" as a tool for managing retirement assets.

¶305 **Increase in Failure to File Return Penalty.** The penalty assessed for failure to file a federal income tax return has been increased, effective for returns due after December 31, 2019, from $330 to the lesser of $435 or 100% of the amount of the tax.

¶310 **Increased Plan Reporting Penalties.** The penalties for failure to file Form 5500, registration statements, required notifications of change, and withholding notices have been substantially increased, effective for returns and statements due after December 31, 2019.

BIPARTISAN AMERICAN MINERS ACT

¶400 **Treasury Transfers to 1974 UMWA Pension Plan.** The Treasury is required to transfer funds to the 1947 United Mineworkers of America Pension Plan to pay retiree benefits. The plan would be treated as if it was in critical status and would be required to comply with its applicable rehabilitation plan. Plan trustees would be subject to extensive annual reporting requirements.

¶405 **Funding Multiemployer Health Benefit Plans.** The Bipartisan American Miners Act of 2019 authorizes the transfer of surplus funds from the Abandoned Mine Land Fund of the Surface Mining Control and Reclamation Act to help finance the health care benefits of miners participating in health plans maintained by employers who declared bankruptcy in 2018 and 2019.

¶410 **Reduction in Minimum Age for Allowable In-Service Distributions.** A pension plan will not fail to be qualified solely because the plan provides, effective for plan years beginning after December 31, 2019, that a distribution may be made to an employee who has attained age 59 (rather than 62) and who is not separated from employment at the time of the distribution. A similar rule will apply to distributions from governmental 457(b) plans.

HEALTH AND WELFARE BENEFITS

¶500 **Repeal of Medical Device Excise Tax.** The 2.3 percent excise tax imposed on sales of medical devices is repealed. The repeal of the tax applies to sales after December 31, 2019.

¶505 **Repeal of Annual Fee on Health Insurance Providers.** The annual fee imposed on health insurers that meet certain criteria is repealed. The repeal of the fee applies to calendar years beginning after December 31, 2020.

¶510 **Repeal of Excise Tax on High Cost Employer-Sponsored Health Coverage.** The excise tax on high cost employer-sponsored health coverage, the so-called "Cadillac" tax, has been repealed, effective for tax years after December 31, 2019.

¶515 **Provision of Pharmacy Benefit Services.** A five-year exemption from some of ERISA's prohibited transaction rules is provided for the offering of pharmacy benefit services to a group health plan that is sponsored by an organization that is tax-exempt and that was established in Chicago, Illinois on August 12, 1881. The relief will be considered effective on the December 20, 2019 date of enactment of the Further Consolidated Appropriations Act.

¶520 **Employer Credit for Paid FMLA Leave.** The employer credit for providing paid Family and Medical Leave Act (FMLA) leave, which was set to expire at the end of 2019, has been extended for one year to apply through 2020.

¶525 **Benefits Provided to Volunteer Firefighters and Emergency Responders.** Federal income tax exclusions authorized for state or local tax benefits and qualified reimbursement payments made to members of volunteer emergency response organizations have been restored for the 2020 tax year. In addition, the exclusion for reimbursement payments has been increased to $50 for each month a volunteer serves.

¶530 **Repeal of Increase in unrelated business taxable income for certain fringe benefit expenses.** Unrelated business taxable income will no longer be increased by the nondeductible amount of certain fringe benefit expenses paid or incurred by an exempt organization.

¶540 **Expansion of 529 Plans.** The rules governing Code Sec. 529 qualified tuition plans are modified, effective for distributions made after December 31, 2018, to allow tax-free distributions for expenses associated with registered apprenticeship programs. Plans also can allow tax-free distributions of certain amounts used to make payments on principal or interest of a qualified education loan of the designated beneficiary or a sibling of the designated beneficiary.

¶545 **Credit for Health Insurance Costs of Eligible Individuals.** The Health Coverage Tax Credit that was set to expire as of January 1, 2020, has been extended for one year, until January 1, 2021.

Expansion of Retirement Savings

¶100	Multiple Employer Plans: Pooled Employer Plans
¶110	Increase in Cap on Automatic Enrollment Safe Harbor Contributions
¶115	Notice Requirement for Nonelective Safe Harbor Plans Eliminated
¶120	Amendment Deadline for Nonelective Safe Harbor Plans Extended
¶125	Expansion of Plan Eligibility to Long-Term, Part-Time Employees
¶130	Increase in Tax Credit for Small Employer Pension Plan Start-Up Costs
¶135	Small Employer Automatic Enrollment Credits
¶140	Treatment of Taxable Non-Tuition Fellowship and Stipend Payments as Compensation for IRA Purposes
¶145	Repeal of Maximum Age for Traditional IRA Contributions
¶150	Difficulty of Care Payments Treated as Compensation in Applying Retirement Contribution Limits
¶155	Prohibition on Plan Loans Through Credit Cards
¶160	Penalty-Free Plan Withdrawals to Cover Birth or Adoption Expenses
¶165	Increased Age for Taking Required Minimum Distributions
¶170	Plan Amendments: Remedial Amendment Periods
¶175	Special Disaster-Related Rules for Use of Retirement Funds
¶180	Portability of Lifetime Income Options
¶185	Treatment of Custodial Accounts on Termination of 403(b) Plans
¶190	Clarification of Retirement Account Rules Related to Church-Controlled Organizations
¶195	Special Rules for Minimum Funding Standards for Frozen Community Newspaper Plans

¶100 Multiple Employer Plans: Pooled Employer Plans

SUMMARY OF NEW LAW

A new "open" Multiple Employer Plan (MEP), called a Pooled Employer Plan (PEP) is authorized, effective for plan years beginning after December 31, 2020. A designated pooled plan provider would, as the named fiduciary, be responsible for plan administration. However, employers would be subject to fiduciary standards in the selection and monitoring of the pooled plan provider. The rules effectively eliminate the "one bad apple" restriction.

BACKGROUND

A Multiple Employer Plan (MEP) is a single plan that covers two or more unrelated employers and is not operated pursuant to a collective bargaining agreement (IRS Reg. 1.413-2(a)(2)). MEPs are typically offered by employer group or associations and by Professional Employer Organizations (PEOs).

Among the administrative advantages afforded by a multiple employer plan is that a plan sponsor is required to file only a single determination letter application and one Form 5500. However, contributions from each employer must be available to pay benefits for any participant, even if the participant is employed by another employer.

ERISA requires a MEP, like any retirement plan, to be established by an employer or an employee organization (ERISA Sec. 3(2)). Longstanding DOL guidance further limited MEPs to employers sharing a common economic or representational nexus that was unrelated to the provision of employee benefits. Absent such nexus, each employer would be treated as maintaining its own ERISA-governed plan, with all the attendant reporting, bonding, and administrative obligations.

Final regulations, effective September 30, 2019, promised to make MEPs more accessible to employers by broadening the conditions under which a group or association will be treated as acting as an employer for purposes of offering a MEP, and clarifying the terms under which a bona fide professional employer organization may sponsor a MEP (ERISA Reg. § 2510.3-55). The rules did not, however, authorize open MEPs, in which participating employer members have no common business connection or purpose beyond their joint participation in the MEP. In addition, the regulations are restricted to 401(k) and other defined contribution plans.

Unified plan ("One bad apple") rule. Despite the advantages afforded by multiple employer 401(k) plans, employers are cautioned that such plans are subject to additional qualification requirements and are more difficult to operate than single employer plans. The main consideration for MEP sponsors is that coverage and nondiscrimination testing and top-heavy determinations must be done on an employer-by-employer basis. The employer deduction and annual compensation limits are also applied on an employer-by-employer basis. As a result, the failure of a qualification requirement by one employer under the plan may, under IRS Reg. § 1.413-2(a)(3)(iv), result in the disqualification of the entire plan (i.e., the "unified plan" or "one bad apple" rule). This risk is especially acute in plans maintained by PEOs. Accordingly, employers participat-

BACKGROUND

ing in the plan must assure that the PEO and any other primary sponsor of the multiple employer 401(k) plan is properly administering the plan.

Proposed regulations would provide an exception to the unified plan rule. Proposed regulations issued by the IRS in July 2019 would provide an exception to the unified plan rule for multiple employer defined contribution plans (IRS Proposed Reg. § 1.413-2(g), at PENSION PLAN GUIDE ¶ 20,264Z). The rules, which would impose new administrative requirements on plan administrators and require plan amendments, however, may not be relied upon until finalized.

NEW LAW EXPLAINED

Multiple Employer Plans: Pooled Employer Plans.—Under the new law, effective for plan years beginning after December 31, 2020, a new class of MEP service provider will be able to create and offer an open MEP called a Pooled Employer Plan (PEP) (Code Sec. 413(e), as added by Division O, Act Sec. 101 of the SECURE Act, enacted as part of the Further Consolidated Appropriations Act, 2020 (P.L. 116-94)). The plans may be structured as a 401(k) or another qualified plan or as an IRA-based plan. Significantly, the new rules effectively eliminate the "one bad apple" restriction.

> **Expert Guidance:** Joan McDonagh, Senior National Regulatory Policy Director at Empower Retirement, and co-author of the *401(k) Answer Book*, highlights the pooled employer plan rules as having potentially the biggest impact on employers that do not currently maintain a plan. The rules, McDonagh advises, allow small business owners to now offer a plan with reduced administrative burdens and fiduciary risks.

Elimination of one bad apple rule. Multiple employer defined contribution plans would not be disqualified merely because one or more employers of employees covered by the plan (qualified plan or IRA) fails to comply with plan qualification requirements. (Code Sec. 413(e)(1), as added by SECURE Act Sec. 101(a)).

The new rule applies to: (1) MEPs with a common interest other than having adopted the plan (i.e., closed MEPs), and (2) open MEPs with a pooled plan provider.

Transfer of plan assets and employer liabilities. In order for the protections to apply, the terms of the plan must provide that the assets of the plan attributable to the employees (or beneficiaries) of a noncompliant employer will be transferred to either: (1) a plan maintained only by that employer (or its successor); (2) an eligible plan, including an IRA, qualified plan, 403(b) annuity, or 457(b) plan; or (3) any other arrangement that the Treasury Secretary determines is appropriate, unless the Secretary determines it is in the best interests of the employees (or their beneficiaries) of such employer to retain the assets in the plan (Code Sec. 413(e)(2)(A)(i), as added by SECURE Act Sec. 101(a)).

Liability of noncompliant employer. The terms of the plan must further provide that a noncompliant employer shall, except to the extent provided by the Secretary, be responsible for any liabilities with respect to the plan attributable to employees of the noncompliant employer (or beneficiaries of such employees). These liabilities are not to

¶100

NEW LAW EXPLAINED

be placed on the plan or any other employer in the plan (Code Sec. 413(e)(2)(A)(ii), as added by SECURE Act Sec. 101(a)).

Pooled plans. A pooled employer plan is an individual account plan providing benefits to the employees of two or more employers. The plan may be structured as a 401(k) or another qualified plan or as an IRA-based plan (ERISA Sec. 3(43)(A)), as added by SECURE Act Sec. 101(c)).

Pooled plans are treated, for purposes of ERISA, as a single plan that is a multiple employer plan. Pooled plans, however, may not be maintained by employers which have a common interest other than having adopted the plan (ERISA Sec. 3(43)(A), as added by SECURE Act Sec. 101(c)). A pooled employer plan also may not include: a multiemployer plan under Code Sec. 413(b); or a plan established before the December 20, 2019 date of enactment of the SECURE Act, unless the plan administrator elects to treat the plan as a pooled employer plan and the plan meets the requirements applicable to a pooled employer plan established on or after such date (ERISA Sec. 3(43)(C), as added by SECURE Act Sec. 101(c)(1)).

Pooled plan providers. A pooled plan provider would be a person who is designated by the terms of the plan as a named fiduciary, as the plan administrator, and as the person responsible for performing all administrative duties (including conducting proper testing with respect to the plan and the employees of each employer in the plan) that are reasonably necessary to ensure compliance with ERISA and the Internal Revenue Code (Code Sec. 413(e)(3), as added by SECURE Act Sec. 101(a)(1); ERISA Sec. 3(44), as added by SECURE Act Sec. 101(c)(1)). The pooled plan provider would need to register with the Department of Labor, acknowledge its status as a named fiduciary in writing, and be appropriately bonded in accord with ERISA Sec. 412.

Required terms of pooled MEP. The terms of a pooled multiple employer plan must: designate a pooled plan provider and provide that the pooled plan provider is a named fiduciary of the plan; designate one or more trustees meeting the requirements of Code Sec. 408(a)(2) to be responsible for the collection of contributions and the holding of plan assets; provide that each employer in the plan retains fiduciary responsibility for the selection and monitoring of the pooled plan provider, and unless delegated to another fiduciary, the investment and management of the portion of the plan's assets attributable to the employees of the employer; provide that employers in the plan, and participants and beneficiaries, are not subject to unreasonable restrictions, fees, or penalties with regard to ceasing participation, receipt of distributions, or otherwise transferring assets; require the pooled plan provider to furnish to employers in the plan any required disclosures or information required to take actions necessary to administer the plan or for the plan to meet any requirements of Code Secs. 401 or 408, whichever is applicable; and provide that any required disclosure or information may be provided in electronic form and will be designed to ensure only reasonable costs are imposed on pooled plan providers and employers in the plan (ERISA Sec. 3(43)(B), as added by SECURE Act Sec. 101(c)(1)).

Form 5500 reporting. The Form 5500 filing for a multiple employer plan (including a pooled employer plan) must include: (1) a list of the employers in the plan, (2) a good faith estimate of the percentage of total contributions made by such employers during the plan year, and (3) the aggregate account balances attributable to each employer in

NEW LAW EXPLAINED

the plan (determined as the sum of the account balances of the employees of each employer (and the beneficiaries of such employees)) (ERISA Sec. 103(g), as amended by SECURE Act Sec. 101(d)). In addition, with respect to a pooled employer plan, filing must provide the identifying information for the person designated under the terms of the plan as the pooled plan provider.

Simplified annual reporting. Finally, a multiple employer plan that covers fewer than 100 participants may be added to the list of pension plans to which simplified reporting may be prescribed by the Secretary of Labor (ERISA Sec. 104(a)(2)(A), as amended by SECURE Act Sec. 101(d)(2)). However, simplified reporting (available to plans covering less than 1,000 participants) would be authorized only if no single employer in the plan has 100 or more participants covered by the plan.

▶ **Effective date.** The amendments shall apply to plan years beginning after December 31, 2020 (including Form 5500 reporting for plan years beginning after December 31, 2020) (SECURE Act Sec. 101(e)).

Law Source: Law at ¶5042, ¶6070, ¶7001, ¶7002, ¶7003 and ¶7008.

— Act Sec. 101(a), Division O, of the Further Consolidated Appropriations Act, 2020 (P.L. 116-94), adding Code Sec. 413(e).

— Act Sec. 101(c), Division O, adding ERISA Sec. 3(43) and ERISA Sec. 3(44).

— Act Sec. 101(d), Division O, amending ERISA Sec. 103(g).

— Act Sec. 101(d)(2), Division O, adding ERISA Sec. 104(a)(2)(A).

— Act. Sec. 101(e), Division O, providing the effective date.

¶110 Increase in Cap on Automatic Enrollment Safe Harbor Contributions

SUMMARY OF NEW LAW

The default maximum applicable to safe harbor qualified automatic contribution arrangements will increase, effective for plan years beginning after December 31, 2019, from 10 percent to 15 percent of an employee's compensation. The increase will apply in the year after an employee's deemed election first applies.

BACKGROUND

401(k) plan sponsors that implement automatic enrollment provisions may comply with the ADP and ACP nondiscrimination tests by making specific contributions under qualified automatic contribution arrangements (Code Sec. 401(k)(13)). Similar to 401(k) safe harbor plans, qualified automatic contribution arrangements provide an additional safe harbor for compliance with the nondiscrimination tests to employers maintaining an eligible automatic enrollment arrangement that provides for a minimum

BACKGROUND

automatic employee contribution and a minimum employer matching or nonelective contribution.

Under a qualified automatic contribution arrangement, an eligible employee, absent a contrary election, is treated as having elected to have the employer make elective contributions in an amount equal to a "qualified percentage" of compensation, not to exceed 10 percent (Code Sec. 401(k)(13)(C)). The default election is the specified qualified percentage multiplied by the employee's compensation from which elective contributions are permitted to be made.

NEW LAW EXPLAINED

Increase in cap on automatic enrollment safe harbor contributions.—The Act, effective for plan years beginning after December 31, 2019, increases the cap on the default rate applicable under an automatic enrollment safe harbor. Specifically, the qualified percentage is raised from 10 percent to 15 percent of an employee's compensation (Code Sec. 401(k)(13)(C)(iii), as amended by Division O, Act Sec. 102(a) of the SECURE Act, enacted as part of the Further Consolidated Appropriations Act, 2020 (P.L. 116-94)).

Note: The qualified percentage will remain at 10 percent for the first year of an employee's enrollment. Thus, the increase in the default cap will apply after the first year that an employee's deemed election applies.

▶ **Effective date.** The amendment applies to plan years beginning after December 31, 2019 (SECURE Act Sec. 102(b)).

Law Source: Law at ¶5043 and ¶6050.

— Act Sec. 102(a), Division O, of the Further Consolidated Appropriations Act, 2020 (P.L. 116-94), amending Code Sec. 401(k)(13)(C)(iii).

— Act Sec. 102(b), Division O, providing the effective date.

¶115 Notice Requirement for Nonelective Safe Harbor Plans Eliminated

SUMMARY OF NEW LAW

The annual notice requirement applicable to nonelective safe harbor plans is eliminated, effective for plan years beginning after December 31, 2019.

BACKGROUND

The ADP nonelective safe harbor may not be adopted unless the employer provides written notice to each employee who is eligible to participate in the plan of their rights and obligations under the plan (Code Sec. 401(k)(12)(D)). The notice, which must be

BACKGROUND

provided within a reasonable period (generally, 30-90 days) before the beginning of each plan year, must be "sufficiently accurate and comprehensive" to inform employees of their rights and obligations under the plan, and must be written in a manner calculated to be understood by the average employee eligible to participate in the plan (IRS Reg. § 1.401(k)-3(d)(2)).

In order to be considered sufficiently accurate and comprehensive, the notice must describe: the safe harbor matching or nonelective contribution formula used under the plan (including a description of the level of matching contributions available under the plan); any other contributions under the plan or matching contributions to another plan (including the potential for discretionary matching contributions) and the conditions under which such contributions are made; the plan to which safe harbor contributions will be made (if different than the plan containing the cash or deferred arrangement); the type and amount of compensation that may be deferred under the plan; the procedures by which cash or deferred elections are to be made, including any applicable administrative requirements; the periods authorized by the plan during which cash or deferred elections may be made; and withdrawal and vesting provisions applicable to contributions under the plan.

NEW LAW EXPLAINED

Notice requirement for nonelective safe harbor plans eliminated.—The Act, effective for plan years beginning after December 31, 2019, eliminates the notice requirement, as long as the nonelective contribution requirements under Code Sec. 401(k)(12)(C) are met (Code Sec 401(k)(12)(A), as amended by Division O, Act Sec. 103(a) of the SECURE Act, enacted as part of the Further Consolidated Appropriations Act, 2020 (P.L. 116-94)). However, eliminating the notice does not eliminate the right of employees to make or change an election at least once per year.

Note: In the event the employer elects to make the matching safe harbor contribution, notice would still be required.

> **Expert Guidance:** Susan Wright, CPA, Managing Editor, Technical Answer Group (TAG), highlights the possible impact the removal of the safe harbor notice requirement for safe harbor nonelective plans may have on the ability of those plans to reduce or suspend safe harbor contributions mid-year. Under the current regulations, a plan can only reduce or suspend safe harbor nonelective contributions during the year if (1) the employer is operating at an economic loss (as described under Code Sec. 412(c)(2)(A)), or (2) the annual safe harbor notice includes a statement that the plan sponsor may amend the plan during the year to reduce or suspend safe harbor contributions. In either case, certain procedural requirements must also be satisfied. When new regulations are issued, Wright advises, we will see whether the mid-year reduction or suspension notice requirement is removed for safe harbor nonelective plans. If not, she cautions, it seems these plans will nevertheless be required to send out an annual notice if the employer would like to reserve the right to reduce or suspend safe harbor nonelective contributions mid-year. The alternative would be to remove the safe

¶115

NEW LAW EXPLAINED

harbor nonelective provision all together and rely on the (new) extended period to adopt the safe harbor nonelective provision for a given plan year.

▶ **Effective date.** The amendment is effective for plan years beginning after December 31, 2019 (Act Sec. 103(d)).

Law Source: Law at ¶5044 and ¶6050.

— Act Sec. 103(a), Division O, of the Further Consolidated Appropriations Act, 2020 (P.L. 116-94), amending Code Sec. 401(k)(12)(A).

— Act Sec. 103(d), Division O, providing the effective date.

¶120 Amendment Deadline for Nonelective Safe Harbor Plans Extended

SUMMARY OF NEW LAW

Plan sponsors may, effective for plan years beginning after December 31, 2019, adopt an amendment implementing a nonelective safe harbor plan, including a Code Sec. 401(k)(13) automatic contribution arrangement, at any time before the 30th day before the close of the plan year. An amendment, however, may be adopted at any time before the last day allowed for the distribution of excess contributions for the plan year (i.e., by the close of the following year) if the amendment requires the employer to provide a nonelective contribution of at least 4 percent of compensation for all eligible employees for that plan year.

BACKGROUND

Under IRS Reg. § 1.401(k)-3(e)(1), the safe harbor provisions of a 401(k) plan must be adopted before the first day of the plan year and remain in effect for the entire 12-month plan year. IRS Reg. §§ 1.401(k)-3(e)(1) and 1.401(m)-3(f) generally prohibit mid-year plan amendments (i.e., changes: (a) first effective during a plan year, but not effective as of the beginning of the plan year, or (b) effective as of the beginning of the plan year, but adopted after the beginning of the plan year). However, effective January 29, 2016, the IRS significantly changed its position, expanding authorization for certain mid-year changes to safe harbor plans (including qualified automatic contribution arrangements (QACAs)) and safe harbor notices (IRS Notice 2016-16, I.R.B. 2016-07, 2-16-16, at PENSION PLAN GUIDE ¶ 17,158I). The relief effectively allowed mid-year changes that, for example: increase future safe harbor nonelective contributions, increase safe harbor matching contributions, authorize age 59½ in-service withdrawals, implement a change in a QACA's default investment fund, and add an automatic contribution feature. The IRS, however, has also specified mid-year changes that are prohibited, such as mid-year changes in the design of a traditional 401(k) plan to a QACA safe harbor plan.

NEW LAW EXPLAINED

Amendment deadline for nonelective safe harbor plans extended.—The Act, effective for plan years beginning after December 31, 2019, authorizes plan sponsors to adopt an amendment implementing a nonelective safe harbor plan, including a Code Sec. 401(k)(13) automatic contribution arrangement, at any time before the 30th day before the close of the plan year (Code Sec. 401(k)(12)(F), as added by Division O, Act Sec. 103(b) of the SECURE Act, enacted as part of the Further Consolidated Appropriations, 2020 (P.L. 116-94)); Code Sec. 401(k)(13)(F), as added by SECURE Act Sec. (103(c)).

An amendment, however, may be adopted at any time before the last day allowed for the distribution of excess contributions for the plan year (i.e., by the close of the following year) if the amendment requires the employer to provide a nonelective contribution of at least 4 percent of compensation (rather than at least 3 percent) for all eligible employees for that plan year (Code Sec. 401(k)(12)(F)(iii), as added by SECURE Act Sec. 103(b)). Note, the plan must actually be amended by that day.

> **Expert Guidance:** Susan Wright, CPA, Managing Editor, Technical Answer Group (TAG) notes, that overall, the extended amendment deadline is a welcome enhancement that affords plan sponsors much greater flexibility. She further cautions that it may not be viewed as a win by plan participants, though, as it may encourage some plan sponsors to remove the safe harbor nonelective provision from their plans and elect to make the safe harbor contribution for a given year based on preliminary or final ADP testing results. If an employer waits until after the statutory deadline (i.e. 30 days before the end of the plan year) to amend their plan, however, participants will be entitled to a 4% safe harbor contribution.
>
> Another interesting issue, highlighted by Wright, is whether plans that are amended in 2020 to suspend or reduce safe harbor nonelective contributions during the year will still have the opportunity to retroactively adopt the safe harbor provision (again) for the 2020 plan year under the new rules. Hopefully, the IRS will issue guidance on this point, but, she advises, absent guidance to the contrary, it seems this option would be permissible.

▶ **Effective date.** The amendments are effective for plan years beginning after December 31, 2019 (SECURE Act Sec. 103(d)).

Law Source: Law at ¶5044 and ¶6050.

— Act Sec. 103(b), Division O, of the Further Consolidated Appropriations Act, 2020 (P.L. 116-94), amending Code Sec. 401(k)(12) by redesignating subparagraph (F) as subparagraph (G).

— Act Sec. 103(b), Division O, adding new Code Sec. 401(k)(12)(F).

— Act Sec. 103(b), Division O, adding Code Sec. 401(k)(12)(F)(iii).

— Act Sec. 103(c), Division O, adding Code Sec. 401(k)(13)(F),

— Act Sec. 103(d), Division O, providing the effective date.

¶125 Expansion of Plan Eligibility to Long-Term, Part-Time Employees

SUMMARY OF NEW LAW

401(k) plans, effective for plan years beginning after December 31, 2020, must have a dual eligibility requirement under which an employee must complete either one-year-of service (not to exceed 1,000 hours) or three consecutive 12-month periods of service in which the employee completes at least 500 hours of service.

BACKGROUND

401(k) plans may not require, as a condition of participation in the plan, that an employee complete a period of service with the employer maintaining the plan that is in excess of one year (Code Sec. 401(k)(2)(D); IRS Reg. §1.401(k)-1(e)(5)). A year of service may not exceed 1,000 hours (Code Sec. 410(a)(3)(A)). However, long-term employees who do not satisfy the 1,000-hour threshold have been effectively precluded from plan participation.

Plans may also establish a minimum age as a condition of participation. The minimum age may not exceed age 21.

NEW LAW EXPLAINED

Expansion of plan eligibility to long-term, part-time employees.—The Act, effective for plan years beginning after December 31, 2020, requires employers maintaining a 401(k) plan to have a dual eligibility requirement under which an employee must complete one-year-of service (not to exceed 1,000 hours) or three consecutive 12-month periods of service in which the "long-term, part-time employee" completes at least 500 hours of service (Code Sec. 401(k)(2)(D), as amended by Divison O, Act Sec. 112(a)(1) of the SECURE Act, enacted as part of the Further Consolidated Appropriations Act, 2020 (P.L. 116-94)).

Note: The expanded eligibility rule would affect only 401(k) plans and would not also apply to employers with collectively bargained plans (Code Sec. 401(k)(15)(C), as added by SECURE Act Sec. 112(a)(2)).

Employee must attain age 21 by end of period. The expanded three consecutive years of service eligibility track would not be available to an employee unless the individual attains age 21 by the close of the last of the three consecutive 12-month periods (Code Sec. 401(k)(15)(A), as added by SECURE Act Sec. 112(a)(2)). Once a long-term part-time employee meets the age and service requirements, the employee must be able to begin participation in the plan no later than the earlier of: (1) the first day of the first plan year beginning after the date on which the employee satisfied the age and service requirements, or (2) the date six months after the date on which the individual satisfied those requirements.

NEW LAW EXPLAINED

> **Expert Guidance:** Bernadine Topazio, the author of the *Flexible Benefits Answer Book* and co-author of the *Coverage and Nondiscrimination Answer Book*, advises that, because the 12-month periods prior to January 1, 2021 do not need to be taken into account, employers will have some time in which to prepare for the change in the plan eligibility rules. However, she cautions, human resource systems will need to be modified to capture these employees over the extended three-year period of time. Depending on the turnover of a company, more employees could become eligible for the plan and then terminate with small balances which might increase the administrative cost for the employer. However, for those employees who do participate and maintain sustained long-term, part-time employment, this can be a viable opportunity for substantial retirement savings.

Nondiscrimination and top-heavy rules do not apply. Employees who qualify for plan participation under the 500-hour rule are likely to be low paid. In recognition of the fact that such low paid employees often make passing the applicable nondiscrimination tests problematic, the Act allows employers to elect to exclude employees, whose plan eligibility is solely a result of the 500-hour track, from nondiscrimination testing (Code Sec. 401(k)(15)(B)(i)(II), as added by SECURE Act Sec. 112(a)(2)). In addition, employers will not be required to make nonelective or matching contributions on behalf of such employees, even if such contributions are made on behalf of other employees (Code Sec. 401(k)(15)(B)(i)(I), as added by SECURE Act Sec. 112(a)(2)).

An employer may also elect to exclude all employees who are eligible to participate in a plan under the 500-hour track from the top-heavy rules of Code Sec. 416 (Code Sec. 401(k)(15)(B)(ii), as added by SECURE Act Sec. 112(a)(2)).

> **Expert Guidance:** Although long-term part-time employees (once eligible) can be excluded from employer contributions and the coverage, non-discrimination testing, and the top-heavy requirements, Susan Wright, CPA, Managing Editor, Technical Answer Group (TAG), cautions that such employees may need to be considered for Form 5500 purposes when determining whether a plan is a large or small plan filer. Including long-term, part-time employees in this determination (absent DOL guidance to the contrary), she notes, could have a significant impact (i.e. subjecting the employer to an annual plan audit requirement) for employers who employ a large number of part-time workers.

Vesting. In determining whether an employee under the 500-hour track has a vested nonforfeitable right to employer contributions under the plan, each 12-month period for which the employee has at least 500 hours of service will be treated as a year of service (Code Sec. 401(k)(15)(B)(iii), as added by SECURE Act Sec. 112(a)(2)).

Break-in-service rules. The break-in-service rules of Code Sec. 411(a)(6) have been modified to provide that a one-year break in service includes a year in which the employee has not completed "at least 500 hours of service" (as opposed to "more than 500 hours of service" (Code Sec. 401(k)(15)(B)(iii), as added by SECURE Act Sec. 112(a)(2)).

Note: The provision of an alternative route to plan eligibility promises to greatly benefit working women who primarily bear the burden of child rearing the United States.

¶125

NEW LAW EXPLAINED

▶ **Effective date.** The amendments generally apply to plan years beginning after December 31, 2020. However, 12-month periods beginning before January 1, 2021, may not be taken into account in determining whether the three consecutive year period of service has been met (SECURE Act Sec. 112(b)).

Law Source: Law at ¶5053 and ¶6050.

— Act Sec. 112(a)(1), Division O, of the Further Consolidated Appropriations Act, 2020 (P.L. 116-94), amending Code Sec. 401(k)(2)(D).

— Act. Sec. 112(a)(2), Division O, adding Code Sec. 401(k)(15)(A)-(D).

— Act Sec. 112(b), Division O, providing the effective date.

¶130 Increase in Tax Credit for Small Employer Pension Plan Start-Up Costs

SUMMARY OF NEW LAW

The tax credit afforded small employers for starting a new retirement plan will increase, effective for tax years beginning after December 31, 2019, from 50 percent of the qualified start-up costs paid or incurred during the taxable year to the greater of: (1) $500, or (2) the lesser of (a) $250 for each nonhighly compensated employee eligible to participate in the plan, or (b) $5,000.

BACKGROUND

Many small employers may be reluctant to provide retirement plans for their employees due to the costs associated with setting up and administering plans. Such costs include fees to change the payroll system, set up an investment vehicle and obtain advice from various consultants.

In order to encourage the adoption of retirement plans, small employers with no more than 100 employees are provided with a nonrefundable tax credit for qualified start-up costs incurred in establishing *new* retirement plans.

Eligible plans. Eligible plans include a qualified defined benefit plan, defined contribution plan (including 401(k) plans), savings incentive match plan for employees (SIMPLE) plans, or simplified employee pension (SEP) plans. However, the plan must cover at least one employee who is not a highly compensated employee.

In order to qualify for the tax credit, the employer must not have employed more than 100 employees who received at least $5,000 of compensation from that employer in the preceding year. In addition, the aggregation rules under Code Secs. 52(a), 52(b), 414(m), and 414(o) apply in determining the number of an employer's employees. Thus, all members of a controlled group of corporations are considered one employer; all trades or businesses under common control are treated as a single employer; and all eligible employer plans are treated as one eligible employer plan.

BACKGROUND

Prior plan may preclude use of credit. A new plan will not be eligible for the credit if a prior qualified employer plan received contributions or accrued benefits for substantially the same employees as the new plan will cover. The aggregation rules are applied to determine whether a prior employer plan existed.

The employer and any predecessor must not have been a member of a controlled group in which a member established or maintained a qualified retirement plan (that received contributions or accrued benefits for the same employees covered by the new plan) during the three-tax-year test period.

Qualified start-up costs. Qualified start-up costs are any ordinary and necessary expenses incurred to establish or administer an eligible plan or to educate employees about retirement planning (Code Sec. 45E(d)(1)(A)).

The credit is limited to 50 percent of the qualified start-up costs paid or incurred during the taxable year. The credit is also subject to a dollar limit, which is a maximum of $500 for the first credit year and each of the two taxable years immediately following the first credit year. In addition, the amount of qualified costs and the allowable credit are determined by applying specified aggregation rules. Thus, an employer's qualified costs include the costs incurred for all eligible employer plans within the employer's control group and the credit is attributable to the employers within the group.

NEW LAW EXPLAINED

Increase in tax credit for small employer pension plan start-up costs.—The Act, effective for tax years beginning after December 31, 2019, increases the tax credit for establishing a new retirement plan. Specifically, for the first credit year and each of the two tax years immediately following the first credit year, the tax credit would be the greater of: (1) $500, or (2) the lesser of (a) $250 for each nonhighly compensated employee eligible to participate in the plan, or (b) $5,000 (Code Sec. 45E(b)(1), as amended by Division O, Act Sec. 104(a) of the SECURE Act, enacted as part of the Further Consolidated Appropriations Act, 2020 (P.L. 116-94)).

Note: An additional $500 credit is provided to encourage small employers to adopt new plans that allow for automatic enrollment. See ¶ 135.

Comment: The increase in the tax credit may aid in the adoption of retirement plans. However, the tax credit is inherently limited. The tax credit is limited to the adoption of new plans and is available for only three years. Thus, the law does not provide an ongoing credit that an employer may use to pay the administration costs of established plans.

Moreover, qualified start-up costs are not deductible to the extent that they are effectively offset by the tax credit. Thus, taxpayers should remember to claim deductions for the remaining qualified costs that are ordinary and necessary business expenses under Code Sec. 162.

▶ **Effective date.** The amendment applies to plan years beginning after December 31, 2019 (SECURE Act Sec. 104(b)).

¶130

NEW LAW EXPLAINED

Law Source: Law at ¶5045 and ¶6010.

— Act Sec. 104(a), Division O, of the Further Consolidated Appropriations Act, 2020 (P.L. 116-94), amending Code Sec. 45E(b)(1).

— Act Sec. 104(b), Division O, providing the effective date.

¶135 Small Employer Automatic Enrollment Credits

SUMMARY OF NEW LAW

Small employers are provided, effective for tax years beginning after December 31, 2019, with a $500 tax credit to pay the start-up costs incurred in adopting a new 401(k) or SIMPLE plan that allows for automatic enrollment. The credit would be available for three years and would be provided in addition to the plan start-up credit authorized under Code Sec. 45E.

BACKGROUND

Employers are allowed a tax credit under Code Sec. 38(b) for current year business expenses. Among authorized tax credits are: investment credits (Code Sec. 46), small employer health insurance credits (Code Sec. 45R), and paid family and medical leave credits (Code Sec. 45S(a)).

Current law does not provide a Code Sec. 38 general business credit for the adoption of a new retirement plan. However, small employers are afforded a nonrefundable tax credit under Code Sec. 45E to offset the qualified start-up cost incurred in establishing a new retirement plan (see ¶130).

Eligible automatic contribution arrangements. Eligible automatic contribution arrangements enable employers to unilaterally enroll employees in their 401(k) plans at a specified percentage of compensation and without being subject to state garnishment law restrictions. Eligible automatic contribution arrangements may be established by any plan under which a participant may make a cash or deferred election. Accordingly, eligible automatic contribution arrangements may be adopted by 401(k) plans, as well 403(b) and 457 plans, simplified employee pension plans (SEPs), and SIMPLE plans.

NEW LAW EXPLAINED

Small employer automatic enrollment credits.—The Act, effective for tax years beginning after December 31, 2019, amends Code Sec. 38 by recognizing, as a current year business credit, up to $500 in costs incurred by small employers in adopting a 401(k) plan or SIMPLE plan with an automatic enrollment feature (Code Sec. 38(b)(33), added by Division O, Act Sec. 105(b) of the SECURE Act, enacted as part of the Further Consolidated Appropriations Act, 2020 (P.L. 116-94); Code Sec. 45T, as added by SECURE Act Sec. 105(a)).

NEW LAW EXPLAINED

$500 credit during credit period. The credit is limited to $500 for any tax year occurring during a specified "credit period." The credit period would be the three-taxable-year period beginning with the first tax year for which the employer included an eligible automatic contribution arrangement in a qualified plan sponsored by the employer (Code Sec. 45T(a) and (b), as added by SECURE Act Sec. 105(a)). However, in order for the credit to apply for a tax year, the eligible automatic contribution arrangement must have been included in the plan for the year (Code Sec. 45T(b)(2), as added by SECURE Act Sec. 105(a)).

Additional credit. The credit is provided in addition to the plan start-up credit authorized under Code Sec. 45E.

Eligible employers. The credit is limited to employers that had no more than 100 employees who received at least $5,000 in compensation from the employer in the preceding year (Code Sec. 45T(c), as added by SECURE Act Sec. 105(a), citing Code Sec. 408(p)(2)(C)(i)).

Qualified employer plan. The credit is limited to qualified employer plans specified under Code Sec. 4972(d). Such plans include 401(k) plans, 403(b) plans, simplified employee pension plans (SEPs), and SIMPLE plans (Code Sec. 45T(b)(1), as added by SECURE Act Sec. 105(a)). The credit, thus, expressly does not apply to governmental plans.

Conversion of existing plan. The conference report indicates that the credit is also available to employers that convert an existing plan to an automatic enrollment design.

▶ **Effective date.** The amendment is effective for tax years beginning after December 31, 2019 (SECURE Act Sec. 105(d)).

Law Source: Law at ¶5046, ¶6005 and ¶6020.

— Act Sec. 105(a), Division O, of the Further Consolidated Appropriations Act, 2020 (P.L. 116-94), adding Code Sec. 45T.

— Act Sec. 105(b), Division O, adding Code Sec. 38(b)(33).

— Act Sec. 105(d), Division O, providing the effective date.

¶140 Treatment of Taxable Non-Tuition Fellowship and Stipend Payments as Compensation for IRA Purposes

SUMMARY OF NEW LAW

Stipends and non-tuition fellowship payments made to graduate and postdoctoral students will be treated, effective for tax years beginning after Dec. 31, 2019, as compensation that may be used as the basis for IRA contributions.

BACKGROUND

In order to establish and contribute to an IRA, a person must receive compensation.

Compensation. Compensation includes wages, salaries, professional fees, and other amounts received for personal services actually rendered, as well as, sales commissions, compensation for services on the basis of a percentage of profits, commissions on insurance premiums, and tips and bonuses (Code Sec. 219(f); IRS Reg. 1.219-1(c)). In addition, taxable alimony and separate maintenance payments received by an individual under a decree of divorce or separate maintenance are considered compensation.

However, compensation, for IRA purposes, does not include earnings and profits from property, such as interest, rents, dividends, disability payments, or other amounts not includible in gross income. In addition, compensation does not encompass deferred incentive awards such as incentive stock options, stock appreciation rights (SARs), nonqualified stock options, pension and annuity payments, or other deferred compensation.

W-2 wages treated as safe harbor compensation. The IRS will treat as "safe harbor" compensation, the amounts properly shown as "Wages, tips, other compensation" on Form W-2, but less any amount properly shown in Box 11 (nonqualified plans), in calculating an individual's compensation for IRA purposes.

Stipends and fellowship payments to graduate students. Stipends and non-tuition fellowship payments received by graduate and postdoctoral students are not treated as compensation. Thus, such payments may not be used as the basis for an IRA, precluding the students from saving for retirement and accumulating tax-favored retirement savings.

NEW LAW EXPLAINED

Treatment of taxable non-tuition fellowship and stipend payments as compensation for IRA purposes.—The Act expands the definition of the term "compensation," for purposes of IRA contributions, to encompass any amount that is included in an individual's gross income that has been paid to aid the individual in the pursuit of graduate or postdoctoral study (Code Sec. 219(f)(1), as amended by Division O, Act Sec. 106(a) of the SECURE Act, enacted as part of the Further Consolidated Appropriations Act, 2020 (P.L. 116-94)). Thus, stipends and non-tuition fellowship payments includible in income may be used by graduate and postdoctoral students as the basis for IRA contributions.

▶ **Effective date.** The amendment will apply to tax years beginning after December 31, 2019 (SECURE Act Sec. 106(b)).

Law Source: Law at ¶5047 and ¶6040.

— Act Sec. 106(a), Division O, of the Further Consolidated Appropriations Act, 2020 (P.L. 116-94), amending Code Sec. 219(f)(1).

— Act Sec. 106(b), Division O, providing the effective date.

¶140

¶145 Repeal of Maximum Age for Traditional IRA Contributions

SUMMARY OF NEW LAW

The rule prohibiting contributions to a traditional IRA by a taxpayer who has attained age 70½ is repealed, effective for tax years beginning after December 31, 2019.

BACKGROUND

Individuals may not deduct contributions to a traditional, non-spousal IRA, for the tax year (or any subsequent year) in which the individual attains age 70½ (Code Sec. 219(d)). However, the age restriction does not apply for Roth IRA contributions (Code Sec. 408A(c)(4)). Thus, taxpayers are allowed to make contributions to a Roth IRA even after they attain age 70½, as long they have received compensation.

Charitable IRA distributions. Individuals age 70½ and older may exclude from income up to $100,000 in "qualified charitable distributions" from either a traditional or Roth IRA (Code Sec. 408(d)(8)(A)). A qualified charitable distribution is any distribution from an individual retirement plan (other than a SEP or a SIMPLE plan), which the trustee makes directly to a "50-percent organization" described in Code Sec. 170(b)(1)(A). The distribution can be made on or after the date the person for whose benefit the plan is maintained attains age 70½. However, the distribution is treated as a qualified charitable distribution only to the extent that the IRA distribution would be otherwise includible in gross income. In addition, such distributions are not to be taken into account for charitable deduction purposes.

NEW LAW EXPLAINED

Repeal of maximum age for traditional IRA contributions.—The Act, effective for contributions made for tax years beginning after December 31, 2019, repeals the prohibition on contributions to a traditional IRA by a taxpayer who has attained age 70½ (Code Sec. 219(d), repealed by Division O, Act Sec. 107(a) of the SECURE Act, enacted as part of the Further Consolidated Appropriations Act, 2020, (P.L. 116-94); Code Sec, 408A(c)(4), repealed by SECURE Act Sec. 107(c)).

> **Expert Guidance:** Michael Melbinger, of Winston & Strawn LLP and author of the *Executive Compensation Update*, notes that the elimination of the 70½ age limit for contributing to an IRA permits continued saving for retirement indefinitely, as long as an individual continues to have earned income. Viewed in conjunction with the increase in the required minimum distribution age to 72 (see ¶ 165), the elimination of the maximum contribution age will support increased retirement savings by allowing for the continued accumulation of earnings within a tax advantaged trust.

Coordination with qualified charitable distributions. The Act clarifies that the amount of qualified charitable distributions that may be excluded from income must be reduced (but not below zero) by an amount equal to the excess of: (1) the aggregate

NEW LAW EXPLAINED

amount of deductions allowed the taxpayer under Code Sec. 219 for all tax years ending on or after the date the taxpayer attains age 70½, over (2) the aggregate amount of reductions allowed for charitable purposes for all tax years preceding the current tax year (Code Sec. 408(d)(8)(A), as amended by Act Sec. 107(b)). The amendment will apply to distributions made for tax years beginning after December 31, 2019.

Note: Taxpayers may continue to make IRA contributions after attaining age 70½. However, those contributions will reduce the amount eligible for the qualified charitable distribution.

▶ **Effective date.** The amendments, repealing Code Sec. 219(d) and Code Sec. 408A(c)(4) are effective for contributions made for tax years beginning after December 31, 2019. (SECURE Act Sec. 107(d)(1)). The amendment of Code Sec. 408(d)(8)(A) is also effective for distributions made for tax years beginning after December 31, 2019 (SECURE Act Sec. 107(d)(2)).

Law Source: Law at ¶5048, ¶6040, ¶6060 and ¶6065.

— Act Sec. 107(a), Division O, of the Further Consolidated Appropriations Act, 2020 (P.L. 116-94), repealing Code Sec. 219(d)(1).

— Act Sec. 107(b), Division O, amending Code Sec. 408(d)(8)(A).

— Act Sec. 107(c), Division O, repealing Code Sec. 408A(c)(4) and redesignating paragraphs (5), (6), and (7) as paragraphs (4), (5), and (6) respectively.

— Act Sec. 107(d), Division O, providing effective date.

¶150 Difficulty of Care Payments Treated as Compensation in Applying Retirement Contribution Limits

SUMMARY OF NEW LAW

Difficulty of care payments will be treated as compensation for purposes of calculating the applicable contribution limits, thereby allowing home health care workers to contribute to an IRA or defined contribution plan.

BACKGROUND

In order to establish and contribute to an IRA, a person must receive compensation. The term "compensation" includes wages, salaries, professional fees, and other amounts received for personal services actually rendered. Compensation also includes such items as sales commissions, compensation for services on the basis of a percentage of profits, commissions on insurance premiums, tips and bonuses, as well as taxable alimony and separate maintenance payments received by an individual under a divorce decree.

Chapter 1—Expansion of Retirement Savings   39

BACKGROUND

However, compensation does not include earnings and profits from property, such as interest, rents, dividends, disability payments, or other amounts not includible in gross income. In addition, compensation for IRA purposes does not include deferred incentive awards such as incentive stock options, stock appreciation rights (SARs), nonqualified stock options, pension and annuity payments, and other deferred compensation.

Nondeductible contributions. Individuals may make nondeductible IRA contributions, up to a specified limit, to the extent they are ineligible to make deductible IRA contributions (Code Sec. 408(o)(2)(B)(i)). However, an individual may elect to treat deductible IRA contributions as nondeductible (Code Sec. 408(o)(2)(B)(ii)). Typically, individuals make such elections if they have no taxable income for the year after taking into account other deductions.

Participation in defined contribution plans require compensation. Similar rules apply to 401(k) plans and other defined contribution plans. Thus, individuals who do not have compensation from an employer or other recognized source cannot participate in a 401(k) plan.

Difficulty of care payments. A taxpayer's gross income does not include amounts received by a foster care provider during the tax year as qualified foster care payments (Code Sec. 131(a)). Qualified foster care payments include any payment made pursuant to a foster care program of a state or political subdivision which is paid by (1) a state or political subdivision thereof or (2) a qualified foster care placement agency, and which is either (1) paid to the foster care provider for caring for a qualified foster individual in the foster care provider's home, or (2) a "difficulty of care" payment (Code Sec. 131(b)(1)).

A "difficulty of care" payment is compensation paid for providing the additional care needed for certain qualified foster individuals. Such payments are provided when a qualified foster individual has a physical, mental or emotional disability for which the state has determined that (1) there is a need for additional compensation to care for the individual, (2) the care is provided in the home of the foster care provider, and (3) the payments are designated by the payor as compensation for such purposes.

Because the compensation of home health care workers that comes from "difficulty of care" payments is exempt from tax under Code Sec. 131, such workers do not have taxable income. Accordingly, as they do not have compensation or earnings upon with contributions may be made, such workers are effectively precluded from participating in a defined contribution plan or contributing to an IRA.

NEW LAW EXPLAINED

Difficulty of care payments treated as compensation in applying retirement contribution limits.—The Act will allow home health care workers to contribute to an IRA or defined contribution plan by treating difficulty of care payments as compensation for purposes of calculating the applicable contribution limits (Code Sec. 408(o)(5), as added by Division O, Act Sec. 116(a)(1) of the SECURE Act, enacted as part of the Further Consolidated Appropriations Act, 2020 (P.L. 116-94); Code Sec. 415(c)(8), as added by SECURE Act Sec. 116(b)(1)).

¶150

NEW LAW EXPLAINED

Defined contribution plan contributions treated as after-tax contributions. Contributions to a defined contribution plan that are allowed because of the modified treatment of difficulty of care payments, must be treated as an investment in contract, and will not cause a plan (and any arrangement which is part of the plan) to be treated as failing to meet the applicable qualification requirements merely by allowing such contributions (Code Sec. 415(c)(8)(B), as added by SECURE Act Sec. 116(b)(1)).

▶ **Effective dates.** The provisions affecting IRAs will be effective for contributions made after the December 20, 2019 enactment of the SECURE Act (SECURE Act Sec. 116(a)(2)). The provisions applicable to defined contribution plans will apply to plan years beginning after December 31, 2015 (SECURE Act Sec. 116(b)(2)).

Law Source: Law at ¶5057, ¶6060 and ¶6075.

— Act Sec. 116(a)(1), Division O, of the Further Consolidated Appropriations Act, 2020 (P.L. 116-94), adding Code Sec. 408(o)(5).

— Act Sec. 116(b)(1), Division O, adding Code Sec. 415(c)(8).

— Act Sec. 116(a)(2) and (b)(2), Division O, providing the effective date.

¶155 Prohibition on Plan Loans Through Credit Cards

SUMMARY OF NEW LAW

Plan loans, effective on the December 20, 2019 date of enactment of the SECURE Act may not be executed through credit cards or similar arrangements.

BACKGROUND

An attractive feature of many 401(k) plans is a provision that allows employees to borrow against their account balances. A loan provision is particularly useful in encouraging low-paid employees to participate in a 401(k) plan. Without such an option, these employees may be reluctant to tie up funds that they may need to purchase a car or to pay for medical costs or other large or unexpected expenses.

Plan loans, however, are not without cost to employees. In addition to set up costs and other administrative fees, an employee must repay a loan, with interest, even if the employee terminates employment. The IRS further cautions that, if there is an express or tacit understanding that a loan will not be repaid, or if the transaction does not otherwise create a debtor-creditor relationship, the amount transferred will be treated as an actual distribution and not as a loan. Under such circumstances, the plan's qualified status would be endangered.

Employers also need to be aware, before adopting a loan program, of several restrictions imposed by the Internal Revenue Code and ERISA that are designed to assure that loans are true loans and not disguised distributions. The restrictions are also intended to protect the assets of the plan from self-dealing by individuals who have power to control the plan.

BACKGROUND

Among the restrictions are: loan terms must be set forth in a written and legally enforceable agreement; the amount of the loan may not exceed the lesser of $50,000 (reduced by previous outstanding loans) or one-half of the present value of the participant's nonforfeitable accrued benefit; the terms of the loan (other than principal residence loans), must require repayment within 5 years; and the loan must be amortized on a substantially level basis with payments made no less frequently than quarterly.

A loan from a qualified 401(k) plan to a participant is not treated as an actual distribution for qualification purposes or for purposes of the 401(k) plan distribution restrictions. However, in order for the plan to remain qualified, loans to participants must: be available to all participants or beneficiaries on a reasonably equivalent basis; not be available to highly compensated employees in an amount greater than the amount made available to other employees; be made in accordance with specific plan provisions; bear a reasonable rate of interest; and be adequately secured. A loan that does not meet the applicable requirements is treated as a deemed distribution and is subject to income tax and, under certain circumstances, the Code Sec. 72(t) penalty 10% tax on early distributions.

However, despite the above conditions, neither the Internal Revenue Code nor ERISA restrict the purposes for which a participant may take a loan from the plan. The ease with which participants may access their accounts is a problem because of the potentially adverse effect such withdrawals could have on retirement savings.

Whether or not a plan allows a participant to recover interest rate changes, the net effect of a loan may be to stunt overall capital accumulation because a partial liquidation immediately reduces the growth factor of compounding. For example, the length of time required to repay a loan on a monthly basis with terms of five years at an interest rate of 10.5% may fail to match the loss of growth due to the liquidation of the account balance to fund the loan. Therefore, although the participant is repaying interest to his or her account, assuming the loans are general plan assets, the participant is generating the interest, not increasing the account balance.

Credit card loans. The above considerations may be especially acute with respect to credit card loans. Credit card loans became a viable option following the issuance by the DOL of an Opinion Letter in 1995 that tacitly sanctioned a loan program pursuant to which participants were able to secure loans, up to a specified limit, from their individual 401(k) accounts through a credit card issued by the administrator of the program (Banc One) (ERISA Opinion Letter 95-17A, June 29, 1995, at PENSION PLAN GUIDE ¶ 19,983T). Proposed regulations issued by the IRS would have imposed a limit of two loans per year on participants. However, in removing the two loan limit from the final rules, the IRS stated that there is no Code Sec. 72(p) barrier to credit card loans that otherwise satisfy the applicable requirements.

Credit card loans have been challenged as enabling the depletion of retirement funds by allowing, if not encouraging, plan participants to indiscriminately borrow from their 401(k) accounts. By contrast, it has also been suggested that, because the repayment of credit card loans is not tied to a payroll deduction, a loan would not be defaulted when a participant terminates employment, which could increase prospects for repayment of the loan.

¶155

NEW LAW EXPLAINED

Prohibition on plan loans through credit cards.—The Act, effective for loans made after the December 20, 2019 date of enactment of the SECURE Act, prohibits plan loans executed through credit cards or similar arrangements (Code Sec. 72(p)(2)(D), as added by Divison O, Act Sec 108(a) of the SECURE Act, enacted as part of the Further Consolidated Appropriations Act, 2020 (P.L. 116-94)).

Note: The restriction on credit card loans, which has long been advocated in the retirement plan community as well as at IRS, may help discourage plan participants from treating their retirement accounts as readily accessible savings accounts.

▶ **Effective date.** The amendment applies to loans made after the December 20, 2019 date of enactment of the Act (SECURE Act Sec. 108(b)).

Law Source: Law at ¶5049 and ¶6025.

— Act Sec. 108(a), Division O, of the Further Consolidated Appropriations Act, 2020 (P.L. 116-94), amending Code Sec. 72(p)(2) by redesignating subparagraph (D) as subparagraph (E).

— Act Sec. 108(a), Division O, adding new Code Sec. 72(p)(2)(D).

— Act. Sec. 108(b), Division O, providing the effective date.

¶160 Penalty-Free Plan Withdrawals to Cover Birth or Adoption Expenses

SUMMARY OF NEW LAW

Individuals are authorized to take penalty free "qualified birth or adoption distributions" of up to $5,000 from an eligible retirement plan (excluding defined benefit plans). Any portion of the distribution may also be recontributed to a retirement plan as an eligible rollover distribution.

BACKGROUND

A 10 percent penalty tax is imposed on an individual under age 59½ who receives a distribution from a plan qualified under Code Sec. 401(a), a 403(b) plan, or from an individual retirement arrangement (Code Sec 72(t)(1)). However, specified distributions are not subject to penalty. Among the distributions exempt from the penalty tax under Code Sec. 72(t)(2) are those made: to a beneficiary (or to the estate of an employee) after the employee's death; because the employee is totally and permanently disabled; to an employee on account of medical expenses, to the extent that the expenses would be deductible under Code Sec. 213 (determined without regard to whether the taxpayer itemizes deductions); for qualified higher education expenses; or to an individual as a qualified reservist distribution.

BACKGROUND

Hardship distributions are not exempt from penalty tax. The only exceptions to the penalty tax on early distributions are those authorized by Code Sec. 72(t)(2). Accordingly, 401(k) participants who receive a hardship distribution from the plan will be subject to penalty tax on the taxable amount of the distribution, unless one of the enumerated exceptions under Code Sec. 72(t)(2) is met.

NEW LAW EXPLAINED

Penalty-free plan withdrawals to cover birth or adoption expenses.—The Act, effective for distributions made after December 31, 2019, authorizes penalty free withdrawals by an individual from an eligible retirement plan (excluding defined benefit plans) for "qualified birth or adoption distributions" of up to $5,000 (Code Sec. 72(t)(2)(H), as added by Division O, Act Sec. 113(a) of the SECURE Act, enacted as part of the Further Consolidated Appropriations Act, 2020 (P.L. 116-94)). Any portion of the distribution may also be recontributed to a retirement plan as an eligible rollover distribution.

Qualified birth or adoption distribution. A qualified birth or adoption distribution would be a distribution from an applicable eligible retirement plan to an individual that is made during the one-year period beginning on the date on which a child of the individual is born or on which the legal adoption by the individual of an "eligible adoptee" is finalized (Code Sec. 72(t)(2)(H)(iii)(I), as added by SECURE Act Sec. 113(a)).

Maximum aggregate amount of distribution. The maximum aggregate amount which may be treated as a qualified birth or adoption distribution by any *individual* with respect to any birth or adoption is $5,000 (Code Sec. 72(t)(2)(H)(ii), as added by SECURE Act Sec. 113(a)).

Note: The maximum aggregate amount applies on an individual basis. Therefore, each spouse may separately receive the maximum aggregate amount of $5,000 in qualified birth or adoption distributions from an eligible retirement plan in which the spouse participates or holds accounts. However, the $5,000 limit is applied on an aggregate basis and covers all plans maintained by the employer and any member of any controlled group which includes the employer (Code Sec. 72(t)(2)(H)(iv), as added by SECURE Act Sec. 113(a)).

Eligible retirement plans. Plans from which the distribution may be made include 401(k) and other qualified retirement plans, 403(b) plans, 457(b) plans, and IRAs (Code Sec. 72(t)(2)(H) (vi), as added by SECURE Act Sec. 113(a)). However, distributions may not be made from a defined benefit plan.

Eligible adoptee. An eligible adoptee would be any individual (other than a child of the taxpayer's spouse) who has not attained age 18 or is physically or mentally incapable of self-support (Code Sec. 72(t)(2)(H)(iii)(II), as added by SECURE Act Sec. 113(a)).

Taxpayer information number. A distribution will not be treated as a qualified birth or adoption distribution unless the taxpayer includes the name, age, and taxpayer identifi-

¶160

NEW LAW EXPLAINED

cation number (TIN) of the child or eligible adoptee on the taxpayer's income tax return for the tax year (Code Sec. 72(t)(2)(H)(vi)(III), as added by SECURE Act Sec. 113(a)).

Recontribution of distribution to plan. An individual who receives a qualified birth or adoption distribution may make one or more contributions in an aggregate amount, not in excess of the distribution, to an eligible retirement plan (including an IRA) of which the individual is a beneficiary and to which a rollover contribution can be made (Code Sec. 72(t)(2)(H)(v), as added by SECURE Act Sec. 113(a)). The taxpayer will be treated as having received the qualified birth or adoption distribution as an eligible rollover distribution and then having transferred the amount to an eligible retirement plan in a direct trustee-to-trustee transfer within 60 days of the distribution (Code Sec. 72(2)(t)(H)(v)(III) and (IV), as added by SECURE Act Sec. 113(a)). Thus, the recontribution of any portion of the distribution will not be taxable to the employee.

Note: The aggregate amount of contributions made by an individual to any applicable eligible retirement plan (other than an individual retirement plan) may not exceed the aggregate amount of qualified birth or adoption distributions that have been made from "such plan" to the individual (Code Sec. 72(t)(2)(H)(v)(II), as added by SECURE Act Sec. 113(a)). In addition, the employee must be otherwise eligible to make contributions (other than recontributions of qualified birth or adoption distributions) to that plan.

However, any portion of a qualified birth or adoption distribution from an individual's eligible retirement plan (whether employer plan or IRA) may be reconstributed to an IRA held by such an individual and to which a rollover may be made.

▶ **Effective date.** The amendments are effective for distributions made after December 31, 2019 (SECURE Act Sec. 113(b)).

Law Source: Law at ¶5054 and ¶6025.

— Act Sec. 113(a), Division O, of the Further Consolidated Appropriations Act, 2020 (P.L. 116-94), adding Code Sec. 72(t)(2)(H).

— Act Sec. 113(b), Division O, providing the effective date.

¶165 Increased Age for Taking Required Minimum Distributions

SUMMARY OF NEW LAW

The age at which required minimum distributions must begin to be made from qualified plans and IRAs is increased, effective for distributions required to be made after December 31, 2019, from 70½ to 72.

BACKGROUND

The interest of an employee participating in a qualified plan or IRA must be distributed no later than his or her "required beginning date." Generally, the interest of an employee must begin to be distributed no later than April 1 of the calendar year following the later of either:

1. the calendar year in which the employee reaches age 70½, or
2. the calendar year in which the employee retires from employment with the employer maintaining the plan (Code Sec. 401(a)(9)(C)).

However, the rule allowing an employee to defer distributions until retirement does not apply to five-percent owners or IRA holders (Code Sec. 401(a)(9)(C)(ii)). Thus, a five-percent owner (any person who owns (or is considered as owning) more than 5% of the outstanding stock of the corporation, or possesses more than 5% of the total combined voting power of all stock of the corporation or the capital or profit interest in the employer) must begin receiving distributions no later than April 1 of the calendar year following the calendar year in which they attain age 70½. Similarly, distributions from an IRA or Individual Retirement Annuity (including a SIMPLE IRA) must begin no later than April 1 of the calendar year following the calendar year in which the IRA holder attains age 70½.

The policy underlying the rule requiring distributions at age 70½ has been to ensure that individuals spend their retirement savings during their lifetime and not use their retirement accounts for estate planning purposes or to transfer wealth to beneficiaries. However, despite the merits of the policy goal, the age 70½ threshold was first applied to retirement plans in the early 1960s and has not been adjusted to account for increases in life expectancy or the increased tendency of Americans to work beyond traditional retirement age.

Financial advisors have maintained that increasing the age at which distributions would begin would increase an employee's account balance, if the employee was in a financial position to delay distributions. However, advisors have also cautioned that, because of the reduced life expectancy attendant implementing a later distribution age, the amount of the required minimum distribution (and associated tax) would also be higher.

NEW LAW EXPLAINED

Increased age for taking required minimum distributions.—The Act, effective for distributions required to be made after December 31, 2019, increases the age at which required minimum distributions must begin to be made from qualified plans and IRAs from 70½ to 72 (Code Sec. 401(a)(9)(C)(i)(I), as amended by Division O, Act Sec. 114(a) of the SECURE Act, enacted as part of the Further Consolidated Appropriations Act, 2020 (P.L. 116-94)).

Note: The law does not alter the provision allowing participants (other than five percent owners and IRA holders) to defer required minimum distributions until retirement.

> **Expert Guidance:** The effect of the law, notes Joan McDonagh, Senior National Regulatory Policy Director at Empower Retirement, and co-author of the *401(k) Answer Book*, is to allow employees who turn 70½ after January 1, 2020 to defer

¶165

NEW LAW EXPLAINED

taking RMDs from the plan or IRA account until April 1 in the year after the year in which they turn age 72.

Bruce J. McNeil , of Stoel Rives, LLP, and Editor-in-Chief of the *Journal of Deferred Compensation* and the *Journal of Pension Planning & Compliance*, adds that the "increase in the age for required distributions will provide employees participating in retirement plans with the opportunity to contribute longer, save more for retirement, and delay their retierment."

The extension also applies for purposes of the date by which a surviving spouse must begin taking required minimum distributions as the designated beneficiary of the employee (Code Secs. 401(a)(9)(B)(iv)(I) and (C)(ii)(I), as amended by SECURE Act Sec. 114(b)). However, this provision may be influenced by the Act's elimination of the 'Stretch IRA" (see ¶ 300).

Note: The provision approximates the goal of reflecting the increase in life expectancy. However, it does not apply to employees and IRA owners who attain age 70½ prior to January 1, 2020. In addition, the new rules may not appease those who have advocated a repeal of the age condition or provide solace to many taxpayers who either are not in a position to defer distributions or will be faced with larger required minimum distributions at age 72.

Expert Guidance: The new rules apply to distributions required to be made after December 31, 2019, with respect to individuals who attain age 70½ after such date. Susan Wright, CPA, Managing Editor, Technical Answer Group (TAG) highlights the possible impact of the effective date on active non-owner participants who had attained age 70½ by December 31, 2019. Assuming the plan does not require RMDs for these participants (which is common), Wright notes, it appears they will be subject to the old rules, meaning they will be required to begin receiving RMDs if they retire, even if they have not yet attained age 72. Hopefully, Wright adds, the IRS will issue guidance on this point.

▶ **Effective date.** The amendments are effective for distributions required to be made after December 31, 2019, with respect to an individual who attains age 70½ after that date (SECURE Act Sec. 114(d)).

Law Source: Law at ¶5055 and ¶6050.

— Act Sec. 114(a), Division O, of the Further Consolidated Appropriations Act, 2020 (P.L. 116-94), amending Code Sec. 401(a)(9)(C)(i)(I)).

— Act Sec. 114(b), Division O, amending Code Secs. 401(a)(9)(B)(iv)(I) and (C)(ii)(I).

— Act Sec. 114(d), Divison O, providing the effective date.

¶165

¶170 Plan Amendments: Remedial Amendment Periods

SUMMARY OF NEW LAW

A remedial amendment period, extending until the last day of the first plan year beginning on or after January 1, 2022, or such later date as Treasury may prescribe, is authorized for plan amendments required by the SECURE Act.

BACKGROUND

A qualified retirement plan must be amended to conform to applicable law and to correct any disqualifying provisions during a prescribed "remedial amendment period."

A plan provision is disqualifying if it results in the failure of the plan to satisfy the qualification requirements, by reason of a change in those requirements, or the disqualifying provision is integral to a qualification requirement that has been changed. A change in qualification requirements includes a statutory change or a change in the requirements provided in regulations or other guidance. In addition, a disqualifying provision includes the absence from a plan of a provision required by (or, if applicable, integral to) the change in the qualification requirements (Code Sec. 401(b); IRS Reg. § 1.401(b)-1)).

The remedial amendment period for a disqualifying provision with respect to a provision of a new plan or the absence of a provision from a new plan is generally the 15th day of the 10th calendar month after the end of the plan's initial plan year. By contrast, the remedial amendment period for a disqualifying provision with respect to an amendment to an existing plan is the end of the second calendar year following the calendar year in which the amendment is adopted or effective, whichever is later.

With respect to a change in the qualification requirements, the remedial amendment period for a disqualifying provision regarding a change in qualification requirements is the end of the second calendar year that begins after the issuance by IRS of the Required Amendments List in which the change in qualification requirements appears.

The remedial amendment period permits a plan to be amended retroactively to comply with a change in plan qualification requirements. However, a plan must be operated in compliance with a change in qualification requirements from the effective date of the change.

NEW LAW EXPLAINED

Plan amendments: remedial amendment periods.—The Act authorizes a remedial plan amendment period until the last day of the first plan year beginning on or after January 1, 2022, or such later date as Treasury may prescribe, for plan amendments required by the SECURE Act (Division O, Act Sec. 601(b) of the SECURE Act, enacted as part of the Further Consolidated Appropriations Act, 2020 (P.L. 116-94)). A plan will be treated as being operated in accordance with terms of the plan and not in violation of

NEW LAW EXPLAINED

the anti-cutback rules of Code Sec. 411(d)(6) or ERISA Sec. 204(g) during the stipulated period (SECURE Act Sec. 601(a)).

The remedial amendment period applicable to governmental plans (Code Sec. 414(d)) and collectively bargained plans (ratified before the December 20, 2019 date of enactment of the SECURE Act) will last until the first plan year beginning on or after January 1, 2024 (SECURE Act Sec. 601(b)).

Retroactive application of amendment. Consistent with generally applicable procedures, a plan must be operated in compliance with a change in qualification requirements, generally from the effective date of the statutory or regulatory amendment to the end of the remedial amendment period (or, if earlier, the date the amendment was adopted) (SECURE Act Sec. 601(b)(2)). In addition, the amendment must apply retroactively during the period (Act Sec. 601(b)(2)).

▶ **Effective date.** The Act does not specify an effective date. Accordingly, the amendment is effective on the December 20, 2019, date of enactment of the SECURE Act.

Law Source: Law at ¶5071.

— Act Sec. 601(a), Division O, of the Further Consolidated Appropriations Act, 2020 (P.L. 116-94), authorizing a remedial plan amendment period.

— Act Sec 601(b), Division O, requiring compliance with change in qualification requirements from date of amendment to end of remedial amendment period.

— Act Sec 601(b)(2), Division O, providing retroactive application.

¶175 Special Disaster-Related Rules for Use of Retirement Funds

SUMMARY OF NEW LAW

An exception to the Code Sec. 72(t) early distribution penalty is provided for qualified disaster distributions from retirement plans of up to $100,000. The qualified distribution will be included in income ratably over a three-year period and taxpayers are further authorized to recontribute the amount of the distribution to an eligible retirement plan. Finally, the Act increases the limits on plan loans made to individuals experiencing qualified disasters from $50,000 to $100,000 and extends applicable loan repayment periods.

BACKGROUND

A 10% additional tax is imposed on an individual under age 59½ who receives a distribution from a plan qualified under Code Sec. 401(a) or from an individual retirement arrangement (Code Sec. 72(t)). The tax applies to the amount of the distribution includible in income.

BACKGROUND

Exceptions to penalty tax: qualified disaster distributions. Exceptions to the penalty tax apply under specified circumstances, including qualified disaster distributions.

The Tax Cuts and Jobs Act of 2017 authorized relief from the 10 percent penalty tax for "qualified 2016 disaster distributions" from qualified plans, 403(b) plans and IRAs of up to $100,000. The provisions essentially mirrored the relief provided under Code Sec. 1400Q. Under the relief, the income attributable to a qualified 2016 disaster distribution could be included in income ratably over three years, and the amount of a qualified disaster distribution could be recontributed to an eligible retirement plan within three years (Tax Cuts and Jobs Act of 2017 (P.L. 115-97) Act Sec. 11028).

A qualified 2016 disaster distribution was defined as a distribution from an eligible retirement plan made on or after January 1, 2016, and before January 1, 2018, to an individual whose principal place of abode at any time during calendar-year 2016 was located in a 2016 disaster area (as declared by the President under the Robert T. Stafford Disaster Relief and Emergency Assistance Act). In addition, however, the individual must have sustained an economic loss by reason of the events giving rise to the disaster declaration.

Recontribution of qualified disaster distribution. Any portion of a qualified 2016 disaster distribution could, at any time during the three-year period beginning the day after the date on which the distribution was received, be recontributed to an eligible retirement plan to which a rollover could be made. An amount recontributed within the three-year period was treated as a rollover and was not includible in income. Thus, if an individual received a qualified 2016 disaster distribution in 2016, that amount was included in income, generally ratably over the year of the distribution and the following two years, but was not subject to the 10 percent early withdrawal tax. Moreover, if the amount of the qualified 2016 disaster distribution was recontributed to an eligible retirement plan in 2018, the individual could file an amended return to claim a refund of the tax attributable to the amount previously included in income (Tax Cuts and Jobs Act of 2017 (P.L. 115-97), Act Sec. 11028(b)(1)(E)).

California wildfire distributions. The Bipartisan Budget Act of 2018 provided disaster relief mirroring the provisions under Code Sec. 1400Q and the authorized recontribution of withdrawals for home purchases under Code Sec. 1400Q(b) for individuals affected by wildfires in California in 2017 (Bipartisan Budget Act of 2018 (P.L. 115-123), Act Secs. 20101 and 2010). The relief applied to distributions from an eligible retirement plan made on or after October 8, 2017, and before January 1, 2019, to an individual whose principal place of abode during any portion of the period from October 8, 2017 to December 31, 2017, was located in a designated California wildfire disaster area. The individual, however, must have sustained an economic loss by reason of the wildfires.

Hardship distributions. Elective deferrals may generally not be distributed prior to a participant's retirement, death, disability, severance from employment, attainment of age 59 ½, or the occurrence of another stipulated event, such as hardship (Code Sec. 401(k)(2)(B); IRS Reg. 1.401(k)-1(d)(1)). Among the recognized hardship distributions are those needed to pay expenses incurred for the repair of damage to the employee's principal residence that would qualify as a deductible casualty expense under Code Sec. 165 (IRS Reg. § 1.401(k)-1(d)(3)(iii)(B)(6)).

¶175

BACKGROUND

Application of restrictions on casualty loss deductions. The Tax Cuts and Jobs Act of 2017 limited the itemized deduction for personal casualty losses, in tax years beginning after December 31, 2017, and before January 1, 2026, to losses attributable to federally declared disasters (Code Sec. 165(h)(5)(A)). Eliminating the deduction for casualty losses that are not attributable to a federally declared disaster initially appeared to similarly restrict the safe harbor distribution authorized under IRS Reg. § 1.401(k)-1(d)(3)(iii)(B)(6). Accordingly, concerns arose that, absent clarification from the IRS, expenses incurred to repair damage to a principal residence that was not attributable to a federally declared disaster would appear to not qualify as an immediate and heavy financial need justifying a hardship distribution under the safe harbor.

Final regulations, effective September 23, 2019, but generally applicable to distributions made on or after January 1, 2020, allay such concerns by expressly stating that the new limits under Code Sec. 165(h)(5) do not apply for purposes of the safe harbor. Thus, the Code Sec. 165 casualty loss rules are applied without regard to whether the loss is attributable to a federally declared disaster (IRS Reg. § 1.401(k)-1(d)(3)(ii)(B)(6)).

Disaster events. Final regulations, effective September 23, 2019, but generally applicable to distributions made on or after January 1, 2020, provide a new safe harbor event for hardship distributions made on account of a disaster declared by the Federal Emergency Management Agency (FEMA) (IRS Reg. § 1.401(k)-1(d)(3)(ii)(B)(7)). Under the final rules, provided an employee's principal residence or principal place of employment at the time of the disaster was located in an area designated by FEMA for individual assistance, expenses and losses (including lost income) incurred by the employee on account of the disaster would qualify for a safe harbor hardship distribution.

Loans. A plan loan to a participant is to be treated as a distribution (i.e., deemed distribution) and taxed to the extent that it exceeds prescribed limits.

Dollar limit on plan loans. A loan from a qualified plan that is repaid within five years is treated as a distribution only to the extent that the amount of the loan, when added to the outstanding loan balance of the employee under all other loans from such plan, exceeds the lesser of: (1) $50,000, reduced by the excess of: (a) the highest outstanding balance of loans for the plan during the one-year period ending on the day before the date the loan is made, over (b) the outstanding balance of the loans for the plan on the date the loan is made; or (2) the greater of one-half of the present value of the employee's nonforfeitable accrued benefit under the plan (i.e. vested interest), or $10,000 (Code Sec. 72(p)(2)(A)).

A temporary increase in the available dollar amount of a plan loan (to $100,000) was authorized for qualified individuals affected by specified hurricanes and California wildfires (Code Sec. 1400Q(c)(1)).

Repayment terms. The terms of the loan (other than principal residence loans), must require repayment within five years (Code Sec. 72(p)(2)(B)). In addition, a loan must be amortized on a substantially level basis with payments made no less frequently than quarterly (Code Sec. 72(p)(2)(C)).

A one-year extension of the repayment date of a loan was authorized for qualified individuals affected by designated hurricanes and for individuals affected by California

¶175

BACKGROUND

wildfires that occurred during a designated period in 2017 (Code Sec. 1400Q(c)(2); Bipartisan Budget Act of 2018 (P.L. 115-123), Act Sec. 20102(c)).

NEW LAW EXPLAINED

Special disaster-related rules for use of retirement funds.—The Act modifies the rules governing early distributions, hardship distributions, and plan loans to allow plan participants access to qualified disaster distributions from their retirement funds (Division Q, Act Sec. 202, of the Further Consolidated Appropriations Act, 2020 (P.L. 116-94)). The relief will be limited to taxpayers who sustained losses in a designated qualified disaster area during the period, beginning January 1, 2018, and ending 60 days after the December 20, 2019 date of enactment of the Appropriations Act (Division Q, Act Sec. 201 of the Appropriations Act).

Qualified disaster distributions. The Act provides an exception to the early distribution penalty under Code Sec. 72(t) for qualified disaster distributions (Division Q, Act Sec. 202(a)(1) of the Appropriations Act). A "qualified disaster distribution" would be a distribution from an eligible retirement plan (including 401(k), 403(b), 457(b) plan, or IRA) made: (1) on or after the first day of the incident period of a qualified disaster and before the date which is 180 days after the December 20, 2019, date of enactment of the Appropriations Act, and (2) to an individual whose principal place of abode at any time during the incident period is located in the qualified disaster area with respect to such qualified disaster (Division Q, Act Sec. 202(a)(4) of the Appropriations Act).

Economic loss required. An individual must also have sustained an economic loss by reason of the qualified disaster in order to qualify for the relief.

Dollar limit on amount of distribution. The aggregate amount of qualified disaster distributions received by an individual for a tax year may not exceed the excess (if any) of: (1) $100,000, over (2) the aggregate amounts treated as qualified disaster distributions received by the individual for all prior tax years (Division Q, Act Sec. 202(a)(2)(A) of the Appropriations Act).

Separate limit applies to multiple disasters. The limitation is applied on an aggregate basis and will cover distributions from all plans maintained by the participant's employer (including any member of the employer's controlled group) (Division Q, Act Sec. 202(a)(2)(B) of the Appropriations Act). However, the limitation will be applied separately with respect to distributions made with respect to each qualified disaster (Division Q, Act Sec. 202(a)(2)(D) of the Appropriations Act).

Recontribution of amount of qualified distribution to plan. Individuals who receive a qualified disaster distribution may, at any time during the three-year period beginning on the day after the date on which the distribution was received, make one or more contributions in an aggregate amount not to exceed the amount of the distribution to an eligible retirement plan of which the individual is a beneficiary and to which a rollover contribution may be made (Division Q, Act Sec. 202(a)(3) of the Appropriations Act). Qualified disaster distributions that are repaid to a plan or IRA will be treated as eligible rollover distributions (Division Q, Act Sec. 202(a)(3)(B)-(C) of the Appropriations Act).

¶175

NEW LAW EXPLAINED

Income tax on qualified distribution spread over three-year period. The income tax on a qualified disaster distribution will be applied ratably to the taxpayer over the three-tax year period beginning with the tax year (Division Q, Act Sec. 202(a)(5)(A) of the Appropriations Act). However, the taxpayer may elect not to have the tax spread ratably over the three-year period.

Exemption from trustee-to-trustee transfer rules. Qualified disaster distributions will not be treated as eligible rollover distributions for purposes of the trustee-to-trustee transfer rules of Code Sec. 401(a)(31) or the rollover notice requirements of Code Sec. 402(f) (Division Q, Act Sec. 202(a)(5) of the Appropriations Act).

Exemption from mandatory withholding. Eligible rollover distributions are generally subject to mandatory 20 percent withholding (Code Sec. 3405(c)). However, qualified disaster distributions will not be treated as eligible rollover distributions subject to mandatory 20 percent withholding (Division Q, Act. Sec 202(a)(6) of the Appropriations Act).

Recontributions of hardship withdrawals for home purchase precluded by qualified disaster. The Act provides relief for taxpayers who took a hardship distribution from an eligible retirement plan in order to purchase or construct a principal residence in a qualified disaster area that was not used because of the disaster. Such taxpayers are authorized to recontribute the amount of the distribution back to the plan without adverse tax consequences (Division Q, Act Sec. 202(b) of the Appropriations Act).

The hardship withdrawal must have been received during the period beginning 180 days before the first day of the incident period of the qualified disaster and ending on the date 30 days after the last day of the incident period (Division Q, Act Sec. 202(b)(2)(C) of the Appropriations Act). In addition, the distribution must be recontributed to the plan within an applicable period, beginning on the first day of the incident period of the qualified disaster and ending on the date which is 180 days after the date of the December 20, 2019 date of enactment of the Appropriations Act (Division Q, Act Sec. 202(b)(3) of the Appropriations Act).

Increase in plan loan amounts to individuals affected by qualified disaster. Individuals whose principal place of residence at any time during the incident period of any qualified disaster is located in the qualified disaster area, and have sustained an economic loss by reason of the disaster, may qualify for an increased loan and are allowed an extended period of time in which to repay the loan (Division Q, Act Sec. 202(c) of the Appropriations Act).

Increase in plan loan limit. Qualified individuals are entitled to a plan loan, made during the 180-day period beginning on the December 20, 2019 date of enactment, not to exceed the lesser of: (1) $100,000 (increased from $50,000), reduced by the excess of: (a) the highest outstanding balance of loans for the plan during the one-year period ending on the day before the date the loan is made, over (b) the outstanding balance of the loans for the plan on the date the loan is made; or (2) the greater of *the present value of the nonforfeitable accrued benefit of the employee under the plan*, or $10,000 (Division Q, Act Sec. 202(c)(1) of the Appropriations Act).

¶175

NEW LAW EXPLAINED

Delayed date of repayment. Qualified individuals with an outstanding plan loan (on or after the first day of the incident period of a qualified disaster) are provided with an extended period during which the loan may be repaid. Specifically, if the due date for any loan repayment occurs during the period, beginning on the first day of the incident period of a qualified disaster and ending on the date 180 days after the last day of the incident period, the due date shall be delayed for one year (or, if later, until the date which is 180 days after the December 20, 2019 date of enactment) (Division Q, Act Sec. 202(c)(2)(A) of the Appropriations Act).

Any subsequent repayments with respect to the loan will be adjusted to reflect the delay in the due date and any interest accruing during the delay (Division Q, Act Sec. 202(c)(2)(B) of the Appropriations Act). The authorized delay will be disregarded in determining the five-year repayment period under Code Sec. 72(p)(2)(B) and amortization under Code Sec. 72(p)(2)(C) (Division Q, Act Sec. 202(c)(2)(C) of the Appropriations Act). Thus, the effect of the delay may be to extend the amortization period.

Adopt required plan amendments by end of 2020 plan year. Nongovernmental plans generally are allowed until the last day of the first plan year beginning on or after January 1, 2020 (or a later date prescribed by Treasury) to adopt plan amendments necessary to comply with the new rules (Division Q, Act Sec. 202(d) of the Appropriations Act). Governmental plans are allowed an additional two years in which to adopt the required amendments.

In addition, as is typically the case, the plan or annuity contract must be operated during a specified period (ending on the last day of the 2020 plan year or the date the amendment was adopted) as if the amendment were in effect. In addition, the amendment to the plan or contract amendment must apply retroactively for the period (Division Q, Act Sec. 202(d)(2)(B) of the Appropriations Act).

▶ **Effective date.** The relief applies to taxpayers who sustained losses in a designated qualified disaster area during the period beginning on January 1, 2018, and on the date that is 60 days after December 20, 2019, which is the date of enactment (Division Q, Act Secs. 201(1)(A) and (2) of the Appropriations Act).

Law Source: Law at ¶5164 and ¶5165.

— Act Sec. 202, Division Q, of the Further Consolidated Appropriations Act, 2020 (P.L. 116-94), modifying early distributions, hardship distributions, and loans..

— Act Sec. 202(a)(1), Division Q, providing an exception to early distribution penalty under Code Sec. 72(t) for qualified disaster distributions.

— Act Sec. 202(a)(2)(A), (B), and (D) Division Q, providing dollar limitations.

— Act Sec. 202(a)(3)(A)-(C), Division Q, providing recontributions of distribution.

— Act Sec. 202(a)(4), Division Q, providing definition of "qualified disaster distribution".

— Act Sec. 202(a)(5)(A), Division Q, providing three-year income tax spread.

— Act Sec. 202(a)(6), Division Q, providing exemption from withholding.

— Act Sec. 202(b), Division Q, providing for recontribution of hardship withdrawals for home purchase precluded by qualified disaster.

¶175

NEW LAW EXPLAINED

— Act Sec. 202(c), Division Q, providing for increase in plan loan amounts repayment period for loans related to qualified disaster.

— Act Sec. 202(d), Division Q, specifying plan amendment timing.

— Act Sec. 201(1)(A) and (2), Division Q, providing the effective date.

¶180 Portability of Lifetime Income Options

SUMMARY OF NEW LAW

Qualified defined contribution plans, 403(b) plans or governmental 457(b) plans are empowered, effective for plan years beginning after December 31, 2019, to make direct trustee-to-trustee transfers to another employer-sponsored retirement plan or IRA of lifetime income investments, or distributions of a lifetime income investment, in the form of a qualified plan distribution annuity, in the event the lifetime income investment is no longer authorized to be held as an investment option under the plan.

BACKGROUND

Amounts held in a 401(k) plan, 403(b) plan, or 457(b) plan, attributable to elective deferrals, may generally not be distributed prior to the participant's retirement, death, disability, severance from employment, or hardship; the termination of the plan; or, in the case of a non-governmental plan, the participant's attainment of age 59 ½ (age 70 ½ for governmental 457 plans). An employee who receives a lump-sum distribution may, however, defer tax on the distribution by transferring (rolling over) all or part of it to another qualified employer-sponsored plan or to an IRA, generally within 60 days of receipt.

Lifetime income options. Lifetime income options included in an employer-sponsored retirement plan, afford employees a minimum level of income (annually or more frequently) for the remainder of the life of the employee or the joint lives of the employee and the employee's designated beneficiary. Lifetime annuities similarly provide payment on behalf of an employee in substantially equal periodic payments over the life of an employee or the joint lives of the employee and the employee's designated beneficiary.

Lifetime income options have been promoted as a means of providing a more secure benefit for participants in defined contribution plans who are increasingly at risk of outliving their retirement savings. However, even when afforded the option, few retirees choose an annuity form of benefit or purchase an annuity with their account balances. Retirees have expressed liquidity concerns, fearing that an annuity (which assesses surrender charges if the investment is liquidated) would be an irrevocable commitment that would limit their flexibility in accessing funds needed to address emerging health and other conditions. In addition to the concerns over the possible loss of funds invested in the long-term annuity upon early death, fear that the cost of a life annuity

BACKGROUND

will exceed the benefit, unwillingness to assume the risk that inflation will erode the value of fixed annuity payments, reluctance to invest too heavily in what is viewed as fixed income product, and risks of under-diversification, plan participants have indicated a lack of confidence that insurance companies will be able to meet payment commitments.

NEW LAW EXPLAINED

Portability of lifetime income options.—The Act, effective for plan years beginning after December 31, 2019, will allow for the portability of lifetime income options, in the event the lifetime income investment is no longer authorized to be held as an investment option under the plan (Code Sec. 401(a)(38), as added by Division O, Act Sec. 109(a) of the SECURE Act, enacted as part of the Further Consolidated Appropriations Act, 2020 (P.L. 116-94)).

Lifetime income investments. A lifetime income investment is an investment option designed to provide an employee with election rights: (1) that are not uniformly available with respect to other investment options under the plan, and (2) that are rights to a lifetime income feature available through a contract or other arrangement offered under the plan (or under another eligible retirement plan, if paid by means of a direct trustee-to-trustee transfer to such other eligible retirement plan) (Code Sec. 401(a)(38)(B)(ii), as added by SECURE Act Sec. 109(a)).

Trustee-to-trustee transfer. In the event the lifetime income investment is no longer authorized as an investment option, qualified defined contribution plans, 403(b) plans or governmental 457(b) plans, will be able to make direct trustee-to-trustee transfers (i.e., qualified distributions) to another employer-sponsored retirement plan or IRA of lifetime income investments or distributions of a lifetime income investment in the form of a qualified plan distribution annuity (Code Sec. 401(a)(38), as added by SECURE Act Sec. 109(a)). The direct trustee-to-trustee transfer (i.e., qualified distribution) would need to occur within 90 days prior to the date on which the lifetime income investment is no longer authorized to be held as an investment option under the plan (Code Sec. 401(a)(38)(A) and (B), as added by SECURE Act Sec. 109(a)).

Note: The amended rules would allow employees, through the trustee-to- trustee rollover, a means around the in-service distribution restrictions.

Plans covered by portability rules. The portability rules will apply to: 401(k) plans (Code Sec. 401(k)(2)(B)(i)(VI), as added by SECURE Act Sec. 109(b)); 403(b) plans (Code Sec. 403(b)(11)(D), as added by SECURE Act Sec. 109(c); and 457(b) plans (Code Sec. 457(d)(1)(A)(iv), as added by SECURE Act Sec. 109(d)).

Note: The portability rules are designed to permit plan participants to preserve investments in lifetime income options, as well as avoid surrender charges and fees. The amendment, along with the safe harbor provided fiduciaries for the selection of life income providers (see ¶ 220), continue the government policy of encouraging the adoption of such plan features.

¶180

NEW LAW EXPLAINED

▶ **Effective date.** The amendments are effective for plan years beginning after December 31, 2019 (SECURE Act Sec. 109(e)).

Law Source: Law at ¶5050, ¶6050, ¶6055 and ¶6085.

— Act Sec. 109(a), Division O, of the Further Consolidated Appropriations Act, 2020 (P.L. 116-94), adding Code Sec. 401(a)(38).
— Act. Sec. 109(b), Division O, adding Code Sec. 401(k)(2)(B)(i)(VI).
— Act Sec. 109(c), Division O, amending Code Sec. 403(b)(11)(D).
— Act Sec. 109(d), Division O, amending Code Sec. 457(d)(1)(A)(iv).
— Act Sec. 109(e), providing the effective date.

¶185 Treatment of Custodial Accounts on Termination of 403(b) Plans

SUMMARY OF NEW LAW

Treasury is instructed to issue guidance under which the distribution needed to effectuate the termination of a 403(b) custodial account may be the distribution of an individual custodial account in kind to a participant or beneficiary. The Treasury guidance will be retroactively effective for tax years beginning after Dec. 31, 2008.

BACKGROUND

Contributions to a 403(b) plan may be excluded from gross income only if made to the following funding arrangements: (1) contracts issued by an insurance company qualified to issue annuities in a State that includes payment in the form of an annuity; (2) custodial accounts that are exclusively invested in stock of a regulated investment company; or (3) a retirement income account for employees of a church-related organization.

Custodial accounts. Custodial accounts are treated as annuity contracts for purposes of Code Sec. 403(b). Amounts contributed to a custodial account and the earnings on those contributions are treated as if they were contributed to a qualified retirement plan and trust under Code Sec. 401(a), and thus exempt from tax (Code Sec. 403(b)(7)). However, contributions to the custodial account may not be distributed before the employee dies, attains age 59 ½, has a severance from employment, or (with respect to elective deferrals) incurs a recognized financial hardship.

Termination of 403(b) plan. A 403(b) plan may be terminated and provide for the distribution of accumulated benefits.

Distribution of accumulated benefits. In order for a 403(b) plan to be considered terminated, all accumulated benefits under the plan must be distributed to all participants and beneficiaries as soon as is "administratively practicable" after the termination of the plan (IRS Reg. 1.403(b)-10(a)(1)). The delivery of a fully paid individual insurance

BACKGROUND

annuity contract is treated as a distribution. However, the mere provision for, and making of, benefit distributions to participants or beneficiaries upon plan termination will not cause a contract to cease to be a 403(b) contract (Rev. Rul. 2011-7, I.R.B. 2011-7, 3-7-11, at PENSION PLAN GUIDE ¶ 19,448Z-299).

Contributions to another 403(b) plan prohibited. 403(b) plans that are subject to the distribution requirements that apply to custodial accounts and elective deferrals may be terminated and accumulated benefits distributed, however, only if the employer (taking into account all entities that are treated as the same employer on the date of termination under the controlled group rules under Code Sec. 414(b), (c), (m), or (o)) does not make contributions to any other 403(b) plan during the period beginning on the date of plan termination and ending 12 months after distribution of all assets from the terminated plan (IRS Reg. 1.403(b)-10(a)(1)). Contributions are made to another 403(b) plan if and only if contributions are made to a 403(b) contract during the period beginning on the date of plan termination and ending 12 months after distribution of all assets from the terminated plan.

Illustration of rules. In Rev. Rul. 2011-7, IRS discussed a situation in which a plan was funded by individual annuity contracts, a group annuity contract, and by amounts held by one or more regulated investment companies in custodial accounts. All amounts held under the plan are a result of employer contributions, including elective deferrals.

On or before January 1, 2012, the employer sponsor adopts a binding resolution to cease future purchases of annuity contracts under the plan and to terminate the plan, effective January 1, 2012. The resolution also provides that all benefits held under the plan are fully vested and nonforfeitable as of January 1, 2012, and directs that all benefits be distributed as soon as practicable thereafter.

The distribution of amounts held in the custodial accounts is made as soon as administratively practical after January 1, 2012. Depending on the elections made by the participant or beneficiary, distributions equal to a recipient's account balance under the custodial account are made (in cash or in kind) either to the participant or beneficiary or to an IRA established for the participant or beneficiary or another eligible retirement plan, in accordance with the rules of IRS Reg. § 1.403(b)-7(b)(1) under which an eligible rollover distribution may be made to an IRA established for the participant or beneficiary or to another eligible retirement plan. Each custodial account provider permits an eligible rollover distribution (as described in Code Sec. 402(c)(4)) to be paid by a direct transfer to an individual retirement account or annuity under Code Sec. 408 or other eligible retirement plan, including an IRA established by the same provider that permits investment in the same mutual fund in which the participant's or beneficiary's custodial account is invested.

IRS concluded that the employer distributed all amounts in the individual and group custodial accounts by payment either to the participant or beneficiary or to an IRA established by the participant or beneficiary or another eligible retirement plan, in accordance with IRS Reg. 403(b)-7(b), or by delivery of a fully paid individual annuity contract. The actions taken by the employer, thus, satisfied the requirements of Code Sec. 403(b) and IRS Reg. 1.403(b)-10(a) for plan termination.

The delivery of a fully paid individual annuity contract to participants or beneficiaries, or of an individual certificate evidencing fully paid benefits under a group annuity contract,

¶185

BACKGROUND

IRS further explained, is not included in gross income until amounts are actually paid to the participant or beneficiary out of the contract, so long as the contract maintains its status as a 403(b) contract. Any other distributions to a participant or beneficiary to effectuate plan termination, whether from an insurance annuity contract, an individual certificate evidencing fully paid benefits under a group annuity contract, or a custodial account, IRS cautioned, are included in gross income, except to the extent the amount is rolled over to an IRA or other eligible retirement plan by a direct rollover or by a transfer made within 60 days after the distribution.

NEW LAW EXPLAINED

Treatment of custodial accounts on termination of 403(b) plans.—Under the Act, no later than six months after the December 20, 2019, date of enactment, Treasury is instructed to issue guidance providing that, in the event an employer terminates the plan under which amounts are contributed to a custodial account, the plan administrator or custodian may distribute an individual custodial account in kind to a participant or beneficiary of the plan (Division O, Act Sec. 110 of the SECURE Act, enacted as part of the Further Consolidated Appropriations Act, 2020 (P.L. 116-94)). The distributed custodial account must be maintained by the custodian on a tax-deferred basis as a 403(b)(7) custodial account, similar to the treatment of fully-paid individual annuity contracts under Rev. Rul. 2011-7, until amounts are actually paid to the participant or beneficiary.

The Treasury guidance must further provide that the 403(b)(7) status of the distributed custodial account will be generally maintained if the custodial account thereafter adheres to the requirements Code Sec. 403(b) that are in effect at the time of the distribution of the account (SECURE Act Sec. 110). In addition, Treasury must clarify that a custodial account will not be considered distributed to the participant or beneficiary if the employer has any material retained rights under the account. However, an employer would not be treated as retaining material rights simply because the custodial account was originally opened under a group contract.

▶ **Effective date.** The Treasury guidance will be retroactively effective for tax years beginning after December 31, 2008. (SECURE Act Sec. 110).

Law Source: Law at ¶5051.

— Act Sec. 110, Division O, of the Further Consolidated Appropriations Act, 2020 (P.L. 116-94), instructing Treasury to issue guidance on treatment of custodial accounts on termination of 403(b) plan.

— Act Sec. 110, providing the effective date.

¶190 Clarification of Retirement Account Rules Related to Church-Controlled Organizations

SUMMARY OF NEW LAW

Individuals eligible to participate in a tax-favored retirement income account maintained by a church include those participating in plans maintained by church-controlled organizations. Thus, effective for plan years beginning on or before December 20, 2019, individuals eligible to participate in the plan would include: duly ordained, commissioned, or licensed ministers, regardless of the source of their compensation; employees of a tax-exempt organization that is controlled by or associated with a church or a convention or association of churches; and certain employees who have separated from service with a church, a convention or association of churches.

BACKGROUND

The tax rules relating to tax-sheltered annuity contracts also apply to retirement income accounts provided by a church or convention of churches for its employees (Code Sec. 403(b)(9); IRS Reg, 1.403(b)-9). Specifically, a retirement income account maintained for employees of a church-related organization (i.e., a church or convention or association of churches) is treated as an annuity contract under the 403(b) rules. Thus, amounts paid by a church employer to a church-maintained retirement income account will be treated the same as amounts contributed by a church employer to a tax-sheltered annuity contract. A church-maintained retirement income account differs only in that the account is not maintained by an insurance company, as is the case with a tax-sheltered annuity contract. Accordingly, the restriction requiring 403(b) assets to be invested in an annuity contract or mutual fund, does not apply to plans maintained by a church or convention of churches.

A retirement income account is a defined contribution program established or maintained by a church-related organization, pursuant to which the following rules apply:

1. The plan must provide for a separate accounting of the retirement income account's interest in the underlying assets. The accounting must be sufficient to: (a) allow for a determination (at all times) of the retirement income account's interest in the underlying assets, and (b) distinguish that interest from an interest that is not part of the retirement income account.

2. Investment performance must be based on gains and losses on the assets held in the retirement income account.

3. The assets held in the account may not be used for, or diverted to, purposes other than for the exclusive benefit of plan participants or their beneficiaries.

The third condition is designed to preclude a loan or extension of credit being made to an employer from assets in the account. However, some confusion existed as to whether individuals eligible to be covered by the plans were limited to church employees or also included those participating in plans maintained by certain church-controlled organizations.

¶190

BACKGROUND

Qualified church-controlled organizations. A qualified church-controlled organization is any church-controlled tax-exempt organization other than an organization that (1) offers goods, services, or facilities for sale, other than on an incidental basis, to the general public, other than goods, services, or facilities that are sold at a nominal charge substantially less than the cost of providing the goods, services, or facilities, and (2) normally receives more than 25 percent of its support from either governmental sources, or receipts from admissions, sales of merchandise, performance of services, or furnishing of facilities, in activities that are not unrelated trades or businesses, or from both.

Church-controlled organizations that are not qualified church-controlled organizations are generally referred to as "nonqualified church-controlled organizations." An emerging issue has been whether employees of nonqualified church-controlled organizations may be covered under a section 403(b) plan that consists of a retirement income account.

NEW LAW EXPLAINED

Clarification of retirement account rules related to church-controlled organizations.—The Act clarifies that covered individuals, eligible to participate in a tax-favored retirement account maintained by a church, include those participating in plans maintained by church-controlled organizations. Incorporating the definition of employee under Code Sec. 414(e)(3)(B), a covered employee for purposes of Code Sec. 403(b)(9) will include: duly ordained, commissioned, or licensed ministers, regardless of the source of compensation; employees of a tax-exempt organization that is controlled by or associated with a church or a convention or association of churches; and certain employees who have separated from service with a church, a convention or association of churches, but for whom the plan retains an accrued benefit or account or continues to receive contributions for the individual for a limited period (Code Sec. 403(b)(9)(B), amended by Division O, Act Sec. 111(a) of the SECURE Act, enacted as part of the Further Consolidated Appropriations Act, 2020 (P.L. 116-94).

▶ **Effective date.** The amendment is effective for plan years beginning before, on, or after the December 20, 2019 date of enactment of the SECURE Act (SECURE Act Sec. 111(b)).

Law Source: Law at ¶5052 and ¶6055.

— Act Sec. 111(a), Division O, of the Further Consolidated Appropriations Act, 2020 (P.L. 116-94), amending Code Sec. 403(b)(9)(B).

— Act Sec. 111(b), Division O, providing the effective date.

¶190

¶195 Special Rules for Minimum Funding Standards for Frozen Community Newspaper Plans

SUMMARY OF NEW LAW

The sponsors of community newspaper pension plans that have been frozen as of December 31, 2017, are provided relief from the governing funding requirements. Under the relief, the interest rate used to calculate funding obligations would increase to 8 percent and the applicable shortfall amortization period would be extended from 7 years to 30 years.

BACKGROUND

Inadequately financed pension plans create the risk that the funds needed to provide employees with promised benefits upon retirement will not be available. Accordingly, employers that maintain defined benefit plans, as well as certain defined contribution plans, such as money purchase plans and target benefit plans, must adhere to funding standards stipulated in ERISA and the Internal Revenue Code. However, arrangements such as profit-sharing plans, welfare benefit plans, stock bonus plans, ESOPs, plans funded exclusively by insurance contracts, church plans, municipal plans, and state plans are exempt from the funding rules.

Minimum required contribution. An employer's contribution to a single-employer defined benefit plan for a plan year may not be less than the "minimum required contribution" (Code Sec. 430(a)(2); ERISA Sec. 303(a)(2)).

The minimum required contribution applicable to plans in which plan assets (reduced by credit balances) are less than the "funding target" of the plan for the year will be the sum of the plan's target normal cost for the plan year, applicable shortfall amortization installments, and applicable waiver amortization installments (Code Sec. 430(a)(1); ERISA Sec. 303(a)(1)).

Target normal cost. For plans that are not at risk for any plan year, the target normal cost is the excess of: (1) the sum of (a) the present value (as of the valuation date) of all benefits that are expected to accrue or to be earned under the plan during the plan year, plus (b) the amount of plan-related expenses expected to be paid from plan assets during the plan year, over (2) the amount of mandatory employee contributions expected to be made during the plan year (Code Sec. 430(b)(1); ERISA Sec. 303(b)(1)).

Shortfall amortization charge for the plan year. The shortfall amortization charge is the total (not less than zero) of the amounts (i.e., the shortfall amortization installments) required to amortize shortfall amortization bases for the plan year and six preceding years (Code Sec. 430(c); ERISA Sec. 303(c)).

Shortfall amortization installments. The shortfall amortization installments are the annual amounts necessary to amortize the shortfall amortization base for the plan year over the seven-year period beginning with the plan year (Code Sec. 430(c)(2)(A); ERISA Sec. 303(c)(2)(A)). The shortfall amortization installment for any plan year in the seven-year period (i.e., the current plan year and the six preceding plan years) with

BACKGROUND

respect to any shortfall amortization base is the annual installment determined for the year for the shortfall amortization base.

Shortfall amortization base. The shortfall amortization base for a plan year is the funding shortfall for the plan year reduced by the present value (determined using the segment rates of ERISA Sec. 303(h)(2)(C) and Code Sec. 430(h)(2)(C)) (see below) of the aggregate total of the shortfall amortization installments and waiver amortization installments that have been determined for the plan year and any succeeding plan year with respect to any shortfall amortization bases and waiver amortization bases for preceding plan years (Code Sec. 430(c)(3); ERISA Sec. 303(c)(3)).

Election of temporary extension of amortizations schedules. The plan sponsor of a single-employer defined benefit pension plan may elect to determine shortfall amortization installments with respect to the shortfall amortization base under two alternative extended amortization schedules: (1) the two plus seven amortization schedule, or (2) the 15-year amortization schedule (Code Sec. 430(c)(2)(D)(iv); ERISA Sec. 303(c)(2)(D)(iv)).

Waiver amortization charge for the plan year. The waiver amortization charge is the aggregate total of the amounts (i.e., the waiver amortization installments) required to amortize the "waiver amortization base" for the plan year over a five-year period (Code Sec. 430(e); ERISA Sec. 303(e)).

Valuation of assets. The value of plan assets is determined as: (1) the fair market value of plan assets on the valuation date, or (2) as the average of the fair market value of assets on the valuation date and the adjusted fair market value of assets, subject to a 90-110 percent corridor (i.e., a plan asset valuation of between 90-110 percent of the fair market value of the assets on the valuation date) (Code Sec. 430(g)(3); ERISA Sec. 303(g)(3)).

Interest rate assumptions: Segmented yield curve. The determination of present value and other funding computations is made on the basis of reasonable actuarial assumptions and methods that take into account the experience of the plan and offer an actuary's best estimate of anticipated experience under the plan (Code Sec. 430(h); ERISA Sec. 303(h)).

The interest rates used in determining the present value of benefits that are included in the target normal cost and the funding target for the plan for the plan year are based on the performance of corporate bonds as reflected in a segmented yield curve that reflects the age of an employer's work force (Code Sec. 430(h)(2)(B); ERISA 303(h)(2)(B)).

The yield curve will essentially consist of different interest rates applicable to benefits payable in three different time periods (i.e., segments). The applicable interest rate will be determined by the segment in which the expected payment due date falls, ranging from 0-5 years, 5-20 years, or over 20 years. Generally, employers with an older work force will be required to use a short-term corporate bond rate, resulting in higher contributions.

The yield curve is an acknowledgment that an employer's funding liabilities are, to a large degree, a function of the demographic profile of the plan's population. Accordingly, an employer with an older plan population nearing retirement age will have a larger funding obligation based on its applicable interest rates, as compared to a new

BACKGROUND

company with a younger plan population, because its liabilities would be discounted at short-term interest rates.

Segment rate stabilization. The segment rates have been modified in a manner that was designed to stabilize the rates (by providing a floor and ceiling to the rates for the current year). Under the governing framework, each of the three segment rates are adjusted to fall within a specified range based on a percentage of the average of the corresponding segment rate for a specified period. The stabilized segment rates were expected to result in an upward adjustment of interest rates, which may lead to a reduction in an employer's required funding contributions.

Specifically, the segment rate stabilization applies if the rate determined under the regular rules is outside a specified range of the average of segment rates for the preceding 25-year period. Each segment rate for the plan year that is determined under Code Sec. 430(h)(2)(C)(i)-(iii) is adjusted so that it is no less than the applicable minimum percentage of the corresponding 25-year average segment rate for the calendar year that contains the first day of the plan year and no more than the applicable maximum percentage of that 25-year segment rate. Thus, if a segment rate determined for an applicable month under the regular rules is less than the applicable minimum percentage, the segment rate will be adjusted upward to match that percentage. Similarly, if the segment rate determined for an applicable month under the regular rules is greater than the applicable maximum percentage, the segment rate will be adjusted down to match that percentage (Code Sec. 430(h)(2)(C); ERISA Sec. 303(h)(2)(C)).

Segment interest corridors. The applicable minimum percentage and the applicable maximum percentage vary in accordance with the plan year. The Bipartisan Budget Act of 2015, effective for plan years beginning after December 31, 2015, extended the funding stabilization percentages, allowing the corridor on interest rates to remain at 10 percent through 2020 (Code Sec. 430(h)(2)(C)(iv); ERISA Sec. 303(h)(2)(C)(iv)) However, the corridor increases by five percent per year through 2024, at which point the corridor permanently remains at 30 percent.

Note: Combined with low interest rates (which produce a higher funding target and target normal cost), the corridors applicable beginning in 2023 will confront businesses that are already facing market pressures that are reducing revenue (e.g., community newspapers) with the need to increase pension contributions or make those contributions over a shorter period of time (which necessarily increases the amount of the required contribution).

At risk plans. Plans with more than 500 participants that have a funded target attainment percentage in the preceding year below designated thresholds will be deemed "at-risk" and subject to increased target liability (Code Sec. 430(i); ERISA Sec. 303(i)). The funding percentage is determined by subtracting credit balances from plan assets.

Variable rate premiums. Single-employer defined benefit plans with unfunded vested benefits, as of the close of the preceding year, must pay an additional variable rate premium (ERISA Sec. 4021)(a). The variable rate premium is based on the amount of potential liability that the plan creates for the PBGC. A plan's per-participant variable rate premium (VRP) is a specified dollar amount for each $1,000 (or fraction thereof) of

¶195

BACKGROUND

unfunded vested benefits under the plan, as of the end of the preceding year (ERISA Sec. 4006(a)(3)).

However, certain categories of single-employer plans are not required to determine or report unfunded vested benefits on their PBGC Comprehensive Premium Filing and do not have to pay the variable rate portion of the PBGC insurance premium. Exemptions are authorized for: plans without vested participants as of the UVB valuation date; Code Sec. 412(e)(3) plans (formerly known as Code Sec. 412(i) plans); certain plans terminating in standard terminations; and certain small new or newly covered plans. (PBGC Reg. § 4006.5).

NEW LAW EXPLAINED

Special rules for minimum funding standards for frozen community newspaper plans.—The Act allows the sponsors of community newspaper pension plans that have been frozen as of December 31, 2017, to elect alternative minimum funding standards that would increase the interest rate used in calculating funding obligations and extend the applicable shortfall amortization period (Code Sec. 430(m), as added by Division O, Act Sec. 115(a) of the SECURE Act, enacted as part of the Further Consolidated Appropriations Act, 2020 (P.L. 116-94); ERISA Sec. 303(m), as added by SECURE Act Sec. 115(b)).

Closed community newspaper plan. The funding relief would be available to the sponsor of a community newspaper plan under which no participant has had their accrued benefit increased (whether because of service or compensation) after December 31, 2017 (Code Sec. 430(m)(1) as added by SECURE Act Sec. 115(a); ERISA Sec. 303(m)(1), as added by SECURE Act Sec. 115(b)). The election would apply to the sponsor's plan and any plan sponsored by any member of the same controlled group.

Community newspaper. The relief would be limited to a "community newspaper plan" which, as of December 31, 2017: (1) publishes and distributes daily, either electronically or in printed form, one or more community newspapers in a single state; (2) is not a company the stock of which is publicly traded (on a stock exchange or in an over-the-counter market), and is not controlled, directly or indirectly, by such a company; (3) is controlled, directly or indirectly: (a) by one or more persons residing primarily in the state in which the community newspaper is published; (b) for not less than 30 years by individuals who are members of the same family; (c) by a trust created or organized in the state in which the community newspaper is published, the sole trustees of which are persons described in (a) or (b); (d) by a tax exempt 501(c)(3) entity, organized and operated in the state in which the community newspaper is published, the primary purpose of which is to benefit communities in that state; or (e) by a combination of persons described in (a), (c), or (d); and (4) does not control directly or indirectly, any newspaper in any other state (Code Sec. 430(m)(4)(A), as added by SECURE Act Sec. 115(a); ERISA Sec. 303(m)(4)(A), as added by SECURE Act Sec. 115(b)).

Control. A person would be treated as controlling another person if the person possesses, directly or indirectly, the power to direct or cause the direction and manage-

¶195

NEW LAW EXPLAINED

ment of such person (including the power to elect a majority of the members of the board of directors of such person) through the ownership of voting securities (Code Sec. 430(m)(4)(C), as added by SECURE Act Sec. 115(a); ERISA Sec. 303(m)(4)(C), as added by SECURE Act Sec. 115(b)).

Controlled group. A controlled group would include all persons treated as a single employer under the standard controlled groups, common control and affiliated service group rules of Code Sec. 414 (Code Sec. 430(m)(5), as added by SECURE Act Sec. 115(a); ERISA Sec. 303(m)(5), as added by SECURE Act Sec. 115(b)).

Circulation scope of at least 100,000. The community newspaper would need to serve a metropolitan statistical area with a population of no less than 100,000 (Code Sec. 430(m)(4)(C), as added by SECURE Act Sec. 115(a); ERISA 303(m)(4)(C), as added by SECURE Act Sec. 115(b)).

Alternative minimum funding standards: Interest rates. The relief would allow a sponsor to elect an alternative interest rate of eight percent for (or, instead of) the first, second, and third segment rates in effect for any month (Code Sec. 430(m)(3)(A)(i), as added by SECURE Act Sec. 115(a); ERISA Sec. 303(m)(3)(A)(i), as added by SECURE Act Sec. 115(b)).

Moreover, for purposes of calculating the funding target and normal cost of a plan, the present value of any benefits accrued or earned under the plan for a plan year for which the election is in effect will be determined on the basis of the United States Treasury obligation yield curve (Code Sec. 430(m)(3)(A)(ii), as added by SECURE Act Sec. 115(a); ERISA Sec. 303(m)(3)(A)(ii), as added by SECURE Act Sec. 115(b))

Comment. The eight percent alternative rate is higher than corporate bond segment rates, which have recently ranged between 3-6 percent. Treasury rates have been lower, ranging from 2.75 to 4 percent.

Alternative minimum funding standards: Shortfall amortization base. The relief modifies the previous shortfall amortization base and the new shortfall amortization base.

Previous shortfall amortization base. Under the relief, previous shortfall amortization bases (i.e., plan years prior to plan year for which the election applies) and all shortfall amortization installments determined with respect to those bases are to be reduced to zero under rules similar to the Code Sec. 430(c)(6) rules for early deemed amortization upon attainment of the funding target (Code Sec. 430(m)(3)(B)(i), as added by SECURE Act Sec. 115(a); ERISA Sec. 303(m)(3)(B)(i), as added by SECURE Act Sec. 115(b)).

Note: Under those rules, for purposes of determining the minimum required contribution for that plan year and subsequent plan years: (1) the shortfall amortization bases for all preceding plan years (and all shortfall amortization installments determined with respect to those bases) are reduced to zero; and (2) the waiver amortization bases for all preceding plan years (and all waiver amortization installments determined with respect to those bases) are reduced to zero (Code Sec. 430(c)(6); IRS Reg. § 1.430(a)-1(e)).

¶195

NEW LAW EXPLAINED

New shortfall amortization base. The new shortfall amortization base for the first plan year is to be determined using the newly prescribed alternative interest rates (Code Sec. 430(m)(3)(B)(ii), as added by SECURE Act Sec. 115(a); ERISA Sec. 303(m)(3)(B)(ii), as added by SECURE Act Sec. 115(b)).

Alternative minimum funding standards: Shortfall amortization installments. Under the relief, the amortization period for shortfall installments would be extended from seven plan years to 30 plan years (Code Sec. 430(m)(3)(C), as added by SECURE Act Sec. 115(a); ERISA Sec. 303(m)(3)(C), as added by SECURE Act Sec. 115(b)).

Note: The special election authorized under Code Sec 430(c)(2)(D) for either the two-plus-seven, or 15-year amortization schedules would not be available for any plan year in which a community newspaper plan sponsor has elected the alternative funding rule (Code Sec. 430(m)(3)(C), as added by SECURE Act Sec. 115(a); ERISA Sec. 303(m)(3)(C), as added by SECURE Act Sec. 115(b)).

At-risk rules would not apply. The rules applicable to at-risk plans under Code Sec. 430(i) and ERISA Sec. 303(i) would not apply to community newspaper plans electing the alternative funding rules (Code Sec. 430(m)(3)(D), as added by SECURE Act Sec. 115(a); ERISA Sec. 303(m)(3)(D), as added by SECURE Act Sec. 115(b)).

Application of variable rate premium. The variable rate premium would be determined as if the election to apply the alternative funding standards had not been made (ERISA Sec. 303(m)(6), as added by SECURE Act Sec. 115(b)).

▶ **Effective date.** The amendments will apply to plan years ending after December 31, 2017 (SECURE Act Sec. 115(c)).

Law Source: Law at ¶5056, ¶6080 and ¶7005.

- Act Sec. 115(a), Division O, of the Further Consolidated Appropriations Act, 2020 (P.L. 116-94), adding Code Sec. 430(m).
- Act Sec. 115(b), Division O, adding ERISA Sec. 303(m).
- Act Sec. 115(c), Division O, providing the effective date.

Administrative Improvements

¶200　Treatment of Plans Adopted by Filing Due Date as in Effect as of Close of Year
¶205　Combined Annual Report for Group of Plans
¶210　Lifetime Income Disclosure
¶220　Fiduciary Safe Harbor for Selection of Lifetime Income Provider
¶225　Expansion of Nondiscrimination Cross-Testing Rules
¶230　Modification of PBGC Premiums for Cooperative and Small Employer Charity (CSEC) Plans

¶200 Treatment of Plans Adopted by Filing Due Date as in Effect as of Close of Year

SUMMARY OF NEW LAW

Employers, effective for tax years beginning after December 31, 2019, will be allowed to treat qualified retirement plans adopted after the close of the tax year, but before the due date of their tax return for the year (including extensions), as having been adopted as of the last day of the tax year.

BACKGROUND

An employer must generally have adopted a qualified plan under Code Sec. 401 by the end of its tax year for a contribution to be deductible for that tax year. However, under Code Sec. 401(b), a stock bonus, pension, profit-sharing, or annuity plan is considered as satisfying the requirements of Code Sec. 401(a) for the period beginning with the date on which it was put into effect, or for the period beginning with the earlier of: (a) the date on which there was adopted or put into effect any amendment which caused the plan to fail to satisfy such requirements, and ending with the time prescribed by law for filing the return of the employer for his taxable year in which such plan or amendment was adopted (including extensions thereof), or (b) such later time as the Secretary may designate, if all provisions of the plan which are necessary to satisfy such requirements are in effect by the end of such period and have been made effective for all purposes for the whole of such period.

BACKGROUND

Thus, a plan may be established on the last day of a tax year, even though the first contribution is not made until the due date of the employer's tax return for the tax year. However, a plan may not be adopted after the end of a tax year and applied retroactively to the tax year prior to the year in which it was adopted.

NEW LAW EXPLAINED

Treatment of plans adopted by filing due date as in effect as of close of year.—The Act, effective for plans adopted for tax years beginning after December 31, 2019, allows employers to treat a stock bonus, pension, profit-sharing or annuity plan adopted after the close of the tax year, but before the due date of their tax return for the year (including extensions) as having been adopted as of the last day of the tax year (Code Sec. 401(b), as amended by Division O, Act Sec. 201(a) of the SECURE Act, enacted as part of the Further Consolidated Appropriations Act, 2020 (P.L. 116-94)).

> **Expert Guidance:** The granting of additional time to establish a plan is designed to provide flexibility for employers (especially small employers) that are considering adopting a plan. It may also provide opportunity for employees to receive contributions for that earlier year and begin to accumulate retirement savings.
>
> James Turpin, co-author of the *Pension Answer Book*, however, cautions that, while the amended rule seems like a great opportunity, it is not the panacea that many expect. First, Turpin advises, it is not possible to retroactively implement the 401(k) features of a profit sharing plan. By the time a plan is adopted, participants might have already been credited with two years of benefit accruals before the plan sponsor has made the first contribution. If the employer adopts a defined benefit plan at the very last moment (i.e., October 14th for an employer with a calendar year for tax purposes), the plan is already out of compliance because the last date to have made a contribution for the initial plan year was September 15.
>
> **Expert Guidance:** Although further guidance may provide clarity or modification, Susan Wright, CPA, Managing Editor, Technical Answer Group (TAG), cautions employers to be careful if they retroactively adopt a plan after the normal Form 5500 filing deadline. The Form 5500 is due by the last day of the seventh month following the close of the plan year. Since employers will now have until the due date of the employer's tax return (including extensions) to adopt a plan retroactively for the prior year, it is possible a plan could be adopted after the plan's Form 5500 filing deadline.
>
> While a Form 5558 could not be filed to retroactively extend the Form 5500 filing deadline, Wright advises, employers do have the option of using the extension for their federal income tax return. This extension is automatically granted as long the following conditions are satisfied: (1) the plan must have the same plan year as the employer's tax year; (2) the employer must have been granted an extension of time to file its federal income tax return; and (3) the employer must maintain a copy of the extension in its records. If an employer is relying on the tax filing extension, Wright stresses, the Form 5500 must be filed no later than the due date of the employer's tax return.

NEW LAW EXPLAINED

Finally, Wright notes that, if an employer wants to adopt a plan retroactively (after the normal Form 5500 filing deadline), the plan year needs to be the same as the employer's tax year to take advantage of the automatic Form 5500 filing extension. Additionally, employers will not be able to wait to adopt a plan until the last minute (as they can do with a SEP) since there will need to be a sufficient amount of time before the deadline for the plan service providers to prepare the plan document, establish a plan trust account, and prepare the Form 5500 so that it can be filed timely.

▶ **Effective date.** The amendment is effective for plans adopted for tax years beginning after December 31, 2019 (SECURE Act Sec. 201(b)).

Law Source: Law at ¶5058 and ¶6050.

— Act Sec. 201(a)(1), Division O, of the Further Consolidated Appropriations Act, 2020 (P.L. 116-94), amending Code Sec. 401(b).

— Act Sec. 201(a)(2), Division O, adding Code Sec. 401(b)(2).

— Act Sec. 201(b), Division O, providing the effective date.

¶205 Combined Annual Report for Group of Plans

SUMMARY OF NEW LAW

The IRS and DOL are directed to allow a group of similar defined contribution plans, effective for returns due for plan years after December 31, 2021, to file a consolidated Form 5500 annual report. The plans must have the same named fiduciary, the same administrator, use the same plan year, and provide the same investments or investment options to participants and beneficiaries.

BACKGROUND

ERISA requires a plan administrator to file a comprehensive annual Form 5500 report, disclosing information relating to the plan's qualified status, financial condition, and operation (ERISA Sec. 104; Code Sec. 6058). In addition, annual reports must be filed by each plan administrator or employer that maintains an employee benefit plan, including defined benefit and defined contribution plans and welfare benefit plans. In addition, annual reports must be filed for a plan, even if the plan is not tax qualified, or benefits no longer accrue, or contributions are no longer made under the plan. Thus, a Form 5500 must be filed for "frozen" plans.

Simplified reporting options are provided for small employers and one-participant plans. However, in order to ensure accurate reflection of the characteristics and operations that applied during the reporting year of the plan or arrangement, a separate Form 5500 must be filed for each plan.

Electronic filing requirement. Filers who are required to file at least 250 returns with the IRS during the calendar year that includes the first day of the plan year must file

BACKGROUND

Form 5500 series returns electronically on magnetic media (Code Sec. 6011(e); IRS Reg. 301.6058-2). Exceptions are authorized for "undue" economic hardship.

NEW LAW EXPLAINED

Combined annual report for group of plans.— The IRS and DOL are directed to allow a group of similar defined contribution plans, effective for returns due for plan years after December 31, 2021, to file a consolidated Form 5500 annual report (Division O, Act Sec. 202 of the SECURE Act, enacted as part of the Further Consolidated Appropriations Act, 2020 (P.L. 116-94)).

Note: The goal of a consolidated return is to reduce aggregate administrative costs, thereby better positioning small employers to sponsor retirement plans.

Identification of plan in aggregated return. In developing the consolidated return, the DOL and IRS are instructed to require such information as will enable a plan participant to identify any aggregate return or report filed with respect to the plan (SECURE Act Sec. 202(b)).

Plans eligible for consolidated return. A group of plans would be eligible to file the consolidated Form 5500 if all of the plans in the group are individual account plans or defined contribution plans (SECURE Act Sec. 202(c)(1)).

In addition, all of the plans in the group must:

(1) have the same trustee, the same named fiduciary or named fiduciaries, and the same plan administrator;

(2) use the same plan year; and

(3) provide the same investments or investment options to participants and beneficiaries (SECURE Act Sec. 202(c)(2) and (3)).

Plans not subject to ERISA. A plan not subject to ERISA may be included in the group if the same person who performs the functions of a trustee, fiduciary, and administrator for all other plans in the group also performs each of these functions for the plan not subject to ERISA (SECURE Act Sec. 202(c)).

Electronic filing requirements. For purposes of applying the 250 return requirement for electronic filing under Code Sec. 6011(e), information regarding each plan for which information is provided on a consolidated return shall be treated as a separate return (Code Sec. 6011(e)(6), as added by SECURE Act Sec. 202(d)(1)). The amendment would apply to returns required to be filed with respect to plan years beginning after December 31, 2019 (SECURE Act Sec. 202(d)(2)).

▶ **Effective date.** The IRS and DOL are required to implement the modifications allowing for a consolidated annual return and report for a group of plans no later than January 1, 2022. The consolidated return would apply to returns and reports for plan years beginning after December 31, 2021 (SECURE Act Sec. 202(e)).

NEW LAW EXPLAINED

Law Source: Law at ¶5059 and ¶6135.

— Act Sec. 202, Division O, of the Further Consolidated Appropriations Act, 2020 (P.L. 116-94), directing the DOL and IRS to develop a consolidated Form 5500 annual report for eligible plans.

— Act Sec. 202(d)(1), Division O, adding Code Sec. 6011(e)(6)

— Act Sec. 202(e), Division O, providing the effective date.

¶210 Lifetime Income Disclosure

SUMMARY OF NEW LAW

Benefit statements provided to defined contribution plan participants would need to include a lifetime income disclosure at least once during any 12-month period. The disclosure would illustrate the monthly payments the participant would receive if the total account balance were used to provide lifetime income streams, including a qualified joint and survivor annuity for the participant and the participant's surviving spouse and a single life annuity. The Secretary of Labor is directed to develop a model disclosure and applicable assumptions. Plan fiduciaries, plan sponsors, or other persons will not incur liability under ERISA to the extent that they provide lifetime income stream equivalents that are derived in accordance with the prescribed assumptions and include the explanations contained in the model disclosure.

BACKGROUND

The plan administrator of a defined contribution plan (other than a one-participant retirement plan) must furnish a pension benefit statement to participants and beneficiaries (ERISA Sec. 105(a)(1)). The pension benefit statement must be provided: (1) at least once each calendar quarter to each participant or beneficiary who has the right to direct the investment of assets in his or her account under the plan; (2) at least once each calendar year to a participant or beneficiary who has his or her own account under the plan but does not have the right to direct the investment of the assets of the account; and (3) upon written request to a plan beneficiary not described in (1) or (2) above.

Content of pension benefit statement. A pension benefit statement must indicate, on the basis of the latest information available, the total benefits accrued and the nonforfeitable benefits, if any, that have accrued or the earliest date on which benefits will become nonforfeitable (ERISA Sec. 105(b)(2)). For a defined contribution (DC) plan, a pension benefit statement must include the value of each investment to which assets in a participant's or beneficiary's account have been allocated, determined as of the most recent valuation date under the plan. The value must include any assets held in the form of employer securities, without regard to whether the securities were contributed by the plan sponsor or acquired at the direction of the plan or the participant or beneficiary.

BACKGROUND

However, the statement is not required to provide information regarding lifetime income that could be provided by funds in the defined contribution plan.

Requirements for quarterly statements for participants with the right to direct investment of account assets. For a pension benefit statement covering a defined contribution plan that must be provided at least once each calendar quarter to participants or beneficiaries who have the right to direct the investment of their account assets, the statement must include an explanation of any limitations or restrictions on any right of the participant or beneficiary to direct the investment. The notice must also provide an explanation, written in a manner calculated to be understood by the average plan participant, regarding the importance of a well-balanced and diversified investment portfolio for the long-term retirement security of the participants and beneficiaries, as well as a statement cautioning the employee that holding more than 20 percent of a portfolio in the securities of one entity (including employer securities) may indicate that the portfolio is not adequately diversified.

Alternative annual statements for participants without the right to direct investment of account assets. The requirement that a notice be provided annually to a participant or beneficiary who has a defined contribution plan account will be met if, at least annually, the plan updates the information that is required to be provided in the pension benefit statement, or provides in a separate statement, information that will enable a participant or beneficiary to determine their nonforfeitable vested benefits.

NEW LAW EXPLAINED

Lifetime income disclosure.—Benefit statements provided to defined contribution plan participants would need to include a lifetime income disclosure at least once during any 12-month period. The disclosure would illustrate the monthly payments the participant would receive if the total account balance were used to provide lifetime income streams, including a qualified joint and survivor annuity for the participant and the participant's surviving spouse and a single life annuity (ERISA Sec. 105(a)(2)(B)(iii) and 105(a)(2)(D), as added by Division O, Act Sec. 203(b) of the SECURE Act, enacted as part of the Further Consolidated Appropriations Act, 2020 (P.L. 116-94)).

Lifetime income stream equivalent of total benefits accrued. The required disclosure will reflect the "lifetime income stream equivalent of the total benefits accrued" with respect to a participant or beneficiary (ERISA Sec. 105(a)(2)(D)(i)(I), as added by SECURE Act Sec. 203(b)).

A lifetime income stream equivalent of the total benefits accrued benefits would be the amount of monthly payments the participant or beneficiary would receive if the total accrued benefits of the participant or a beneficiary were used to provide "lifetime income streams," based on assumptions to be specified by the Secretary of Labor (ERISA Sec. 105(a)(2)(D)(i)(II), as added by SECURE Act Sec. 203(b)).

Lifetime income streams refer to a qualified joint and survivor annuity (for the participant and the participant's surviving spouse), based on assumptions specified by the Secretary of Labor, including the assumption that the participant or beneficiary has a spouse of equal age, and a single life annuity (ERISA Sec. 105(a)(2)(D)(i)(III), as added

¶210

NEW LAW EXPLAINED

by SECURE Act Sec. 203(b)). The lifetime income streams may have a term certain or other features, as permitted by the rules to be prescribed by the Secretary of Labor.

> **Expert Guidance:** Bruce J. McNeil, of Stoel Rives, LLP, Editor-in-Chief of the *Journal of Deferred Compensation* and the *Journal of Pension Planning & Compliance*, notes that the required disclosure of lifetime income to participants once every 12 months is "really a snapshot of the income and not a projection with tables and actuarial assumptions." Accordingly, McNeil cautions the "information disclosed may be misleading and not very helpful."

Model disclosure. The Secretary of Labor is directed, within one year of the December 20, 2019 date enactment of the SECURE Act, to issue a model lifetime income disclosure (ERISA Sec. 105(a)(2)(D)(ii), as added by SECURE Act Sec. 203(b)). The model disclosure must be written in a manner so as to be understood by the average plan participant and explain: (1) that the lifetime income stream equivalent is only provided as an illustration; (2) that the actual payments under the lifetime income stream which may be purchased with the total benefits accrued will depend on numerous factors and may vary substantially from the lifetime income stream equivalent in the disclosures; and (3) the assumptions upon which the lifetime income stream equivalent was determined. The DOL is further empowered to provide such other similar explanations as it considers appropriate.

Assumptions and rules. The Secretary of Labor is further instructed, within one year of the December 20, 2019 enactment of the SECURE Act, to prescribe assumptions which administrators of individual account plans may use in converting total accrued benefits into lifetime income stream equivalents (ERISA Sec. 105(a)(2)(D)(iii), as added by SECURE Act Sec. 203(b)). The DOL must also issue interim final rules implementing the assumptions.

The DOL is authorized to issue a single set of specific assumptions (including tables or factors which facilitate such conversions), or ranges of permissible assumptions. In addition, to the extent that an accrued benefit is or may be invested in a lifetime income stream, the assumptions may permit administrators of individual account plans to use the amounts payable under such lifetime income stream as a lifetime income stream equivalent.

Limitation on liability for providing lifetime income stream equivalent. Plan fiduciaries, plan sponsors, or other persons will not have liability under ERISA solely because they provide lifetime income stream equivalents that are derived in accordance with the prescribed assumptions and include the explanations contained in the model disclosure (ERISA Sec. 105(a)(2)(D)(iv), as added by SECURE Act Sec. 203(b)).

▶ **Effective date.** The amendment applies to pension benefit statements furnished more than 12 months after the latest of the issuance by the DOL of the interim final rules, the model disclosure, or the required assumptions (ERISA Sec. 105(a)(2)(D)(v), as added by SECURE Act Sec. 203(b)).

Law Source: Law at ¶5060 and ¶7004.

— Act Sec. 203, Division O, of the Further Consolidated Appropriations Act, 2020 (P.L. 116-94), adding ERISA Sec. 105(a)(2)(D).

— Act Sec. 203, Division O, providing the effective date at ERISA Sec. 105(a)(2)(D)(v).

¶220 Fiduciary Safe Harbor for Selection of Lifetime Income Provider

SUMMARY OF NEW LAW

Plan fiduciaries are afforded an optional safe harbor to satisfy the prudence requirements of ERISA with respect to the selection of insurers for a guaranteed retirement income contract. In the event the fiduciary receives certain assurances from the insurer regarding its compliance with state insurance requirements, a fiduciary would be shielded from liability for any loss that may be incurred by a participant or beneficiary due to the insurer's failure to satisfy its financial obligations under the contract.

BACKGROUND

Employee benefit plans purchase benefit distribution annuities for several purposes. Annuities typically are purchased for participants and beneficiaries in connection with the termination of a plan or for participants who are retiring or separating from service with accrued vested benefits.

The selection of an annuity provider is a fiduciary decision, and the DOL has brought several actions against fiduciaries who have failed to follow adequate procedures in selecting the safest available annuity provider. Of concern to the DOL has been the inability of some insurance carriers to satisfy their annuity liabilities because of substantial investment in high risk, high yield debt securities or troubled real estate loans. Accordingly, the DOL has provided guidance for fiduciaries to follow when selecting an annuity provider for purposes of benefit distribution where the plan intends to transfer liability for benefits to the annuity provider.

Safest available annuity standard not applicable to individual account plans. In selecting an annuity provider for purposes of benefit distribution under a defined benefit pension plan, fiduciaries must take steps calculated to select the "safest annuity available," unless it would be in the interest of participants and beneficiaries to do otherwise (ERISA Reg. § 2509.95-1; Interpretive Bulletin 95-1, 3-6-95 (60 FR 12328), at PENSION PLAN GUIDE ¶ 19,972C).

Fiduciaries may not select an annuity provider without an "objective, thorough, and analytical" search and an evaluation of factors relating to the annuity provider's credit worthiness and ability to pay claims.

However, the safest available annuity requirement is not applicable to individual account plans. Governing ERISA regulations expressly limit the application of the safest available annuity rule to the selection of annuity providers for benefit distributions from defined benefit plans (ERISA Reg. § 2509.95-1(a)).

The selection of the annuity contract as an optional form of distribution from an individual account plan does, however, remain subject to all otherwise applicable fiduciary standards. Thus, although a plan fiduciary is not required to select the safest

BACKGROUND

available annuity, it must choose the most prudent option specific to the plan and the plan's participants and beneficiaries.

Safe harbor for selection of annuity providers. A governing safe harbor enables plan fiduciaries to comply with the fiduciary requirements applicable to the selection of an annuity provider for the distribution of benefits under individual account plans (ERISA Reg. § 2550.404a-4).

Under the safe harbor, a fiduciary may not rely solely on ratings provided by insurance rating services in selecting an annuity provider. However, the regulations do not specify minimum requirements or establish the safe harbor as the exclusive means by which the requirements of ERISA Sec. 404(a)(1)(B), with respect to the selection of an annuity provider, may be satisfied (ERISA Reg. § 2550.404a-4(a)(2)).

Note: The final regulations do not reference the general fiduciary standards of ERISA Sec. 404(a)(1). However, the general fiduciary rules still apply and the final regulations do not substantively change the applicable principles. Thus, a plan sponsor may, for example, transfer liability for the payment of benefits to an annuity provider but may not relieve itself of its obligations under ERISA to act in the exclusive interest of participants and beneficiaries and with care, skill, prudence, and diligence in selecting the provider.

Safe harbor conditions. Under the safe harbor, a fiduciary will be deemed to have acted prudently in the selection of an annuity provider for purposes of benefit distribution from an individual account plan or benefit distribution options made available to participants and beneficiaries under the plan, if it has satisfied the following specified conditions (ERISA Reg. § 2550.404a-4(b)):

1. Engaged in an objective, thorough, and analytical search for the purpose of identifying and selecting the annuity provider from which to purchase annuities.

2. Given appropriate consideration to information that is sufficient to assess the ability of the annuity provider to make all future payments under the annuity contract.

3. Given appropriate consideration to the cost (including fees and commissions) of the annuity contract in relation to the benefits and administrative services to be provided under the contract.

Time of selection. In order to clarify that the safe harbor conditions apply solely to a fiduciary's decision to purchase a distribution annuity from an annuity provider, the final regulations allow fiduciaries flexibility with respect to when the safe harbor conditions must be satisfied. Specifically, the final rules provide that the time of selection may be either: (1) the time that the annuity provider and contract are selected for the distribution of benefits to a specific participant or beneficiary; or (2) the time that the annuity provider is selected to provide annuity contracts at future dates.

Periodic review of annuity provider. In order to eliminate possible confusion that could discourage employers from offering annuities as lifetime income distribution options in their plans, the DOL has clarified that a fiduciary's selection and monitoring of an annuity provider is to be judged based on the information available at the time of the selection, and at each periodic review, and not in light of subsequent events (DOL Field Assistance Bulletin 2015-02, July 13, 2015, at PENSION PLAN GUIDE ¶ 19,981Z-50).

NEW LAW EXPLAINED

Fiduciary safe harbor for selection of lifetime income provider.—Plan fiduciaries are afforded an optional safe harbor to satisfy the prudence requirements of ERISA with respect to the selection of insurers for a guaranteed retirement income contract (ERISA Sec. 404(e), as added by Division O, Act Sec. 204 of the SECURE Act, enacted as part of the Further Consolidated Appropriations Act, 2020 (P.L. 116-94)). In the event the fiduciary receives certain assurances from the insurer regarding its compliance with state insurance requirements, a fiduciary would be shielded from liability for any loss that may be incurred by a participant or beneficiary due to the insurer's failure to satisfy its financial obligations under the contract.

Note: The safe harbor relieves fiduciaries of liability with respect to the selection of the insurer and, thus, may encourage the adoption of lifetime income options in defined contribution plans. However, the safe harbor does not relieve fiduciaries from the responsibility to make a separate determination of the prudence of the guaranteed retirement income contract, including its terms and conditions.

Guaranteed retirement income contract. A guaranteed retirement income contract is an annuity contract for a fixed term or a contract (or provision or feature thereof) which provides guaranteed benefits annually (or more frequently) for at least the remainder of the life of the participant or the joint lives of the participant and the participant's designated beneficiary as part of an individual account plan (ERISA Sec. 404(e)(6), as added by SECURE Act Sec. 204)).

Safe harbor for selection of guaranteed retirement income contract. The safe harbor would deem a fiduciary to have satisfied the prudence requirements under ERISA Sec. 404(a)(1)(B) in the selection of the insurer of a guaranteed retirement income contract, if the fiduciary: (1) engages in an "objective, thorough, and analytical search" for the purpose of identifying insurers from which to purchase such contracts; (2) with respect to each insurer of a guaranteed retirement income contract: (a) considers the financial capability of the insurer to satisfy its obligations under the contract, and (b) considers the cost (including fees and commissions) of the guaranteed retirement income contract offered by the insurer in relation to the benefits and product features of the contract and administrative services to be provided under such contract; and (3) on the basis of such considerations, concludes that: (a) at the time of the selection, the insurer is financially capable of satisfying its obligations under the guaranteed retirement income contract, and (b) the relative cost (including fees and commissions) of the selected guaranteed retirement income contract is reasonable (ERISA Sec. 404(e)(1), as added by SECURE Act Sec. 204).

Determination of financial capability of insurer. A fiduciary would be deemed to have satisfied its fiduciary duties under ERISA in determining the financial capabilities of an insurer to satisfy its obligations under the guaranteed retirement income contract under specified conditions (ERISA Sec. 404(e)(2), as added by SECURE Act Sec. 204).

Written representation by insurer of financial capability. The fiduciary must obtain written representations from the insurer that the insurer: (1) is licensed to offer guaranteed retirement income contracts; (2) at the time of selection and for each of the

NEW LAW EXPLAINED

immediately preceding seven plan years: (a) operates under a certificate of authority from the insurance commissioner of its domiciliary state which has not been revoked or suspended, (b) has filed audited financial statements in accordance with the laws of its domiciliary state under applicable statutory accounting principles, (c) maintains (and has maintained) reserves which satisfy all the statutory requirements of all states where the insurer does business, and (d) is not operating under an order of supervision, rehabilitation, or liquidation; (3) undergoes, at least every five years, a financial examination (within the meaning of the law of its domiciliary state) by the insurance commissioner of the domiciliary state (or representative, designee, or other party approved by such commissioner); and (4) will notify the fiduciary of any change in circumstances occurring after the required representations have been provided which would preclude the insurer from making such representations at the time of the issuance of the guaranteed retirement income contract (ERISA Sec. 404(e)(2)(A), as added by SECURE Act Sec. 204).

In addition, the fiduciary, after receiving the required representations, and as of the time of selection, must not be in possession of any other information which would cause the fiduciary to question the representations provided (ERISA Sec. 404(e)(2)(B), as added by SECURE Act Sec. 204).

Fiduciary not required to select lowest cost contract. The safe harbor does not require a fiduciary to select the lowest cost contract (ERISA Sec. 404(e)(3), as added by SECURE Act Sec. 204). Thus, a fiduciary may consider the value of a contract, including features and benefits of the contract and attributes of the insurer (including, without limitation, the insurer's financial strength) in conjunction with the cost of the contract.

Time of selection of insurer and contract. The safe harbor requires compliance with the applicable conditions at the time the insurer and the contract are selected. The time of selection is generally defined as the time that the insurer and the contract are selected for distribution of benefits to a specific participant or beneficiary (ERISA Sec. 404(e)(4)(A), as added by SECURE Act Sec. 204). However, if the fiduciary periodically reviews the continuing appropriateness of the selected insurer, the time of selection would be the time that the insurer and the contract are selected to provide benefits at future dates to participants or beneficiaries under the plan.

Note: Significantly, a fiduciary is not *required* under the safe harbor to review the appropriateness of a selection after the purchase of a contract for a participant or beneficiary.

Scope of periodic review. In the event a fiduciary elects to engage a periodic review of the appropriateness of a selection, it would generally only need to obtain the required written representations (see above) from the insurer on an annual basis (ERISA Sec. 404(e)(4)(B), as added by SECURE Act Sec. 204). However, the safe harbor suggests that a greater review would be needed in the event the fiduciary receives notice of changed circumstance and becomes aware of facts that would cause the fiduciary to question such representations.

Liability limitation. Fiduciaries who comply with the conditions of the safe harbor would be shielded from liability following the distribution of any benefit, or the

¶220

NEW LAW EXPLAINED

investment by or on behalf of a participant or beneficiary pursuant to the selected guaranteed retirement income contract, for any losses that may result to the participant or beneficiary due to the insurer's inability to satisfy its financial obligations under the terms of the contract (ERISA Sec. 404(e)(5), as added by SECURE Act Sec. 204).

▶ **Effective date.** The Act does not provide an effective date. Accordingly, the amendment is considered effective on the December 20, 2019 date of enactment of the SECURE Act.

Law Source: Law at ¶5061 and ¶7006.

— Act Sec. 204, Division O, of the Further Consolidated Appropriations Act, 2020 (P.L. 116-94), adding ERISA Sec. 404(e).

¶225 Expansion of Nondiscrimination Cross-Testing Rules

SUMMARY OF NEW LAW

The governing nondiscrimination rules would be amended, effective upon the December 20, 2019 date of enactment of the SECURE Act, to allow expanded cross-testing between an employer's closed defined benefit plan and defined contribution plans. The modifications will help closed plans pass the applicable nondiscrimination tests and enable existing participants in such plans to continue to accrue benefits.

BACKGROUND

An employer may maintain a defined benefit (DB) and a defined contribution (DC) plan and aggregate them for purposes of satisfying the minimum coverage rules. Such DB/DC plans are subject to a separate set of rules for testing discrimination in amount of contributions or benefits and discrimination in the availability of benefits, rights, and features (BR&Fs) (IRS Reg. § 1.401(a)(4)-9(b))). The general rule for DB/DC plans is that they are to be treated as a single plan for testing purposes.

Determining aggregate allocation rates. An employee's aggregate normal and most valuable allocation rates are determined by treating all DC plans that are part of a DB/DC plan as a single plan, and all DB plans that are part of a DB/DC plan as a separate single plan (IRS Reg. § 1.401(a)(4)-9(b)(2)(ii)(A)).

Determination of aggregate accrual rates. An employee's aggregate normal and most valuable accrual rates are determined by treating all DC plans that are part of a DB/DC plan as a single plan, and all DB plans that are part of a DB/DC plan as a separate single plan (IRS Reg. § 1.401(a)(4)-9(b)(2)(ii)(B)).

Nondiscrimination relief for closed DB plans. The IRS has provided temporary nondiscrimination relief for certain "closed" DB plans (i.e., plans that are closed to new entrants as of a specified date, but continue to provide ongoing accruals for existing participants) (IRS Notice 2019-49, I.R.B. 2019-37, 9-9-19, at PENSION PLAN GUIDE

BACKGROUND

¶ 17,167L, modifying IRS Notice 2018-69, I.R.B. 2018-37, 9-10-18, at PENSION PLAN GUIDE ¶ 17,164S, modifying IRS Notice 2017-45, I.R.B. 2017-38, 9-18-2017, at PENSION PLAN GUIDE ¶ 17,162, modifying IRS Notice 2016-57, I.R.B. 2016-40, 10-3-2016, at PENSION PLAN GUIDE, ¶ 17,159R, modifying IRS Notice 2015-28, I.R.B. 2015-14, 4-19-15, at PENSION PLAN GUIDE ¶ 17,156E, modifying IRS Notice 2014-5, I.R.B. 2014-2, 1-6-2014, at PENSION PLAN GUIDE ¶ 17,153B). Closing a DB plan can also often coincide with an amendment that provides new or greater contributions under a DC plan that is intended to replace accruals under the DB plan for new hires or other employees to whom the DB plan is closed. However, such arrangements invite discrimination concerns.

In the event a closed defined benefit plan cannot satisfy the coverage requirement of Code Sec. 410(b) on its own, it must be aggregated with another plan. If the defined benefit plan is aggregated with a defined contribution plan that covers the employer's new hires in order to satisfy the coverage requirement, it must also be aggregated with the defined contribution plan for purposes of satisfying the nondiscrimination requirements of Code Sec. 401(a)(4). In the typical case, the aggregated plans will fail the requirements of Code Sec. 401(a)(4) unless they are permitted to demonstrate compliance with the nondiscrimination requirements on the basis of equivalent benefits. The aggregated plans usually may demonstrate nondiscrimination on the basis of equivalent benefits in the initial years of aggregation without the need for benefit changes.

Proposed regulations providing relief for closed plans were issued in January 2016 (IRS Proposed Reg. §§ 1.401(a)(4)-4, 1.401(a)(4)-8, 1.401(a)(4)-9) (1-29-16 (81 FR 4976), at PENSION PLAN GUIDE ¶ 20,264H). The IRS expected initially that the regulations would have been finalized and effective for plan years beginning on or after January 1, 2018. However, the final regulations have not been released and the IRS does not anticipate the rules being issued before 2020 or 2021.

While regulatory changes to the nondiscrimination rules are under consideration, the IRS will permit certain employers that sponsor a closed DB plan and a DC plan to demonstrate that the aggregated plans comply with the nondiscrimination requirements of Code Sec. 401(a)(4) on the basis of equivalent benefits, even if the aggregated plans do not satisfy the current conditions for testing on that basis, if certain conditions are met. Specifically, the IRS has provided a temporary additional eligibility criterion that permits a DB/DC plan to demonstrate satisfaction of the nondiscrimination in amount of contributions or benefits requirement of IRS Reg. § 1.401(a)(4)-1(b)(2) on the basis of equivalent benefits even if the DB/DC plan does not meet any of the existing eligibility conditions for testing on that basis under IRS Reg. § 1.401(a)(4)-9(b)(2)(v) (i.e., minimum aggregate allocation gateway) (IRS Notice 2019-49). Under this alternative, the DB/DC plan may nonetheless make that demonstration on the basis of equivalent benefits for a plan year that begins before 2021, if it includes a DB plan providing ongoing accruals that was amended to provide that only employees who participated in the DB plan on a specified date continue to accrue benefits under the plan. Each of the DB plans in the DB/DC plan must satisfy one of the following conditions set forth in Notice 2014-5:

1. For the plan year beginning in 2013, the DB plan was part of a DB/DC plan that either was primarily defined benefit in character (within the meaning of IRS Reg.

¶225

BACKGROUND

§ 1.401(a)(4)-9(b)(2)(v)(B)) or consisted of broadly available separate plans (within the meaning of IRS Reg. § 1.401(a)(4)-9(b)(2)(v)(C)); or

2. In the case of a DB plan that was amended, by an amendment adopted before December 13, 2013, to provide that only employees who participated in the DB plan on a specified date continue to accrue benefits under the plan, the DB plan was not part of a DB/DC plan for the plan year beginning in 2013 because the DB plan satisfied the coverage and nondiscrimination requirements without aggregation with any DC plan.

Additional temporary relief for closed DB plans with respect to benefits, rights, or features. The proposed rules and IRS Notice 2014-5 provided closed DB plans with relief from nondiscrimination testing with respect to a benefit, right, or feature that was made available only to a grandfathered group of employees. If specified eligibility conditions were met, a special testing rule would treat a benefit, right, or feature that was provided only to the employees as satisfying the current and effective availability tests of IRS Reg. § 1.401(a)(4)-4(b) and (c). However, the relief effectively did not apply to defined benefit plans that were closed to new entrants but had not undergone a change in benefit formula with respect to existing participants. The IRS subsequently addressed the limits to the existing relief by providing closed defined benefit plans with additional temporary relief from the current and effective availability requirements of IRS Reg. § 1.401(a)(4)-4, relating to benefits, rights, or features (IRS Notice 2019-60, I.R.B. 2019-49, 12-2-19, at PENSION PLAN GUIDE ¶ 17,167W. Under the temporary relief, which will apply for plan years ending after November 13, 2019, and beginning before January 1, 2021, a plan will be treated as satisfying the current and effective availability tests of IRS Reg. § 1.401(a)(4)-4(b) and (c) for the plan year with respect to a benefit, right, or feature that was provided under the plan at the time the amendment closing the plan was adopted.

NEW LAW EXPLAINED

Expansion of nondiscrimination cross-testing rules.— The SECURE Act, effective upon the December 20, 2019 date of enactment, would allow expanded cross-testing between an employer's closed defined benefit plan and a defined contribution plan. (Code Sec. 401(o), as added by Division O, Act Sec. 205(a) of the SECURE Act, enacted as part of the Further Consolidated Appropriations Act, 2020 (P.L. 116-94)). Plan sponsors would be afforded the option of electing to apply the new rules to plan years beginning after December 31, 2013 (Act Sec. 205(c)(2)). The modifications, which substantially expand upon prior relief, are designed to help closed plans pass the applicable nondiscrimination tests and enable existing participants in such plans to continue to accrue benefits.

Testing of defined benefit plans with closed class of participants. A closed plan would be eligible for the expanded rules regarding cross-testing and aggregation if either: (1) the class was closed before April 5, 2017, or (2) taking into account predecessor plans, the plan has been in effect for at least five years as of the date the class is closed, and during the five-year period preceding the date the class is closed,

¶225

NEW LAW EXPLAINED

there has not been a "substantial increase" in the coverage or value of the benefits, rights, or features (Code 401(o)(1)(A)(iii), Code Sec. 401(o)(1)(B)(iii)(IV), and Code Sec 401(o)(1)(C), as added by SECURE Act Sec. 205(a)).

In addition, the plan must provide benefits to a closed class of participants; for the plan year as of which the class closes and the two succeeding plan years, the plan must satisfy the coverage and nondiscrimination requirements taking into account special rules; and after the date as of which the class was closed, any plan amendment which modifies the closed class or the benefits provided to such closed class may not discriminate significantly in favor of highly compensated employees (Code Sec. 401(o)(1)(B)(iii), as added by SECURE Act Sec. 205(a)).

Nondiscrimination testing. A defined benefit plan that provides benefits, rights, or features to a closed class of participants will not fail nondiscrimination testing under Code Sec. 401(a)(4) because of the composition of the closed class or the benefits, rights, or features provided to the closed class, if: (1) the plan passes the Code Sec. 401(a)(4) nondiscrimination testing for the plan year the class was closed and the two succeeding plan years, taking into account a set of special specified rules (Code Sec. 401(o)(1)(A)(i), as added by SECURE Act Sec. 205(a)); and (2) any amendments modifying the closed class or benefits, rights, or features after the date the class was closed do not discriminate significantly in favor of highly compensated employees (Code Sec. 401(o)(1)(A)(ii), as added by SECURE Act Sec. 205(a)).

Aggregation with a defined contribution plan on basis of benefits. For purposes of determining compliance with the nondiscrimination requirements and the Code Sec. 410(b) coverage rules, an eligible defined benefit plan may be aggregated and tested on a benefits basis with one or more defined contribution plans (Code Sec. 401(o)(1)(B)(i), as added by SECURE Act Sec. 205(a)).

Closed defined benefit plan. The plan must provide benefits to a closed class of participants; for the plan year as of which the class closes and the two succeeding plan years, the plan must satisfy the coverage rules of Code Sec. 410(b); and after the date on which the plan closed, no plan amendment modifying the class or the benefits provided to the class, may significantly discriminate in favor of highly compensated employees (Code Sec. 401(o)(1)(B)(iii), as added by SECURE Act Sec. 205(a)).

The class must generally have closed before April 5, 2017. However, the relief will continue to apply if, taking into account a predecessor plan, such plan has been in effect for at least five years as of the date the class is closed, and during the five-year period preceding the date the class is closed, there has not been a substantial increase in the coverage or value of the benefits, rights, or features, or in the coverage of benefits under the plan (Code Sec. 401(o)(1)(C), as added by SECURE Act Sec. 205(a)).

Aggregation with specified plans. The closed defined benefit plan may be aggregated with the portion of one or more defined contribution plans which: provide matching contributions (under Code Sec. 401(m)(4)(A)); provide annuity contracts (under Code Sec. 403(b)) which are purchased with matching contributions or nonelective contributions; or consist of an employee stock ownership plan (under Code Sec. 4975(e)(7)), or a tax

¶225

NEW LAW EXPLAINED

credit employee stock ownership plan (under Code Sec. 409(a) (Code Sec. 401(o)(1)(B)(i), as added by SECURE Act Sec. 205(a)).

Matching contributions. In the event a defined benefit plan is aggregated with a portion of a defined contribution plan providing matching contributions, the defined benefit plan must also be aggregated with any portion of such defined contribution plan which provides elective deferrals (Code Sec. 401(o)(1)(B)(ii)(I), as added by SECURE Act Sec. 205(a)). In addition, the matching contributions must be treated in the same manner as nonelective contributions (Code Sec. 401(o)(1)(B)(ii)(II), as added by SECURE Act Sec. 205(a)).

Special testing rules. For purposes of nondiscrimination and coverage testing for closed plans eligible for the modified requirements under Code Sec. 401(o)(1)(A) and (B), the following rules apply: in applying Code Sec. 410(b)(6)(C), the closing of the class of participants shall not be treated as a significant change in coverage under Code Sec. 410(b)(6)(C)(i)(II); two or more plans shall not fail to be eligible to be aggregated and treated as a single plan solely because they have different plan years (this rule also applies for determining whether plans may be aggregated and treated as one plan for purposes of applying the nondiscrimination and coverage rules); changes in the employee population will be disregarded to the extent attributable to individuals who become employees or cease to be employees, after the date the class is closed, by reason of a merger, acquisition, divestiture, or similar event; and aggregation and all other testing methodologies otherwise applicable nondiscrimination and coverage testing may be taken into account (Code Sec. 401(o)(1)(I), as added by SECURE Act Sec. 205(a)).

Substantial increase for benefit, rights, and features. For purposes of the rules under Code Sec. 401(o)(1)(C) discussed above (i.e., plans in effect for at least five years as of the closing date) a plan will be treated as having had a substantial increase in coverage or value of the benefits, rights, or features during the applicable five-year period only if, during such period: (1) the number of participants covered by such benefits, rights, or features on the date such period ends is more than 50 percent greater than the number of such participants on the first day of the plan year in which such period began, or (2) the benefits, rights, and features have been modified by one or more plan amendments in such a way that, as of the date the class is closed, the value of such benefits, rights, and features to the closed class as a whole is substantially greater than the value as of the first day of such five-year period, solely as a result of such amendments (Code Sec. 401(o)(1)(D), as added by SECURE Act Sec. 205(a)).

Substantial increase for aggregate testing on benefits basis. In applying Code Sec. 401(o)(1)(C), for purposes of aggregation testing on a benefits basis, a plan will be treated as having had a substantial increase in coverage or benefits during the applicable five-year period only if, during such period: (1) the number of participants benefitting under the plan on the date such period ends is more than 50 percent greater than the number of such participants on the first day of the plan year in which such period began, or (2) the average benefit provided to such participants on the date such period ends is more than 50 percent greater than the average benefit provided on the first day

¶225

NEW LAW EXPLAINED

of the plan year in which such period began (Code Sec. 401(o)(1)(E),(G) and (H), as added by SECURE Act Sec. 205(a)).

Employees disregarded in determination of substantial increase. Specified employees are disregarded for purposes of determining whether a substantial increase in coverage value or coverage or benefits occurred. Employees that may be disregarded include employees who became participants: (1) as a result of a merger, acquisition, or similar event which occurred during the seven-year period preceding the date on which the class was closed, or (2) by reason of a merger of the plan with another plan which had been in effect for at least five years as of the date of the merger (if the benefits, rights, or features under one plan are conformed to the benefits, rights, or features of the other plan prospectively) (Code Sec. 401(o)(1)(F), as added by SECURE Act Sec. 205(a)).

Spun-off plans. The modified cross-testing rules apply to the portion of a closed defined benefit plan (as defined under Code Sec. 401(o)(1)(A) and (B)(iii)) that is spun off to another plan. Thus, if the spun-off plan continues to adhere to the applicable requirements of either Code Sec. 401(o)(1) (A)(i) or (ii) or Code Sec. 401(o)(a)(B)(iii)(II) or (III), the treatment of the spun-off plan will continue with respect to the other employer (Code Sec. 401(o)(1)(J), as added by SECURE Act Sec. 205(a)).

Testing of defined contribution plans on a benefits basis. A defined contribution plan may be tested on a benefits basis if: (1) the plan provides "make-whole contributions" to a closed class of participants whose accruals under a defined benefit plan have been reduced or eliminated; (2) for the plan year of the defined contribution plan as of which the class eligible to receive such make-whole contributions closes and the two succeeding plan years, the closed class of participants satisfies the coverage requirements of Code Sec. 410(b)(2)(A)(i) (determined by applying the special rules of Code Sec. 401(o)(1)(I)); (3) after the date as of which the class was closed, any amendment to the defined contribution plan which modifies the closed class or the allocations, benefits, rights, and features provided to such closed class does not discriminate significantly in favor of highly compensated employees; and (4) the class was closed before April 5, 2017, or meets the rule for defined benefit plans that were closed at a different date under Code Sec. 401(o)(1)(C) (Code Sec. 401(o)(2)(A), as added by SECURE Act Sec. 205(a)).

Closed class of participants. A closed class of participants will be treated as being closed before April 5, 2017, if the plan sponsor's intention to create the closed class was reflected in formal written documents and communicated to participants before such date (SECURE Act Sec. 205(c)(2)(B)). In addition, references to a closed class of participants and similar references to a closed class include arrangements under which one or more classes of participants are closed. However, one or more classes of participants closed on different dates may not be aggregated for purposes of determining the date any such class was closed (Code Sec. 401(o)(3)(B), as addded by SECURE Act Sec. 205(a)).

Make-whole contributions. Make-whole contributions are nonelective allocations made for each employee in the class which are reasonably calculated, in a consistent manner, to replace some or all of the retirement benefits which the employee would have

¶225

NEW LAW EXPLAINED

received under the defined benefit plan and any other plan or qualified cash or deferred arrangement under 401(k)(2) if no change had been made to such defined benefit plan and such other plan or arrangement (Code Sec. 401(o)(3)(A), as added by SECURE Act Sec. 205(a)).

Note: Consistency is not required with respect to employees who were subject to different benefit formulas under the defined benefit plan.

Aggregation with plans including matching contributions. The portion of one or more defined contribution plans which provides make-whole contributions or other nonelective contributions may be aggregated and tested on a benefits basis with the portion of one or more other defined contribution plans which: (1) provides matching contributions (as defined under Code Sec. 401(m)(4)(A)); (2) provides annuity contracts (defined under Code Sec. 403(b)) which are purchased with matching contributions or nonelective contributions; or (3) consists of an employee stock ownership plan or a tax credit employee stock ownership plan (Code Sec. 401(o)(2)(B), as added by SECURE Act Sec. 205(a)).

Spun-off plans. The rules continue to apply to portions of a defined contribution plan that are spun off to another employer, under specified conditions (Code Sec. 401(o)(2)(C), as added by SECURE Act Sec. 205(a)).

Participation requirements for protected participants. Closed defined benefit plans are provided a measure of relief from the participation requirements of Code Sec. 401(a)(26). A plan will be deemed to satisfy the minimum participation rules if: (1) the plan is amended to cease all benefit accruals, or to provide future benefit accruals only to a closed class of participants; (2) the plan satisfies Code Sec. 401(a)(26)(A) as of the effective date of the amendment; and (3) the amendment was adopted before April 5, 2017, or the plan would be described in Code Sec. 401(o)(1)(C), as applied for aggregation purposes, and by treating the effective date of the amendment as the date the class was closed (Code Sec. 401(a)(26)(I), as added by SECURE Act Sec. 205(b)).

Significant change in coverage. The amendments are not treated as a significant change in coverage under Code Sec. 410(b)(6)(C)(i)(II) (Code Sec. 401(a)(26)(I)(iii), as added by SECURE Act Sec. 205(b)).

Spun-off plans. The rules continue to apply to portions of a plan that are spun off to another employer (Code Sec. 401(a)(26)(I)(iv), as added by SECURE Act Sec. 205(b)).

Post-enactment amendments. A plan will not fail to be eligible for the special cross-testing, aggregation, and participation rules (under Code Sec. 401(o)(1)(A), Code Sec. 401(o)(1)(B)(iii), or Code Sec. 401(a)(26)) solely because, in the case of cross-testing, the plan was amended before the December 20, 2019 date of enactment of the SECURE Act, to eliminate one or more benefits, rights, or features, and is further amended after that date of enactment to provide such previously eliminated benefits, rights, or features to a closed class of participants. Nor would the rules cease to apply, in the case of aggregation or participation, if the plan was amended before the date of the enactment to cease all benefit accruals, and further amended after such date of enactment to

NEW LAW EXPLAINED

provide benefit accruals to a closed class of participants (SECURE Act Sec. 205(c)(2)(C)).

> **Expert Guidance:** Michael Melbinger, partner at Winston & Strawn LLP, and author of *Executive Compensation Update*, stresses that the SECURE Act has made it easier for closed pension plans (and savings plans that provide make-whole contributions to former pension plan participants) to satisfy nondiscrimination testing and, thus, continue benefit accruals, through cross-testing.

▶ **Effective date.** The amendments generally take effect on the December 20, 2019 date of the enactment of the Act, without regard to whether any plan modifications referred to in such amendments are adopted or effective before, on, or after such date of enactment. (SECURE Act Sec. 205(c)(1)). However, a plan sponsor may elect to apply the amendments to plan years beginning after December 31, 2013 (SECURE Act Sec. 205(c)(2)).

Law Source: Law at ¶5062 and ¶6050.

— Act Sec. 205(a)(1), Division O, of the Further Consolidated Appropriations Act, 2020 (P.L. 116-94), amending Code Sec. 401 by redesignating subsection (o) as subsection (p).

— Act Sec. 205(a)(2), Division O, adding Code Sec. 401(o).

— Act Sec. 205(b), Division O, adding Code Sec. 401(a)(26)(I).

— Act Sec. 205(c)(1) and (2), Division O, providing the effective date.

¶230 Modification of PBGC Premiums for Cooperative and Small Employer Charity (CSEC) Plans

SUMMARY OF NEW LAW

Individualized rules are established for the calculation of PBGC premiums for Cooperative and Small Employer Charity (CSEC) plans. Such plans, effective for plan years beginning after December 31, 2018, would be subject to a flat-rate premium of $19 per participant, and a variable rate premium of $9 for each $1,000 of unfunded vested benefits.

BACKGROUND

Single-employer defined benefit plans that are covered by ERISA's termination insurance program are required to pay annual termination insurance premiums to the Pension Benefit Guaranty Corporation (PBGC) (ERISA Sec. 4006)). The PBGC, in turn, guarantees benefits for plan participants in the event a plan terminates with insufficient assets to pay benefit liabilities. Single-employer plans and multiple employer plans, including Cooperative and Small Employer Charity (CSEC) plans, are subject to the same PBGC premium requirements.

Premium payment rules. The premium payment program for single-employer (and multiple employer) defined benefit plans consists of two components:

BACKGROUND

1. a flat-rate premium; and
2. a variable rate premium.

Flat-rate premium rate. The flat rate premium is equal to the applicable flat premium rate multiplied by the plan's participant count (ERISA Sec. 4006(a)(3); PBGC Reg. 4006.3(a)). The rates are subject to indexing. For the 2020 plan year, the flat-rate premium is $83 per participant (up from $80 in 2019) (ERISA Sec. 4006(a)(3)(A)(i); PBGC Website (https://www.pbgc.gov), October 11, 2019).

Variable rate premium. Plans with unfunded vested benefits, as of the close of the preceding year, must pay an additional variable rate premium (ERISA Sec. 4006(a)(3)(E)).

Determining the variable rate premium. The variable rate premium is based on the amount of potential liability that the plan creates for the PBGC. A plan's per-participant variable rate premium (VRP) is a specified dollar amount for each $1,000 (or fraction thereof) of unfunded vested benefits under the plan, as of the end of the preceding year (ERISA Sec. 4006(a)(3)(E)(i) and (ii)). The per-participant VRP is multiplied by the number of plan participants during the plan year to yield the total VRP.

Note: Under the rules in effect prior to the adoption of the Pension Protection Act of 2006, a plan's VRP was generally $9 for each $1,000 (or fraction thereof) of unfunded vested benefits under the plan as of the end of the preceding year. Although the rules for calculating the amount of unfunded vested benefits for determining the variable rate premium were modified by PPA, the variable rate premium, for plan years beginning before 2015, remained $9 per $1000 of unfunded vested benefits (ERISA Sec. 4006(a)(8)(A)(i)).

Rules for calculating variable rate premium. Unfunded vested benefits for a plan year will be the excess (if any) of (1) the funding target of the plan (including at-risk assumptions) as determined under ERISA Sec. 303(d) for the plan year by taking into account only vested benefits and using a specified interest rate, over (2) the fair market value of plan assets for the plan year which are held by the plan on the valuation date (ERISA Sec. 4006(a)(3)(E)(iii)).

Amount of variable rate premium. The variable rate premium is indexed (ERISA Sec. 4006(a)(3)(E)(ii); ERISA Sec. 4006(a)(8)). For plan years beginning in 2020, the variable rate premium is $45 per $1,000 of unfunded vested benefits (up from the 2019 rate of $43 per $1,000 of unfunded vested benefits) (ERISA Sec. 4006(a)(8)(C)(i)-(vi); PBGC Website (https://www.pbgc.gov), October 11, 2019).

Cooperative and small employer charity plans. Eligible cooperative plans and eligible charity plans are permanently relieved from having to comply with the funding rules generally applicable to single-employer plans (ERISA Sec. 306 and Code Sec. 433). These plans are treated as a new category of qualified plans referred to as Cooperative and Small Employer Charity (CSEC) plans, and are subject to funding rules substantially similar to the pre-PPA funding rules. Thus, employers will need to make contributions sufficient to ensure that the plan does not have an accumulated funding deficiency as of the end of the plan year. The plan must maintain a funding standard account, and the employer will need to make quarterly payments if the plan has a funded current liability percentage for the preceding year of less than 100 percent. The funding

BACKGROUND

standard account is to be credited and charged solely as provided under the CSEC funding rules (ERISA Sec. 306(b)(1)).

A cooperative and small employer charity pension plan is a defined benefit plan (*other than a multiemployer plan*) that is either: (1) an eligible cooperative plan; (2) a defined benefit plan that, as of June 25, 2010, was maintained by more than one employer, all which were Code Sec. 501(c)(3) organizations; or (3) as of June 25, 2010, was maintained by a single employer that was a Code Sec. 501(c)(3) organization chartered under Part B of Subtitle II of Title 36, United States Code, whose primary exempt purpose is to provide services with respect to children, and which has employees in at least 40 states (ERISA Sec. 210(f)(1) and Code Sec. 414(y)(1)).

NEW LAW EXPLAINED

Modification of PBGC premiums for cooperative and small employer charity (CSEC) plans.—The Act, effective for plan years beginning after December 31, 2018, modifies the flat rate premiums and variable rate premiums applicable to CSEC pension plans (ERISA Sec. 4006(a)(3) and (8), as added by Division O, Act Sec. 206 of the SECURE Act, enacted as part of the Further Consolidated Appropriations Act, 2020 (P.L. 116-94)). The amendments reflect the modified funding rules applicable to CSEC plans, allowing for consistency in the application of the overlapping rules.

Flat rate premiums

The flat rate premium, applicable to CSEC plans for plan years beginning after December 31, 2018, will be $19 per participant (ERISA Sec. 4006(a)(3)(A)(vii), as added by SECURE Act Sec. 206(a)).

Variable rate premiums. As noted above, under ERISA Sec. 4006(a)(3)(E)(iii), in determining the applicable variable rate premium, unfunded vested benefits for a plan year are defined as the excess (if any) of: (1) the funding target of the plan (including at-risk assumptions) as determined "under ERISA Sec. 303(d)" for the plan year by taking into account only vested benefits and using a specified interest rate, over (2) the fair market value of plan assets for the plan year which are held by the plan on the valuation date. The SECURE Act consistent with the modified funding rules applicable to CSEC plans, clarifies that, effective for plan years beginning after December 31, 2018, unfunded vested benefits refers to the excess (if any) of: (I) the funding liability of the plan, as determined under the rules of ERISA Sec. 306(j)(5)(C) for the plan year by only taking into account vested benefits, over (II) the fair market value of plan assets for the plan year which are held by the plan on the valuation date (ERISA Sec. 4006(a)(3)(E)(v), as added by SECURE Act Sec. 206(b)(1)).

Amount of variable rate premium. The applicable dollar amount for purposes of determining the amount of the variable rate premium applicable to a CSEC plan will, effective for plan years beginning after December 31, 2018, be $9 for each $1,000 (or fraction thereof) of unfunded vested benefits under the plan as of the end of the preceding year (ERISA Sec. 4006(a)(8)(E), as added by SECURE Act Sec. 206(b)(2)).

¶230

NEW LAW EXPLAINED

▶ **Effective date.** The amendments will apply to CSEC plans with plan years beginning after December 31, 2018 (SECURE Act Sec. 206(a) and (b)).

Law Source: Law at ¶5063 and ¶7009.

— Act Sec. 206(a), Division O, of the Further Consolidated Appropriations Act, 2020 (P.L. 116-94), adding ERISA Sec. 4006(a)(3)(A)(vii).

— Act Sec. 206(b)(1), Division O, adding ERISA Sec. 4006(a)(3)(E)(v).

— Act Sec. 206(b)(2), Division O, adding ERISA Sec. 4006(a)(8)(E).

— Act Sec. 206(a) and (b), Division O, providing the effective date.

Revenue Provisions

¶300 Modification of Required Distribution Rules for Designated Beneficiaries
¶305 Increase in Failure to File Return Penalty
¶310 Increased Plan Reporting Penalties

¶300 Modification of Required Distribution Rules for Designated Beneficiaries

SUMMARY OF NEW LAW

Under modified required minimum distribution rules, effective for distributions made with respect to defined contribution plan participants and IRA owners who die after December 31, 2019, distributions to individuals other than the surviving spouse of the employee (or IRA owner), disabled or chronically ill individuals, individuals who are not more than 10 years younger than the employee (or IRA owner), or a child of the employee (or IRA owner) who has not reached the age of majority, must generally be distributed by the end of the 10th calendar year following the year of the employee or IRA owner's death. Limited exceptions are authorized, but the provision will effectively limit, if not eliminate, the "stretch IRA" as a tool for managing retirement assets.

BACKGROUND

Required minimum distribution (RMD) rules apply to lifetime and post-mortem distributions from qualified retirement plans and IRAs. While the participant or IRA owner is alive, the amount of such distributions is calculated based on the life expectancy of that individual using the Uniform Life Table (IRS Reg. 1.401(a)(9)-9, Q/A-2). However, if a spouse is named as beneficiary of the account and is more than 10 years younger than the participant or IRA owner, the joint life expectancy of the couple is used to determine the RMD amount (IRS Reg 1.401(a)(9)-9, Q/A-3).

Different rules apply in the event an employee dies before distributions have begun. Two methods apply for distributing the employee's interest.

Five-year rule. Under the five-year rule, the entire interest of an employee who dies before distributions have begun must be distributed as of December 31 of the calendar

BACKGROUND

year containing the fifth anniversary of the date of the employee's death (Code Sec. 401(a)(9)(B)(ii); IRS Reg. § 1.401(a)(9)-3, Q/A-1 and A-25).

Life expectancy rule. Under the life expectancy rule, if any portion of the employee's interest is payable to (or for the benefit of) a designated beneficiary, the portion of the employee's interest to which the beneficiary is entitled will be distributed over the life of the beneficiary (or over a period not extending beyond the life expectancy of the beneficiary) (Code Sec. 401(a)(9)(B)(iii)). Distributions must commence no later than one year after the date of the employee's death.

Surviving spouse. If the designated beneficiary is the employee's surviving spouse, distributions must begin on or before the later of: (1) December 31 of the calendar year immediately following the calendar year in which the employee died, or (2) December 31 of the calendar year in which the employee would have reached age 70 ½ (Code Sec. 401(a)(9)(B)(iv)(I); IRS Reg. § 1.401(a)(9)-3, Q/A-3(b)).

Surviving spouse may claim IRA as own account. The surviving spouse beneficiary of an IRA holder may elect to treat the entire interest in the trust as his or her own IRA (IRS Reg. § 1.408-8, Q/A-5). In the event that such an election is made, the surviving spouse is considered to be the individual for whose benefit the trust is maintained. The surviving spouse's interest in the IRA would be subject to the required minimum distribution rules of Code Sec. 401(a)(9)(A) and distributed over the life of the surviving spouse or over the lives of the surviving spouse and a designated beneficiary.

Absence of governing plan provision. If an employee dies before his or her required beginning date and the employee has a designated beneficiary, the life expectancy rule (rather than the 5-year rule) would be the default distribution rule (IRS Reg. § 1.401(a)(9)-3, Q/A-4(a)). Thus, absent a plan provision or election of the 5-year rule, the life expectancy rule applies in all cases where an employee has a designated beneficiary and the 5-year rule applies if an employee does not have a designated beneficiary.

Stretch IRAs. The rules have enabled retirees to leave plan and IRA assets to children, grandchildren and other nonspousal beneficiaries, without subjecting the beneficiaries to potentially large tax assessments attendant large distributions. Thus, a retiree can effectively "stretch" the IRA over the lifetime of a nonspousal beneficiary, providing potentially years of compounded tax-favored investment growth.

Roth IRAs. Roth IRAs are not subject to lifetime RMDs (Code Sec. 408A(c)(5)). However, beneficiaries of Roth IRAs are required to take RMDs, although such distributions will be tax free if the five-year holding period has been met (IRS Reg 1.408A-6, Q/A-14).

Penalties. Failure to comply with the RMD rules can result in imposition of a 50-percent excise tax based on the amount of RMDs that were supposed to be, but were not, distributed (Code Sec. 4974). No penalty is applicable to Roth IRA owners because they are not required to take lifetime RMDs. However, a penalty may apply to beneficiaries of Roth IRAs for failure to take such distributions.

NEW LAW EXPLAINED

¶300

NEW LAW EXPLAINED

Modification of required distribution rules for designated beneficiaries.—The Act, effective for distributions made with respect to defined contribution plan participants and IRA owners who die after December 31, 2019, will require distributions to individuals other than the surviving spouse of the employee (or IRA owner), disabled or chronically ill individuals, individuals who are not more than 10 years younger than the employee (or IRA owner), or child of the employee (or IRA owner) who has not reached the age of majority, to generally be distributed by the end of the 10th calendar year following the year of the employee or IRA owner's death (Code Sec. 401(a)(9)(H), as added by Division O, Act Sec. 401(a)(1) of the SECURE Act, enacted as part of the Further Consolidated Appropriations Act, 2020 (P.L. 116-94)).

Note: Unlike prior law, the 10-year period will apply regardless of whether the plan participant or IRA owner dies before or after reaching the required beginning date (Code Sec. 401(a)(9)(H)(i)(II), as added by SECURE Act Sec. 401(a)(1)).

Plans subject to modified rule. The modified RMD rules apply to qualified defined contribution plans, 403(b) plans, 457(b) plans IRAs, and Roth IRAs. All eligible retirement plans, other than defined benefit plans, are treated as a defined contribution plan (Code Sec. 401(a)(9)(H)(vi), as added by SECURE Act. Sec. 401(a)(1)).

Eligible designated beneficiaries. The modified rules will not apply to "eligible designated beneficiaries" (Code Sec. 401(a)(9)(H)(ii), as added by SECURE Act Sec. 401(a)(1)). Thus, distributions to such individuals may be generally extended over the life or life expectancy of the eligible beneficiary. The special rules applicable to surviving spouses (detailed above) continue to apply.

A new term, "eligible designated beneficiaries" will be limited to: the surviving spouse of the employee; a minor child of the employee; a disabled person under Code Sec. 72(m)(7) (i.e., a person unable to engage in any substantial gainful activity due to a medically determinable physical or mental impairment); a chronically ill individual (as defined by Code Sec. 7702B(c)(2)), whose period of inability to perform (without substantial assistance) at least two activities of daily living, such as bathing, dressing, or toileting, has been certified as indefinite and is expected to be lengthy; and an individual who is not more than 10 years younger than the deceased participant or IRA owner (Code Sec. 401(a)(9)(E), as amended by SECURE Act Sec. 401(a)(2)).

Note: Special rules apply in the case of applicable multi-beneficiary trusts maintained for disabled or chronically ill beneficiaries (Code Sec. 401(a)(9)(H)(iv), as added by SECURE Act Sec. 401(a)(1)).

Determination of eligible designated beneficiary status. The determination of whether a designated beneficiary (i.e., a beneficiary designated by an employee) is an "eligible designated beneficiary" will be made as of the date of the employee's death (Code Sec. 401(a)(9)(E)(ii), as amended by SECURE Act Sec. 401(a)(2)).

Note: Under prior law, an improper beneficiary designation could be "cured" by September 30 of the year following the year the plan participant or IRA owner died. The amended rules foreclose this option. However, it may still be possible to substitute a

¶300

NEW LAW EXPLAINED

beneficiary by means of a qualified disclaimer under Code Sec. 2518, if the time limitation and other applicable requirements are met.

Children reaching age of majority. The exception applicable to minor children of the employee will cease to apply once a child reaches the age of majority. Thus, once a minor child reaches the age of majority, any remainder of the child's interest in the plan or IRA distributions must be completed within 10 years after the date on which the age of majority is attained (Code Sec. 401(a)(9)(E)(iii), as amended by SECURE Act Sec. 401(a)(2)).

Death of eligible designated beneficiary. In the event an eligible designated beneficiary dies before the portion of the employee's interest is entirely distributed, the exception to the 10-year distribution rule will not be further extended to the beneficiary of the eligible designated beneficiary. The remainder of the portion of the employee's interest would need to be distributed within 10 years after the death of the eligible designated beneficiary (Code Sec. 401(a)(9)(H)(iii), as added by SECURE Act Sec. 401(a)(1)).

Collective bargaining agreements. The amended rules are generally effective for distributions with respect to employees who die after December 31, 2019 (SECURE Act Sec. 401(b)(1)). However, with respect to plans maintained pursuant to a collective bargaining agreement ratified before the December 20, 2019 date of enactment of the SECURE Act, the modified rules will apply to distributions with respect to employees who die in calendar years beginning after the earlier of: (A) the later of (i) the date on which the collective bargaining agreement terminates, or (ii) December 31, 2019, or (B) December 31, 2021 (SECURE Act Sec. 401(b)(2)). However, any amendment adopted to conform the plan to the modified rules will not be treated as a termination of the collective bargaining agreement.

Governmental plans. The rules will apply to distributions made under governmental plans (defined by Code Sec. 414(d)) with respect to employees who die after December 31, 2021 (SECURE Act Sec. 401(b)(3)).

Exception for existing qualified annuity contracts. The 10-year distribution rule will not apply to binding qualified annuity contracts that were in effect on the December 20, 2019 date of enactment of the SECURE Act (SECURE Act Sec. 401(b)(4)).

A qualified annuity, for purposes of the exception, would be: (i) a commercial annuity (under Code Sec. 3405(e)(6)); (ii) under which annuity payments are made over the life of the employee (or the joint lives of the employee and a designated beneficiary) in accordance with Code Sec. 401(a)(9)(A)(ii) (prior to amendment); and (iii) pursuant to which the employee (whether or not annuity payments have begun before or after the December 20, 2019 date of enactment of the SECURE Act) made an irrevocable election before the date of enactment as to the method and amount of annuity payments to be made to the employee or any designated beneficiary (SECURE Act Sec. 401(b)(4)(B)).

Death of employee before effective date of amendment. Special rules apply in the event a plan participant or IRA owner dies before the effective date of the SECURE Act (defined as the "first day of the first calendar year to which the amendments made by this section apply to a plan with respect to employees dying on or after such date") and

NEW LAW EXPLAINED

the designated beneficiary of the employee dies after the date of enactment (SECURE Act Sec. 401(b)(5)). Under such circumstances, the amended rules will apply to any beneficiary of the deceased beneficiary. Moreover, the designated beneficiary will be treated as an eligible designated beneficiary for purposes of the new rules under Code Sec. 401(a)(9)(H)(ii) (as added by SECURE Act Sec. 401(a)(1)).

> **Expert Guidance:** The new 10-year default rule will severely limit, if not eliminate, the use of the "stretch IRA" as an effective estate planning tool. The amended rules will subject non-spousal beneficiaries to potentially large tax liability on an accelerated time frame. However, taxpayers may consider other strategies, such as charitable remainder trusts, that can achieve similar, if not exactly the same, financially beneficial results.
>
> James Turpin, co-author of the *Pension Answer Book*, adds that the new rules on beneficiaries and the application of the 10-year limitation on distributions to most non-spouse beneficiaries may make naming the trust less desirable. When a participant in a qualified plan or the owner of an IRA designates a trust as their beneficiary upon death, Turpin cautions, the terms of the trust will need to be revisited to assure that the original intent will still be effective and whether the trust is a conduit trust or an accumulation trust, it may need to be revised to reflect the intended distribution of the account upon death.

▶ **Effective date.** The amendments are generally effective (with the exception of circumstances noted above) for distributions made with respect to plan participants and IRA owners who die after December 31, 2019 (SECURE Act Sec. 401(b)).

Law source: Law at ¶5066 and ¶6050.

— Act Sec. 401(a)(1), Division O, of the Further Consolidated Appropriations Act, 2020 (P.L. 116-94), adding Code Sec. 401(a)(9)(H).

— Act Sec. 401(a)(2), Divison O, amending Code Sec. 401(a)(9)(E).

— Act Sec. 401(b), Division O, providing the effective date.

¶305 Increase in Failure to File Return Penalty

SUMMARY OF NEW LAW

The penalty assessed for failure to file a federal income tax return has been increased, effective for returns due after December 31, 2019, from $330 to the lesser of $435 or 100% of the amount of the tax.

BACKGROUND

An employer that fails to file a federal tax return within 60 days of the prescribed date (including filing extensions), is subject, absent a showing of reasonable cause, to a penalty of no less than the lesser of $330 or 100 percent of the amount required to be

BACKGROUND

shown as tax on such return (Code Sec. 6651(a)). The dollar amount is subject to an inflation adjustment (Code Sec. 6651(j)).

NEW LAW EXPLAINED

Increase in failure to file penalty.—The Act, effective for returns due after December 31, 2019, increases the failure to file penalty from $330 to the lesser of $435 or 100% of the amount of the tax due. (Code Sec. 6651(a), as amended by Division O, Act Sec. 402(a) of the SECURE Act, enacted as part of the Further Consolidated Appropriations Act, 2020 (P.L. 116-94); Code Sec. 6651(j)(1), as amended by SECURE Act Sec. 402(b)).

▶ **Effective date.** The amendment is effective for returns due after December 31, 2019 (including extensions) (SECURE Act Sec. 402(c)).

Law source: Law at ¶5067 and ¶6150.

— Act. Sec. 402(a), Division O, of the Further Consolidated Appropriations Act, 2020 (P.L. 116-94), amending Code Sec. 6651(a).

— Act Sec. 402(b), Division O, amending Code Sec. 6651(j)(1).

— Act Sec. 402(c), providing the effective date.

¶310 Increased Plan Reporting Penalties

SUMMARY OF NEW LAW

The penalties for failure to file Form 5500, registration statements, required notifications of change, and withholding notices have been substantially increased, effective for returns and statements due after December 31, 2019.

BACKGROUND

A plan administrator or employer is subject to a penalty $25 per day (up to $15,000) for the failure to comply with the annual Form 5500 reporting requirements (Code Sec. 6652(e)). A penalty of $1 per participant per day (up to $5,000) may be imposed for the failure to file a registration statement or a notification of changes (Code Sec. 6652(d)). Finally, the failure to file a required withholding notice will, absent reasonable cause, subject an employer to a penalty of $10 for each such failure, up to $5,000 for the calendar year (Code Sec. 6652(h)).

NEW LAW EXPLAINED

Increased plan reporting penalties.— The Act significantly increases the applicable reporting penalties. The Form 5500 penalty would be increased to $250 per day, not to exceed $150,000 (Code Sec. 6652(e), as amended by Division O, Act Sec. 403(a) of the

NEW LAW EXPLAINED

SECURE Act, enacted as part of the Further Consolidated Appropriations Act, 2020 (P.L. 116-94)). The failure to file a registration statement would increase to $10 per participant, up to $50,000 (Code Sec. 6652(d), as amended by SECURE Act Sec. 403(b)). The failure to file a required notification of change would result in a penalty of $10 per day, not to exceed $10,000 for any failure (Code Sec. 6652(d), as amended by SECURE Act Sec. 403(b)). Finally, the failure to provide a required withholding notice would result in a $100 penalty for each failure, up to $50,000 for all failures during the calendar year (Code Sec. 6652(h), as amended by SECURE Act Sec. 403(c)).

▶ **Effective date.** The amendments would be effective for returns, statements, and notifications required to be filed, and notices required to be provided, after December 31, 2019 (SECURE Act Sec. 403(d)).

Law source: Law at ¶5068 and ¶6155.

— Act Sec. 403(a), Division O, of the Further Consolidated Appropriations Act, 2020 (P.L. 116-94), amending Code Sec. 6652(e).
— Act Sec. 403(b), Division O, amending Code Sec. 6652(d).
— Act Sec. 403(c), Division O, amending Code Sec. 6652(h).
— Act Sec. 403(d), Division O, providing the effective date.

Bipartisan American Miners Act

¶400 Treasury Transfers to 1974 UMWA Pension Plan
¶405 Funding Multiemployer Health Benefit Plans
¶410 Reduction in Minimum Age for Allowable In-Service Distributions

¶400 Treasury Transfers to 1974 UMWA Pension Plan

SUMMARY OF NEW LAW

The Treasury is required to transfer funds to the 1974 United Mineworkers of America Pension Plan to pay retiree benefits. The plan would be treated as if it was in critical status and would be required to comply with its applicable rehabilitation plan. Plan trustees would be subject to extensive annual reporting requirements.

BACKGROUND

The Surface Mining Control and Reclamation Act of 1977 (SMCRA) (30 U.S.C. 1232) authorized the Treasury to transfer funds, not otherwise appropriated, to health benefit plans maintained for the United Mine Workers of America. Treasury was authorized to pay to the United Mine Workers of America Combined Benefit Fund (Combined Fund), the amount that the trustees of the Combined Fund estimated would be expended from premium accounts maintained by the Combined Fund for the fiscal year to provide benefits for beneficiaries who are unassigned beneficiaries (solely as a result of the application of Code Sec. 9706(h)(1)), subject to specified limitations (SMCRA Sec. 1232(i)).

The total amount that could be transferred under Act Sec. 1232(i) was limited to $490,000. In addition, SMCRA did not authorize the transfer of funds to satisfy pension liabilities.

Multiemployer plans in critical status subject to rehabilitation plans. Multiemployer plans that are so underfunded as to be in "endangered" or "critical" status are required, under the Internal Revenue Code and ERISA, to adopt funding improvement and rehabilitation plans and take certain actions to improve their funding status over a multi-year period (Code Sec. 432; ERISA Sec. 305). Excise taxes and civil penalties may apply if a plan does not adopt or comply with a required funding improvement or rehabilitation plan.

BACKGROUND

Critical status. A multiemployer plan is in critical status for a plan year if the plan actuary determines that it meets any one of four specified tests as of the beginning of the plan year (Code Sec. 432(b)(2); ERISA Sec. 305(b)(2)). Generally, a plan that is less than 65% funded will be in critical status if it is projected that the plan: (1) will have an accumulated funding deficiency within five years; or (2) will not have sufficient assets to pay the promised benefits within seven years.

Rehabilitation plan. A plan in critical status must adopt and implement a rehabilitation plan designed to enable the plan to emerge from critical status (and must satisfy specified operational requirements) throughout the rehabilitation plan adoption and rehabilitation periods (Code Sec. 432(a)(2); ERISA Sec. 305(a)(2)). The rehabilitation plan must provide contribution and benefit schedules, including a default schedule, that set out reductions in future benefit accruals necessary for the plan to emerge from critical status by the end of the rehabilitation period.

Withdrawal liability. Reductions in benefits under a rehabilitation plan are disregarded in determining a plan's unfunded vested benefits (i.e., the amount by which the value of nonforfeitable benefits under the plan exceeds the value of plan assets) for purposes of determining an employer's withdrawal liability (Code Sec. 432(e)(9)(A); ERISA Sec. 305(e)(9)(A)).

NEW LAW EXPLAINED

Treasury transfers to 1974 UMWA Pension Plan.—The Bipartisan American Miners Act, effective for fiscal years beginning after September 30, 2016, authorizes Treasury to transfer funds to the 1974 United Mineworkers of America Pension Plan to pay retiree benefits (Division M, Act Sec. 102 of the Bipartisan American Miners Act of 2019, enacted as part of the Further Consolidated Appropriations Act, 2020 (P.L. 116-94)).

Note: The Act effectively establishes the precedent of allowing federal tax funds to be used to support the retiree benefits of a private sector pension plan.

Transfer cap increased. The Act increases the cap of the total amount that may be transferred from $490 million to $750 million (SMCRA Sec. 402(i)(3)(A), as amended by Division M, Act Sec. 102(a) of the Miners Act).

Transfer to UMWA Pension Plan. In the event the dollar limitation (as now increased to $750 million) exceeds the aggregate amount required to be transferred (under SMCRA Sec. 402(i)) for a fiscal year, Treasury "shall" transfer an additional amount equal to the difference between the dollar limitation and the aggregate amount to the trustees of the 1974 UMWA Pension Plan to pay benefits required under the plan (SMCRA Sec. 402(i)(4), as added by Division M, Act Sec. 102(a) of the Miners Act).

Limited period of transfer. The authorized transfers must cease as of the first fiscal year beginning after the first plan year for which the funded percentage (as defined in Code Sec. 432(j)(2)) of the 1974 UMWA Pension Plan) is at least 100 percent (SMCRA Sec. 402(i)(4)(B), as added by Act Sec. 102(a) of the Miners Act).

¶400

NEW LAW EXPLAINED

Benefit increases prohibited. During a fiscal year in which the 1974 UMWA Pension Plan is receiving transfers, the plan may not be amended to increase liabilities by reason of any increase in benefits, any change in the accrual of benefits, or any change in the rate at which benefits become nonforfeitable under the plan may be adopted (SMCRA Sec. 402(i)(4)(C), as added by Division M, Act Sec. 102(a) of the Miners Act). An exception is provided for amendments required as a condition of qualification.

Maintain critical status. The plan will be treated as if it were in in critical status until such time as it is no longer eligible for the transfers (SMCRA Sec. 402(i)(4)(D)(i), as added by Division M, Act Sec. 102(a) of the Miners Act).

Compliance with rehabilitation plan. The Plan, until it is no longer eligible for transfers, is further required to maintain and comply with its rehabilitation plan under Code Sec. 432(e) and ERISA Sec. 305(e), including any updates thereto (SMCRA Sec. 402(i)(4)(D)(ii), as added by Division M, Act Sec. 102(a) of the Miners Act).

Transfers disregarded in determining withdrawal liability. The amount of any transfer (and any earnings attributable thereto) shall be disregarded in determining the unfunded vested benefits of the 1974 UMWA Pension Plan and the allocation of unfunded vested benefits to an employer for purposes of determining the employer's withdrawal liability under ERISA Sec. 4201 (SMCRA Sec. 402(i)(4)(E), as added by Division M, Act Sec. 102(a) of the Miners Act).

Employers required to maintain contribution. A transfer may not be made for a fiscal year unless the persons that are obligated to contribute to the 1974 UMWA Pension Plan on the date of the transfer are obligated to make the contributions at rates that are no less than those in effect on the date which is 30 days before the December 20, 2019 of enactment of the Bipartisan American Miners Act (SMCRA Sec. 402(i)(4)(F), as added by Division M, Act Sec. 102(a) of the Miners Act).

Annual reporting requirements. Plan trustees would be subject, effective for plan years beginning after the December 20, 2019 date of enactment of the Miners Act, to extensive annual reporting requirements. In general, no later than the 90th day of *each* plan year beginning after the December 20 2019 date of enactment of the Act, plan trustees would be required to file reports (including appropriate documentation and actuarial certifications) with the Secretary of the Treasury (or the Secretary's delegate) and the Pension Benefit Guaranty Corporation (SMCRA Sec. 402(i)(4)(G), as added by Division M, Act Sec. 102(a) of the Miners Act).

Required information. Plan trustees must disclose: (1) whether the plan is in endangered or critical status as of the first day of the year; (2) the funded percentage as of the first day of the plan year, and the underlying actuarial value of assets and liabilities taken into account in determining the percentage; (3) the market value of plan assets as of the last day of the plan year preceding such plan year; (4) the total value of all contributions made during the plan year preceding such plan year; (5) the total value of all benefits paid during the plan year preceding such plan year; (6) cash flow projections for such plan year and either the 6 or 10 succeeding plan years, at the election of the trustees, and the assumptions relied upon in making such projections; (7) funding standard account projections for such plan year and the 9 succeeding plan years, and

¶400

NEW LAW EXPLAINED

the assumptions relied upon in making such projections; (8) the total value of all investment gains or losses during the plan year preceding such plan year; (9) any significant reduction in the number of active participants during the plan year preceding such plan year, and the reason for the reduction; (10) a list of employers that withdrew from the plan in the plan year preceding such plan year, and the resulting reduction in contributions; (11) a list of employers that paid withdrawal liability to the plan during the plan year preceding such plan year and, for each employer, a total assessment of the withdrawal liability paid, the annual payment amount, and the number of years remaining in the payment schedule with respect to such withdrawal liability; (12) any material changes to benefits, accrual rates, or contribution rates during the plan year preceding such plan year; (13) any scheduled benefit increase or decrease in the plan year preceding such plan year having a material effect on plan liabilities; (14) details regarding any funding improvement plan or rehabilitation plan and updates to such plan; (15) the number of participants and beneficiaries during the plan year preceding such plan year who are active participants, the number of participants and beneficiaries in pay status, and the number of terminated vested participants and beneficiaries; (16) the information contained on the most recent annual funding notice submitted by the plan under ERISA Sec. 101(f); (17) the information contained on the most recent Form 5500 filed for the plan; and (18) copies of the plan document and amendments, other retirement benefit or ancillary benefit plans relating to the plan and contribution obligations under such plans, a break-down of the plan's administrative expenses, participant census data and distribution of benefits, the most recent actuarial valuation report as of the plan year, copies of collective bargaining agreements, and financial reports and such other information as the Secretary of the Treasury or the Secretary's delegate, in consultation with the Secretary of Labor and the Director of the Pension Benefit Guaranty Corporation, may require (SMCRA Sec. 402(i)(4)(G)(i), as added by Division M, Act Sec. 102(a) of the Miners Act).

Submit information electronically. The required report must be submitted electronically (SMCRA Sec. 402(i)(4)(G)(ii), as added by Division M, Act Sec. 102(a) of the Miners Act).

Treasury will share information with Labor. Treasury would be required to share the reported information with the Labor Department (SMCRA Sec. 402(i)(4)(G)(iii), as added by Division M, Act Sec. 102(a) of the Miners Act).

Failure to file penalties. The failure to file any required report by the stipulated due date will trigger a penalty of $100 for each day the failure continues (SMCRA Sec. 402(i)(4)(G)(iv), as added by Division M, Act Sec. 102(a) of the Miners Act). An exception would apply if Treasury determined that reasonable diligence had been exercised by the plan trustees of such plan in attempting to timely file such report.

▶ **Effective dates.** The amendments generally apply to fiscal years beginning after September 30, 2016 (Division M, Act Sec. 102(b)(1) of the Miners Act). However, the reporting requirements will apply to plan years beginning after the December 20, 2019 date of the enactment (Division M, Act Sec. 102(b)(2) of the Miners Act).

NEW LAW EXPLAINED

Law Source: Law at ¶5004.

— Act Sec. 102(a)(1), Division M, of the Further Consolidated Appropriations Act, 2020 (P.L. 116-94), amending Act Sec. 402(i)(3)(A) of the Surface Mining Control and Reclamation Act of 1977(SMCRA).

— Act Sec. 102(a)(2), Division M, amending SMCRA Sec. 402(i) by redesignating paragraph (4) as paragraph (5).

— Act Sec. 102(a)(3), Division M, adding new SMCRA Sec. 402(i)(4).

— Act Sec. 102(b), Division M, providing the effective date.

¶405 Funding Multiemployer Health Benefit Plans

SUMMARY OF NEW LAW

The Bipartisan American Miners Act of 2019 authorizes the transfer of surplus funds from the Abandoned Mine Land Fund of the Surface Mining Control and Reclamation Act to help finance the health care benefits of miners participating in health plans maintained by employers who declared bankruptcy in 2018 and 2019.

BACKGROUND

The Surface Mining Control and Reclamation Act of 1977 (SMCRA) (30 U.S.C. 1231) authorized an Abandoned Mine Reclamation Fund to be administered by the Secretary of the Interior. The fund was comprised of amounts deposited in the fund derived from: reclamation fees levied under SMCRA Sec. 402; user charges imposed on or for reclaimed lands after the deduction of maintenance expenditures for maintenance have been deducted; donations by persons, corporations, associations, and foundations; certain recovered moneys; and interest credited to the fund.

Moneys in the Abandoned Mine Reclamation Fund could be used for only stipulated purposes, including transfers to specified benefit funds. (SMCRA Sec. 402(h)). The SMCRA generally authorized the transfer of interest earned by the Fund to a Multiemployer Health Benefit Plan established after July 20, 1992 by parties that are settlors of the United Mine Workers of America 1992 Benefit Plan. Specifically, a transfer was allowed in an amount equal to the *excess* (if any) of: (1) the amount that the trustees of the Plan estimate will be expended from the Plan during the next calendar year, to provide benefits no greater than those provided by the Plan as of December 31, 2006; over (2) the amount that the trustees estimated the Plan will receive during the next calendar year in payments paid by Federal agencies in connection with benefits provided by the Plan (SMCRA Sec. 402(h)(2)(C)(i)).

The "excess" amount that could be transferred was calculated by taking into account only: (1) beneficiaries actually enrolled in the Plan as of May 5, 2017, who are eligible to receive health benefits under the Plan on the first day of the calendar year for which the transfer is made, other than those beneficiaries enrolled in the Plan under the terms of a

BACKGROUND

participation agreement with the current or former employer of such beneficiaries; and (2) beneficiaries whose health benefits, defined as those benefits payable, following death or retirement or upon a finding of disability, directly by an employer in the bituminous coal industry under a coal wage agreement (as defined in Code Sec 9701(b)(1)) would be denied or reduced as a result of a bankruptcy proceeding commenced in 2012 or 2015.

In applying the rules, a beneficiary enrolled in the Plan as of May 5, 2017, was deemed to have been eligible to receive health benefits under the Plan on January 1, 2017.

The Fund has been a means of securing the health benefits of retired miners, especially under a legislative fix adopted in 2017. However, the pending bankruptcies of mine companies in 2018 and 2019, placed the benefits of miners beyond the authorized statutory relief.

NEW LAW EXPLAINED

Funding multiemployer health benefit plans.—The Bipartisan American Miners Act of 2019 authorizes the transfer of surplus funds from the Abandoned Mine Land Fund of the Surface Mining Control and Reclamation Act to help finance the health care benefits of miners participating in health plans maintained by employers who declared bankruptcy in 2018 and 2019 (Division M, Act Sec. 103 of the Bipartisan Miners Act, enacted as part of the Further Consolidated Appropriations Act, 2020 (P.L. 116-94)).

Specifically, SMCRA Sec. 402(h)(2)(C) would be amended to authorize, in determining the excess amount that could be transferred, consideration of "beneficiaries whose health benefits, defined as those benefits payable, following death or retirement or upon a finding of disability, directly by an employer in the bituminous coal industry under a coal wage agreement (as defined in Code Sec. 9701(b)(1)), *or a related coal wage agreement*, would be denied or reduced as a result of a bankruptcy proceeding commenced in *2012, 2015, 2018, or 2019*" (SMCRA Sec. 402(h)(2)(C)(ii)(II), as amended by Division M, Act Sec. 103 of the Miners Act).

Related coal wage agreement. A related coal wage agreement would be an agreement between the United Mine Workers of America and an employer in the bituminous coal industry that: (1) is a signatory operator; or (2) is or was a debtor in a bankruptcy proceeding that was consolidated, administered, or otherwise, with the bankruptcy proceeding of a signatory operator or a related person to a signatory operation (as defined under Code Sec. 9701(c) (SMCRA Sec. 402(h)(2)(C)(vi), as added by Division M, Act Sec. 103 of the Miners Act).

Accounting for dispute resolution costs. The excess amount will be calculated by further taking into account the cost of administering the resolution of dispute process administered (as of the December 20, 2019 date of enactment) by the plan trustees (SMCRA Sec. 402(h)(2)(C)(ii)(III), as added by Division M, Act Sec. 103 of the Miners Act).

Deemed participation. Finally, in applying the rules, a beneficiary enrolled in the Plan as of May 5, 2017, will be deemed to have been eligible to receive health benefits under

NEW LAW EXPLAINED

the Plan on January 1, 2019 (SMCRA Sec. 402(h)(2)(C)(ii), as amended by Division M, Act Sec. 103 of the Miners Act).

▶ **Effective date.** The Act does not specify an effective date for the amendments. Accordingly, the amendments are treated as effective on the December 20, 2019 date of enactment of the Bipartisan American Miners Act.

Law Source: Law at ¶5005.

— Act Sec. 103(1), (2) and (4), Division M, of the Further Consolidated Appropriations Act, 2020 (P.L. 116-94), amending Act Sec. 402(h)(2)(C)(ii) of the Surface Mining Control and Reclamation Act of 1977(SMCRA).

— Act Sec. 103(3), Division M, adding SMCRA Sec. 402(h)(2)(C)(ii)(III).

— Act Sec. 103(5), Division M, adding SMCRA Sec. 402(h)(2)(C)(vi).

¶410 Reduction in Minimum Age for Allowable In-Service Distributions

SUMMARY OF NEW LAW

A pension plan will not fail to be qualified solely because the plan provides, effective for plan years beginning after December 31, 2019, that a distribution may be made to an employee who has attained age 59 ½ (rather than 62) and who is not separated from employment at the time of the distribution. A similar rule will apply to distributions from governmental 457(b) plans.

BACKGROUND

A qualified plan must be established and maintained by an employer primarily to provide systematically for the payment of definitely determinable benefits to its employees over a period of years, usually for life, after retirement or attainment of normal retirement age. A plan does not fail to satisfy this requirement merely because the plan provides that a distribution may be made from the plan to an employee who has attained age 62 and who is not separated from employment at the time of such distribution (IRS Reg. § 1.401(a)-1(b)(1)).

The Pension Protection Act further authorized a phased retirement program, under which, for purposes of the definition of pension plan under ERISA, a distribution from a plan, fund, or program is not treated as made in a form other than retirement income or as a distribution prior to termination of covered employment solely because the distribution is made to an employee who has attained age 62 and who is not separated from employment at the time of such distribution (ERISA Sec. 3(2)(A)). In addition, under Code Sec. 401(a)(36), a pension plan will not fail to be a qualified retirement plan solely because the plan provides that a distribution may be made to an employee who has attained age 62 and who is not separated from employment at the time of the distribution.

BACKGROUND

457(b) plans. The distribution rules applicable to 457(b) plans are more restrictive. An eligible plan may not allow an amount to be paid or made available under the plan earlier than: (1) the calendar year in which the participant attains age 70 ½; (2) upon a severance from employment with the employer; or (3) upon the occurrence of an unforeseeable emergency (Code Sec. 457(d)(1)(A); IRS Reg. § 1.457-6(a)).

NEW LAW EXPLAINED

Reduction in minimum age for allowable in-service distributions.—The Act, effective for plan years beginning after December 31, 2019, reduces the minimum age at which in-service distributions may be made under Code Sec. 401(a)(36) to 59 1/2 from 62 (Code Sec. 401(a)(36), as amended by Division M, Act Sec. 104(a) of the Bipartisan Miners Act, enacted as part of the Further Consolidated Appropriations Act, 2020 (P.L 116-94)).

The distribution rules applicable to 457(b) plans have also been modified. The Act, effective for plan years beginning after December 31, 2019, authorizes distributions to be made from a governmental 457(b) plan in the calendar year in which the participant attains age 59 ½ (Code Sec. 457(d)(1)(A)(i), as amended by Division M, Act Sec. 104(b) of the Miners Act).

▶ **Effective dates.** The amendments apply to plan years beginning after December 31, 2019 (Division M, Act Sec. 104(c) of the Miners Act).

Law Source: Law at ¶5006, ¶6050 and ¶6085.

— Act Sec. 104(a), Division M, of the Further Consolidated Appropriations Act, 2020 (P.L. 116-94), amending Code Sec. 401(a)(36).

— Act Sec. 104(b), Division M, amending Code Sec. 457(d)(1)(A)(i).

— Act Sec. 104(c), Division M, providing the effective date.

Health and Welfare Benefits   5

¶500   Repeal of Medical Device Excise Tax
¶505   Repeal of Annual Fee on Health Insurance Providers
¶510   Repeal of Excise Tax on High Cost Employer-Sponsored Health Coverage
¶515   Pharmacy Benefit Services Exemption from Certain ERISA Requirements
¶520   Employer Credit for Paid Family and Medical Leave
¶525   Benefits Provided to Volunteer Firefighters and Emergency Responders
¶530   Repeal of Increase in Unrelated Business Taxable Income for Certain Fringe Benefit Expenses
¶540   Expansion of Section 529 Plans
¶545   Credit for Health Insurance Costs of Eligible Individuals

¶500 Repeal of Medical Device Excise Tax

SUMMARY OF NEW LAW

The 2.3 percent excise tax imposed on sales of medical devices is repealed. The repeal of the tax applies to sales after December 31, 2019.

BACKGROUND

The Patient Protection and Affordable Care Act (P.L. 111-148) originally included an annual fee on manufacturers and importers of medical devices. The Health Care and Education Reconciliation Act of 2010 (P.L. 111-152) repealed the annual fee and replaced it with an excise tax. Starting in 2013, the tax was imposed on any manufacturer,

BACKGROUND

producer or importer of certain medical devices. The tax is equal to 2.3 percent of the price for which the medical device is sold.

For purposes of the medical device excise tax, a taxable medical device means any "device"—as defined in Section 201(h) of the Federal Food Drug and Cosmetic Act—intended for humans. Sales of eyeglasses, contact lenses, and hearing aids are exempt from the tax. In addition, any other medical device determined to be of a type that is generally purchased by the general public at retail for individual use is not subject to the excise tax. This is referred to as the "retail exemption."

The medical device tax is a manufacturers' excise tax, and as a result, the manufacturer or importer of a taxable medical device is responsible for filing Form 720, Quarterly Federal Excise Tax Return, and paying the tax. Generally, consumers have no reporting or recordkeeping requirements.

NEW LAW EXPLAINED

Repeal of medical device excise tax.—Starting in 2020, the 2.3 percent excise tax imposed on any manufacturer, producer or importer of certain medical devices is repealed (Subchapter E of Chapter 32 of the Internal Revenue Code, repealed by Division N, Act Sec. 501(a) of the Further Consolidated Appropriations Act, 2020 (P.L. 116-94).

▶ **Effective date.** The amendments made by this section apply to sales after December 31, 2019 (Division N, Act Sec. 501(d) of the Appropriations Act).

Law source: Law at ¶5029, ¶6105, ¶6110 and ¶6145.

— Act Sec. 501(a), Division N, of the Further Consolidated Appropriations Act, 2020 (P.L. 116-94), striking subchapter E [Code Sec. 4191] of Chapter 32 of the Internal Revenue Code.

— Act Sec. 501(b)(1), Division N, amending Code Sec. 4221(a).

— Act Sec. 501(b)(2), Division N, amending Code Sec. 6416(b)(2).

— Act Sec. 501(d), Division N, providing the effective date.

¶505 Repeal of Annual Fee on Health Insurance Providers

SUMMARY OF NEW LAW

The annual fee imposed on health insurers that meet certain criteria is repealed. The repeal of the fee applies to calendar years beginning after December 31, 2020.

BACKGROUND

The Patient Protection and Affordable Care Act imposed a fee on "covered entities" engaged in the business of providing health insurance. A "covered entity" is defined as any entity with net premiums written for health insurance for United States health risks in the fee year if the entity is one of the following:

- a health insurance issuer under Code Sec. 9832(b)(2);
- a health maintenance organization (HMO) under Code Sec. 9832(b)(3);
- an insurance company subject to tax under Part I or II of Chapter 1 subchapter L of the Tax Code;
- an entity that provides health insurance under Medicare Advantage, Medicare Part D, or Medicaid; or
- a multiple employer welfare arrangement (MEWA) under section 3(40) of ERISA, to the extent not fully insured.

For purposes of the fee, "health insurance" does not include insurance coverage for long-term care, disability, accidents, specified illnesses, hospital indemnity or other fixed indemnity insurance, or Medicare supplemental health insurance.

In general, the term "health insurance" has the same meaning as the term "health insurance coverage" in Code Sec. 9832(b)(1)(A). In turn, Code Sec. 9832(b)(1)(A) defines health insurance as benefits consisting of medical care under any hospital or medical service policy or certificate, hospital or medical service plan contract, or health maintenance organization contract, when these benefits are offered by an entity meeting the definition of a covered entity under IRS Reg. §57(b)(1). The term "health insurance" includes limited scope dental and vision benefits under Code Sec. 9832(c)(2)(A) and retiree-only health insurance (IRS Reg. §57.2(h)(1)).

There was a moratorium on the fee for 2017, and there was a suspension on the fee for 2019.

NEW LAW EXPLAINED

Repeal of annual fee on health insurance providers.—Starting in 2021, the annual fee on health insurance providers ("covered entities") is repealed (Division N, Act Sec. 502(a) of the Further Consolidated Appropriations Act, 2020 (P.L. 116-94), striking Sec. 9010 of the Patient Protection and Affordable Care Act).

▶ **Effective date.** The amendments made by this section apply to calendar years beginning after December 31, 2020 (Division N, Act Sec. 502(b) of the Appropriations Act).

Law source: Law at ¶5030.

— Act Sec. 502(a), Division N, of the Further Consolidated Appropriations Act, 2020 (P.L. 116-94), striking Sec. 9010 of the Patient Protection and Affordable Care Act.

— Act Sec. 502(b), Division N, providing the effective date.

¶505

¶510 Repeal of Excise Tax on High Cost Employer-Sponsored Health Coverage

SUMMARY OF NEW LAW

The excise tax on high cost employer-sponsored health coverage, the so-called "Cadillac" tax, has been repealed, effective for tax years after December 31, 2019.

BACKGROUND

The Patient Protection and Affordable Care Act (ACA) imposed an excise tax on the cost of high cost employer-sponsored health coverage. The unpopular "Cadillac" tax was originally designed to curtail the preferred tax treatment of employer-sponsored plans and reduce excess health spending.

The tax would have required plan sponsors and insurers to pay a 40 percent excise tax on the excess cost of employer-sponsored health coverage for employees—amounts over $11,100 for employee-only and $29,750 for family coverage, adjusted for inflation annually. The excise tax was originally meant to apply to tax years beginning after December 31, 2017. However, the tax was delayed several times, most recently to 2022.

The Cadillac tax would have affected 21 percent of employers when it was scheduled to take effect in 2022, according to research from the Kaiser Family Foundation.

NEW LAW EXPLAINED

Repeal of excise tax on high cost employer-sponsored health coverage. — The 40 percent excise tax on high cost employer-sponsored coverage is repealed (Division N, Act Sec. 503(a) of the Further Consolidated Appropriations Act, 2020 (P.L. 116-94), repealing Code Sec. 4980I).

Note: The excise tax was designed to help pay for the ACA. The Congressional Budget Office has projected that the repeal of the Cadillac tax will cost nearly $200 billion over 10 years.

▶ **Effective date.** The amendments made by this section apply to tax years beginning after December 31, 2019 (Division N, Act Sec. 503(c) of the Appropriations Act).

Law source: Law at ¶5031, ¶6130 and ¶6140.

— Act Sec. 503(a), Division N, of the Further Consolidated Appropriations Act, 2020 (P.L. 116-94), striking Code Sec. 4980I.

— Act Sec. 503(b), Division N, amending Code Sec. 6051(a)(14) and adding new subsection (g).

— Act Sec. 503(c), Division N, providing the effective date.

¶515 Pharmacy Benefit Services Exemption from Certain ERISA Requirements

SUMMARY OF NEW LAW

A five-year exemption from some of ERISA's prohibited transaction rules is provided for the offering of pharmacy benefit services to a group health plan that is sponsored by an organization that is tax-exempt and that was established in Chicago, Illinois on August 12, 1881.

BACKGROUND

Persons who are considered fiduciaries with respect to employee benefit plans have special responsibilities under ERISA. Failure to meet these responsibilities could lead to fiduciary liability. Under ERISA, a fiduciary is a person who:

1. exercises discretionary authority or control respecting management of the plan or exercises any authority or control over the management or disposition of its assets,
2. renders investment advice for a fee or other compensation (direct or indirect) as to any monies or other property of the plan, or has any authority or responsibility to do so, or
3. has discretionary authority or discretionary responsibility in the administration of the plan.

The determination of an individual's fiduciary status is an inherently factual inquiry and will require analysis of the specific facts and circumstances of each case (ERISA Sec. 3(21)).

ERISA's prohibited transaction rules bar a fiduciary from engaging in certain transactions, such as dealing with plan assets, for the fiduciary's own interest. These prohibited transaction rules apply to a party in interest (called a disqualified person by the Internal Revenue Code). A person who participates in a prohibited transaction is subject to a 15-percent excise tax on the amount involved. If the prohibited transaction is not timely corrected, an excise tax of 100 percent of the amount involved is imposed.

A plan fiduciary may not cause a plan to engage in any transaction which he or she knows, or should know, constitutes a direct or indirect:

1. sale, exchange, or lease of any property between the plan and a party in interest;
2. loan of money or other extension of credit between the plan and a party in interest;
3. furnishing of goods, services, or facilities between the plan and a party in interest;
4. transfer of any plan assets to, or use by or for the benefit of, a party in interest, or
5. acquisition, on behalf of any plan, of any employer security or employer real property in violation of the 10-percent limitation imposed by ERISA on the acquisition and holding of employer securities and employer real property (ERISA Sec. 406(a)).

A fiduciary with respect to the plan is also prohibited from:

BACKGROUND

1. dealing with plan assets in the fiduciary's own interest or for the fiduciary's own account,
2. acting, in any transaction involving the plan, on behalf of a party whose interests are adverse to the interests of the plan or the interests of its participants or beneficiaries, and
3. receiving any consideration for his or her personal account from any party dealing with the plan in connection with a transaction involving the income or assets of the plan (ERISA Sec. 406(b)).

Exemptions from the prohibited transaction rules are available. A number of exemptions are provided by statute.

Employee benefit plans often include a group health insurance plan and pharmacy benefits. Plan sponsors can manage the benefits and adjudicate claims internally or outsource the benefits management to a pharmacy benefit manager (PBM).

The Commonwealth Fund explains that "PBMs operate in the middle of the distribution chain for prescription drugs." Also, according to the Commonwealth Fund, "By negotiating with drug manufacturers and pharmacies to control drug spending, PBMs have a significant behind-the-scenes impact in determining total drug costs for insurers, shaping patients' access to medications, and determining how much pharmacies are paid. PBMs have faced growing scrutiny about their role in rising prescription drug costs and spending."

An issue of contention has been whether plan administrators, employers serving as plan administrators, and PBMs are considered fiduciaries subject to the prohibited transaction rules.

NEW LAW EXPLAINED

Pharmacy benefit services exemption.—The prohibited transaction rules in ERISA Secs. 406(a), (b)(1) and (b)(2) will not apply, for five years, to the offering of pharmacy benefit services to (or the purchase of such services by participants of) a group health plan that is sponsored by an entity described in ERISA Sec. (3)(37)(G)(vi) (i.e., a plan sponsored by an organization that is described in Code Sec. 501(c)(5) (i.e., labor, agricultural, or horticultural organizations) and exempt from tax under Code Sec. 501(a) and that was established in Chicago, Illinois, on August 12, 1881) or to any other group health plan that is sponsored by a regional council, local union, or other labor organization affiliated with such entity (ERISA Sec. 408(h)(1) as added by Division P, Act Sec. 1302(a) of the Further Consolidated Appropriations Act, 2020 (P.L. 116-94)).

The exemption applies to any arrangement where the entity or organization provides pharmacy benefit services that include:

- prior authorization and appeals,
- a retail pharmacy network,
- pharmacy benefit administration,
- mail order fulfillment,

¶515

NEW LAW EXPLAINED

- formulary support,
- manufacturer payments,
- audits, and
- specialty pharmacy and goods

to the group health plan, provided that certain conditions are met (ERISA Sec. 408(h)(1), as added by Division P, Act Sec. 1302(a) of the Appropriations Act).

Conditions. The conditions that must be met are the following:

1. the terms of the arrangement are at least as favorable to the group health plan as such group health plan could obtain in a similar arm's length arrangement with an unrelated third party;
2. at least 50 percent of the providers participating in the pharmacy benefit services offered by the arrangement are unrelated to the contributing employers or any other party in interest with respect to the group health plan;
3. the group health plan retains an independent fiduciary who will be responsible for monitoring the group health plan's consultants, contractors, subcontractors, and other service providers;
4. any decisions regarding the provision of pharmacy benefit services are made by the group health plan's independent fiduciary, based on objective standards developed by the independent fiduciary in reliance on information provided by the arrangement;
5. the independent fiduciary of the group health plan provides an annual report to the Secretary and the congressional committees of jurisdiction attesting these conditions have been met for the applicable plan year, together with a statement that use of the arrangement's services are in the best interest of the participants and beneficiaries in the aggregate for that plan year compared to other similar arrangements the group health plan could have obtained in transactions with an unrelated third party; and
6. the arrangement is not designed to benefit any party in interest with respect to the group health plan (ERISA Sec. 408(h)(2) as added by Division P, Act Sec. 1302(a) of the Appropriations Act).

Violations. If an entity described in ERISA Sec. 3(37)(G)(vi) or any affiliate of such entity violates any of the conditions of the exemption, such exemption will not apply with respect to such entity or affiliate and all enforcement and claims available under ERISA will apply (ERISA Sec. 408(h)(3), as added by Division P, Act Sec. 1302(a) of the Appropriations Act).

Rule of construction. Nothing in this subsection shall be construed to modify any obligation of a group health plan otherwise set forth in ERISA (ERISA Sec. 408(h)(4), as added by Division P, Act Sec. 1302(a) of the Appropriations Act).

Tax exemption. Any party to an arrangement that satisfies the requirements of ERISA Sec. 408(h) will be exempt from the tax imposed by Code Sec. 4975(c) with respect to

¶515

NEW LAW EXPLAINED

such arrangement (Code Sec. 4975(c)(7), as added by Division P, Act Sec. 1302(b) of the Appropriations Act).

Applicability. With respect to a group health plan subject to ERISA Sec. 408(h) (as amended by Code Secs. 4975(a) and (c)), beginning at the end of the fifth plan year of such group health plan that begins after the December 20, 2019 date of enactment of the Appropriations Act, such ERISA Sec. 408(h) and Code Sec. 4975(c) shall have no force or effect.

▶ **Effective date.** No specific effective date is provided. The amendments made by this section are therefore considered effective on December 20, 2019, the date of enactment of the Appropriations Act.

Law source: Law at ¶5107, ¶6125 and ¶7007.

— Act Sec. 1302(a) Division P, of the Further Consolidated Appropriations Act, 2020 (P.L. 116-94), adding ERISA Sec. 408(h).

— Act Sec. 1302(b), Division P, adding Code Sec. 4975(c)(7).

— Act Sec. 1302(c), Division P, defining the term of applicability.

¶520 Employer Credit for Paid Family and Medical Leave

SUMMARY OF NEW LAW

The employer credit for providing paid Family and Medical Leave Act (FMLA) leave, which was set to expire at the end of 2019, has been extended for one year to apply through 2020.

BACKGROUND

The Family and Medical Leave Act of 1993 (P.L. 103-3) requires an employer with 50 or more employees (within a 75-mile radius) to give eligible employees 12 weeks of unpaid leave for births, adoptions, and family illnesses. While this leave can be unpaid, many employers provide paid FMLA leave.

The Tax Cuts and Jobs Act (P.L. 115-97) implemented a tax credit for employers that provided paid leave under the FMLA after 2017 (Code Sec. 45S). Note that the Tax Cuts and Jobs Act does not require employers to provide paid leave, but rather offers the tax credit as an incentive for employers that provide a certain level of paid FMLA leave to their employees.

Eligible employers can claim a general business credit equal to 12.5 percent of the amount of wages paid to qualifying employees during any period in which such employees are on FMLA leave if the rate of payment under the program is 50 percent of the wages normally paid to an employee. The credit is increased by 0.25 percentage

BACKGROUND

points (but not above 25 percent) for each percentage point by which the rate of payment exceeds 50 percent.

"Qualifying employees" are defined as those that have been employed by the employer for one year or more, and who for the preceding year, had compensation not in excess of 60 percent of the compensation threshold for highly compensated employees, or $78,000 in 2020 (60 percent of $130,000). The maximum amount of leave subject to the credit for any employee for any tax year may not exceed 12 weeks.

The credit is part of the general business credit and was only available for wages paid in tax years beginning after December 31, 2017, and before January 1, 2020.

NEW LAW EXPLAINED

Employer credit for paid FMLA leave.—The employer credit for paid FMLA leave has been extended for one year (Code Sec. 45S(i), as amended by Division Q, Act Sec. 142(a) of the Further Consolidated Appropriations Act, 2020 (P.L. 116-94)). The credit has been extended through 2020 and is now set to expire on December 31, 2020.

▶ **Effective date.** The amendments in this section apply to wages paid in tax years beginning after December 31, 2019 (Division Q, Act Sec. 142(b) of the Appropriations Act).

Law source: Law at ¶5159 and ¶6015.

— Act Sec. 142(a), Division Q, of the Further Consolidated Appropriations Act, 2020 (P.L. 116-94), amending Code Sec. 45S(i).

— Act Sec. 142(b), Division Q, providing the effective date.

¶525 Benefits Provided to Volunteer Firefighters and Emergency Responders

SUMMARY OF NEW LAW

Federal income tax exclusions authorized for state or local tax benefits and qualified reimbursement payments made to members of volunteer emergency response organizations have been restored for the 2020 tax year. In addition, the exclusion for reimbursement payments has been increased to $50 for each month a volunteer serves.

BACKGROUND

For tax years 2008 through 2010, under Code Sec. 139B(a), volunteer firefighters and emergency medical responders were generally allowed to exclude from income any state and local tax benefit or qualified reimbursement payment they received in exchange for their volunteer services. The exclusion applied to tax years beginning after December 31, 2007 and before January 1, 2011.

BACKGROUND

Since this exclusion expired, volunteer firefighters and emergency responders have had to pay federal income tax on the benefits they receive from their communities.

NEW LAW EXPLAINED

Benefits provided to volunteer firefighters and emergency responders.—Federal income tax exclusions authorized for state or local tax benefits and qualified reimbursement payments made to members of volunteer emergency response organizations have been restored for the 2020 tax year (Code Sec. 139B(d), as amended by Division O, Act Sec. 301(b) of SECURE Act, enacted as part of the Further Consolidated Appropriations Act, 2020 (P.L. 116-94)). In addition, the exclusion for reimbursement payments has been increased from $30 to $50 for each month a volunteer serves (Code Sec. 139B(c)(2), as amended by SECURE Act Sec. 301(a)).

▶ **Effective date.** The amendments in this section apply to taxable years beginning after December 31, 2019 (SECURE Act Sec. 301(d)).

Law source: Law at ¶5064, ¶6030 and ¶6100.

— Act Sec. 301(a), Division O, of the SECURE Act, as enacted by the Further Consolidated Appropriations Act, 2020 (P.L. 116-94), amending Code Sec. 139B(c)(2)(B).

— Act Sec. 301(b), Division O, amending Code Sec. 139(B)(d);

— Act Sec. 301(c), Division O, amending Code Sec. 3121(a)(23);

— Act. Sec. 301(d), Division O, providing the effective date.

¶530 Repeal of Increase in Unrelated Business Taxable Income for Certain Fringe Benefit Expenses

SUMMARY OF NEW LAW

Unrelated business taxable income will no longer be increased by the nondeductible amount of certain fringe benefit expenses paid or incurred by an exempt organization.

BACKGROUND

The income of an exempt organization is subject to the tax on unrelated business income if two conditions are present: (1) the income must be from a trade or business regularly carried on by the organization, and (2) the trade or business must not be substantially related—aside from the need of the organization for funds or the use it makes of the profits—to the organization's exercise or performance of the purposes or functions on which its exemption is based (Code Secs. 511 and 512).

¶530

BACKGROUND

Unrelated business taxable income (UBTI), which is subject to the tax under Code Sec. 511, is the gross income derived by any organization from any unrelated trade or business regularly carried on by it, less the regular deductions allowed for income tax purposes which are directly connected with the carrying on of such trade or business (Code Sec. 512(a)).

Ordinary and necessary business expenses are generally tax deductible, while expenses incurred for personal reasons or pleasure are not deductible (Code Secs. 162 and 262). This distinction can be difficult to make when expenses have both personal and business components, such as entertainment, gift and travel expenses incurred to promote business. Code Sec. 274 addresses this problem by imposing additional limits on expenses that are otherwise deductible under other Internal Revenue Code provisions.

The Tax Cuts and Jobs Act of 2017 (P.L. 115-97) provided that the UBTI of an exempt organization would be increased by the nondeductible amount of certain fringe benefit expenses incurred by the organization in that tax year, effective for amounts paid or incurred after December 31, 2017 (Code Sec. 512(a)(7), as added by Act Sec. 13703(a) of the Tax Cuts and Jobs Act). These fringe benefits are expenses for which a deduction is not available due to Code Sec. 274, and specifically include:

- any qualified transportation fringe, as defined in Code Sec. 132(f);
- any parking facility used in connection with qualified parking, as defined in Code Sec. 132(f)(5)(C); and
- any on-premises athletic facility, as defined in Code Sec. 132(j)(4)(B).

Fringe benefits are a form of compensation and, as such, must be included in income and are subject to withholding unless explicitly excluded under the Internal Revenue Code. Eight basic types of fringe benefits are excluded from an employee's gross income, including a no-additional-cost service, a qualified employee discount, a working condition fringe, a de minimis fringe, a qualified transportation fringe, a qualified moving expense reimbursement, qualified retirement planning services, and qualified military base realignment and closure fringe benefit payments (Code Sec. 132). Special rules also exclude eating and athletic facilities, and the use of certain demonstrator automobiles.

NEW LAW EXPLAINED

Repeal of increase in unrelated business taxable income for certain fringe benefit expenses.—Unrelated business taxable income will no longer be increased by the nondeductible amount of certain fringe benefit expenses paid or incurred by an exempt organization (Code Sec. 512(a)(7), repealed by Division Q, Act Sec. 302(a) of the Further Consolidated Appropriations Act, 2020 (P.L. 116-94)).

▶ **Effective date.** The amendments made by this section take effect as if included in the amendments made by Section 13703 of the Tax Cuts and Jobs Act of 2017 (P.L. 115–97) (applicable to amounts paid or incurred after December 31, 2017) (Division Q, Act Sec. 302(b) of the Appropriations Act).

¶530

NEW LAW EXPLAINED

Law source: Law at ¶5173.

— Act Sec. 302(a), Division Q, of the Further Consolidated Appropriations Act, 2020 (P.L. 116-94), striking Code Sec. 512(a)(7);

— Act Sec. 302(b), Division Q, providing the effective date.

¶540 Expansion of Section 529 Plans

SUMMARY OF NEW LAW

The rules governing Code Sec. 529 qualified tuition plans are modified, retroactively effective to distributions made after 2018, to allow tax-free distributions for expenses associated with registered apprenticeship programs. Plans also can allow tax-free distributions of certain amounts used to make payments on principal or interest of a qualified education loan of the designated beneficiary or a sibling of the designated beneficiary.

BACKGROUND

A qualified tuition program (commonly referred to as a QTP, qualified tuition plan, or 529 plan) is exempt from all federal income tax, except the tax on the unrelated business income of a charitable organization. There are two basic types of QTPs: prepaid tuition programs and college savings programs.

Distributions can be made for qualified higher education expenses, which are defined as:

1. the tuition, fees, books, supplies, and equipment required for the enrollment or attendance of a designated beneficiary at an eligible educational institution;
2. the expenses incurred for special needs services for a special needs beneficiary in connection with enrollment or attendance at an eligible educational institution;
3. the expenses for the purchase of computer or peripheral equipment, computer software, or Internet access and related services, if such equipment, software, or services are to be used primarily by the beneficiary during any of the years the beneficiary is enrolled at an eligible educational institution; and
4. room and board incurred by a designated beneficiary who is enrolled at least half time at an eligible educational institution (Code Sec. 529(e)(3)(A)-(B)).

For distributions made after December 31, 2017, a designated beneficiary may, on an annual basis, receive up to $10,000 in aggregate Code Sec. 529 distributions to be used in connection with expenses for tuition in connection with enrollment or attendance at an elementary or secondary public, private, or religious school (Code Sec. 529(c)(7)).

Certain individuals who have paid interest on qualified education loans may claim an above-the-line deduction for such interest expenses, subject to a maximum annual

BACKGROUND

deduction limit of $2,500 (Code Sec. 221). However, funds in 529 plans may not be used to make student loan payments.

NEW LAW EXPLAINED

Distributions allowed for expenses associated with registered apprenticeship programs.—The rules governing qualified tuition plans are modified to allow tax-free treatment for distributions that are used to pay costs incurred for fees, books, supplies, and equipment required for the participation of a designated beneficiary in an apprenticeship program. In order to qualify as a higher education expense, however, the apprenticeship program must be registered and certified with the Secretary of Labor under Section 1 of the National Apprenticeship Act (Code Sec. 529(c)(8), as added by Division O, Act Sec. 302(a) of the SECURE Act, enacted as part of Further Consolidated Appropriations Act, 2020 (P.L. 116-94)).

Distributions allowed for qualified education loan repayments. The rules applicable to qualified tuition plans are modified to allow tax-free treatment to apply to distributions of certain amounts used to make payments on the principal or interest of a qualified education loan (Code Sec. 529(c)(9)(A), as added by SECURE Act Sec. 302(b)(1)). No individual may receive more than $10,000 of such distributions, in aggregate, over the course of the individual's lifetime (Code Sec. 529(c)(9)(B), as added by SECURE Act Sec. 302(b)(1)).

> **Comment:** To the extent that an individual receives in excess of $10,000 of such distributions, they are subject to the usual tax treatment of Code Sec. 529 distributions (i.e., the earnings are included in income and subject to a 10-percent penalty) (House Committee Report on H.R. 1994, H. Rept. 116–65).

Distribution to repay loan of sibling of designated beneficiary. A special rule allows such amounts to be distributed to a sibling of a designated beneficiary (i.e., a brother, sister, stepbrother, or stepsister) (Code Sec. 529(c)(9)(C), as added by SECURE Act Sec. 302(b)(1)). This rule allows a Code Sec. 529 account holder to make a student loan distribution to a sibling of the designated beneficiary without changing the designated beneficiary of the account.

For purposes of the $10,000 lifetime limit on student loan distributions, a distribution to a sibling of a designated beneficiary is applied towards the sibling's lifetime limit, and not the designated beneficiary's lifetime limit (Code Sec. 529(c)(9)(C), as added by SECURE Act Sec. 302(b)(1)). Thus, $10,000 may be directed towards the loan of the designated beneficiary and $10,000 may be directed towards the loan of a sibling.

Coordination with deduction for student loan interest. The deduction available for interest paid by the taxpayer during the taxable year on any qualified education loan would be reduced (but not below zero) to the extent such interest was paid from a tax-free distribution from a Code Sec. 529 plan (Code Sec. 221(e)(1), as amended by SECURE Act Sec. 302(b)(2)).

▶ **Effective date.** The amendments made by this section apply to distributions made after December 31, 2018 (SECURE Act Sec. 302(c)).

¶540

NEW LAW EXPLAINED

Law source: Law at ¶5065, ¶6045 and ¶6095.

— Act Sec. 302(a), Division O, Further Consolidated Appropriations Act, 2020 (P.L. 116-94), adding Code Sec. 529(c)(8).

— Act Sec. 302(b)(1), Division O, adding Code Sec. 529(c)(9).

— Act Sec. 302(b)(2), Division O, amending Code Sec. 221(e)(1).

— Act Sec. 302(c), Division O, providing the effective date.

¶545 Credit for Health Insurance Costs of Eligible Individuals

SUMMARY OF NEW LAW

The Health Coverage Tax Credit that was set to expire as of January 1, 2020 has been extended for one year, until January 1, 2021.

BACKGROUND

The Trade Act of 2002 (P.L. 107-210) created the Health Coverage Tax Credit (HCTC) to help pay for private health coverage for displaced workers certified to receive certain Trade Adjustment Assistance (TAA) benefits and for individuals receiving pension benefits from the Pension Benefit Guaranty Corporation. The HCTC is a tax credit that pays 72.5 percent of the qualified premium amount paid by eligible individuals for qualified health coverage. The HCTC is a refundable credit that eligible individuals can claim when they file their federal tax returns, even if they owe no tax. The HCTC was set to expire on January 1, 2020.

NEW LAW EXPLAINED

Credit for health insurance costs of eligible individuals.—The HCTC has been extended for one year to January 1, 2021 (Code Sec. 35(b)(1)(B), as amended by Division Q, Act Sec. 146(a) of the Further Consolidated Appropriations Act, 2020 (P.L. 116-94)).

▶ **Effective date.** The amendment made by this section applies for months beginning after December 31, 2019 (Division Q, Act Sec. 146(b) of the Appropriations Act).

Law source: Law at ¶5163 and ¶6001.

— Act Sec. 146(a), Division Q, of the Further Consolidated Appropriations Act, 2020 (P.L. 116-94), amending Code Sec. 35(b)(1)(B).

— Act. Sec. 146(b), Division Q, providing the effective date.

Further Consolidated Appropriations Act, 2020
(P.L. 116-94, enacted December 20, 2019)

[¶ 5000] INTRODUCTION

Selected provisions of the Further Consolidated Appropriations Act, 2020, (P.L. 116-94) are reproduced below. On December 20, 2019, President Donald Trump signed the bipartisan, year-end government spending and tax package. The 2020 Appropriations Act includes the Setting Every Community Up for Retirement Enhancement Act of 2019 (SECURE Act), which makes substantial changes to retirement saving rules. On December 17, 2019, the House of Representatives passed the 2020 Appropriations Act, by a vote of 297-120, and on December 19, 2019, the Senate passed the measure by a vote of 71 to 23.

[¶ 5001] SEC. 1. SHORT TITLE, ETC.

This Act may be cited as the "Further Consolidated Appropriations Act, 2020".

[¶ 5002] SEC. 2. TABLE OF CONTENTS.

Sec. 1. Short title.
Sec. 2. Table of contents.

* * *

DIVISION M—BIPARTISAN AMERICAN MINERS
DIVISION N—HEALTH AND HUMAN SERVICES EXTENDERS
DIVISION O—SETTING EVERY COMMUNITY UP FOR RETIREMENT ENHANCEMENT
DIVISION P—OTHER MATTER

Title I—Platte River Recovery Implementation Program
Title II—Great Lakes
Title III—Morris K. Udall and Stewart L. Udall Foundation
Title IV—White Horse Hill National Game Preserve
Title V—Pittman-Robertson Fund
Title VI—John F. Kennedy Center
Title VII—Preserving America's Battlefields
Title VIII—Veterans Affairs Report on Disability Compensation and the Positive Association With Exposure to an Herbicide Agent
Title IX—Disaster Recovery Workforce
Title X—Television Viewer Protection
Title XI—Eligibility to Receive Signals Under a Distant-Signal Satellite License
Title XII—Groundfish Trawl Fishery
Title XIII—Temporary Relief from Certain ERISA Requirements
Title XIV—Library of Congress Technical Corrections
Title XV—Senate Entities
Title XVI—Legislative Branch Inspectors General Independence
Title XVII—Managing Political Fund Activity
Title XVIII—Kentucky Wildlands National Heritage Area Study
Title XIX—International Bank for Reconstruction and Development

Title XX—European Energy Security and Diversification Act of 2019
DIVISION Q—REVENUE PROVISIONS
***

DIVISION M—BIPARTISAN AMERICAN MINERS

[¶ 5003] **SEC. 101. SHORT TITLE.**

This division may be cited as the "Bipartisan American Miners Act of 2019".

[¶ 5004] **SEC. 102. TRANSFERS TO 1974 UMWA PENSION PLAN.**

(a) IN GENERAL.—Subsection (i) of section 402 of the Surface Mining Control and Reclamation Act of 1977 (30 U.S.C. 1232) is amended—

    (1) in paragraph (3)(A), by striking "$490,000,000" and inserting "$750,000,000";

    (2) by redesignating paragraph (4) as paragraph (5); and

    (3) by inserting after paragraph (3) the following:

"(4) ADDITIONAL AMOUNTS.—

"(A) CALCULATION.—If the dollar limitation specified in paragraph (3)(A) exceeds the aggregate amount required to be transferred under paragraphs (1) and (2) for a fiscal year, the Secretary of the Treasury shall transfer an additional amount equal to the difference between such dollar limitation and such aggregate amount to the trustees of the 1974 UMWA Pension Plan to pay benefits required under that plan.

"(B) CESSATION OF TRANSFERS.—The transfers described in subparagraph (A) shall cease as of the first fiscal year beginning after the first plan year for which the funded percentage (as defined in section 432(j)(2) of the Internal Revenue Code of 1986) of the 1974 UMWA Pension Plan is at least 100 percent.

"(C) PROHIBITION ON BENEFIT INCREASES, ETC.—During a fiscal year in which the 1974 UMWA Pension Plan is receiving transfers under subparagraph (A), no amendment of such plan which increases the liabilities of the plan by reason of any increase in benefits, any change in the accrual of benefits, or any change in the rate at which benefits become nonforfeitable under the plan may be adopted unless the amendment is required as a condition of qualification under part I of subchapter D of chapter 1 of the Internal Revenue Code of 1986.

"(D) CRITICAL STATUS TO BE MAINTAINED.—Until such time as the 1974 UMWA Pension Plan ceases to be eligible for the transfers described in subparagraph (A)—

"(i) the Plan shall be treated as if it were in critical status for purposes of sections 412(b)(3), 432(e)(3), and 4971(g)(1)(A) of the Internal Revenue Code of 1986 and sections 302(b)(3) and 305(e)(3) of the Employee Retirement Income Security Act;

"(ii) the Plan shall maintain and comply with its rehabilitation plan under section 432(e) of such Code and section 305(e) of such Act, including any updates thereto; and

"(iii) the provisions of subsections (c) and (d) of section 432 of such Code and subsections (c) and (d) of section 305 of such Act shall not apply.

"(E) TREATMENT OF TRANSFERS FOR PURPOSES OF WITHDRAWAL LIABILITY UNDER ERISA.—The amount of any transfer made under subparagraph (A) (and any earnings attributable thereto) shall be disregarded in determining the unfunded vested benefits of the 1974 UMWA Pension Plan and the allocation of such unfunded vested benefits to an employer for purposes of determining the employer's withdrawal liability under section 4201 of the Employee Retirement Income Security Act of 1974.

"(F) REQUIREMENT TO MAINTAIN CONTRIBUTION RATE.—A transfer under subparagraph (A) shall not be made for a fiscal year unless the persons that are obligated to contribute to the 1974 UMWA Pension Plan on the date of the transfer are obligated to make the contributions at rates that are no less than those in effect on the date which is 30 days before the date of enactment of the Bipartisan American Miners Act of 2019.

"(G) ENHANCED ANNUAL REPORTING.—

"(i) IN GENERAL.—Not later than the 90th day of each plan year beginning after the date of enactment of the Bipartisan American Miners Act of 2019, the trustees of the 1974 UMWA Pension Plan shall file with the Secretary of the Treasury or the Secretary's delegate and the Pension Benefit Guaranty Corporation a report (including appropriate documentation and actuarial certifications from the plan actuary, as required by the Secretary of the Treasury or the Secretary's delegate) that contains—

"(I) whether the plan is in endangered or critical status under section 305 of the Employee Retirement Income Security Act of 1974 and section 432 of the Internal Revenue Code of 1986 as of the first day of such plan year;

"(II) the funded percentage (as defined in section 432(j)(2) of such Code) as of the first day of such plan year, and the underlying actuarial value of assets and liabilities taken into account in determining such percentage;

"(III) the market value of the assets of the plan as of the last day of the plan year preceding such plan year;

"(IV) the total value of all contributions made during the plan year preceding such plan year;

"(V) the total value of all benefits paid during the plan year preceding such plan year;

"(VI) cash flow projections for such plan year and either the 6 or 10 succeeding plan years, at the election of the trustees, and the assumptions relied upon in making such projections;

"(VII) funding standard account projections for such plan year and the 9 succeeding plan years, and the assumptions relied upon in making such projections;

"(VIII) the total value of all investment gains or losses during the plan year preceding such plan year;

"(IX) any significant reduction in the number of active participants during the plan year preceding such plan year, and the reason for such reduction;

"(X) a list of employers that withdrew from the plan in the plan year preceding such plan year, and the resulting reduction in contributions;

"(XI) a list of employers that paid withdrawal liability to the plan during the plan year preceding such plan year and, for each employer, a total assessment of the withdrawal liability paid, the annual payment amount, and the number of years remaining in the payment schedule with respect to such withdrawal liability;

"(XII) any material changes to benefits, accrual rates, or contribution rates during the plan year preceding such plan year;

"(XIII) any scheduled benefit increase or decrease in the plan year preceding such plan year having a material effect on liabilities of the plan;

"(XIV) details regarding any funding improvement plan or rehabilitation plan and updates to such plan;

"(XV) the number of participants and beneficiaries during the plan year preceding such plan year who are active participants, the number of participants and beneficiaries in pay status, and the number of terminated vested participants and beneficiaries;

"(XVI) the information contained on the most recent annual funding notice submitted by the plan under section 101(f) of the Employee Retirement Income Security Act of 1974;

"(XVII) the information contained on the most recent Department of Labor Form 5500 of the plan; and

"(XVIII) copies of the plan document and amendments, other retirement benefit or ancillary benefit plans relating to the plan and contribution obligations under such plans, a breakdown of administrative expenses of the plan, participant census data and distribution of benefits, the most recent actuarial valuation report as of the plan year, copies of collective bargaining agreements, and financial reports, and such other information as the Secretary of the Treasury or the Secretary's delegate, in consultation with the Secretary of Labor and the Director of the Pension Benefit Guaranty Corporation, may require.

"(ii) ELECTRONIC SUBMISSION.—The report required under clause (i) shall be submitted electronically.

"(iii) INFORMATION SHARING.—The Secretary of the Treasury or the Secretary's delegate shall share the information in the report under clause (i) with the Secretary of Labor.

"(iv) PENALTY.—Any failure to file the report required under clause (i) on or before the date described in such clause shall be treated as a failure to file a report required to be filed under section 6058(a) of the Internal Revenue Code of 1986, except that section 6652(e) of such Code shall be applied with respect to any such failure by substituting '$100' for '$25'. The preceding sentence shall not apply if the Secretary of the Treasury or the Secretary's delegate determines that reasonable diligence has been exercised by the trustees of such plan in attempting to timely file such report.

"(H) 1974 UMWA PENSION PLAN DEFINED.—For purposes of this paragraph, the term '1974 UMWA Pension Plan' has the meaning given the term in section 9701(a)(3) of the Internal Revenue Code of 1986, but without regard to the limitation on participation to individuals who retired in 1976 and thereafter.".

(b) EFFECTIVE DATES.—

(1) IN GENERAL.—The amendments made by this section shall apply to fiscal years beginning after September 30, 2016.

(2) REPORTING REQUIREMENTS.—Section 402(i)(4)(G) of the Surface Mining Control and Reclamation Act of 1977 (30 U.S.C. 1232(i)(4)(G)), as added by this section, shall apply to plan years beginning after the date of the enactment of this Act.

[¶ 5005] SEC. 103. INCLUSION IN MULTIEMPLOYER HEALTH BENEFIT PLAN.

Section 402(h)(2)(C) of the Surface Mining Control and Reclamation Act of 1977 (30 U.S.C. 1232(h)(2)(C)) is amended—

(1) by striking "the Health Benefits for Miners Act of 2017" both places it appears in clause (ii) and inserting "the Bipartisan American Miners Act of 2019";

(2) by striking ", would be denied or reduced as a result of a bankruptcy proceeding commenced in 2012 or 2015" in clause(ii)(II) and inserting "or a related coal wage agreement, would be denied or reduced as a result of a bankruptcy proceeding commenced in 2012, 2015, 2018, or 2019";

(3) by striking "and" at the end of clause (ii)(I), by striking the period at the end of clause (ii)(II) and inserting "; and", and by inserting after clause (ii)(II) the following new subclause:

"(III) the cost of administering the resolution of disputes process administered (as of the date of the enactment of the Bipartisan American Miners Act of 2019) by the Trustees of the Plan.",

(4) by striking "January 1, 2017" in clause (ii) and inserting "January 1, 2019"; and

(5) by adding at the end the following new clause:

"(vi) RELATED COAL WAGE AGREEMENT.—For purposes of clause (ii), the term 'related coal wage agreement' means an agreement between the United Mine Workers of America and an employer in the bituminous coal industry that—

"(I) is a signatory operator; or

"(II) is or was a debtor in a bankruptcy proceeding that was consolidated, administratively or otherwise, with the bankruptcy proceeding of a signatory operator or a related person to a signatory operator (as those terms are defined in section 9701(c) of the Internal Revenue Code of 1986).".

[¶ 5006] SEC. 104. REDUCTION IN MINIMUM AGE FOR ALLOWABLE IN-SERVICE DISTRIBUTIONS.

(a) IN GENERAL.—Section 401(a)(36) of the Internal Revenue Code of 1986 is amended by striking "age 62" and inserting "age $59\frac{1}{2}$".

(b) APPLICATION TO GOVERNMENTAL SECTION 457(b) PLANS.—Clause (i) of section 457(d)(1)(A) of the Internal Revenue Code of 1986 is amended by inserting "(in the case of a plan maintained by an employer described in subsection (e)(1)(A), age $59\frac{1}{2}$)" before the comma at the end.

(c) EFFECTIVE DATE.—The amendments made by this section shall apply to plan years beginning after December 31, 2019.

DIVISION N—HEALTH AND HUMAN SERVICES EXTENDERS
TITLE I—HEALTH AND HUMAN SERVICES EXTENDERS
Subtitle A—Medicare Provisions

Sec. 101. Extension of the work geographic index floor under the Medicare program.

Sec. 102. Extension of funding for quality measure endorsement, input, and selection.

Sec. 103. Extension of funding outreach and assistance for low-income programs.

Sec. 104. Extension of appropriations to the Patient-Centered Outcomes Research Trust Fund; extension of certain health insurance fees.

Sec. 105. Laboratory Access for Beneficiaries.

Sec. 106. Exclusion of complex rehabilitative manual wheelchairs from medicare competitive acquisition program; non-application of medicare fee-schedule adjustments for certain wheelchair accessories and cushions.

Sec. 107. Extending pass-through status for certain drugs under part B of the Medicare program.

Sec. 108. Hematopoietic stem cell acquisition payments.

Subtitle B—Medicaid Provisions

Sec. 201. Extension of Community Mental Health Services demonstration program.

Sec. 202. Medicaid funding for the territories.

Sec. 203. Delay of DSH reductions.

Sec. 204. Extension of spousal impoverishment protections.

Sec. 205. Extension of the Money Follows the Person rebalancing demonstration program.

Subtitle C—Human Services and Other Health Programs

Sec. 301. Extension of demonstration projects to address health professions workforce needs.

Sec. 302. Extension of the temporary assistance for needy families program and related programs.

Sec. 303. Extension of sexual risk avoidance education program.

Sec. 304. Extension of personal responsibility education program.

Subtitle D—Public Health Provisions

Sec. 401. Extension for community health centers, the national health service corps, and teaching health centers that operate GME programs.

Sec. 402. Diabetes programs.

Sec. 403. Poison Center Network Enhancement.

Sec. 404. Kay Hagan Tick Act.

Subtitle E—Revenue Provisions

Sec. 501. Repeal of medical device excise tax.

Sec. 502. Repeal of annual fee on health insurance providers.

Sec. 503. Repeal of excise tax on high cost employer-sponsored health coverage.

Subtitle F—Miscellaneous Provisions

Sec. 602. Addressing expiration of child welfare demonstration projects and supporting Family First implementation.

Sec. 603 Minimum age of sale of tobacco products.

Sec. 604. Sale of tobacco products to individuals under the age of 21.

Sec. 605. Biological product definition.

Sec. 606. Protecting access to biological products.

Sec. 607. Streamlining the transition of biological products.

Sec. 608. Reenrollment of certain individuals in qualified health plans in certain Exchanges.

SEC. 104(c)   ¶5006

Sec. 609. Protection of silver loading practice.

Sec. 610. Actions for delays of generic drugs and biosimilar biological products.

Subtitle A—Medicare Provisions

[¶ 5007] SEC. 101. EXTENSION OF THE WORK GEOGRAPHIC INDEX FLOOR UNDER THE MEDICARE PROGRAM.

Section 1848(e)(1)(E) of the Social Security Act (42 U.S.C. 1395w-4(e)(1)(E)) is amended by striking "January 1, 2020" and inserting "May 23, 2020".

[¶ 5008] SEC. 102. EXTENSION OF FUNDING FOR QUALITY MEASURE ENDORSEMENT, INPUT, AND SELECTION.

(a) IN GENERAL.—Section 1890(d)(2) of the Social Security Act (42 U.S.C. 1395aaa(d)(2)) is amended—

(1) in the first sentence, by striking "$1,665,000 for the period beginning on October 1, 2019, and ending on December 20, 2019" and inserting "$4,830,000 for the period beginning on October 1, 2019, and ending on May 22, 2020"; and

(2) in the third sentence, by striking "December 20, 2019," and inserting "May 22, 2020".

(b) EFFECTIVE DATE.—The amendments made by subsection (a) shall take effect as if included in the enactment of the Further Continuing Appropriations Act, 2020, and Further Health Extenders Act of 2019 (Public Law 116-69).

[¶ 5009] SEC. 103. EXTENSION OF FUNDING OUTREACH AND ASSISTANCE FOR LOW-INCOME PROGRAMS.

(a) ADDITIONAL FUNDING FOR STATE HEALTH INSURANCE PROGRAMS.—Subsection (a)(1)(B) of section 119 of the Medicare Improvements for Patients and Providers Act of 2008 (42 U.S.C. 1395b-3 note), as amended by section 3306 of the Patient Protection and Affordable Care Act (Public Law 111-148), section 610 of the American Taxpayer Relief Act of 2012 (Public Law 112-240), section 1110 of the Pathway for SGR Reform Act of 2013 (Public Law 113-67), section 110 of the Protecting Access to Medicare Act of 2014 (Public Law 113-93), section 208 of the Medicare Access and CHIP Reauthorization Act of 2015 (Public Law 114-10), section 50207 of division E of the Bipartisan Budget Act of 2018 (Public Law 115-123), section 1402 of the Continuing Appropriations Act, 2020, and Health Extenders Act of 2019 (Public Law 116-59), and section 1402 of the Further Continuing Appropriations Act, 2020, and Further Health Extenders Act of 2019 (Public Law 116-69), is amended—

(1) in clause (x), by striking "and" at the end;

(2) in clause (xi), by striking the period at the end and inserting "; and"; and

(3) by inserting after clause (xi) the following new clause:

"(xii) for the period beginning on December 21, 2019, and ending on May 22, 2020, of $5,485,000.".

(b) ADDITIONAL FUNDING FOR AREA AGENCIES ON AGING.—Subsection (b)(1)(B) of such section 119, as so amended, is amended—

(1) in clause (x), by striking "and" at the end;

(2) in clause (xi), by striking the period at the end and inserting "; and"; and

(3) by inserting after clause (xi) the following new clause:

"(xii) for the period beginning on December 21, 2019, and ending on May 22, 2020, of $3,165,000.".

(c) ADDITIONAL FUNDING FOR AGING AND DISABILITY RESOURCE CENTERS.—Subsection (c)(1)(B) of such section 119, as so amended, is amended—

(1) in clause (x), by striking "and" at the end;

(2) in clause (xi), by striking the period at the end and inserting "; and"; and

(3) by inserting after clause (xi) the following new clause:

"(xii) for the period beginning on December 21, 2019, and ending on May 22, 2020, of $2,110,000.".

(d) ADDITIONAL FUNDING FOR CONTRACT WITH THE NATIONAL CENTER FOR BENEFITS AND OUTREACH ENROLLMENT.—Subsection (d)(2) of such section 119, as so amended, is amended—

(1) in clause (x), by striking "and" at the end;

(2) in clause (xi), by striking the period at the end and inserting "; and"; and

(3) by inserting after clause (xi) the following new clause:

"(xii) for the period beginning on December 21, 2019, and ending on May 22, 2020, of $5,063,000.".

[¶ 5010] SEC. 104. EXTENSION OF APPROPRIATIONS TO THE PATIENT-CENTERED OUTCOMES RESEARCH TRUST FUND; EXTENSION OF CERTAIN HEALTH INSURANCE FEES.

(a) IN GENERAL.—Section 9511 of the Internal Revenue Code of 1986 is amended—

(1) in subsection (b)—

(A) in paragraph (1)—

(i) by inserting after subparagraph (E) the following new subparagraph:

"(F) For each of fiscal years 2020 through 2029—

"(i) an amount equivalent to the net revenues received in the Treasury from the fees imposed under subchapter B of chapter 34 (relating to fees on health insurance and self-insured plans) for such fiscal year; and

"(ii) the applicable amount (as defined in paragraph (4)) for the fiscal year."; and

(ii) by striking "and (E)(ii)" in the last sentence and inserting "(E)(ii), and (F)(ii)"; and

(B) by adding at the end the following new paragraph:

"(4) APPLICABLE AMOUNT DEFINED.—In paragraph (1)(F)(ii), the term 'applicable amount' means—

"(A) for fiscal year 2020, $275,500,000;

"(B) for fiscal year 2021, $285,000,000;

"(C) for fiscal year 2022, $293,500,000;

"(D) for fiscal year 2023, $311,500,000;

"(E) for fiscal year 2024, $320,000,000;

"(F) for fiscal year 2025, $338,000,000;

"(G) for fiscal year 2026, $355,500,000;

"(H) for fiscal year 2027, $363,500,000;

"(I) for fiscal year 2028, $381,000,000; and

"(J) for fiscal year 2029, $399,000,000.";

(2) in subsection (d)(2)(A), by striking "2019" and inserting "2029"; and

(3) in subsection (f), by striking "December 20, 2019" and inserting "September 30, 2029".

(b) HEALTH INSURANCE POLICIES.—Section 4375(e) of the Internal Revenue Code of 1986 is amended by striking "2019" and inserting "2029".

(c) SELF-INSURED HEALTH PLANS.—Section 4376(e) of the Internal Revenue Code of 1986 is amended by striking "2019" and inserting "2029".

(d) IDENTIFICATION OF RESEARCH PRIORITIES.—Subsection (d)(1)(A) of section 1181 of the Social Security Act (42 U.S.C. 1320e) is amended by adding at the end the following: "Such national priorities shall include research with respect to intellectual and developmental disabilities and maternal mortality. Such priorities should reflect a balance between long-term priorities and short-term priorities, and be responsive to changes in medical evidence and in health care treatments.".

(e) CONSIDERATION OF FULL RANGE OF OUTCOMES DATA.—Subsection (d)(2) of such section 1181 is amended by adding at the end the following subparagraph:

"(F) CONSIDERATION OF FULL RANGE OF OUTCOMES DATA.—Research shall be designed, as appropriate, to take into account and capture the full range of clinical and patient-centered outcomes relevant to, and that meet the needs of, patients, clinicians, purchasers, and policy-makers in making informed health decisions. In addition to the relative health outcomes and clinical effectiveness, clinical and patient-centered outcomes shall include the potential burdens and economic impacts of the utilization of medical treatments, items, and services on different stakeholders and decision-makers respectively. These potential burdens and economic impacts include medical out-of-pocket costs, including health plan benefit and formulary design, non-medical costs to the patient and family, including caregiving, effects on future costs of care, workplace productivity and absenteeism, and healthcare utilization.".

(f) BOARD COMPOSITION.—Subsection (f) of such section 1181 is amended—

(1) in paragraph (1)—

(A) in subparagraph (C)—

(i) in the matter preceding clause (i)—

(I) by striking "Seventeen" and inserting "At least nineteen, but no more than twenty-one"; and

(II) by striking ", not later than 6 months after the date of enactment of this section,"; and

(ii) in clause (iii), by striking "3" and inserting "at least 3, but no more than 5"; and

(2) in paragraph (3)—

(A) in the first sentence—

(i) by striking the "the members" and inserting "members"; and

(ii) by inserting the following before the period at the end: "to the extent necessary to preserve the evenly staggered terms of the Board."; and

(B) by inserting the following after the first sentence: "Any member appointed to fill a vacancy occurring before the expiration of the term for which the member's predecessor was appointed shall be appointed for the remainder of that term and thereafter may be eligible for reappointment to a full term. A member may serve after the expiration of that member's term until a successor has been appointed.".

(g) METHODOLOGY COMMITTEE APPOINTMENTS.—Such section 1181 is amended—

(1) in subsection (d)(6)(B), by striking "Comptroller General of the United States" and inserting "Board"; and

(2) in subsection (h)(4)—

(A) in subparagraph (A)(ii), by striking "Comptroller General" and inserting "Board"; and

(B) in the first sentence of subparagraph (B), by striking "and of the Government Accountability Office".

(h) REPORTS BY THE COMPTROLLER GENERAL OF THE UNITED STATES.—Subsection (g)(2)(A) of such section 1181 is amended—

(1) by striking clause (iv) and inserting the following:

"(iv) Not less frequently than every 5 years, the overall effectiveness of activities conducted under this section and the dissemination, training, and capacity building activities conducted under section 937 of the Public Health Service Act. Such review shall include the following:

"(I) A description of those activities and the financial commitments related to research, training, data capacity building, and dissemination and uptake of research findings.

"(II) The extent to which the Institute and the Agency for Healthcare Research and Quality have collaborated with stakeholders, including provider and payer organizations, to facilitate the dissemination and uptake of research findings.

"(III) An analysis of available data and performance metrics, such as the estimated public availability and dissemination of research findings and uptake and utilization of research findings in clinical guidelines and decision support tools, on the extent to which such research findings are used by health care decision-makers, the effect of the dissemination of such findings on changes in medical practice and reducing practice variation and disparities in health care, and the effect of the research conducted and disseminated on innovation and the health care economy of the United States."; and

(2) by adding at the end the following new clause:

"(vi) Not less frequently than every 5 years, any barriers that researchers funded by the Institute have encountered in conducting studies or clinical trials, including challenges covering the cost of any medical treatments, services, and items described in subsection (a)(2)(B) for purposes of the research study.".

[¶ 5011] SEC. 105. LABORATORY ACCESS FOR BENEFICIARIES.

(a) AMENDMENTS RELATING TO REPORTING REQUIREMENTS WITH RESPECT TO CLINICAL DIAGNOSTIC LABORATORY TESTS.—

(1) REVISED REPORTING PERIOD FOR REPORTING OF PRIVATE SECTOR PAYMENT RATES FOR ESTABLISHMENT OF MEDICARE PAYMENT RATES.—Section 1834A(a) of the Social Security Act (42 U.S.C. 1395m-1(a)) is amended—

(A) in paragraph (1)—

(i) by striking "Beginning January 1, 2016" and inserting the following:

"(A) GENERAL REPORTING REQUIREMENTS.—Subject to subparagraph (B), beginning January 1, 2016";

(ii) in subparagraph (A), as added by subparagraph (A) of this paragraph, by inserting "(referred to in this subsection as the 'reporting period')" after "at a time specified by the Secretary"; and

(iii) by adding at the end the following:

"(B) REVISED REPORTING PERIOD.—In the case of reporting with respect to clinical diagnostic laboratory tests that are not advanced diagnostic laboratory tests, the Secretary shall revise the reporting period under subparagraph (A) such that—

"(i) no reporting is required during the period beginning January 1, 2020, and ending December 31, 2020;

"(ii) reporting is required during the period beginning January 1, 2021, and ending March 31, 2021; and

"(iii) reporting is required every three years after the period described in clause (ii)."; and

(B) in paragraph (4)—

(i) by striking "In this section" and inserting the following:

"(A) IN GENERAL.—Subject to subparagraph (B), in this section"; and

(ii) by adding at the end the following:

"(B) EXCEPTION.—In the case of the reporting period described in paragraph (1)(B)(ii) with respect to clinical diagnostic laboratory tests that are not advanced diagnostic laboratory tests, the term 'data collection period' means the period beginning January 1, 2019, and ending June 30, 2019.".

(2) CORRECTIONS RELATING TO PHASE-IN OF REDUCTIONS FROM PRIVATE PAYOR RATE IMPLEMENTATION.—Section 1834A(b)(3) of the Social Security Act (42 U.S.C. 1395m-1(b)(3)) is amended—

(A) in subparagraph (A), by striking "through 2022" and inserting "through 2023"; and

(B) in subparagraph (B)—

(i) in clause (i), by striking "through 2019" and inserting "through 2020"; and

(ii) in clause (ii), by striking "2020 through 2022" and inserting "2021 through 2023".

(b) STUDY AND REPORT BY MEDPAC.—

(1) IN GENERAL.—The Medicare Payment Advisory Commission (in this subsection referred to as the "Commission") shall conduct a study to review the methodology the Administrator of the Centers for Medicare & Medicaid Services has implemented for the private payor rate-based clinical laboratory fee schedule under the Medicare program under title XVIII of the Social Security Act (42 U.S.C. 1395 et seq.).

(2) SCOPE OF STUDY.—In carrying out the study described in paragraph (1), the Commission shall consider the following:

(A) How best to implement the least burdensome data collection process required under section 1834A(a)(1) of such Act (42 U.S.C. 1395m-1(a)(1)) that would—

(i) result in a representative and statistically valid data sample of private market rates from all laboratory market segments, including hospital outreach laboratories, physician office laboratories, and independent laboratories; and

(ii) consider the variability of private payor payment rates across market segments.

(B) Appropriate statistical methods for estimating rates that are representative of the market.

(3) REPORT TO CONGRESS.—Not later than 18 months after the date of the enactment of this Act, the Commission shall submit to the Administrator, the Committee on Finance of the Senate, and the Committees on Ways and Means and Energy and Commerce of the House of Representatives a report that includes—

(A) conclusions about the methodology described in paragraph (1); and

(B) any recommendations the Commission deems appropriate.

[¶5012] SEC. 106. EXCLUSION OF COMPLEX REHABILITATIVE MANUAL WHEELCHAIRS FROM MEDICARE COMPETITIVE ACQUISITION PROGRAM; NON-APPLICATION OF MEDICARE FEE-SCHEDULE ADJUSTMENTS FOR CERTAIN WHEELCHAIR ACCESSORIES AND CUSHIONS.

(a) EXCLUSION OF COMPLEX REHABILITATIVE MANUAL WHEELCHAIRS FROM COMPETITIVE ACQUISITION PROGRAM.—Section 1847(a)(2)(A) of the Social Security Act (42 U.S.C. 1395w-3(a)(2)(A)) is amended—

(1) by inserting ", complex rehabilitative manual wheelchairs(as determined by the Secretary), and certain manual wheelchairs(identified, as of October 1, 2018, by HCPCS codes E1235, E1236, E1237, E1238, and K0008 or any successor to such codes)" after "group 3 or higher"; and

(2) by striking "such wheelchairs" and inserting "such complex rehabilitative power wheelchairs, complex rehabilitative manual wheelchairs, and certain manual wheelchairs".

(b) NON-APPLICATION OF MEDICARE FEE SCHEDULE ADJUSTMENTS FOR WHEELCHAIR ACCESSORIES AND SEAT AND BACK CUSHIONS WHEN FURNISHED IN CONNECTION WITH COMPLEX REHABILITATIVE MANUAL WHEELCHAIRS.—

(1) IN GENERAL.—Notwithstanding any other provision of law, the Secretary of Health and Human Services shall not, during the period beginning on January 1, 2020, and ending on June 30, 2021, use information on the payment determined under the competitive acquisition programs under section 1847 of the Social Security Act (42 U.S.C. 1395w-3) to adjust the payment amount that would otherwise be recognized under section 1834(a)(1)(B)(ii) of such Act (42 U.S.C. 1395m(a)(1)(B)(ii)) for wheelchair accessories(including seating systems) and seat and back cushions when furnished in connection with complex rehabilitative manual wheelchairs (as determined by the Secretary), and certain manual wheelchairs (identified, as of October 1, 2018, by HCPCS codes E1235, E1236, E1237, E1238, and K0008 or any successor to such codes).

(2) IMPLEMENTATION.—Notwithstanding any other provision of law, the Secretary may implement this subsection by program instruction or otherwise.

[¶ 5013] **SEC. 107. EXTENDING PASS-THROUGH STATUS FOR CERTAIN DRUGS UNDER PART B OF THE MEDICARE PROGRAM.**

(a) IN GENERAL.—Section 1833(t)(6) of the Social Security Act (42 U.S.C. 1395l(t)(6)) is amended—

(1) in subparagraph (E)(i), by striking "2018" and inserting "2018 or 2020"; and

(2) by adding at the end the following new subparagraph:

"(J) ADDITIONAL PASS-THROUGH EXTENSION AND SPECIAL PAYMENT ADJUSTMENT RULE FOR CERTAIN DIAGNOSTIC RADIOPHARMACEUTICALS.—In the case of a drug or biological furnished in the context of a clinical study on diagnostic imaging tests approved under a coverage with evidence development determination whose period of pass-through status under this paragraph concluded on December 31, 2018, and for which payment under this subsection was packaged into a payment for a covered OPD service (or group of services) furnished beginning January 1, 2019, the Secretary shall—

"(i) extend such pass-through status for such drug or biological for the 9-month period beginning on January 1, 2020;

"(ii) remove, during such period, the packaged costs of such drug or biological (as determined by the Secretary) from the payment amount under this subsection for the covered OPD service (or group of services) with which it is packaged; and

"(iii) not make any adjustments to payment amounts under this subsection for a covered OPD service (or group of services) for which no costs were removed under clause (ii).".

(b) IMPLEMENTATION.—Notwithstanding any other provision of law, the Secretary of Health and Human Service may implement the amendments made by subsection (a) by program instruction or otherwise.

[¶ 5014] **SEC. 108. HEMATOPOIETIC STEM CELL ACQUISITION PAYMENTS.**

Section 1886 of the Social Security Act (42 U.S.C. 1395ww) is amended—

(1) in subsection (a)(4), in the second sentence, by inserting "for cost reporting periods beginning on or after October 1, 2020, costs related to hematopoietic stem cell acquisition for the purpose of an allogeneic hematopoietic stem cell transplant (as described in subsection (d)(5)(M))," after "October 1, 1987),";

(2) in subsection (d)—

(A) in paragraph (4)(C)(iii)—

(i) by inserting "or payments under paragraph (5)(M) (beginning with fiscal year 2021)" after "fiscal year 1991)"; and

(ii) by inserting "or payments under paragraph (5)(M)" before the period at the end; and

(B) in paragraph (5), by adding at the end the following new subparagraph:

"(M)(i) For cost reporting periods beginning on or after October 1, 2020, in the case of a subsection (d) hospital that furnishes an allogeneic hematopoietic stem cell transplant to an individual during such a period, payment to such hospital for hematopoietic stem cell acquisition shall be made on a reasonable cost basis. The items included in such hematopoietic stem cell acquisition shall be specified by the Secretary through rulemaking.

"(ii) For purposes of this subparagraph, the term 'allogeneic hematopoietic stem cell transplant' means, with respect to an individual, the intravenous infusion of hematopoietic cells derived from bone marrow, peripheral blood stem cells, or cord blood, but not including embryonic stem cells, of a donor to an individual that are or may be used to restore hematopoietic function in such individual having an inherited or acquired deficiency or defect.".

Subtitle B—Medicaid Provisions

[¶ 5015] **SEC. 201. EXTENSION OF COMMUNITY MENTAL HEALTH SERVICES DEMONSTRATION PROGRAM.**

Section 223(d)(3) of the Protecting Access to Medicare Act of 2014 (42 U.S.C. 1396a note) is amended by striking "December 20, 2019" and inserting "May 22, 2020".

[¶ 5016] **SEC. 202. MEDICAID FUNDING FOR THE TERRITORIES.**

(a) TREATMENT OF CAP.—Section 1108(g) of the Social Security Act (42 U.S.C. 1308(g)) is amended—

(1) in paragraph (2)—

(A) in the matter preceding subparagraph (A), by striking "subject to and section 1323(a)(2) of the Patient Protection and Affordable Care Act paragraphs (3) and (5)" and inserting "subject to section 1323(a)(2) of the Patient Protection and Affordable Care Act and paragraphs (3) and (5)";

(B) in subparagraph (A)—

(i) by striking "Puerto Rico shall not exceed the sum of" and inserting "Puerto Rico shall not exceed—

"(i) except as provided in clause (ii), the sum of";

(ii) by striking "$100,000;" and inserting "$100,000; and"; and

(iii) by adding at the end the following new clause:

"(ii) for each of fiscal years 2020 through 2021, the amount specified in paragraph (6) for each such fiscal year;";

(C) in subparagraph (B)—

(i) by striking "the Virgin Islands shall not exceed the sum of" and inserting "the Virgin Islands shall not exceed—

"(i) except as provided in clause (ii), the sum of";

(ii) by striking "$10,000;" and inserting "$10,000; and"; and

(iii) by adding at the end the following new clause:

"(ii) for each of fiscal years 2020 through 2021, $126,000,000;";

(D) in subparagraph (C)—

(i) by striking "Guam shall not exceed the sum of" and inserting "Guam shall not exceed—

"(i) except as provided in clause (ii), the sum of";

(ii) by striking "$10,000;" and inserting "$10,000; and"; and

(iii) by adding at the end the following new clause:

"(ii) for each of fiscal years 2020 through 2021, $127,000,000;";

(E) in subparagraph (D)—

(i) by striking "the Northern Mariana Islands shall not exceed the sum of" and inserting "the Northern Mariana Islands shall not exceed—

"(i) except as provided in clause (ii), the sum of"; and

(ii) by adding at the end the following new clause:

"(ii) for each of fiscal years 2020 through 2021, $60,000,000; and";

(F) in subparagraph (E)—

(i) by striking "American Samoa shall not exceed the sum of" and inserting "American Samoa shall not exceed—

"(i) except as provided in clause (ii), the sum of";

(ii) by striking "$10,000." and inserting "$10,000; and"; and

(iii) by adding at the end the following new clause:

"(ii) for each of fiscal years 2020 through 2021, $84,000,000."; and

(G) by adding at the end the following flush sentence:

"For each fiscal year after fiscal year 2021, the total amount certified for Puerto Rico, the Virgin Islands, Guam, the Northern Mariana Islands, and American Samoa under subsection (f) and this subsection for the fiscal year shall be determined as if the preceding subparagraphs were applied to each of fiscal years 2020 through 2021 without regard to clause (ii) of each such subparagraph."; and

(2) by adding at the end the following new paragraphs:

"(6) APPLICATION TO PUERTO RICO FOR FISCAL YEARS 2020 THROUGH 2021.—

"(A) IN GENERAL.—Subject to subparagraph (B), the amount specified in this paragraph is—

"(i) for fiscal year 2020, $2,623,188,000; and

"(ii) for fiscal year 2021, $2,719,072,000.

"(B) ADDITIONAL INCREASE FOR PUERTO RICO.—

"(i) IN GENERAL.—For each of fiscal years 2020 through 2021, the amount specified in this paragraph for the fiscal year shall be equal to the amount specified for such fiscal year under subparagraph (A) increased by $200,000,000 if the Secretary certifies that, with respect to such fiscal year, Puerto Rico's State plan under title XIX (or a waiver of such plan) establishes a reimbursement floor, implemented through a directed payment arrangement plan, for physician services that are covered under the Medicare part B fee schedule in the Puerto Rico locality established under section 1848(b) that is not less than 70 percent of the payment that would apply to such services if they were furnished under part B of title XVIII during such fiscal year.

"(ii) APPLICATION TO MANAGED CARE.—In certifying whether Puerto Rico has established a reimbursement floor under a directed payment arrangement plan that satisfies the requirements of clause (i)—

"(I) for fiscal year 2020, the Secretary shall apply such requirements to payments for physician services under a managed care contract entered into or renewed after the date of enactment of this paragraph and disregard payments for physician services under any managed care contract that was entered into prior to such date; and

"(II) for each of fiscal years 2020 through 2021—

"(aa) the Secretary shall disregard payments made under sub-capitated arrangements for services such as primary care case management; and

"(bb) if the reimbursement floor for physician services applicable under a managed care contract satisfies the requirements of clause (i) for the fiscal year in which the contract is entered into or renewed, such reimbursement floor shall be deemed to satisfy such requirements for the subsequent fiscal year.

"(7) PUERTO RICO PROGRAM INTEGRITY REQUIREMENTS.—

"(A) IN GENERAL.—

"(i) PROGRAM INTEGRITY LEAD.—Not later than 6 months after the date of enactment of this paragraph, the agency responsible for the administration of Puerto Rico's Medicaid program under title XIX shall designate an officer (other than the director of such agency) to serve as the Program Integrity Lead for such program.

"(ii) PERM REQUIREMENT.—Not later than 18 months after the date of enactment of this paragraph, Puerto Rico shall publish a plan, developed by Puerto Rico in coordination with the Administrator of the Centers for Medicare & Medicaid Services and approved by the Administrator, for how Puerto Rico will develop measures to satisfy the payment error rate measurement (PERM) requirements under subpart Q of part 431 of title 42, Code of Federal Regulations (or any successor regulation).

"(iii) CONTRACTING REFORM.—Not later than 12 months after the date of enactment of this paragraph, Puerto Rico shall publish a contracting reform plan to combat fraudulent, wasteful, or abusive contracts under Puerto Rico's Medicaid program under title XIX that includes—

"(I) metrics for evaluating the success of the plan; and

"(II) a schedule for publicly releasing status reports on the plan.

"(iv) MEQC.—Not later than 18 months after the date of enactment of this paragraph, Puerto Rico shall publish a plan, developed by Puerto Rico in coordination with the Administrator of the Centers for Medicare & Medicaid Services and approved by the Administrator, for how Puerto Rico will comply with the Medicaid eligibility quality control (MEQC) requirements of subpart P of part 431 of title 42, Code of Federal Regulations (or any successor regulation).

"(B) FMAP REDUCTION FOR FAILURE TO MEET ADDITIONAL REQUIREMENTS.—

"(i) IN GENERAL.—For each fiscal quarter during the period beginning on January 1, 2020, and ending on September 30, 2021:

"(I) For every clause under subparagraph (A) with respect to which Puerto Rico does not fully satisfy the requirements described in the clause (including requirements imposed under the terms of a plan described in the clause) in the fiscal quarter, the Federal medical assistance percentage applicable to Puerto Rico under section 1905(ff) shall be reduced by the number of percentage points determined for the clause and fiscal quarter under subclause (II).

"(II) The number of percentage points determined under this subclause with respect to a clause under subparagraph (A) and a fiscal quarter shall be the number of percentage points (not to exceed 2.5 percentage points) equal to—

"(aa) 0.25 percentage points; multiplied by

"(bb) the total number of consecutive fiscal quarters for which Puerto Rico has not fully satisfied the requirements described in such clause.

"(ii) EXCEPTION FOR EXTENUATING CIRCUMSTANCES OR REASONABLE PROGRESS.—For purposes of clause (i), Puerto Rico shall be deemed to have fully satisfied the requirements of a clause under subparagraph (A) (including requirements imposed under the terms of a plan described in the clause) for a fiscal quarter if—

"(I) the Secretary approves an application from Puerto Rico describing extenuating circumstances that prevented Puerto Rico from fully satisfying the requirements of the clause; or

"(II) in the case of a requirement imposed under the terms of a plan described in a clause under subparagraph (A), Puerto Rico has made objectively reasonable progress towards satisfying such terms and has submitted a timely request for an exception to the imposition of a penalty to the Secretary.

"(8) PROGRAM INTEGRITY LEAD REQUIREMENT FOR THE VIRGIN ISLANDS, GUAM, THE NORTHERN MARIANA ISLANDS, AND AMERICAN SAMOA.—

"(A) PROGRAM INTEGRITY LEAD REQUIREMENT.—Not later than October 1, 2020, the agency responsible for the administration of the Medicaid program under title XIX of each territory specified in subparagraph (C) shall designate an officer (other than the director of such agency) to serve as the Program Integrity Lead for such program.

"(B) FMAP REDUCTION.—For each fiscal quarter during fiscal year 2021, if the territory fails to satisfy the requirement of subparagraph (A) for the fiscal quarter, the Federal medical assistance percentage applicable to the territory under section 1905(ff) for such fiscal quarter shall be reduced by the number of percentage points (not to exceed 5 percentage points) equal to—

"(i) 0.25 percentage points; multiplied by

"(ii) the total number of fiscal quarters during the fiscal year in which the territory failed to satisfy such requirement.

"(C) SCOPE.—This paragraph shall apply to the Virgin Islands, Guam, the Northern Mariana Islands, and American Samoa.".

(b) TREATMENT OF FUNDING UNDER ENHANCED ALLOTMENT PROGRAM.—Section 1935(e) of the Social Security Act (42 U.S.C. 1396u-5(e)) is amended—

(1) in paragraph (1)(B), by striking "if the State" and inserting "subject to paragraph (4), if the State";

(2) by redesignating paragraph (4) as paragraph (5); and

(3) by inserting after paragraph (3) the following new paragraph:

"(4) TREATMENT OF FUNDING FOR CERTAIN FISCAL YEARS.—Notwithstanding paragraph (1)(B), in the case that Puerto Rico, the Virgin Islands, Guam, the Northern Mariana Islands, or American Samoa establishes and submits to the Secretary a plan described in paragraph (2) with respect to any of fiscal years 2020 through 2021, the amount specified for such a year in paragraph (3) for Puerto Rico, the Virgin Islands, Guam, the Northern Mariana Islands, or American Samoa, as the case may be, shall be taken into account in applying, as applicable, subparagraph (A)(ii), (B)(ii), (C)(ii), (D)(ii), or (E)(ii) of section 1108(g)(2) for such year.".

(c) INCREASED FMAP.—Subsection (ff) of section 1905 of the Social Security Act (42 U.S.C. 1396d) is amended to read as follows:

"(ff) TEMPORARY INCREASE IN FMAP FOR TERRITORIES FOR CERTAIN FISCAL YEARS.—Notwithstanding subsection (b) or (z)(2)—

"(1) for the period beginning October 1, 2019, and ending December 20, 2019, the Federal medical assistance percentage for Puerto Rico, the Virgin Islands, Guam, the Northern Mariana Islands, and American Samoa shall be equal to 100 percent;

"(2) subject to section 1108(g)(7)(C), for the period beginning December 21, 2019, and ending September 30, 2021, the Federal medical assistance percentage for Puerto Rico shall be equal to 76 percent; and

"(3) subject to section 1108(g)(8)(B), for the period beginning December 21, 2019, and ending September 30, 2021, the Federal medical assistance percentage for the Virgin Islands, Guam, the Northern Mariana Islands, and American Samoa shall be equal to 83 percent.".

(d) ANNUAL REPORT.—Section 1108(g) of the Social Security Act (42 U.S.C. 1308(g)), as amended by subsection (a), is further amended by adding at the end the following new paragraph:

"(9) ANNUAL REPORT.—

"(A) IN GENERAL.—Not later than the date that is 30 days after the end of each fiscal year (beginning with fiscal year 2020 and ending with fiscal year 2021), in the case that a specified territory receives a Medicaid cap increase, or an increase in the Federal medical assistance percentage for such territory under section 1905(ff), for such fiscal year, such territory shall submit to the Chair and Ranking Member of the Committee on Energy and Commerce of the House of Representatives and the Chair and Ranking Member of the Committee on Finance of the Senate a report, employing the most up-to-date information available, that describes how such territory has used such Medicaid cap increase, or such increase in the Federal medical assistance percentage, as applicable, to increase access to health care under the State Medicaid plan of such territory under title XIX (or a waiver of such plan). Such report may include—

"(i) the extent to which such territory has, with respect to such plan (or waiver)—

"(I) increased payments to health care providers;

"(II) increased covered benefits;

"(III) expanded health care provider networks; or

"(IV) improved in any other manner the carrying out of such plan (or waiver); and

"(ii) any other information as determined necessary by such territory.

"(B) DEFINITIONS.—In this paragraph:

"(i) MEDICAID CAP INCREASE.—The term 'Medicaid cap increase' means, with respect to a specified territory and fiscal year, any increase in the amounts otherwise determined under this subsection for such territory for such fiscal year by reason of the amendments made by section 202 of division N of the Further Consolidated Appropriations Act, 2020.

"(ii) SPECIFIED TERRITORY.—The term 'specified territory' means Puerto Rico, the Virgin Islands, Guam, the Northern Mariana Islands, and American Samoa.".

(e) APPLICATION OF CERTAIN DATA REPORTING AND PROGRAM INTEGRITY REQUIREMENTS TO NORTHERN MARIANA ISLANDS, AMERICAN SAMOA, AND GUAM.—

(1) IN GENERAL.—Section 1902 of the Social Security Act (42 U.S.C. 1396a) is amended by adding at the end the following new subsection:

"(qq) APPLICATION OF CERTAIN DATA REPORTING AND PROGRAM INTEGRITY REQUIREMENTS TO NORTHERN MARIANA ISLANDS, AMERICAN SAMOA, AND GUAM.—

"(1) IN GENERAL.—Not later than October 1, 2021, the Northern Mariana Islands, American Samoa, and Guam shall—

"(A) demonstrate progress in implementing methods, satisfactory to the Secretary, for the collection and reporting of reliable data to the Transformed Medicaid Statistical Information System (T-MSIS) (or a successor system); and

"(B) demonstrate progress in establishing a State medicaid fraud control unit described in section 1903(q).

"(2) DETERMINATION OF PROGRESS.—For purposes of paragraph (1), the Secretary shall deem that a territory described in such paragraph has demonstrated satisfactory progress in implementing methods for the collection and reporting of reliable data or establishing a State medicaid fraud control unit if the territory has made a good faith effort to implement such methods or establish such a unit, given the circumstances of the territory.".

(2) CONFORMING AMENDMENT.—Section 1902(j) of the Social Security Act (42 U.S.C. 1396a(j)) is amended—

(A) by striking "or the requirement" and inserting ", the requirement"; and

(B) by inserting before the period at the end the following: ", or the requirement under subsection (qq)(1) (relating to data reporting)".

(3) REEVALUATION OF WAIVERS OF MEDICAID FRAUD CONTROL UNIT REQUIREMENT.—

(A) IN GENERAL.—Not later than the date that is 1 year after the date of enactment of this Act, the Secretary of Health and Human Services shall reevaluate any waiver approved (and in effect as of the date of enactment of this Act) for Guam, the Northern Mariana Islands, or American Samoa under subsection (a)(61) or subsection (j) of section 1902 of the Social Security Act (42 U.S.C.1396a) with respect to the requirement to establish a State medicaid fraud control unit (as described in section 1903(q) of such Act (42 U.S.C. 1396b(q))).

(B) RULE OF CONSTRUCTION.—Nothing in this paragraph shall be construed as requiring the Secretary of Health and Human Services to terminate or refuse to extend a waiver described in subparagraph (A).

(f) ADDITIONAL PROGRAM INTEGRITY REQUIREMENTS.—

(1) DEFINITIONS.—In this subsection:

(A) INSPECTOR GENERAL.—The term "Inspector General" means the Inspector General of the Department of Health and Human Services.

(B) PUERTO RICO'S MEDICAID PROGRAM.—The term "Puerto Rico's Medicaid program" means, collectively, Puerto Rico's State plan under title XIX of the Social Security Act (42 U.S.C. 1396 et seq.) and any waiver of such plan.

(2) REPORT ON CONTRACTING OVERSIGHT AND APPROVAL.—Not later than 1 year after the date of enactment of this Act, the Comptroller General of the United States shall issue, and submit to the Chair and Ranking Member of the Committee on Energy and Commerce of the House of Representatives and the Chair and Ranking Member of the Committee on Finance of the Senate, a report on contracting oversight and approval with respect to Puerto Rico's State plan under title XIX of the Social Security Act (42 U.S.C. 1396 et seq.) (or a waiver of such plan). Such report shall—

(A) examine—

(i) the process used by Puerto Rico to evaluate bids and award contracts under such plan (or waiver);

(ii) which contracts are not subject to competitive bidding or requests for proposals under such plan (or waiver); and

(iii) oversight by the Centers for Medicare & Medicaid Services of contracts awarded under such plan (or waiver); and

(B) include any recommendations for Congress, the Secretary of Health and Human Services, or Puerto Rico relating to changes that the Comptroller General determines necessary to improve the program integrity of such plan (or waiver).

(3) AUDITS OF MANAGED CARE PAYMENTS.—Not later than the date that is 1 year after the date of enactment of this Act, the Inspector General shall develop and submit to Congress—

(A) a report identifying payments made under Puerto Rico's Medicaid program to managed care organizations that the Inspector General determines to be at high risk for waste, fraud, or abuse; and

(B) a plan for auditing and investigating such payments.

(4) SYSTEM FOR TRACKING FEDERAL FUNDING PROVIDED TO PUERTO RICO; MEDICAID AND CHIP SCORECARD REPORTING.—Section 1902 of the Social Security Act (42 U.S.C. 1396a), as amended by subsection(e), is further amended by adding at the end the following new subsection:

"(rr) PROGRAM INTEGRITY REQUIREMENTS FOR PUERTO RICO.—

"(1) SYSTEM FOR TRACKING FEDERAL MEDICAID FUNDING PROVIDED TO PUERTO RICO.—

"(A) IN GENERAL.—Puerto Rico shall establish and maintain a system, which may include the use of a quarterly Form CMS-64, for tracking any amounts paid by the Federal Government to Puerto Rico with respect to the State plan of Puerto Rico (or a waiver of such plan). Under such system, Puerto Rico shall ensure that information is available, with respect to each quarter in a fiscal year (beginning with the first quarter beginning on or after the date that is 1 year after the date of the enactment of this subsection), on the following:

"(i) In the case of a quarter other than the first quarter of such fiscal year—

"(I) the total amount expended by Puerto Rico during any previous quarter of such fiscal year under the State plan of Puerto Rico (or a waiver of such plan); and

"(II) a description of how such amount was so expended.

"(ii) The total amount that Puerto Rico expects to expend during the quarter under the State plan of Puerto Rico (or a waiver of such plan), and a description of how Puerto Rico expects to expend such amount.

"(B) REPORT TO CMS.—For each quarter with respect to which Puerto Rico is required under subparagraph (A) to ensure that information described in such subparagraph is available, Puerto Rico shall submit to the Administrator of the Centers for Medicare & Medicaid Services a report on such information for such quarter, which may include the submission of a quarterly Form CMS-37.

"(2) SUBMISSION OF DOCUMENTATION ON CONTRACTS UPON REQUEST.—

Puerto Rico shall, upon request, submit to the Administrator of the Centers for Medicare & Medicaid Services all documentation requested with respect to contracts awarded under the State plan of Puerto Rico (or a waiver of such plan).

"(3) REPORTING ON MEDICAID AND CHIP SCORECARD MEASURES.—Beginning 12 months after the date of enactment of this subsection, Puerto Rico shall begin to report to the Administrator of the Centers for Medicare & Medicaid Services on selected measures included in the Medicaid and CHIP Scorecard developed by the Centers for Medicare & Medicaid Services.".

(5) APPROPRIATION.—Out of any funds in the Treasury not otherwise appropriated, there is appropriated to the Secretary of Health and Human Services $5,000,000 for each of fiscal years 2020 through 2021 to carry out this subsection.

[¶ 5017] SEC. 203. DELAY OF DSH REDUCTIONS.

Section 1923(f)(7)(A) of the Social Security Act (42 U.S.C. 1396r-4(f)(7)(A)) is amended by striking "December 21, 2019" each place it appears and inserting "May 23, 2020".

[¶ 5018] SEC. 204. EXTENSION OF SPOUSAL IMPOVERISHMENT PROTECTIONS.

(a) IN GENERAL.—Section 2404 of Public Law 111-148 (42 U.S.C. 1396r-5 note) is amended by striking "December 31, 2019" and inserting "May 22, 2020".

(b) RULE OF CONSTRUCTION.—Nothing in section 2404 of Public Law 111-148 (42 U.S.C. 1396r-5 note) or section 1902(a)(17) or 1924 of the Social Security Act (42 U.S.C. 1396a(a)(17), 1396r-5) shall be construed as prohibiting a State from—

(1) applying an income or resource disregard under a methodology authorized under section 1902(r)(2) of such Act (42 U.S.C. 1396a(r)(2))—

(A) to the income or resources of an individual described in section 1902(a)(10)(A)(ii)(VI) of such Act (42 U.S.C. 1396a(a)(10)(A)(ii)(VI)) (including a disregard of the income or resources of such individual's spouse); or

(B) on the basis of an individual's need for home and community-based services authorized under subsection (c), (d), (i), or (k) of section 1915 of such Act (42 U.S.C. 1396n) or under section 1115 of such Act (42 U.S.C. 1315); or

(2) disregarding an individual's spousal income and assets under a plan amendment to provide medical assistance for home and community-based services for individuals by reason of being determined eligible under section 1902(a)(10)(C) of such Act (42 U.S.C. 1396a(a)(10)(C)) or by reason of section 1902(f) of such Act (42 U.S.C. 1396a(f)) or otherwise on the basis of a reduction of income based on costs incurred for medical or other remedial care under which the State disregarded the income and assets of the individual's spouse in determining the initial and ongoing financial eligibility of an individual for such services in place of the spousal impoverishment provisions applied under section 1924 of such Act (42 U.S.C. 1396r-5).

[¶ 5019] SEC. 205. EXTENSION OF THE MONEY FOLLOWS THE PERSON REBALANCING DEMONSTRATION PROGRAM.

Section 6071(h) of the Deficit Reduction Act of 2005 (42 U.S.C. 1396a note) is amended—

(1) in paragraph (1)—

(A) in subparagraph (E), by striking "and" after the semicolon;

(B) in subparagraph (F), by striking the period at the end and inserting "; and"; and

(C) by adding at the end the following:

"(G) subject to paragraph (3), $176,000,000 for the period beginning on January 1, 2020, and ending on May 22, 2020."; and

(2) in paragraph (3)—

(A) in the paragraph header, by striking "FOR FY 2019"; and

(B) by striking "paragraph (1)(F)" and inserting "subparagraphs (F) and (G) of paragraph (1)".

Subtitle C—Human Services and Other Health Programs

[¶ 5020] SEC. 301. EXTENSION OF DEMONSTRATION PROJECTS TO ADDRESS HEALTH PROFESSIONS WORKFORCE NEEDS.

Activities authorized by section 2008 of the Social Security Act shall continue through May 22, 2020, in the manner authorized for fiscal year 2019, and out of any money in the Treasury of the United States not otherwise appropriated, there are hereby appropriated such sums as may be necessary for such purpose. Grants and payments may be made pursuant to this authority through the date so specified at the pro rata portion of the total amount authorized for such activities in fiscal year 2019.

[¶ 5021] SEC. 302. EXTENSION OF THE TEMPORARY ASSISTANCE FOR NEEDY FAMILIES PROGRAM AND RELATED PROGRAMS.

Activities authorized by part A of title IV and section 1108(b) of the Social Security Act shall continue through May 22, 2020, in the manner authorized for fiscal year 2019, and out of any money in the Treasury of the United States not otherwise appropriated, there are hereby appropriated such sums as may be necessary for such purpose.

[¶ 5022] SEC. 303. EXTENSION OF SEXUAL RISK AVOIDANCE EDUCATION PROGRAM.

Section 510 of the Social Security Act (42 U.S.C. 710) is amended—

(1) in subsection (a)—

(A) in paragraph (1), in the matter preceding subparagraph (A), by striking "December 20, 2019" and inserting "May 22, 2020";

(B) in paragraph (2)(A), by striking "December 20, 2019" and inserting "May 22, 2020"; and

¶ 5019 SEC. 204(b)(1)(A)

(2) in subsection (f)(1), by striking "$16,643,836 for the period beginning October 1, 2019, and ending December 20, 2019" and inserting "$48,287,671 for the period beginning October 1, 2019, and ending May 22, 2020".

[¶ 5023] SEC. 304. EXTENSION OF PERSONAL RESPONSIBILITY EDUCATION PROGRAM.

Section 513 of the Social Security Act (42 U.S.C. 713) is amended—

(1) in subsection (a)(1)—

(A) in subparagraph (A), in the matter preceding clause (i), by striking "December 20, 2019" and inserting "May 22, 2020";

(B) in subparagraph (B)(i), by striking by striking "December 20, 2019" and inserting "May 22, 2020"; and

(2) in subsection (f), by striking "$16,643,836 for the period beginning October 1, 2019, and ending December 20, 2019" and inserting "$48,287,671 for the period beginning October 1, 2019, and ending May 22, 2020".

Subtitle D—Public Health Provisions

[¶ 5024] SEC. 401. EXTENSION FOR COMMUNITY HEALTH CENTERS, THE NATIONAL HEALTH SERVICE CORPS, AND TEACHING HEALTH CENTERS THAT OPERATE GME PROGRAMS.

(a) COMMUNITY HEALTH CENTERS.—Section 10503(b)(1)(F) of the Patient Protection and Affordable Care Act (42 U.S.C. 254b-2(b)(1)(F)) is amended by—

(1) striking "$887,671,223" and inserting "$2,575,342,466"; and

(2) striking "December 20, 2019" and inserting "May 22, 2020".

(b) NATIONAL HEALTH SERVICE CORPS.—Section 10503(b)(2)(G) of the Patient Protection and Affordable Care Act (42 U.S.C. 254b-2(b)(2)(G)) is amended—

(1) by striking "$68,794,521" and inserting "$199,589,041"; and

(2) by striking "December 20, 2019" and inserting "May 22, 2020".

(c) TEACHING HEALTH CENTERS THAT OPERATE GRADUATE MEDICAL EDUCATION PROGRAMS.—Section 340H(g)(1) of the Public Health Service Act (42 U.S.C. 256h(g)(1)) is amended—

(1) by striking "$28,072,603" and inserting "$81,445,205"; and

(2) by striking "December 20, 2019" and inserting "May 22, 2020".

(d) APPLICATION OF PROVISIONS.—Amounts appropriated pursuant to the amendments made by this section for the period beginning on October 1, 2019, and ending on May 22, 2020, shall be subject to the requirements contained in Public Law 115-245 for funds for programs authorized under sections 330 through 340 of the Public Health Service Act (42 U.S.C. 254 through 256).

(e) CONFORMING AMENDMENT.—Paragraph (4) of section 3014(h) of title 18, United States Code, as amended by section 1101(e) of division B of Public Law 116-69, is amended by striking "section 1101(d) of division B of the Continuing Appropriations Act, 2020, and Health Extenders Act of 2019, and section 1101(d) of the Further Continuing Appropriations Act, 2020, and Further Health Extenders Act of 2019" and inserting ", and section 401(d) of division N of the Further Consolidated Appropriations Act, 2020".

[¶ 5025] SEC. 402. DIABETES PROGRAMS.

(a) TYPE I.—Section 330B(b)(2)(D) of the Public Health Service Act (42 U.S.C. 254c-2(b)(2)(D)) is amended—

(1) by striking "$33,287,671" and inserting "$96,575,342"; and

(2) by striking "December 20, 2019" and inserting "May 22, 2020".

(b) INDIANS.—Section 330C(c)(2)(D) of the Public Health Service Act (42 U.S.C. 254c-3(c)(2)(D)) is amended—

(1) by striking "$33,287,671" and inserting "$96,575,342"; and

(2) by striking "December 20, 2019" and inserting "May 22, 2020".

[¶ 5026] SEC. 403. POISON CENTER NETWORK ENHANCEMENT.

(a) NATIONAL TOLL-FREE NUMBER.—Section 1271 of the Public Health Service Act (42 U.S.C. 300d–71) is amended—

(1) in the section heading, by inserting before the period the following: "AND OTHER COMMUNICATION CAPABILITIES"; and

(2) by striking subsection (a) and inserting the following:

"(a) IN GENERAL.—The Secretary—

"(1) shall provide coordination and assistance to poison control centers for the establishment and maintenance of a nationwide toll-free phone number, to be used to access such centers; and

"(2) may provide coordination and assistance to poison control centers and consult with professional organizations for the establishment, implementation, and maintenance of other communication technologies to be used to access such centers.";

(3) by redesignating subsection (b) as subsection (c);

(4) by inserting after subsection (a) the following:

"(b) ROUTING CONTACTS WITH POISON CONTROL CENTERS.—Not later than 18 months after the date of enactment of this subsection, the Secretary shall coordinate with the Chairman of the Federal Communications Commission, to the extent technically and economically feasible, to ensure that communications with the national toll-free number are routed to the appropriate poison control center based on the physical location of the contact rather than the area code of the contact device."; and

(5) in subsection (c), as so redesignated—

(A) by striking "2015 through 2019" and inserting "2020 through 2024"; and

(B) by striking "maintenance of the nationwide toll free phone number under subsection (a)" and inserting "establishment, implementation, and maintenance activities carried out under subsections (a) and (b)".

(b) NATIONWIDE MEDIA CAMPAIGN.—Section 1272 of the Public Health Service Act (42 U.S.C. 300d–72) is amended—

(1) in the section heading, by striking "NATIONWIDE MEDIA CAMPAIGN TO PROMOTE" and inserting "PROMOTING";

(2) in subsection (a)—

(A) by inserting "and support outreach to" after "educate";

(B) by striking "poison prevention" and inserting "poisoning and toxic exposure prevention"; and

(C) by striking "established under" and inserting "and other available communication technologies established, implemented, or maintained under";

(3) in subsection (b)—

(A) in the matter preceding paragraph (1), by striking "nationwide poison prevention" and inserting "nationwide poisoning and toxic exposure prevention"; and

(B) in paragraph (1), by striking "poison prevention and poison control center" and inserting "poisoning and toxic exposure prevention awareness materials, applicable public health emergency preparedness and response information, and poison control center" after "distribution of"; and

(4) by striking subsection (c);

(5) by redesignating subsection (d) as subsection (c); and

(6) in subsection (c) (as so redesignated), by striking "2015 through 2019" and inserting "2020 through 2024".

¶ 5026   SEC. 402(b)(1)

(c) MAINTENANCE OF PROGRAM.—Section 1273 of the Public Health Service Act (42 U.S.C. 300d-73) is amended—

(1) in subsection (a), by inserting "and toxic exposures" after "poisonings"; and

(2) in subsection (b)—

(A) in paragraph (1)—

(i) by striking "for poison" and inserting "for poisoning and toxic exposure"; and

(ii) by striking "and preparedness" and inserting "preparedness and response";

(B) in paragraph (3)—

(i) by striking "United States and" and inserting "United States,"; and

(ii) by inserting before the semicolon the following: ", and other government agencies as determined to be appropriate and nonduplicative by the Secretary"; and

(C) in paragraph (8), by striking "calls" and inserting "contacts";

(3) in subsection (d), by striking paragraph (3) and inserting the following:

"(3) LIMITATION.—

"(A) IN GENERAL.—The sum of the number of years for a waiver under paragraph (1) and a renewal under paragraph (2) may not exceed 5 years.

"(B) PUBLIC HEALTH EMERGENCY.—Notwithstanding any previous waivers, in the case of a poison control center whose accreditation is affected by a public health emergency declared pursuant to section 319, the Secretary may, as the circumstances of the emergency reasonably require, provide a waiver under paragraph (1) or a renewal under paragraph (2), not to exceed 2 years. The Secretary may require quarterly reports and other information related to such a waiver or renewal under this paragraph.";

(4) by striking subsection (f) and inserting the following:

"(f) MAINTENANCE OF EFFORT.—With respect to activities for which a grant is awarded under this section, the Secretary may require that poison control centers agree to maintain the expenditures of the center for such activities at a level that is not less than the level of expenditures maintained by the center for the fiscal year preceding the fiscal year for which the grant is received.";

(5) In subsection (g), by striking "2015 through 2019" and inserting "2020 through 2024"; and

(6) by adding at the end the following:

"(h) BIENNIAL REPORT TO CONGRESS.—Not later than 2 years after the date of enactment of this subsection, and every 2 years thereafter, the Secretary shall submit to the Committee on Health, Education, Labor, and Pensions of the Senate and Committee on Energy and Commerce of the House of Representatives a report concerning the operations of, and trends identified by, the Poison Control Network. Such report shall include—

"(1) descriptions of the activities carried out pursuant to sections 1271, 1272, and 1273, and the alignment of such activities with the purposes provided under subsection (a);

"(2) a description of trends in volume of contacts to poison control centers;

"(3) a description of trends in poisonings and toxic exposures reported to poison control centers, as applicable and appropriate;

"(4) an assessment of the impact of the public awareness campaign, including any geographic variations;

"(5) a description of barriers, if any, preventing poison control centers from achieving the purposes and programs under this section and sections 1271 and 1272;

"(6) a description of the standards for accreditation described in subsection (c), including any variations in those standards, and any efforts to create and maintain consistent standards across organizations that accredit poison control centers; and

"(7) the number of and reason for any waivers provided under subsection (d).".

[¶ 5027] SEC. 404. KAY HAGAN TICK ACT.

(a) SHORT TITLE.—This section may be cited as the "Kay Hagan Tick Act".

(b) COMBATING VECTOR-BORNE DISEASES.—Title III of the Public Health Service Act is amended by inserting after section 317T (42 U.S.C. 247b-22) the following:

"SEC. 317U. NATIONAL STRATEGY AND REGIONAL CENTERS OF EXCELLENCE IN VECTOR-BORNE DISEASES.

"(a) IN GENERAL.—The Secretary shall—

"(1)(A) ensure the development and implementation of a national strategy to address vector-borne diseases, including tick-borne diseases, that—

"(i) identifies and assesses gaps and any unnecessary duplication in federally-funded programs; and

"(ii) identifies strategic goals to address such diseases and appropriate benchmarks to measure progress toward achieving such goals; and

"(B) update such strategy, as appropriate; and

"(2) coordinate programs and activities, including related to data collection, research, and the development of diagnostics, treatments, vaccines, and other related activities, to address vector-borne diseases, including tick-borne diseases, across the Department of Health and Human Services and with other Federal agencies or departments, as appropriate.

"(b) CONSULTATION.—In carrying out subsection (a)(1), the Secretary shall consult with the Tick-Borne Disease Working Group established under section 2062 of the 21st Century Cures Act (42 U.S.C. 284s) and other individuals, as appropriate, such as—

"(1) epidemiologists with experience in vector-borne diseases;

"(2) representatives of patient advocacy and research organizations that focus on vector-borne diseases, including such organizations that have demonstrated experience in related research, public health, data collection, or patient access to care;

"(3) health information technology experts or other information management specialists;

"(4) clinicians, entomologists, vector management professionals, public health professionals, and others with expertise in vector-borne diseases; and

"(5) researchers, including researchers with experience conducting translational research.

"(c) CENTERS OF EXCELLENCE.—The Secretary, in coordination with the Director of the Centers for Disease Control and Prevention, shall award grants, contracts, or cooperative agreements to institutions of higher education for the establishment or continued support of regional centers of excellence in vector-borne diseases to address vector-borne diseases, including tick-borne diseases, by—

"(1) facilitating collaboration between academia and public health organizations for public health surveillance, prevention, and response activities related to vector-borne diseases, including tick-borne diseases;

"(2) providing training for public health entomologists and other health care professionals, as appropriate, to address vector-borne diseases, including tick-borne diseases;

"(3) conducting research to develop and validate prevention and control tools and methods, including evidence-based and innovative, evidence-informed tools and methods to anticipate and respond to disease outbreaks; or

"(4) preparing for and responding to outbreaks of vector-borne diseases, including tick-borne diseases.

"(d) ELIGIBILITY.—To be eligible to receive a grant, contract, or cooperative agreement under subsection (c), an entity shall submit to the Secretary an application at such time, in such manner, and containing such information as the Secretary may require, including a description of how the entity will conduct the activities described in such subsection.

"(e) REPORTS.—

"(1) PROGRAM SUMMARY.—An entity receiving an award under subsection (c) shall, not later than one year after receiving such award, and annually thereafter, submit to the Secretary a summary of programs and activities funded under the award.

"(2) Progress Report.—Not later than 4 years after the date of enactment of this section, the Secretary shall submit to the Committee on Health, Education, Labor, and Pensions of the Senate and the Committee on Energy and Commerce of the House of Representatives, a report on the progress made in addressing vector-borne diseases, including tick-borne diseases, through activities carried out under this section.

"(f) Authorization of Appropriations.—For the purpose of carrying out this section, there are authorized to be appropriated $10,000,000 for each of fiscal years 2021 through 2025.".

(c) Enhancing Capacity to Address Vector-Borne Diseases.—Subtitle C of title XXVIII of the Public Health Service Act (42 U.S.C. 300hh-31 et seq.) is amended by adding at the end the following:

"SEC. 2822. ENHANCED SUPPORT TO ASSIST HEALTH DEPARTMENTS IN ADDRESSING VECTOR-BORNE DISEASES.

"(a) In General.—The Secretary, acting through the Director of the Centers for Disease Control and Prevention, may enter into cooperative agreements with health departments of States, political subdivisions of States, and Indian Tribes and Tribal organizations in areas at high risk of vector-borne diseases in order to increase capacity to identify, report, prevent, and respond to such diseases and related outbreaks.

"(b) Eligibility.—To be eligible to enter into a cooperative agreement under this section, an entity described in subsection (a) shall prepare and submit to the Secretary an application at such time, in such manner, and containing such information as the Secretary may require, including a plan that describes—

"(1) how the applicant proposes to develop or expand programs to address vector-borne disease risks, including through—

"(A) related training and workforce development;

"(B) programmatic efforts to improve capacity to identify, report, prevent, and respond to such disease and related outbreaks; and

"(C) other relevant activities identified by the Director of the Centers for Disease Control and Prevention, as appropriate;

"(2) the manner in which the applicant will coordinate with other Federal, Tribal, and State agencies and programs, as applicable, related to vector-borne diseases, as well as other relevant public and private organizations or agencies; and

"(3) the manner in which the applicant will evaluate the effectiveness of any program carried out under the cooperative agreement.

"(c) Authorization of Appropriations.—For the purposes of carrying out this section, there are authorized to be appropriated $20,000,000 for each of fiscal years 2021 through 2025.".

Subtitle E—Revenue Provisions

[¶ 5029] SEC. 501. REPEAL OF MEDICAL DEVICE EXCISE TAX.

(a) In General.—Chapter 32 of the Internal Revenue Code of 1986 is amended by striking subchapter E.

(b) Conforming Amendments.—

(1) Subsection (a) of section 4221 of the Internal Revenue Code of 1986 is amended by striking the last sentence.

(2) Paragraph (2) of section 6416(b) of such Code is amended by striking the last sentence.

(c) Clerical Amendment.—The table of subchapters for chapter 32 of the Internal Revenue Code of 1986 is amended by striking the item relating to subchapter E.

(d) Effective Date.—The amendments made by this section shall apply to sales after December 31, 2019.

[¶ 5030] **SEC. 502. REPEAL OF ANNUAL FEE ON HEALTH INSURANCE PROVIDERS.**

(a) IN GENERAL.—Subtitle A of title IX of the Patient Protection and Affordable Care Act is amended by striking section 9010.

(b) EFFECTIVE DATE.—The amendment made by this section shall apply to calendar years beginning after December 31, 2020.

[¶ 5031] **SEC. 503. REPEAL OF EXCISE TAX ON HIGH COST EMPLOYER-SPONSORED HEALTH COVERAGE.**

(a) IN GENERAL.—Chapter 43 of the Internal Revenue Code of 1986 is amended by striking section 4980I.

(b) CONFORMING AMENDMENTS.—

(1) Section 6051 of such Code is amended—

(A) by striking "section 4980I(d)(1)" in subsection (a)(14) and inserting "subsection (g)", and

(B) by adding at the end the following new subsection:

"(g) APPLICABLE EMPLOYER-SPONSORED COVERAGE.—For purposes of subsection (a)(14)—

"(1) IN GENERAL.—The term 'applicable employer-sponsored coverage' means, with respect to any employee, coverage under any group health plan made available to the employee by an employer which is excludable from the employee's gross income under section 106, or would be so excludable if it were employer-provided coverage (within the meaning of such section 106).

"(2) EXCEPTIONS.—The term 'applicable employer-sponsored coverage' shall not include—

"(A) any coverage (whether through insurance or otherwise) described in section 9832(c)(1) (other than subparagraph (G) thereof) or for long-term care,

"(B) any coverage under a separate policy, certificate, or contract of insurance which provides benefits substantially all of which are for treatment of the mouth (including any organ or structure within the mouth) or for treatment of the eye, or

"(C) any coverage described in section 9832(c)(3) the payment for which is not excludable from gross income and for which a deduction under section 162(l) is not allowable.

"(3) COVERAGE INCLUDES EMPLOYEE PAID PORTION.—Coverage shall be treated as applicable employer-sponsored coverage without regard to whether the employer or employee pays for the coverage.

"(4) GOVERNMENTAL PLANS INCLUDED.—Applicable employer-sponsored coverage shall include coverage under any group health plan established and maintained primarily for its civilian employees by the Government of the United States, by the government of any State or political subdivision thereof, or by any agency or instrumentality of any such government.".

(2) Section 9831(d)(1) of such Code is amended by striking "except as provided in section 4980I(f)(4)".

(3) The table of sections for chapter 43 of such Code is amended by striking the item relating to section 4980I.

(c) EFFECTIVE DATE.—The amendments made by this section shall apply to taxable years beginning after December 31, 2019.

Subtitle F—Miscellaneous Provisions

[¶ 5032] SEC. 602. ADDRESSING EXPIRATION OF CHILD WELFARE DEMONSTRATION PROJECTS AND SUPPORTING FAMILY FIRST IMPLEMENTATION.

(a) SHORT TITLE.—This section may be cited as the "Family First Transition Act".

(b) EVIDENCE STANDARD TRANSITION.—

(1) TEMPORARY SUSPENSION OF REQUIREMENT THAT AT LEAST 50 PERCENT OF A STATE'S REIMBURSEMENT FOR PREVENTION AND FAMILY SERVICES AND PROGRAMS BE FOR PROGRAMS AND SERVICES THAT MEET THE WELL-SUPPORTED PRACTICE REQUIREMENT.—With respect to quarters in fiscal years 2020 and 2021, section 474(a)(6)(A) of the Social Security Act (42 U.S.C. 674(a)(6)(A)) shall be applied without regard to clause (ii) of such section.

(2) SUPPORTED PRACTICES TEMPORARILY TREATED AS WELL-SUPPORTED PRACTICES.—With respect to quarters in fiscal years 2022 and 2023, practices that meet the criteria specified for supported practices in section 471(e)(4)(C) of the Social Security Act (42 U.S.C. 671(e)(4)(C)) shall be considered well-supported practices for purposes of section 474(a)(6)(A)(ii) of such Act (42 U.S.C. 674(a)(6)(A)(ii)).

(c) ENHANCED FUNDING FOR TRANSITION ACTIVITIES.—

(1) TRANSITION FUNDING.—

(A) APPROPRIATION.—Out of any money in the Treasury of the United States not otherwise appropriated, there are appropriated to the Secretary of Health and Human Services (in this section referred to as the "Secretary") to carry out this subsection $500,000,000 for fiscal year 2020, which shall remain available through fiscal year 2021.

(B) DISTRIBUTION OF FUNDS.—

(i) IN GENERAL.—The Secretary shall allot the amount appropriated by subparagraph (A) of this paragraph in accordance with section 423 of the Social Security Act (42 U.S.C. 623), and shall pay each State to which an allotment is so made, the total amount so allotted, subject to clause (ii) of this subparagraph.

(ii) RESERVATION OF FUNDS FOR INDIAN TRIBES AND TRIBAL ORGANIZATIONS.—Before applying clause (i) of this subparagraph, the Secretary shall reserve 3 percent of the amount appropriated by subparagraph (A) of this paragraph for allotment to the Indian tribes and tribal organizations with a plan approved under subpart 1 of part B of title IV of the Social Security Act, based on each tribe or tribal organization's share of the total tribal child population among all such tribes and tribal organizations.

(2) FUNDING CERTAINTY FOR STATES WITH EXPIRING DEMONSTRATION PROJECTS.—

(A) IN GENERAL.—Out of any money in the Treasury of the United States not otherwise appropriated, there are appropriated to the Secretary, for payment to each State that was operating a demonstration project approved under section 1130 of the Social Security Act on September 30, 2019, for each fiscal year specified in subparagraph (B) of this paragraph, an amount equal to the amount (if any) by which—

(i)(I) the applicable percentage for the fiscal year so specified of the maximum capped allocation due to the State or sub-State jurisdiction for fiscal year 2019 for foster care maintenance, administration, or training costs, under the demonstration project, as specified in section 4.3 of the State waiver terms and conditions document capped allocation payment table in effect on August 31, 2019; or

(II) if the terms and conditions do not specify a maximum amount payable for fiscal year 2019 for the State or sub-State jurisdiction (due to the use of a comparison jurisdiction to ensure cost neutrality), the final cost neutrality limit for the State or sub-State jurisdiction for fiscal year 2018, as most recently reported by the State or sub-State jurisdiction as of September 30, 2019, for foster care maintenance, administration, or training costs under the demonstration project that were included in the waiver; exceeds

(ii) the total amount payable to the State or sub-State jurisdiction under part E of title IV of such Act for the fiscal year so specified for foster care expenditures (whether payable under paragraph (1) or (3) of section 474(a) of such Act) that were maintenance, administration, or training costs of the demonstration project taken into account by the Secretary in determining the total amount referred to in clause (i) of this subparagraph.

(B) APPLICABLE PERCENTAGE DEFINED.—In this subparagraph, the term "applicable percentage" means—

(i) 90 percent, in the case of fiscal year 2020; or

(ii) 75 percent, in the case of fiscal year 2021.

(C) SPECIAL RULE.—The calculation under subparagraph (A) with respect to a State shall be made without regard to—

(i) any change approved after August 31, 2019, in the capped allocation or the terms and conditions referred to in clause (i) of subparagraph (A) with respect to the State; or

(ii) any change made after such date to the financial form submitted by the State that is used in determining the capped allocation.

(D) DISTRIBUTION OF FUNDS.—Each State that receives funds under this paragraph shall distribute the funds to jurisdictions in the State that were operating demonstration projects under section 1130 of the Social Security Act in a manner consistent with each sub-State jurisdiction's proportionate loss as compared with fiscal year 2019.

(E) RECONCILIATION PROCESS.—Each State seeking a payment under this paragraph shall report expenditures pursuant to part E of title IV of the Social Security Act (42 U.S.C. 670 et seq.) in a manner determined by the Secretary and the Secretary shall account for any revisions to spending for fiscal years 2020 and 2021 after the end of the respective fiscal year that are reported by the State agency administering the State plan approved under such part, and received by the Department of Health and Human Services, within 2 years after the last day of the fiscal quarter in which the expenditure was made.

(F) AVAILABILITY OF FUNDS.—The amounts made available for payments to States under this paragraph for a fiscal year shall remain available through the end of the third succeeding fiscal year.

(3) USE OF FUNDS.—

(A) IN GENERAL.—In addition to the purposes specified in part B of title IV of the Social Security Act (42 U.S.C. 671 et seq.), a State may use funds provided under this subsection for activities previously funded under a demonstration project under section 1130 of such Act (42 U.S.C. 1320a-9) to reduce any adverse fiscal impacts as jurisdictions transition funding sources for the projects, and for activities directly associated with the implementation of title VII of division E of Public Law 115-123 (also known as the Family First Prevention Services Act).

(B) LIMITATION.—None of the funds provided under this subsection may be used to match Federal funds under any program.

(d) REPORTING ON ENHANCED FUNDING FOR TRANSITION ACTIVITIES.—

(1) IN GENERAL.—Each State to which funds are paid under subsection (c) of this section shall submit to the Secretary, in a manner specified by the Secretary, a written report on—

(A) how the grant is used to implement each part of title VII of division E of Public Law 115-123 (also known as the Family First Prevention Services Act), with a separate statement with respect to each such part;

(B) all programs, services, and operational costs to which the grant is put;

(C) the characteristics of the families and children served by use of the grant; and

(D)(i) the use by the State of amounts provided for each fiscal year to continue activities previously funded under a waiver provided under section 1130 of the Social Security Act (42 U.S.C. 1320a-9); and

(ii)(I) the plan of the State to transition the activities so that needed activities can be provided under the State plan approved under part E of title IV of the Social Security Act (42 U.S.C. 670 et seq.); or

(II) if expenditures for the activities would not be eligible for payment under the State plan approved under such part E—

(aa) the reason therefor; and

(bb) the funding sources the State plans to use to cover the costs of needed activities.

(2) APPLICABILITY OF OTHER LAWS.—For purposes of subpart 2 of part B of title IV of the Social Security Act (42 U.S.C. 629 et seq.), each report required by paragraph (1) of this subsection shall be considered to be required by section 432(a)(8) of such Act (42 U.S.C. 629b(a)(8)), and shall contain such additional information as the Secretary may require.

(e) DEFINITION OF STATE.—In this section, the term "State" has the meaning given the term in section 431(a)(4) of the Social Security Act (42 U.S.C. 629a(a)(4)).

(f) RENAMING OF TITLE IV-B-2 OF THE SOCIAL SECURITY ACT.—The subpart heading for subpart 2 of part B of title IV of the Social Security Act is amended by striking "Promoting Safe and Stable Families" and inserting "MaryLee Allen Promoting Safe and Stable Families Program".

(g) EFFECTIVE DATE.—This section and the amendments made by this section shall take effect as if included in the Bipartisan Budget Act of 2018 on the date of the enactment of such Act.

(h) TECHNICAL CORRECTION.—Section 50701 of the Bipartisan Budget Act of 2018 (42 U.S.C. 1305 note; Public Law 115-123) is amended by striking "Bipartisan Budget Act of 2018" and inserting "Family First Prevention Services Act".

[¶ 5033] SEC. 603. MINIMUM AGE OF SALE OF TOBACCO PRODUCTS.

(a) IN GENERAL.—Section 906(d) of the Federal Food, Drug, and Cosmetic Act (21 U.S.C. 387f(d)) is amended—

(1) in paragraph (3)(A)(ii), by striking "18 years" and inserting "21 years"; and

(2) by adding at the end the following:

"(5) MINIMUM AGE OF SALE.—It shall be unlawful for any retailer to sell a tobacco product to any person younger than 21 years of age.".

(b) REGULATIONS.—

(1) IN GENERAL.—Not later than 180 days after the date of enactment of this Act, the Secretary of Health and Human Services(referred to in this section as the "Secretary") shall publish in the Federal Register a final rule to update the regulations issued under chapter IX of the Federal Food, Drug, and Cosmetic Act (21 U.S.C. 387 et seq.) as appropriate, only to carry out the amendments made by subsection (a), including to update all references to persons younger than 18 years of age in subpart B of part 1140 of title 21, Code of Federal Regulations, and to update the relevant age verification requirements under such part 1140 to require age verification for individuals under the age of 30. Such final rule shall—

(A) take full effect not later than 90 days after the date on which such final rule is published; and

(B) be deemed to be in compliance with all applicable provisions of chapter 5 of title 5, United States Code and all other provisions of law relating to rulemaking procedures.

(2) OTHER REGULATIONS.—Prior to making amendments to part 1140 of title 21, Code of Federal Regulations other than the amendments described in paragraph (1), the Secretary shall promulgate a proposed rule in accordance with chapter 5 of title 5, United States Code.

(c) NOTIFICATION.—Not later than 90 days after the date of enactment of this Act, the Secretary shall provide written notification to the Committee on Health, Education, Labor, and Pensions of the Senate and the Committee on Energy and Commerce of the House of Representatives regarding the progress of the Department of Health and Human Services towards promulgating the final rule under subsection (b). If, 180 days after the date of enactment of this Act, such rule has not been promulgated in accordance with subsection (b), the Secretary shall provide a written notification and a justification for the delay in rulemaking to such committees.

(d) PENALTIES FOR VIOLATIONS.—

(1) IN GENERAL.—Section 103(q)(2) of the Family Smoking Prevention and Tobacco Control Act (Public Law 111–31) is amended—

(A) in subparagraph (A), in the matter preceding clause (i), by inserting "section 906(d)(5) or of" after "violations of"; and

(B) in subparagraph (C), by inserting "section 906(d)(5) or of" after "a retailer of".

(2) REPEATED VIOLATIONS.—Section 303(f)(8) of the Federal Food, Drug, and Cosmetic Act (21 U.S.C. 333(f)(8)) is amended by inserting "section 906(d)(5) or of" after "repeated violations of".

(3) MISBRANDED PRODUCTS.—Section 903(a)(7)(B) of the Federal Food, Drug, and Cosmetic Act (21 U.S.C. 387c) is amended by inserting "section 906(d)(5) or of" after "violation of".

[¶ 5034] SEC. 604. SALE OF TOBACCO PRODUCTS TO INDIVIDUALS UNDER THE AGE OF 21.

(a) IN GENERAL.—Section 1926 of the Public Health Service Act (42 U.S.C. 300x–26) is amended—

(1) in the heading—

(A) by striking "STATE LAW REGARDING"; and

(B) by striking "18" and inserting "21";

(2) by striking subsections (a) and (d);

(3) by redesignating subsections (b) and (c) as subsections (a) and (b), respectively;

(4) by amending subsection (a), as so redesignated, to read as follows:

"(a) IN GENERAL.—A funding agreement for a grant under section 1921 is that the State involved will—

"(1) annually conduct random, unannounced inspections to ensure that retailers do not sell tobacco products to individuals under the age of 21; and

"(2) annually submit to the Secretary a report describing—

"(A) the activities carried out by the State to ensure that retailers do not sell tobacco products to individuals under the age of 21;

"(B) the extent of success the State has achieved in ensuring that retailers do not sell tobacco products to individuals under the age of 21; and

"(C) the strategies to be utilized by the State to ensure that retailers do not sell tobacco products to individuals under the age of 21 during the fiscal year for which the grant is sought.";

(5) in subsection (b), as so redesignated—

(A) by striking paragraphs (1), (2), (3), and (4);

(B) by striking "Before making" and inserting the following:

"(1) IN GENERAL.—Before making";

(C) by striking "for the first applicable fiscal year or any subsequent fiscal year";

(D) by striking "subsections (a) and (b)" and inserting "subsection (a)";

(E) by striking "equal to—"and inserting "up to 10 percent of the amount determined under section 1933 for the State for the applicable fiscal year."; and

(F) by adding at the end the following:

"(2) LIMITATION.—

"(A) IN GENERAL.—A State shall not have funds withheld pursuant to paragraph (1) if such State for which the Secretary has made a determination of noncompliance under such paragraph—

"(i) certifies to the Secretary by May 1 of the fiscal year for which the funds are appropriated, consistent with subparagraph (B), that the State will commit additional State funds, in accordance with paragraph (1), to ensure that retailers do not sell tobacco products to individuals under 21 years of age;

"(ii) agrees to comply with a negotiated agreement for a corrective action plan that is approved by the Secretary and carried out in accordance with guidelines issued by the Secretary; or

"(iii) is a territory that receives less than $1,000,000 for a fiscal year under section 1921.

"(B) CERTIFICATION.—

"(i) IN GENERAL.—The amount of funds to be committed by a State pursuant to subparagraph (A)(i) shall be equal to 1 percent of such State's substance abuse allocation determined under section 1933 for each percentage point by which the State misses the retailer compliance rate goal established by the Secretary.

"(ii) STATE EXPENDITURES.—For a fiscal year in which a State commits funds as described in clause (i), such State shall maintain State expenditures for tobacco prevention programs and for compliance activities at a level that is not less than the level of such expenditures maintained by the State for the preceding fiscal year, plus the additional funds for tobacco compliance activities required under clause (i). The State shall submit a report to the Secretary on all State obligations of funds for such fiscal year and all State expenditures for the preceding fiscal year for tobacco prevention and compliance activities by program activity by July 31 of such fiscal year.

"(iii) DISCRETION.—The Secretary shall exercise discretion in enforcing the timing of the State obligation of the additional funds required by the certification described in subparagraph (A)(i) as late as July 31 of such fiscal year.

"(C) FAILURE TO CERTIFY.—If a State described in subparagraph (A) fails to certify to the Secretary pursuant to subparagraph (A)(i) or enter into, or comply with, a negotiated agreement under subparagraph (A)(ii), the Secretary may take action pursuant to paragraph (1)."; and

(6) by adding at the end the following:

"(c) IMPLEMENTATION OF REPORTING REQUIREMENTS.—

"(1) TRANSITION PERIOD.—The Secretary shall—

"(A) not withhold amounts under subsection (b) for the 3-year period immediately following the date of enactment of division N of the Further Consolidated Appropriations Act, 2020; and

"(B) use discretion in exercising its authority under subsection (b) during the 2-year period immediately following the 3-year period described in subparagraph (A), to allow for a transition period for implementation of the reporting requirements under subsection (a)(2).

"(2) REGULATIONS OR GUIDANCE.—Not later than 180 days after the date of enactment of division N of the Further Consolidated Appropriations Act, 2020, the Secretary shall update regulations under part 96 of title 45, Code of Federal Regulations or guidance on the retailer compliance rate goal under subsection (b), the use of funds provided under section 1921 for purposes of meeting the requirements of this section, and reporting requirements under subsection (a)(2).

"(3) COORDINATION.—The Secretary shall ensure the Assistant Secretary for Mental Health and Substance Use coordinates, as appropriate, with the Commissioner of Food and Drugs to ensure that the technical assistance provided to States under subsection (e) is consistent with applicable regulations for retailers issued under part 1140 of title 21, Code of Federal Regulations.

"(d) TRANSITIONAL GRANTS.—

"(1) IN GENERAL.—The Secretary shall award grants under this subsection to each State that receives funding under section 1921 to ensure compliance of each such State with this section.

"(2) USE OF FUNDS.—A State receiving a grant under this subsection—

"(A) shall use amounts received under such grant for activities to plan for or ensure compliance in the State with subsection (a); and

"(B) in the case of a State for which the Secretary has made a determination under subsection (b) that the State is prepared to meet, or has met, the requirements of subsection (a), may use such funds for tobacco cessation activities, strategies to prevent the use of tobacco products by individuals under the age of 21, or allowable uses under section 1921.

"(3) SUPPLEMENT NOT SUPPLANT.—Grants under this subsection shall be used to supplement and not supplant other Federal, State, and local public funds provided for activities under paragraph (2).

"(4) AUTHORIZATION OF APPROPRIATIONS.—To carry out this subsection, there are authorized to be appropriated $18,580,790 for each of fiscal years 2020 through 2024.

"(5) SUNSET.—This subsection shall have no force or effect after September 30, 2024.

"(e) TECHNICAL ASSISTANCE.—The Secretary shall provide technical assistance to States related to the activities required under this section.".

(b) REPORT TO CONGRESS.—Not later than 3 years after the date of enactment of this Act, the Secretary shall submit to the Committee on Health, Education, Labor, and Pensions of the Senate and the Committee on Energy and Commerce of the House of Representatives a report on the status of implementing the requirements of section 1926 of the Public Health Service Act (42 U.S.C. 300x-26), as amended by subsection (a), and a description of any technical assistance provided under subsection (e) of such section, including the number of meetings requested and held related to technical assistance.

(c) CONFORMING AMENDMENT.—Section 212 of division D of the Consolidated Appropriations Act, 2010 (Public Law 111-117) is repealed.

[¶ 5035] SEC. 605. BIOLOGICAL PRODUCT DEFINITION.

Section 351(i)(1) of the Public Health Service Act (42 U.S.C. 262(i)(1)) is amended by striking "(except any chemically synthesized polypeptide)".

[¶ 5036] SEC. 606. PROTECTING ACCESS TO BIOLOGICAL PRODUCTS.

Section 351(k)(7) of the Public Health Service Act (42 U.S.C. 262(k)(7)) is amended by adding at the end the following:

"(D) DEEMED LICENSES.—

"(i) NO ADDITIONAL EXCLUSIVITY THROUGH DEEMING.—An approved application that is deemed to be a license for a biological product under this section pursuant to section 7002(e)(4) of the Biologics Price Competition and Innovation Act of 2009 shall not be treated as having been first licensed under subsection (a) for purposes of subparagraphs (A) and (B).

"(ii) APPLICATION OF LIMITATIONS ON EXCLUSIVITY.—Subparagraph (C) shall apply with respect to a reference product referred to in such subparagraph that was the subject of an approved application that was deemed to be a license pursuant to section 7002(e)(4) of the Biologics Price Competition and Innovation Act of 2009.

"(iii) APPLICABILITY.—The exclusivity periods described in section 527, section 505A(b)(1)(A)(ii), and section 505A(c)(1)(A)(ii) of the Federal Food, Drug, and Cosmetic Act shall continue to apply to a biological product after an approved application for the biological product is deemed to be a license for the biological product under subsection (a) pursuant to section 7002(e)(4) of the Biologics Price Competition and Innovation Act of 2009.".

[¶ 5037] SEC. 607. STREAMLINING THE TRANSITION OF BIOLOGICAL PRODUCTS.

Section 7002(e)(4) of the Biologics Price Competition and Innovation Act of 2009 (Public Law 111-148) is amended—

(1) by striking "An approved application" and inserting the following:

"(A) IN GENERAL.—An approved application"; and

(2) by adding at the end the following:

"(B) TREATMENT OF CERTAIN APPLICATIONS.—

"(i) IN GENERAL.—With respect to an application for a biological product submitted under subsection (b) or (j) of section 505 of the Federal Food, Drug, and Cosmetic Act (21 U.S.C. 355) that is filed not later than March 23, 2019, and is not approved as of March 23, 2020, the Secretary shall continue to review such application under such section 505 after March 23, 2020.

"(ii) EFFECT ON LISTED DRUGS.—Only for purposes of carrying out clause (i), with respect to any applicable listed drug with respect to such application, the following shall apply:

"(I) Any drug that is a biological product that has been deemed licensed under section 351 of the Public Health Service Act (42 U.S.C. 262) pursuant to subparagraph (A) and that is referenced in an application described in clause (i), shall continue to be identified as a listed drug on the list published pursuant to section 505(j)(7) of the Federal Food, Drug, and Cosmetic Act, and the information for such drug on such list shall not be revised after March 20, 2020, until—

"(aa) such drug is removed from such list in accordance with subclause (III) or subparagraph (C) of such section 505(j)(7); or

"(bb) this subparagraph no longer has force or effect.

"(II) Any drug that is a biological product that has been deemed licensed under section 351 of the Public Health Service Act (42 U.S.C. 262) pursuant to subparagraph (A) and that is referenced in an application described in clause (i) shall be subject only to requirements applicable to biological products licensed under such section.

"(III) Upon approval under subsection (c) or (j) of section 505 of the Federal Food, Drug, and Cosmetic Act of an application described in clause (i), the Secretary shall remove from the list published pursuant to section 505(j)(7) of the Federal Food, Drug, and Cosmetic Act any listed drug that is a biological product that has been deemed licensed under section 351 of the Public Health Service Act pursuant to subparagraph (A) and that is referenced in such approved application, unless such listed drug is referenced in one or more additional applications described in clause (i).

"(iii) DEEMED LICENSURE.—Upon approval of an application described in clause (i), such approved application shall be deemed to be a license for the biological product under section 351 of the Public Health Service Act.

"(iv) RULE OF CONSTRUCTION.—

"(I) APPLICATION OF CERTAIN PROVISIONS.—

"(aa) PATENT CERTIFICATION OR STATEMENT.—An application described in clause (i) shall contain a patent certification or statement described in, as applicable, section 505(b)(2) of the Federal Food, Drug, and Cosmetic Act or clauses (vii) and (viii) of section 505(j)(2)(A) of such Act and, with respect to any listed drug referenced in such application, comply with related requirements concerning any timely filed patent information listed pursuant to section 505(j)(7) of such Act.

"(bb) DATE OF APPROVAL.—The earliest possible date on which any pending application described in clause (i) may be approved shall be determined based on—

"(AA) the last expiration date of any applicable period of exclusivity that would prevent such approval and that is described in section 505(c)(3)(E), 505(j)(5)(B)(iv), 505(j)(5)(F), 505A, 505E, or 527 of the Federal Food, Drug, and Cosmetic Act; and

"(BB) if the application was submitted pursuant to section 505(b)(2) of the Federal Food, Drug, and Cosmetic Act and references any listed drug, the last applicable date determined under subparagraph (A), (B), or (C) of section 505(c)(3) of such Act, or, if the application was submitted under section 505(j) of such Act, the last applicable date determined under clause (i), (ii), or (iii) of section 505(j)(5)(B) of such Act.

"(II) EXCLUSIVITY.—Nothing in this subparagraph shall be construed to affect section 351(k)(7)(D) of the Public Health Service Act.

"(v) LISTING.—The Secretary may continue to review an application after March 23, 2020, pursuant to clause (i), and continue to identify any applicable listed drug pursuant to clause (ii) on the list published pursuant to section 505(j)(7) of the Federal Food, Drug, and Cosmetic Act, even if such review or listing may reveal the existence of such application and the identity of any listed drug for which the investigations described in section 505(b)(1)(A) of the Federal Food, Drug, and Cosmetic Act are relied upon by the applicant for approval of the pending application. Nothing in

SEC. 607(2) ¶5037

this subparagraph shall be construed as authorizing the Secretary to disclose any other information that is a trade secret or confidential information described in section 552(b)(4) of title 5, United States Code.

"(vi) SUNSET.—Beginning on October 1, 2022, this subparagraph shall have no force or effect and any applications described in clause (i) that have not been approved shall be deemed withdrawn.".

[¶ 5038] SEC. 608. REENROLLMENT OF CERTAIN INDIVIDUALS IN QUALIFIED HEALTH PLANS IN CERTAIN EXCHANGES.

Section 1311(c) of the Patient Protection and Affordable Care Act (42 U.S.C. 18031(c)) is amended by adding the end the following new paragraph:

"(7) REENROLLMENT OF CERTAIN INDIVIDUALS IN QUALIFIED HEALTH PLANS IN CERTAIN EXCHANGES.—

"(A) IN GENERAL.—In the case of an Exchange that the Secretary operates pursuant to section 1321(c)(1), the Secretary shall establish a process under which an individual described in subparagraph (B) is reenrolled for plan year 2021 in a qualified health plan offered through such Exchange. Such qualified health plan under which such individual is so reenrolled shall be—

"(i) if available for plan year 2021, the qualified health plan under which such individual is enrolled during the annual open enrollment period for such plan year; and

"(ii) if such qualified health plan is not available for plan year 2021, a qualified health plan offered through such Exchange determined appropriate by the Secretary.

"(B) INDIVIDUAL DESCRIBED.—An individual described in this subsection is an individual who, with respect to plan year 2020—

"(i) resides in a State with an Exchange described in subparagraph (A);

"(ii) is enrolled in a qualified health plan during such plan year and does not enroll in a qualified health plan for plan year 2021 during the annual open enrollment period for such plan year 2021; and

"(iii) does not elect to disenroll under a qualified health plan for plan year 2021 during such annual open enrollment period.".

[¶ 5039] SEC. 609. PROTECTION OF SILVER LOADING PRACTICE.

With respect to plan year 2021, the Secretary of Health and Human Services may not take any action to prohibit or otherwise restrict the practice commonly known as "silver loading" (as described in the rule entitled "Patient Protection and Affordable Care Act; HHS Notice of Benefit and Payment Parameters for 2020" published on April 25, 2019 (84 Fed. Reg. 17533)).

[¶ 5040] SEC. 610. ACTIONS FOR DELAYS OF GENERIC DRUGS AND BIOSIMILAR BIOLOGICAL PRODUCTS.

(a) DEFINITIONS.—In this section—

(1) the term "commercially reasonable, market-based terms" means—

(A) a nondiscriminatory price for the sale of the covered product at or below, but not greater than, the most recent wholesale acquisition cost for the drug, as defined in section 1847A(c)(6)(B) of the Social Security Act (42 U.S.C. 1395w-3a(c)(6)(B));

(B) a schedule for delivery that results in the transfer of the covered product to the eligible product developer consistent with the timing under subsection (b)(2)(A)(iv); and

(C) no additional conditions are imposed on the sale of the covered product;

(2) the term "covered product"—

(A) means—

(i) any drug approved under subsection (c) or (j) of section 505 of the Federal Food, Drug, and Cosmetic Act (21 U.S.C. 355) or biological product licensed under subsection (a) or (k) of section 351 of the Public Health Service Act (42 U.S.C. 262);

(ii) any combination of a drug or biological product described in clause (i); or

(iii) when reasonably necessary to support approval of an application under section 505 of the Federal Food, Drug, and Cosmetic Act (21 U.S.C. 355), or section 351 of the Public Health Service Act (42 U.S.C. 262), as applicable, or otherwise meet the requirements for approval under either such section, any product, including any device, that is marketed or intended for use with such a drug or biological product; and

(B) does not include any drug or biological product that appears on the drug shortage list in effect under section 506E of the Federal Food, Drug, and Cosmetic Act (21 U.S.C. 356e), unless—

(i) the drug or biological product has been on the drug shortage list in effect under such section 506E continuously for more than 6 months; or

(ii) the Secretary determines that inclusion of the drug or biological product as a covered product is likely to contribute to alleviating or preventing a shortage.

(3) the term "device" has the meaning given the term in section 201 of the Federal Food, Drug, and Cosmetic Act (21 U.S.C. 321);

(4) the term "eligible product developer" means a person that seeks to develop a product for approval pursuant to an application for approval under subsection (b)(2) or (j) of section 505 of the Federal Food, Drug, and Cosmetic Act (21 U.S.C. 355) or for licensing pursuant to an application under section 351(k) of the Public Health Service Act (42 U.S.C. 262(k));

(5) the term "license holder" means the holder of an application approved under subsection (c) or (j) of section 505 of the Federal Food, Drug, and Cosmetic Act (21 U.S.C. 355) or the holder of a license under subsection (a) or (k) of section 351 of the Public Health Service Act (42 U.S.C. 262) for a covered product;

(6) the term "REMS" means a risk evaluation and mitigation strategy under section 505-1 of the Federal Food, Drug, and Cosmetic Act (21 U.S.C. 355-1);

(7) the term "REMS with ETASU" means a REMS that contains elements to assure safe use under section 505-1(f) of the Federal Food, Drug, and Cosmetic Act (21 U.S.C. 355-1(f));

(8) the term "Secretary" means the Secretary of Health and Human Services;

(9) the term "single, shared system of elements to assure safe use" means a single, shared system of elements to assure safe use under section 505-1(f) of the Federal Food, Drug, and Cosmetic Act (21 U.S.C. 355-1(f)); and

(10) the term "sufficient quantities" means an amount of a covered product that the eligible product developer determines allows it to—

(A) conduct testing to support an application under—

(i) subsection (b)(2) or (j) of section 505 of the Federal Food, Drug, and Cosmetic Act (21 U.S.C. 355); or

(ii) section 351(k) of the Public Health Service Act (42 U.S.C. 262(k)); and

(B) fulfill any regulatory requirements relating to approval of such an application.

(b) CIVIL ACTION FOR FAILURE TO PROVIDE SUFFICIENT QUANTITIES OF A COVERED PRODUCT.—

(1) IN GENERAL.—An eligible product developer may bring a civil action against the license holder for a covered product seeking relief under this subsection in an appropriate district court of the United States alleging that the license holder has declined to provide sufficient quantities of the covered product to the eligible product developer on commercially reasonable, market-based terms.

(2) ELEMENTS.—

(A) IN GENERAL.—To prevail in a civil action brought under paragraph (1), an eligible product developer shall prove, by a preponderance of the evidence—

(i) that—

(I) the covered product is not subject to a REMS with ETASU; or

(II) if the covered product is subject to a REMS with ETASU—

(aa) the eligible product developer has obtained a covered product authorization from the Secretary in accordance with subparagraph (B); and

(bb) the eligible product developer has provided a copy of the covered product authorization to the license holder;

SEC. 610(b)(2)(A)(i)(II)(bb)   ¶5040

(ii) that, as of the date on which the civil action is filed, the eligible product developer has not obtained sufficient quantities of the covered product on commercially reasonable, market-based terms;

(iii) that the eligible product developer has submitted a written request to purchase sufficient quantities of the covered product to the license holder, and such request—

(I) was sent to a named corporate officer of the license holder;

(II) was made by certified or registered mail with return receipt requested;

(III) specified an individual as the point of contact for the license holder to direct communications related to the sale of the covered product to the eligible product developer and a means for electronic and written communications with that individual; and

(IV) specified an address to which the covered product was to be shipped upon reaching an agreement to transfer the covered product; and

(iv) that the license holder has not delivered to the eligible product developer sufficient quantities of the covered product on commercially reasonable, market-based terms—

(I) for a covered product that is not subject to a REMS with ETASU, by the date that is 31 days after the date on which the license holder received the request for the covered product; and

(II) for a covered product that is subject to a REMS with ETASU, by 31 days after the later of—

(aa) the date on which the license holder received the request for the covered product; or

(bb) the date on which the license holder received a copy of the covered product authorization issued by the Secretary in accordance with subparagraph (B).

(B) AUTHORIZATION FOR COVERED PRODUCT SUBJECT TO A REMS WITH ETASU.—

(i) REQUEST.—An eligible product developer may submit to the Secretary a written request for the eligible product developer to be authorized to obtain sufficient quantities of an individual covered product subject to a REMS with ETASU.

(ii) AUTHORIZATION.—Not later than 120 days after the date on which a request under clause (i) is received, the Secretary shall, by written notice, authorize the eligible product developer to obtain sufficient quantities of an individual covered product subject to a REMS with ETASU for purposes of—

(I) development and testing that does not involve human clinical trials, if the eligible product developer has agreed to comply with any conditions the Secretary determines necessary; or

(II) development and testing that involves human clinical trials, if the eligible product developer has—

(aa)(AA) submitted protocols, informed consent documents, and informational materials for testing that include protections that provide safety protections comparable to those provided by the REMS for the covered product; or

(BB) otherwise satisfied the Secretary that such protections will be provided; and

(bb) met any other requirements the Secretary may establish.

(iii) NOTICE.—A covered product authorization issued under this subparagraph shall state that the provision of the covered product by the license holder under the terms of the authorization will not be a violation of the REMS for the covered product.

(3) AFFIRMATIVE DEFENSE.—In a civil action brought under paragraph (1), it shall be an affirmative defense, on which the defendant has the burden of persuasion by a preponderance of the evidence—

(A) that, on the date on which the eligible product developer requested to purchase sufficient quantities of the covered product from the license holder—

(i) neither the license holder nor any of its agents, wholesalers, or distributors was engaged in the manufacturing or commercial marketing of the covered product; and

(ii) neither the license holder nor any of its agents, wholesalers, or distributors otherwise had access to inventory of the covered product to supply to the eligible product developer on commercially reasonable, market-based terms;

(B) that—

(i) the license holder sells the covered product through agents, distributors, or wholesalers;

(ii) the license holder has placed no restrictions, explicit or implicit, on its agents, distributors, or wholesalers to sell covered products to eligible product developers; and

(iii) the covered product can be purchased by the eligible product developer in sufficient quantities on commercially reasonable, market-based terms from the agents, distributors, or wholesalers of the license holder; or

(C) that the license holder made an offer to the individual specified pursuant to paragraph (2)(A)(iii)(III), by a means of communication (electronic, written, or both) specified pursuant to such paragraph, to sell sufficient quantities of the covered product to the eligible product developer at commercially reasonable market-based terms—

(i) for a covered product that is not subject to a REMS with ETASU, by the date that is 14 days after the date on which the license holder received the request for the covered product, and the eligible product developer did not accept such offer by the date that is 7 days after the date on which the eligible product developer received such offer from the license holder; or

(ii) for a covered product that is subject to a REMS with ETASU, by the date that is 20 days after the date on which the license holder received the request for the covered product, and the eligible product developer did not accept such offer by the date that is 10 days after the date on which the eligible product developer received such offer from the license holder.

(4) REMEDIES.—

(A) IN GENERAL.—If an eligible product developer prevails in a civil action brought under paragraph (1), the court shall—

(i) order the license holder to provide to the eligible product developer without delay sufficient quantities of the covered product on commercially reasonable, market-based terms;

(ii) award to the eligible product developer reasonable attorney's fees and costs of the civil action; and

(iii) award to the eligible product developer a monetary amount sufficient to deter the license holder from failing to provide eligible product developers with sufficient quantities of a covered product on commercially reasonable, market-based terms, if the court finds, by a preponderance of the evidence—

(I) that the license holder delayed providing sufficient quantities of the covered product to the eligible product developer without a legitimate business justification; or

(II) that the license holder failed to comply with an order issued under clause (i).

(B) MAXIMUM MONETARY AMOUNT.—A monetary amount awarded under subparagraph (A)(iii) shall not be greater than the revenue that the license holder earned on the covered product during the period—

(i) beginning on—

(I) for a covered product that is not subject to a REMS with ETASU, the date that is 31 days after the date on which the license holder received the request; or

(II) for a covered product that is subject to a REMS with ETASU, the date that is 31 days after the later of—

(aa) the date on which the license holder received the request; or

(bb) the date on which the license holder received a copy of the covered product authorization issued by the Secretary in accordance with paragraph (2)(B); and

(ii) ending on the date on which the eligible product developer received sufficient quantities of the covered product.

(C) AVOIDANCE OF DELAY.—The court may issue an order under subparagraph (A)(i) before conducting further proceedings that may be necessary to determine whether the eligible product developer is entitled to an award under clause (ii) or (iii) of subparagraph (A), or the amount of any such award.

(c) LIMITATION OF LIABILITY.—A license holder for a covered product shall not be liable for any claim under Federal, State, or local law arising out of the failure of an eligible product developer to follow adequate safeguards to assure safe use of the covered product during development or testing activities described in this section, including transportation, handling, use, or disposal of the covered product by the eligible product developer.

(d) NO VIOLATION OF REMS.—Section 505-1 of the Federal Food, Drug, and Cosmetic Act (21 U.S.C. 355-1) is amended by adding at the end the following new subsection:

"(l) PROVISION OF SAMPLES NOT A VIOLATION OF STRATEGY.—The provision of samples of a covered product to an eligible product developer (as those terms are defined in section 610(a) of division N of the Further Consolidated Appropriations Act, 2020) shall not be considered a violation of the requirements of any risk evaluation and mitigation strategy that may be in place under this section for such drug.".

(e) RULE OF CONSTRUCTION.—

(1) DEFINITION.—In this subsection, the term "antitrust laws"—

(A) has the meaning given the term in subsection (a) of the first section of the Clayton Act (15 U.S.C. 12); and

(B) includes section 5 of the Federal Trade Commission Act (15 U.S.C. 45) to the extent that such section applies to unfair methods of competition.

(2) ANTITRUST LAWS.—Nothing in this section shall be construed to limit the operation of any provision of the antitrust laws.

(f) REMS APPROVAL PROCESS FOR SUBSEQUENT FILERS.—Section 505-1 of the Federal Food, Drug, and Cosmetic Act (21 U.S.C. 355-1), as amended by subsection (d), is further amended—

(1) in subsection (g)(4)(B)—

(A) in clause (i) by striking "or" after the semicolon;

(B) in clause (ii) by striking the period at the end and inserting "; or"; and

(C) by adding at the end the following:

"(iii) accommodate different, comparable aspects of the elements to assure safe use for a drug that is the subject of an application under section 505(j), and the applicable listed drug.";

(2) in subsection (i)(1), by striking subparagraph (C) and inserting the following:

"(C)(i) Elements to assure safe use, if required under subsection (f) for the listed drug, which, subject to clause (ii), for a drug that is the subject of an application under section 505(j) may use—

"(I) a single, shared system with the listed drug under subsection (f); or

"(II) a different, comparable aspect of the elements to assure safe use under subsection (f).

"(ii) The Secretary may require a drug that is the subject of an application under section 505(j) and the listed drug to use a single, shared system under subsection (f), if the Secretary determines that no different, comparable aspect of the elements to assure safe use could satisfy the requirements of subsection (f).";

(3) in subsection (i), by adding at the end the following:

"(3) SHARED REMS.—If the Secretary approves, in accordance with paragraph (1)(C)(i)(II), a different, comparable aspect of the elements to assure safe use under subsection (f) for a drug that is the subject of an abbreviated new drug application under section 505(j), the Secretary may require that such different comparable aspect of the elements to assure safe use can be used with respect to any other drug that is the subject of an application under section 505(j) or 505(b) that references the same listed drug."; and

(4) by adding at the end the following:

"(m) SEPARATE REMS.—When used in this section, the term 'different, comparable aspect of the elements to assure safe use' means a risk evaluation and mitigation strategy for a drug that is the subject of an application under section 505(j) that uses different methods or operational means than the strategy required under subsection (a) for the applicable listed drug, or other application under section 505(j) with the same such listed drug, but achieves the same level of safety as such strategy.".

(g) RULE OF CONSTRUCTION.—Nothing in this section, the amendments made by this section, or in section 505-1 of the Federal Food, Drug, and Cosmetic Act (21 U.S.C. 355-1), shall be construed as—

(1) prohibiting a license holder from providing an eligible product developer access to a covered product in the absence of an authorization under this section; or

(2) in any way negating the applicability of a REMS with ETASU, as otherwise required under such section 505-1, with respect to such covered product.

DIVISION O—SETTING EVERY COMMUNITY UP FOR RETIREMENT ENHANCEMENT

[¶5041] SEC. 1. SHORT TITLE, ETC.

(a) SHORT TITLE.—This Act may be cited as the "Setting Every Community Up for Retirement Enhancement Act of 2019".

(b) TABLE OF CONTENTS.—The table of contents of this Act is as follows:

Sec. 1. Short title, etc.

TITLE I—EXPANDING AND PRESERVING RETIREMENT SAVINGS

Sec. 101. Multiple employer plans; pooled employer plans.
Sec. 102. Increase in 10 percent cap for automatic enrollment safe harbor after 1st plan year.
Sec. 103. Rules relating to election of safe harbor 401(k) status.
Sec. 104. Increase in credit limitation for small employer pension plan startup costs.
Sec. 105. Small employer automatic enrollment credit.
Sec. 106. Certain taxable non-tuition fellowship and stipend payments treated as compensation for IRA purposes.
Sec. 107. Repeal of maximum age for traditional IRA contributions.
Sec. 108. Qualified employer plans prohibited from making loans through credit cards and other similar arrangements.
Sec. 109. Portability of lifetime income options.
Sec. 110. Treatment of custodial accounts on termination of section 403(b) plans.
Sec. 111. Clarification of retirement income account rules relating to church-controlled organizations.
Sec. 112. Qualified cash or deferred arrangements must allow long-term employees working more than 500 but less than 1,000 hours per year to participate.
Sec. 113. Penalty-free withdrawals from retirement plans for individuals in case of birth of child or adoption.

Sec. 114. Increase in age for required beginning date for mandatory distributions.
Sec. 115. Special rules for minimum funding standards for community newspaper plans.
Sec. 116. Treating excluded difficulty of care payments as compensation for determining retirement contribution limitations.

TITLE II—ADMINISTRATIVE IMPROVEMENTS

Sec. 201. Plan adopted by filing due date for year may be treated as in effect as of close of year.
Sec. 202. Combined annual report for group of plans.
Sec. 203. Disclosure regarding lifetime income.
Sec. 204. Fiduciary safe harbor for selection of lifetime income provider.
Sec. 205. Modification of nondiscrimination rules to protect older, longer service participants.
Sec. 206. Modification of PBGC premiums for CSEC plans.

TITLE III—OTHER BENEFITS

Sec. 301. Benefits provided to volunteer firefighters and emergency medical responders.
Sec. 302. Expansion of section 529 plans.

TITLE IV—REVENUE PROVISIONS

Sec. 401. Modification of required distribution rules for designated beneficiaries.
Sec. 402. Increase in penalty for failure to file.
Sec. 403. Increased penalties for failure to file retirement plan returns.
Sec. 404. Increase information sharing to administer excise taxes.

TITLE V—TAX RELIEF FOR CERTAIN CHILDREN

Sec. 501. Modification of rules relating to the taxation of unearned income of certain children.

TITLE VI—ADMINISTRATIVE PROVISIONS

Sec. 601. Provisions relating to plan amendments.

TITLE I—EXPANDING AND PRESERVING RETIREMENT SAVINGS

[¶ 5042] SEC. 101. MULTIPLE EMPLOYER PLANS; POOLED EMPLOYER PLANS.

(a) QUALIFICATION REQUIREMENTS.—

(1) IN GENERAL.—Section 413 of the Internal Revenue Code of 1986 is amended by adding at the end the following new subsection:

"(e) APPLICATION OF QUALIFICATION REQUIREMENTS FOR CERTAIN MULTIPLE EMPLOYER PLANS WITH POOLED PLAN PROVIDERS.—

"(1) IN GENERAL.—Except as provided in paragraph (2), if a defined contribution plan to which subsection (c) applies—

"(A) is maintained by employers which have a common interest other than having adopted the plan, or

"(B) in the case of a plan not described in subparagraph (A), has a pooled plan provider,

then the plan shall not be treated as failing to meet the requirements under this title applicable to a plan described in section 401(a) or to a plan that consists of individual retirement accounts described in section 408 (including by reason of subsection (c) thereof), whichever is applicable, merely because one or more employers of employees covered by the plan fail to take such actions as are required of such employers for the plan to meet such requirements.

"(2) LIMITATIONS.—

"(A) IN GENERAL.—Paragraph (1) shall not apply to any plan unless the terms of the plan provide that in the case of any employer in the plan failing to take the actions described in paragraph (1)—

"(i) the assets of the plan attributable to employees of such employer (or beneficiaries of such employees) will be transferred to a plan maintained only by such employer (or its successor), to an eligible retirement plan as defined in section 402(c)(8)(B) for each individual whose account is transferred, or to any other arrangement that the Secretary determines is appropriate, unless the Secretary determines it is in the best interests of the employees of such employer (and the beneficiaries of such employees) to retain the assets in the plan, and

"(ii) such employer (and not the plan with respect to which the failure occurred or any other employer in such plan) shall, except to the extent provided by the Secretary, be liable for any liabilities with respect to such plan attributable to employees of such employer (or beneficiaries of such employees).

"(B) FAILURES BY POOLED PLAN PROVIDERS.—If the pooled plan provider of a plan described in paragraph (1)(B) does not perform substantially all of the administrative duties which are required of the provider under paragraph (3)(A)(i) for any plan year, the Secretary may provide that the determination as to whether the plan meets the requirements under this title applicable to a plan described in section 401(a) or to a plan that consists of individual retirement accounts described in section 408 (including by reason of subsection (c) thereof), whichever is applicable, shall be made in the same manner as would be made without regard to paragraph (1).

"(3) POOLED PLAN PROVIDER.—

"(A) IN GENERAL.—For purposes of this subsection, the term 'pooled plan provider' means, with respect to any plan, a person who—

"(i) is designated by the terms of the plan as a named fiduciary (within the meaning of section 402(a)(2) of the Employee Retirement Income Security Act of 1974), as the plan administrator, and as the person responsible to perform all administrative duties (including conducting proper testing with respect to the plan and the employees of each employer in the plan) which are reasonably necessary to ensure that—

"(I) the plan meets any requirement applicable under the Employee Retirement Income Security Act of 1974 or this title to a plan described in section 401(a) or to a plan that consists of individual retirement accounts described in section 408 (including by reason of subsection (c) thereof), whichever is applicable, and

"(II) each employer in the plan takes such actions as the Secretary or such person determines are necessary for the plan to meet the requirements described in subclause (I), including providing to such person any disclosures or other information which the Secretary may require or which such person otherwise determines are necessary to administer the plan or to allow the plan to meet such requirements,

"(ii) registers as a pooled plan provider with the Secretary, and provides such other information to the Secretary as the Secretary may require, before beginning operations as a pooled plan provider,

"(iii) acknowledges in writing that such person is a named fiduciary (within the meaning of section 402(a)(2) of the Employee Retirement Income Security Act of 1974), and the plan administrator, with respect to the plan, and

"(iv) is responsible for ensuring that all persons who handle assets of, or who are fiduciaries of, the plan are bonded in accordance with section 412 of the Employee Retirement Income Security Act of 1974.

"(B) AUDITS, EXAMINATIONS AND INVESTIGATIONS.—The Secretary may perform audits, examinations, and investigations of pooled plan providers as may be necessary to enforce and carry out the purposes of this subsection.

"(C) AGGREGATION RULES.—For purposes of this paragraph, in determining whether a person meets the requirements of this paragraph to be a pooled plan provider with respect to any plan, all persons who perform services for the plan and who are treated as a single employer under subsection (b), (c), (m), or (o) of section 414 shall be treated as one person.

"(D) TREATMENT OF EMPLOYERS AS PLAN SPONSORS.—Except with respect to the administrative duties of the pooled plan provider described in subparagraph (A)(i), each employer in a plan which has a pooled plan provider shall be treated as the plan sponsor with respect to the portion of the plan attributable to employees of such employer (or beneficiaries of such employees).

"(4) GUIDANCE.—

"(A) IN GENERAL.—The Secretary shall issue such guidance as the Secretary determines appropriate to carry out this subsection, including guidance—

"(i) to identify the administrative duties and other actions required to be performed by a pooled plan provider under this subsection,

"(ii) which describes the procedures to be taken to terminate a plan which fails to meet the requirements to be a plan described in paragraph (1), including the proper treatment of, and actions needed to be taken by, any employer in the plan and the assets and liabilities of the plan attributable to employees of such employer (or beneficiaries of such employees), and

"(iii) identifying appropriate cases to which the rules of paragraph (2)(A) will apply to employers in the plan failing to take the actions described in paragraph (1).

The Secretary shall take into account under clause (iii) whether the failure of an employer or pooled plan provider to provide any disclosures or other information, or to take any other action, necessary to administer a plan or to allow a plan to meet requirements applicable to the plan under section 401(a) or 408, whichever is applicable, has continued over a period of time that demonstrates a lack of commitment to compliance.

"(B) GOOD FAITH COMPLIANCE WITH LAW BEFORE GUIDANCE.—An employer or pooled plan provider shall not be treated as failing to meet a requirement of guidance issued by the Secretary under this paragraph if, before the issuance of such guidance, the employer or pooled plan provider complies in good faith with a reasonable interpretation of the provisions of this subsection to which such guidance relates.

"(5) MODEL PLAN.—The Secretary shall publish model plan language which meets the requirements of this subsection and of paragraphs (43) and (44) of section 3 of the Employee Retirement Income Security Act of 1974 and which may be adopted in order for a plan to be treated as a plan described in paragraph (1)(B).".

(2) CONFORMING AMENDMENT.—Section 413(c)(2) of such Code is amended by striking "section 401(a)" and inserting "sections 401(a) and 408(c)".

(3) TECHNICAL AMENDMENT.—Section 408(c) of such Code is amended by inserting after paragraph (2) the following new paragraph:

"(3) There is a separate accounting for any interest of an employee or member (or spouse of an employee or member) in a Roth IRA.".

(b) NO COMMON INTEREST REQUIRED FOR POOLED EMPLOYER PLANS.—Section 3(2) of the Employee Retirement Income Security Act of 1974 (29 U.S.C. 1002(2)) is amended by adding at the end the following:

"(C) A pooled employer plan shall be treated as—

"(i) a single employee pension benefit plan or single pension plan; and

"(ii) a plan to which section 210(a) applies.".

(c) POOLED EMPLOYER PLAN AND PROVIDER DEFINED.—

(1) IN GENERAL.—Section 3 of the Employee Retirement Income Security Act of 1974 (29 U.S.C. 1002) is amended by adding at the end the following:

"(43) POOLED EMPLOYER PLAN.—

"(A) IN GENERAL.—The term 'pooled employer plan' means a plan—

"(i) which is an individual account plan established or maintained for the purpose of providing benefits to the employees of 2 or more employers;

"(ii) which is a plan described in section 401(a) of the Internal Revenue Code of 1986 which includes a trust exempt from tax under section 501(a) of such Code or a plan that consists of individual retirement accounts described in section 408 of such Code (including by reason of subsection (c) thereof); and

"(iii) the terms of which meet the requirements of subparagraph (B).

Such term shall not include a plan maintained by employers which have a common interest other than having adopted the plan.

"(B) REQUIREMENTS FOR PLAN TERMS.—The requirements of this subparagraph are met with respect to any plan if the terms of the plan—

"(i) designate a pooled plan provider and provide that the pooled plan provider is a named fiduciary of the plan;

"(ii) designate one or more trustees meeting the requirements of section 408(a)(2) of the Internal Revenue Code of 1986 (other than an employer in the plan) to be responsible for collecting contributions to, and holding the assets of, the plan and require such trustees to implement written contribution collection procedures that are reasonable, diligent, and systematic;

"(iii) provide that each employer in the plan retains fiduciary responsibility for—

"(I) the selection and monitoring in accordance with section 404(a) of the person designated as the pooled plan provider and any other person who, in addition to the pooled plan provider, is designated as a named fiduciary of the plan; and

"(II) to the extent not otherwise delegated to another fiduciary by the pooled plan provider and subject to the provisions of section 404(c), the investment and management of the portion of the plan's assets attributable to the employees of the employer (or beneficiaries of such employees);

"(iv) provide that employers in the plan, and participants and beneficiaries, are not subject to unreasonable restrictions, fees, or penalties with regard to ceasing participation, receipt of distributions, or otherwise transferring assets of the plan in accordance with section 208 or paragraph (44)(C)(i)(II);

"(v) require—

"(I) the pooled plan provider to provide to employers in the plan any disclosures or other information which the Secretary may require, including any disclosures or other information to facilitate the selection or any monitoring of the pooled plan provider by employers in the plan; and

"(II) each employer in the plan to take such actions as the Secretary or the pooled plan provider determines are necessary to administer the plan or for the plan to meet any requirement applicable under this Act or the Internal Revenue Code of 1986 to a plan described in section 401(a) of such Code or to a plan that consists of individual retirement accounts described in section 408 of such Code (including by reason of subsection (c) thereof), whichever is applicable, including providing any disclosures or other information which the Secretary may require or which the pooled plan provider otherwise determines are necessary to administer the plan or to allow the plan to meet such requirements; and

"(vi) provide that any disclosure or other information required to be provided under clause (v) may be provided in electronic form and will be designed to ensure only reasonable costs are imposed on pooled plan providers and employers in the plan.

"(C) EXCEPTIONS.—The term 'pooled employer plan' does not include—

"(i) a multiemployer plan; or

"(ii) a plan established before the date of the enactment of the Setting Every Community Up for Retirement Enhancement Act of 2019 unless the plan administrator elects that the plan will be treated as a pooled employer plan and the plan meets the requirements of this title applicable to a pooled employer plan established on or after such date.

"(D) TREATMENT OF EMPLOYERS AS PLAN SPONSORS.—Except with respect to the administrative duties of the pooled plan provider described in paragraph (44)(A)(i), each employer in a pooled employer plan shall be treated as the plan sponsor with respect to the portion of the plan attributable to employees of such employer (or beneficiaries of such employees).

"(44) POOLED PLAN PROVIDER.—

"(A) IN GENERAL.—The term 'pooled plan provider' means a person who—

"(i) is designated by the terms of a pooled employer plan as a named fiduciary, as the plan administrator, and as the person responsible for the performance of all administrative duties (including conducting proper testing with respect to the plan and the employees of each employer in the plan) which are reasonably necessary to ensure that—

"(I) the plan meets any requirement applicable under this Act or the Internal Revenue Code of 1986 to a plan described in section 401(a) of such Code or to a plan that consists of individual retirement accounts described in section 408 of such Code (including by reason of subsection (c) thereof), whichever is applicable; and

"(II) each employer in the plan takes such actions as the Secretary or pooled plan provider determines are necessary for the plan to meet the requirements described in subclause (I), including providing the disclosures and information described in paragraph (43)(B)(v)(II);

"(ii) registers as a pooled plan provider with the Secretary, and provides to the Secretary such other information as the Secretary may require, before beginning operations as a pooled plan provider;

"(iii) acknowledges in writing that such person is a named fiduciary, and the plan administrator, with respect to the pooled employer plan; and

"(iv) is responsible for ensuring that all persons who handle assets of, or who are fiduciaries of, the pooled employer plan are bonded in accordance with section 412.

"(B) AUDITS, EXAMINATIONS AND INVESTIGATIONS.—The Secretary may perform audits, examinations, and investigations of pooled plan providers as may be necessary to enforce and carry out the purposes of this paragraph and paragraph (43).

"(C) GUIDANCE.—The Secretary shall issue such guidance as the Secretary determines appropriate to carry out this paragraph and paragraph (43), including guidance—

"(i) to identify the administrative duties and other actions required to be performed by a pooled plan provider under either such paragraph; and

"(ii) which requires in appropriate cases that if an employer in the plan fails to take the actions required under subparagraph (A)(i)(II)—

"(I) the assets of the plan attributable to employees of such employer (or beneficiaries of such employees) are transferred to a plan maintained only by such employer (or its successor), to an eligible retirement plan as defined in section 402(c)(8)(B) of the Internal Revenue Code of 1986 for each individual whose account is transferred, or to any other arrangement that the Secretary determines is appropriate in such guidance; and

"(II) such employer (and not the plan with respect to which the failure occurred or any other employer in such plan) shall, except to the extent provided in such guidance, be liable for any liabilities with respect to such plan attributable to employees of such employer (or beneficiaries of such employees).

The Secretary shall take into account under clause (ii) whether the failure of an employer or pooled plan provider to provide any disclosures or other information, or to take any other action, necessary to administer a plan or to allow a plan to meet requirements described in subparagraph (A)(i)(II) has continued over a period of time that demonstrates a lack of commitment to compliance. The Secretary may waive the requirements of subclause (ii)(I) in appropriate circumstances if the Secretary determines it is in the best interests of the employees of the employer referred to in such clause (and the beneficiaries of such employees) to retain the assets in the plan with respect to which the employer's failure occurred.

"(D) GOOD FAITH COMPLIANCE WITH LAW BEFORE GUIDANCE.—An employer or pooled plan provider shall not be treated as failing to meet a requirement of guidance issued by the Secretary under subparagraph (C) if, before the issuance of such guidance, the employer or pooled plan provider complies in good faith with a reasonable interpretation of the provisions of this paragraph, or paragraph (43), to which such guidance relates.

"(E) AGGREGATION RULES.—For purposes of this paragraph, in determining whether a person meets the requirements of this paragraph to be a pooled plan provider with respect to any plan, all persons who perform services for the plan and who are treated as a single employer under subsection (b), (c), (m), or (o) of section 414 of the Internal Revenue Code of 1986 shall be treated as one person.".

(2) BONDING REQUIREMENTS FOR POOLED EMPLOYER PLANS.—The last sentence of section 412(a) of the Employee Retirement Income Security Act of 1974 (29 U.S.C. 1112(a)) is amended by inserting "or in the case of a pooled employer plan (as defined in section 3(43))" after "section 407(d)(1))".

(3) CONFORMING AND TECHNICAL AMENDMENTS.—Section 3 of the Employee Retirement Income Security Act of 1974 (29 U.S.C. 1002) is amended—

(A) in paragraph (16)(B)—

(i) by striking "or" at the end of clause (ii); and

(ii) by striking the period at the end and inserting ", or (iv) in the case of a pooled employer plan, the pooled plan provider."; and

(B) by striking the second paragraph (41).

(d) POOLED EMPLOYER AND MULTIPLE EMPLOYER PLAN REPORTING.—

(1) ADDITIONAL INFORMATION.—Section 103 of the Employee Retirement Income Security Act of 1974 (29 U.S.C. 1023) is amended—

(A) in subsection (a)(1)(B), by striking "applicable subsections (d), (e), and (f)" and inserting "applicable subsections (d), (e), (f), and (g)"; and

(B) by amending subsection (g) to read as follows:

"(g) ADDITIONAL INFORMATION WITH RESPECT TO POOLED EMPLOYER AND MULTIPLE EMPLOYER PLANS.—An annual report under this section for a plan year shall include—

"(1) with respect to any plan to which section 210(a) applies(including a pooled employer plan), a list of employers in the plan and a good faith estimate of the percentage of total contributions made by such employers during the plan year and the aggregate account balances attributable to each employer in the plan (determined as the sum of the account balances of the employees of such employer (and the beneficiaries of such employees)); and

"(2) with respect to a pooled employer plan, the identifying information for the person designated under the terms of the plan as the pooled plan provider.".

(2) SIMPLIFIED ANNUAL REPORTS.—Section 104(a) of the Employee Retirement Income Security Act of 1974 (29 U.S.C. 1024(a)) is amended by striking paragraph (2)(A) and inserting the following:

"(2)(A) With respect to annual reports required to be filed with the Secretary under this part, the Secretary may by regulation prescribe simplified annual reports for any pension plan that—

"(i) covers fewer than 100 participants; or

"(ii) is a plan described in section 210(a) that covers fewer than 1,000 participants, but only if no single employer in the plan has 100 or more participants covered by the plan.".

(e) EFFECTIVE DATE.—

(1) IN GENERAL.—The amendments made by this section shall apply to plan years beginning after December 31, 2020.

(2) RULE OF CONSTRUCTION.—Nothing in the amendments made by subsection (a) shall be construed as limiting the authority of the Secretary of the Treasury or the Secretary's delegate (determined without regard to such amendment) to provide for the proper treatment of a failure to meet any requirement applicable under the Internal Revenue Code of 1986 with respect to one employer (and its employees) in a multiple employer plan.

[¶ 5043] SEC. 102. INCREASE IN 10 PERCENT CAP FOR AUTOMATIC ENROLLMENT SAFE HARBOR AFTER 1ST PLAN YEAR.

(a) IN GENERAL.—Section 401(k)(13)(C)(iii) of the Internal Revenue Code of 1986 is amended by striking "does not exceed 10 percent" and inserting "does not exceed 15 percent (10 percent during the period described in subclause (I))".

(b) EFFECTIVE DATE.—The amendments made by this section shall apply to plan years beginning after December 31, 2019.

[¶ 5044] SEC. 103. RULES RELATING TO ELECTION OF SAFE HARBOR 401(k) STATUS.

(a) LIMITATION OF ANNUAL SAFE HARBOR NOTICE TO MATCHING CONTRIBUTION PLANS.—

(1) IN GENERAL.—Subparagraph (A) of section 401(k)(12) of the Internal Revenue Code of 1986 is amended by striking "if such arrangement" and all that follows and inserting "if such arrangement—

"(i) meets the contribution requirements of subparagraph (B) and the notice requirements of subparagraph (D), or

"(ii) meets the contribution requirements of subparagraph (C).".

(2) AUTOMATIC CONTRIBUTION ARRANGEMENTS.—Subparagraph (B) of section 401(k)(13) of such Code is amended by striking "means" and all that follows and inserting "means a cash or deferred arrangement—

"(i) which is described in subparagraph (D)(i)(I) and meets the applicable requirements of subparagraphs (C) through (E), or

"(ii) which is described in subparagraph (D)(i)(II) and meets the applicable requirements of subparagraphs (C) and (D).".

(b) NONELECTIVE CONTRIBUTIONS.—Section 401(k)(12) of the Internal Revenue Code of 1986 is amended by redesignating subparagraph (F) as subparagraph (G), and by inserting after subparagraph (E) the following new subparagraph:

"(F) TIMING OF PLAN AMENDMENT FOR EMPLOYER MAKING NONELECTIVE CONTRIBUTIONS.—

"(i) IN GENERAL.—Except as provided in clause (ii), a plan may be amended after the beginning of a plan year to provide that the requirements of subparagraph (C) shall apply to the arrangement for the plan year, but only if the amendment is adopted—

"(I) at any time before the 30th day before the close of the plan year, or

"(II) at any time before the last day under paragraph (8)(A) for distributing excess contributions for the plan year.

"(ii) EXCEPTION WHERE PLAN PROVIDED FOR MATCHING CONTRIBUTIONS.—Clause (i) shall not apply to any plan year if the plan provided at any time during the plan year that the requirements of subparagraph (B) or paragraph (13)(D)(i)(I) applied to the plan year.

"(iii) 4-PERCENT CONTRIBUTION REQUIREMENT.—Clause (i)(II) shall not apply to an arrangement unless the amount of the contributions described in subparagraph (C) which the employer is required to make under the arrangement for the plan year with respect to any employee is an amount equal to at least 4 percent of the employee's compensation.".

(c) AUTOMATIC CONTRIBUTION ARRANGEMENTS.—Section 401(k)(13) of the Internal Revenue Code of 1986 is amended by adding at the end the following:

"(F) TIMING OF PLAN AMENDMENT FOR EMPLOYER MAKING NONELECTIVE CONTRIBUTIONS.—

"(i) IN GENERAL.—Except as provided in clause (ii), a plan may be amended after the beginning of a plan year to provide that the requirements of subparagraph (D)(i)(II) shall apply to the arrangement for the plan year, but only if the amendment is adopted—

"(I) at any time before the 30th day before the close of the plan year, or

"(II) at any time before the last day under paragraph (8)(A) for distributing excess contributions for the plan year.

"(ii) EXCEPTION WHERE PLAN PROVIDED FOR MATCHING CONTRIBUTIONS.—Clause (i) shall not apply to any plan year if the plan provided at any time during the plan year that the requirements of subparagraph (D)(i)(I) or paragraph (12)(B) applied to the plan year.

"(iii) 4-PERCENT CONTRIBUTION REQUIREMENT.—Clause (i)(II) shall not apply to an arrangement unless the amount of the contributions described in subparagraph (D)(i)(II) which the employer is required to make under the arrangement for the plan year with respect to any employee is an amount equal to at least 4 percent of the employee's compensation.".

(d) EFFECTIVE DATE.—The amendments made by this section shall apply to plan years beginning after December 31, 2019.

[¶5045] SEC. 104. INCREASE IN CREDIT LIMITATION FOR SMALL EMPLOYER PENSION PLAN STARTUP COSTS.

(a) IN GENERAL.—Paragraph (1) of section 45E(b) of the Internal Revenue Code of 1986 is amended to read as follows:

"(1) for the first credit year and each of the 2 taxable years immediately following the first credit year, the greater of—

"(A) $500, or

"(B) the lesser of—

"(i) $250 for each employee of the eligible employer who is not a highly compensated employee (as defined in section 414(q)) and who is eligible to participate in the eligible employer plan maintained by the eligible employer, or

"(ii) $5,000, and".

(b) EFFECTIVE DATE.—The amendment made by this section shall apply to taxable years beginning after December 31, 2019.

[¶5046] SEC. 105. SMALL EMPLOYER AUTOMATIC ENROLLMENT CREDIT.

(a) IN GENERAL.—Subpart D of part IV of subchapter A of chapter 1 of the Internal Revenue Code of 1986 is amended by adding at the end the following new section:

"SEC. 45T. AUTO-ENROLLMENT OPTION FOR RETIREMENT SAVINGS OPTIONS PROVIDED BY SMALL EMPLOYERS.

"(a) IN GENERAL.—For purposes of section 38, in the case of an eligible employer, the retirement auto-enrollment credit determined under this section for any taxable year is an amount equal to—

"(1) $500 for any taxable year occurring during the credit period, and

"(2) zero for any other taxable year.

"(b) CREDIT PERIOD.—For purposes of subsection (a)—

"(1) IN GENERAL.—The credit period with respect to any eligible employer is the 3-taxable-year period beginning with the first taxable year for which the employer includes an eligible automatic contribution arrangement (as defined in section 414(w)(3)) in a qualified employer plan (as defined in section 4972(d)) sponsored by the employer.

"(2) MAINTENANCE OF ARRANGEMENT.—No taxable year with respect to an employer shall be treated as occurring within the credit period unless the arrangement described in paragraph (1) is included in the plan for such year.

"(c) ELIGIBLE EMPLOYER.—For purposes of this section, the term 'eligible employer' has the meaning given such term in section 408(p)(2)(C)(i).".

(b) CREDIT TO BE PART OF GENERAL BUSINESS CREDIT.—Subsection (b) of section 38 of the Internal Revenue Code of 1986 is amended by striking "plus" at the end of paragraph (31), by striking the period at the end of paragraph (32) and inserting ", plus", and by adding at the end the following new paragraph:

"(33) in the case of an eligible employer (as defined in section 45T(c)), the retirement auto-enrollment credit determined under section 45T(a).".

(c) CLERICAL AMENDMENT.—The table of sections for subpart D of part IV of subchapter A of chapter 1 of the Internal Revenue Code of 1986 is amended by inserting after the item relating to section 45S the following new item:

"Sec. 45T. Auto-enrollment option for retirement savings options provided by small employers.".

(d) EFFECTIVE DATE.—The amendments made by this section shall apply to taxable years beginning after December 31, 2019.

[¶ 5047] **SEC. 106. CERTAIN TAXABLE NON-TUITION FELLOWSHIP AND STIPEND PAYMENTS TREATED AS COMPENSATION FOR IRA PURPOSES.**

(a) IN GENERAL.—Paragraph (1) of section 219(f) of the Internal Revenue Code of 1986 is amended by adding at the end the following: "The term 'compensation' shall include any amount which is included in the individual's gross income and paid to the individual to aid the individual in the pursuit of graduate or postdoctoral study.".

(b) EFFECTIVE DATE.—The amendment made by this section shall apply to taxable years beginning after December 31, 2019.

[¶ 5048] **SEC. 107. REPEAL OF MAXIMUM AGE FOR TRADITIONAL IRA CONTRIBUTIONS.**

(a) IN GENERAL.—Paragraph (1) of section 219(d) of the Internal Revenue Code of 1986 is repealed.

(b) COORDINATION WITH QUALIFIED CHARITABLE DISTRIBUTIONS.—Add at the end of section 408(d)(8)(A) of such Code the following: "The amount of distributions not includible in gross income by reason of the preceding sentence for a taxable year (determined without regard to this sentence) shall be reduced (but not below zero) by an amount equal to the excess of—

"(i) the aggregate amount of deductions allowed to the taxpayer under section 219 for all taxable years ending on or after the date the taxpayer attains age $70^1/_2$, over

"(ii) the aggregate amount of reductions under this sentence for all taxable years preceding the current taxable year.".

(c) CONFORMING AMENDMENT.—Subsection (c) of section 408A of the Internal Revenue Code of 1986 is amended by striking paragraph (4) and by redesignating paragraphs (5), (6), and (7) as paragraphs (4), (5), and (6), respectively.

(d) EFFECTIVE DATE.—

(1) IN GENERAL.—Except as provided in paragraph (2), the amendments made by this section shall apply to contributions made for taxable years beginning after December 31, 2019.

(2) SUBSECTION (b).—The amendment made by subsection (b) shall apply to distributions made for taxable years beginning after December 31, 2019.

[¶ 5049] **SEC. 108. QUALIFIED EMPLOYER PLANS PROHIBITED FROM MAKING LOANS THROUGH CREDIT CARDS AND OTHER SIMILAR ARRANGEMENTS.**

(a) IN GENERAL.—Paragraph (2) of section 72(p) of the Internal Revenue Code of 1986 is amended by redesignating subparagraph (D) as subparagraph (E) and by inserting after subparagraph (C) the following new subparagraph:

"(D) PROHIBITION OF LOANS THROUGH CREDIT CARDS AND OTHER SIMILAR ARRANGEMENTS.—Subparagraph (A) shall not apply to any loan which is made through the use of any credit card or any other similar arrangement.".

(b) EFFECTIVE DATE.—The amendments made by subsection (a) shall apply to loans made after the date of the enactment of this Act.

[¶ 5050] **SEC. 109. PORTABILITY OF LIFETIME INCOME OPTIONS.**

(a) IN GENERAL.—Subsection (a) of section 401 of the Internal Revenue Code of 1986 is amended by inserting after paragraph (37) the following new paragraph:

"(38) PORTABILITY OF LIFETIME INCOME.—

"(A) IN GENERAL.—Except as may be otherwise provided by regulations, a trust forming part of a defined contribution plan shall not be treated as failing to constitute a qualified trust under this section solely by reason of allowing—

"(i) qualified distributions of a lifetime income investment, or

"(ii) distributions of a lifetime income investment in the form of a qualified plan distribution annuity contract,

on or after the date that is 90 days prior to the date on which such lifetime income investment is no longer authorized to be held as an investment option under the plan.

"(B) DEFINITIONS.—For purposes of this subsection—

"(i) the term 'qualified distribution' means a direct trustee-to-trustee transfer described in paragraph (31)(A) to an eligible retirement plan (as defined in section 402(c)(8)(B)),

"(ii) the term 'lifetime income investment' means an investment option which is designed to provide an employee with election rights—

"(I) which are not uniformly available with respect to other investment options under the plan, and

"(II) which are to a lifetime income feature available through a contract or other arrangement offered under the plan (or under another eligible retirement plan (as so defined), if paid by means of a direct trustee-to-trustee transfer described in paragraph (31)(A) to such other eligible retirement plan),

"(iii) the term 'lifetime income feature' means—

"(I) a feature which guarantees a minimum level of income annually (or more frequently) for at least the remainder of the life of the employee or the joint lives of the employee and the employee's designated beneficiary, or

"(II) an annuity payable on behalf of the employee under which payments are made in substantially equal periodic payments (not less frequently than annually) over the life of the employee or the joint lives of the employee and the employee's designated beneficiary, and

"(iv) the term 'qualified plan distribution annuity contract' means an annuity contract purchased for a participant and distributed to the participant by a plan or contract described in subparagraph (B) of section 402(c)(8) (without regard to clauses (i) and (ii) thereof).".

(b) CASH OR DEFERRED ARRANGEMENT.—

(1) IN GENERAL.—Clause (i) of section 401(k)(2)(B) of the Internal Revenue Code of 1986 is amended by striking "or" at the end of subclause (IV), by striking "and" at the end of subclause(V) and inserting "or", and by adding at the end the following new subclause:

"(VI) except as may be otherwise provided by regulations, with respect to amounts invested in a lifetime income investment (as defined in subsection (a)(38)(B)(ii)), the date that is 90 days prior to the date that such lifetime income investment may no longer be held as an investment option under the arrangement, and".

(2) DISTRIBUTION REQUIREMENT.—Subparagraph (B) of section 401(k)(2) of such Code, as amended by paragraph (1), is amended by striking "and" at the end of clause (i), by striking the semicolon at the end of clause (ii) and inserting ", and", and by adding at the end the following new clause:

"(iii) except as may be otherwise provided by regulations, in the case of amounts described in clause (i)(VI), will be distributed only in the form of a qualified distribution (as defined in subsection (a)(38)(B)(i)) or a qualified plan distribution annuity contract (as defined in subsection (a)(38)(B)(iv)),".

(c) SECTION 403(b) PLANS.—

(1) ANNUITY CONTRACTS.—Paragraph (11) of section 403(b) of the Internal Revenue Code of 1986 is amended by striking "or" at the end of subparagraph (B), by striking the period at the end of subparagraph (C) and inserting ", or", and by inserting after subparagraph (C) the following new subparagraph:

"(D) except as may be otherwise provided by regulations, with respect to amounts invested in a lifetime income investment (as defined in section 401(a)(38)(B)(ii))—

"(i) on or after the date that is 90 days prior to the date that such lifetime income investment may no longer be held as an investment option under the contract, and "(ii) in the form of a qualified distribution (as defined in section 401(a)(38)(B)(i)) or a qualified plan distribution annuity contract (as defined in section 401(a)(38)(B)(iv)).".

(2) CUSTODIAL ACCOUNTS.—Subparagraph (A) of section 403(b)(7) of such Code is amended by striking "if—"and all that follows and inserting "if the amounts are to be invested in regulated investment company stock to be held in that custodial account, and under the custodial account—

"(i) no such amounts may be paid or made available to any distributee (unless such amount is a distribution to which section 72(t)(2)(G) applies) before—

"(I) the employee dies,

"(II) the employee attains age $59^1/_2$,

"(III) the employee has a severance from employment,

"(IV) the employee becomes disabled (within the meaning of section 72(m)(7)),

"(V) in the case of contributions made pursuant to a salary reduction agreement (within the meaning of section 3121(a)(5)(D)), the employee encounters financial hardship, or

"(VI) except as may be otherwise provided by regulations, with respect to amounts invested in a lifetime income investment (as defined in section 401(a)(38)(B)(ii)), the date that is 90 days prior to the date that such lifetime income investment may no longer be held as an investment option under the contract, and

"(ii) in the case of amounts described in clause (i)(VI), such amounts will be distributed only in the form of a qualified distribution (as defined in section 401(a)(38)(B)(i)) or a qualified plan distribution annuity contract (as defined in section 401(a)(38)(B)(iv)).".

(d) ELIGIBLE DEFERRED COMPENSATION PLANS.—

(1) IN GENERAL.—Subparagraph (A) of section 457(d)(1) of the Internal Revenue Code of 1986 is amended by striking "or" at the end of clause (ii), by inserting "or" at the end of clause (iii), and by adding after clause (iii) the following:

"(iv) except as may be otherwise provided by regulations, in the case of a plan maintained by an employer described in subsection (e)(1)(A), with respect to amounts invested in a lifetime income investment (as defined in section 401(a)(38)(B)(ii)), the date that is 90 days prior to the date that such lifetime income investment may no longer be held as an investment option under the plan,".

(2) DISTRIBUTION REQUIREMENT.—Paragraph (1) of section 457(d) of such Code is amended by striking "and" at the end of subparagraph (B), by striking the period at the end of subparagraph (C) and inserting ", and", and by inserting after subparagraph (C) the following new subparagraph:

"(D) except as may be otherwise provided by regulations, in the case of amounts described in subparagraph (A)(iv), such amounts will be distributed only in the form of a qualified distribution (as defined in section 401(a)(38)(B)(i)) or a qualified plan distribution annuity contract (as defined in section 401(a)(38)(B)(iv)).".

(e) EFFECTIVE DATE.—The amendments made by this section shall apply to plan years beginning after December 31, 2019.

[¶ 5051] SEC. 110. TREATMENT OF CUSTODIAL ACCOUNTS ON TERMINATION OF SECTION 403(b) PLANS.

Not later than six months after the date of enactment of this Act, the Secretary of the Treasury shall issue guidance to provide that, if an employer terminates the plan under which amounts are contributed to a custodial account under subparagraph (A) of section 403(b)(7), the plan administrator or custodian may distribute an individual custodial account in kind to a participant or beneficiary of the plan and the distributed custodial account shall be maintained by the custodian on a tax-deferred basis as a section 403(b)(7) custodial account, similar to the treatment of fully-paid individual annuity contracts under Revenue Ruling 2011-7, until amounts are actually paid to the participant or beneficiary. The guidance shall provide further (i) that the section 403(b)(7) status of the distributed custodial account is generally maintained if the custodial account thereafter adheres to the requirements of section 403(b) that are in effect at the time of the distribution of the account and (ii) that a custodial account would not be considered distributed to the participant or beneficiary if the employer has any material retained rights under the account (but the employer would not be treated as retaining material rights simply because the custodial account was originally opened under a group contract). Such guidance shall be retroactively effective for taxable years beginning after December 31, 2008.

[¶ 5052] **SEC. 111. CLARIFICATION OF RETIREMENT INCOME ACCOUNT RULES RELATING TO CHURCH-CONTROLLED ORGANIZATIONS.**

(a) IN GENERAL.—Subparagraph (B) of section 403(b)(9) of the Internal Revenue Code of 1986 is amended by inserting "(including an employee described in section 414(e)(3)(B))" after "employee described in paragraph (1)".

(b) EFFECTIVE DATE.—The amendment made by this section shall apply to years beginning before, on, or after the date of the enactment of this Act.

[¶ 5053] **SEC. 112. QUALIFIED CASH OR DEFERRED ARRANGEMENTS MUST ALLOW LONG-TERM EMPLOYEES WORKING MORE THAN 500 BUT LESS THAN 1,000 HOURS PER YEAR TO PARTICIPATE.**

(a) PARTICIPATION REQUIREMENT.—

(1) IN GENERAL.—Section 401(k)(2)(D) of the Internal Revenue Code of 1986 is amended to read as follows:

"(D) which does not require, as a condition of participation in the arrangement, that an employee complete a period of service with the employer (or employers) maintaining the plan extending beyond the close of the earlier of—

"(i) the period permitted under section 410(a)(1) (determined without regard to subparagraph (B)(i) thereof), or

"(ii) subject to the provisions of paragraph (15), the first period of 3 consecutive 12-month periods during each of which the employee has at least 500 hours of service.".

(2) SPECIAL RULES.—Section 401(k) of such Code is amended by adding at the end the following new paragraph:

"(15) SPECIAL RULES FOR PARTICIPATION REQUIREMENT FOR LONG-TERM, PART-TIME WORKERS.—For purposes of paragraph (2)(D)(ii)—

"(A) AGE REQUIREMENT MUST BE MET.—Paragraph (2)(D)(ii) shall not apply to an employee unless the employee has met the requirement of section 410(a)(1)(A)(i) by the close of the last of the 12-month periods described in such paragraph.

"(B) NONDISCRIMINATION AND TOP-HEAVY RULES NOT TO APPLY.—

"(i) NONDISCRIMINATION RULES.—In the case of employees who are eligible to participate in the arrangement solely by reason of paragraph (2)(D)(ii)—

"(I) notwithstanding subsection (a)(4), an employer shall not be required to make nonelective or matching contributions on behalf of such employees even if such contributions are made on behalf of other employees eligible to participate in the arrangement, and

"(II) an employer may elect to exclude such employees from the application of subsection (a)(4), paragraphs (3), (12), and (13), subsection (m)(2), and section 410(b).

"(ii) TOP-HEAVY RULES.—An employer may elect to exclude all employees who are eligible to participate in a plan maintained by the employer solely by reason of paragraph (2)(D)(ii) from the application of the vesting and benefit requirements under subsections (b) and (c) of section 416.

"(iii) VESTING.—For purposes of determining whether an employee described in clause (i) has a nonforfeitable right to employer contributions (other than contributions described in paragraph (3)(D)(i)) under the arrangement, each 12-month period for which the employee has at least 500 hours of service shall be treated as a year of service, and section 411(a)(6) shall be applied by substituting 'at least 500 hours of service' for 'more than 500 hours of service' in subparagraph (A) thereof.

"(iv) EMPLOYEES WHO BECOME FULL-TIME EMPLOYEES.—This subparagraph (other than clause (iii)) shall cease to apply to any employee as of the first plan year beginning after the plan year in which the employee meets the requirements of section 410(a)(1)(A)(ii) without regard to paragraph (2)(D)(ii).

"(C) EXCEPTION FOR EMPLOYEES UNDER COLLECTIVELY BARGAINED PLANS, ETC.—Paragraph (2)(D)(ii) shall not apply to employees described in section 410(b)(3).

"(D) SPECIAL RULES.—

"(i) TIME OF PARTICIPATION.—The rules of section 410(a)(4) shall apply to an employee eligible to participate in an arrangement solely by reason of paragraph (2)(D)(ii).

"(ii) 12-MONTH PERIODS.—12-month periods shall be determined in the same manner as under the last sentence of section 410(a)(3)(A).".

(b) EFFECTIVE DATE.—The amendments made by this section shall apply to plan years beginning after December 31, 2020, except that, for purposes of section 401(k)(2)(D)(ii) of the Internal Revenue Code of 1986 (as added by such amendments), 12-month periods beginning before January 1, 2021, shall not be taken into account.

[¶5054] SEC. 113. PENALTY-FREE WITHDRAWALS FROM RETIREMENT PLANS FOR INDIVIDUALS IN CASE OF BIRTH OF CHILD OR ADOPTION.

(a) IN GENERAL.—Section 72(t)(2) of the Internal Revenue Code of 1986 is amended by adding at the end the following new subparagraph:

"(H) DISTRIBUTIONS FROM RETIREMENT PLANS IN CASE OF BIRTH OF CHILD OR ADOPTION.—

"(i) IN GENERAL.—Any qualified birth or adoption distribution.

"(ii) LIMITATION.—The aggregate amount which may be treated as qualified birth or adoption distributions by any individual with respect to any birth or adoption shall not exceed $5,000.

"(iii) QUALIFIED BIRTH OR ADOPTION DISTRIBUTION.—For purposes of this subparagraph—

"(I) IN GENERAL.—The term 'qualified birth or adoption distribution' means any distribution from an applicable eligible retirement plan to an individual if made during the 1-year period beginning on the date on which a child of the individual is born or on which the legal adoption by the individual of an eligible adoptee is finalized.

"(II) ELIGIBLE ADOPTEE.—The term 'eligible adoptee' means any individual (other than a child of the taxpayer's spouse) who has not attained age 18 or is physically or mentally incapable of self-support.

"(iv) TREATMENT OF PLAN DISTRIBUTIONS.—

"(I) IN GENERAL.—If a distribution to an individual would (without regard to clause (ii)) be a qualified birth or adoption distribution, a plan shall not be treated as failing to meet any requirement of this title merely because the plan treats the distribution as a qualified birth or adoption distribution, unless the aggregate amount of such distributions from all plans maintained by the employer (and any member of any controlled group which includes the employer) to such individual exceeds $5,000.

"(II) CONTROLLED GROUP.—For purposes of subclause (I), the term 'controlled group' means any group treated as a single employer under subsection (b), (c), (m), or (o) of section 414.

"(v) AMOUNT DISTRIBUTED MAY BE REPAID.—

"(I) IN GENERAL.—Any individual who receives a qualified birth or adoption distribution may make one or more contributions in an aggregate amount not to exceed the amount of such distribution to an applicable eligible retirement plan of which such individual is a beneficiary and to which a rollover contribution of such distribution could be made under section 402(c), 403(a)(4), 403(b)(8), 408(d)(3), or 457(e)(16), as the case may be.

"(II) LIMITATION ON CONTRIBUTIONS TO APPLICABLE ELIGIBLE RETIREMENT PLANS OTHER THAN IRAS.—The aggregate amount of contributions made by an individual under subclause (I) to any applicable eligible retirement plan which is not an individual retirement plan shall not exceed the aggregate amount of qualified birth or adoption distributions which are made from such plan to such individual. Subclause (I) shall not apply to contributions to any applicable eligible retirement plan which is not an individual retirement plan unless the individual is eligible to make contributions (other than those described in subclause (I)) to such applicable eligible retirement plan.

"(III) TREATMENT OF REPAYMENTS OF DISTRIBUTIONS FROM APPLICABLE ELIGIBLE RETIREMENT PLANS OTHER THAN IRAS.—If a contribution is made under subclause (I) with respect to a qualified birth or adoption distribution from an applicable eligible retirement plan other than an individual retirement plan, then the taxpayer shall, to the extent of the amount of the contribution, be treated as having received such distribution in an eligible rollover distribution (as defined in section 402(c)(4)) and as having transferred the amount to the applicable eligible retirement plan in a direct trustee to trustee transfer within 60 days of the distribution.

"(IV) TREATMENT OF REPAYMENTS FOR DISTRIBUTIONS FROM IRAS.—If a contribution is made under subclause (I) with respect to a qualified birth or adoption distribution from an individual retirement plan, then, to the extent of the amount of the contribution, such distribution shall be treated as a distribution described in section 408(d)(3) and as having been transferred to the applicable eligible retirement plan in a direct trustee to trustee transfer within 60 days of the distribution.

"(vi) DEFINITION AND SPECIAL RULES.—For purposes of this subparagraph—

"(I) APPLICABLE ELIGIBLE RETIREMENT PLAN.—The term 'applicable eligible retirement plan' means an eligible retirement plan (as defined in section 402(c)(8)(B)) other than a defined benefit plan.

"(II) EXEMPTION OF DISTRIBUTIONS FROM TRUSTEE TO TRUSTEE TRANSFER AND WITHHOLDING RULES.—For purposes of sections 401(a)(31), 402(f), and 3405, a qualified birth or adoption distribution shall not be treated as an eligible rollover distribution.

"(III) TAXPAYER MUST INCLUDE TIN.—A distribution shall not be treated as a qualified birth or adoption distribution with respect to any child or eligible adoptee unless the taxpayer includes the name, age, and TIN of such child or eligible adoptee on the taxpayer's return of tax for the taxable year.

"(IV) DISTRIBUTIONS TREATED AS MEETING PLAN DISTRIBUTION REQUIREMENTS.—Any qualified birth or adoption distribution shall be treated as meeting the requirements of sections 401(k)(2)(B)(i), 403(b)(7)(A)(ii), 403(b)(11), and 457(d)(1)(A).".

(b) EFFECTIVE DATE.—The amendments made by this section shall apply to distributions made after December 31, 2019.

[¶5055] SEC. 114. INCREASE IN AGE FOR REQUIRED BEGINNING DATE FOR MANDATORY DISTRIBUTIONS.

(a) IN GENERAL.—Section 401(a)(9)(C)(i)(I) of the Internal Revenue Code of 1986 is amended by striking "age 70$\frac{1}{2}$" and inserting "age 72".

(b) SPOUSE BENEFICIARIES; SPECIAL RULE FOR OWNERS.—Subparagraphs (B)(iv)(I) and (C)(ii)(I) of section 401(a)(9) of such Code are each amended by striking "age 70$\frac{1}{2}$" and inserting "age 72".

(c) CONFORMING AMENDMENTS.—The last sentence of section 408(b) of such Code is amended by striking "age 70$\frac{1}{2}$" and inserting "age 72".

(d) EFFECTIVE DATE.—The amendments made by this section shall apply to distributions required to be made after December 31, 2019, with respect to individuals who attain age 70$\frac{1}{2}$ after such date.

[¶5056] SEC. 115. SPECIAL RULES FOR MINIMUM FUNDING STANDARDS FOR COMMUNITY NEWSPAPER PLANS.

(a) AMENDMENT TO INTERNAL REVENUE CODE OF 1986.—Section 430 of the Internal Revenue Code of 1986 is amended by adding at the end the following new subsection:

"(m) SPECIAL RULES FOR COMMUNITY NEWSPAPER PLANS.—

"(1) IN GENERAL.—The plan sponsor of a community newspaper plan under which no participant has had the participant's accrued benefit increased (whether because of service or compensation) after December 31, 2017, may elect to have the alternative standards described in paragraph (3) apply to such plan, and any plan sponsored by any member of the same controlled group.

"(2) ELECTION.—An election under paragraph (1) shall be made at such time and in such manner as prescribed by the Secretary. Such election, once made with respect to a plan year, shall apply to all subsequent plan years unless revoked with the consent of the Secretary.

"(3) ALTERNATIVE MINIMUM FUNDING STANDARDS.—The alternative standards described in this paragraph are the following:

"(A) INTEREST RATES.—

"(i) IN GENERAL.—Notwithstanding subsection (h)(2)(C) and except as provided in clause (ii), the first, second, and third segment rates in effect for any month for purposes of this section shall be 8 percent.

"(ii) NEW BENEFIT ACCRUALS.—Notwithstanding subsection (h)(2), for purposes of determining the funding target and normal cost of a plan for any plan year, the present value of any benefits accrued or earned under the plan for a plan year with respect to which an election under paragraph (1) is in effect shall be determined on the basis of the United States Treasury obligation yield curve for the day that is the valuation date of such plan for such plan year.

"(iii) UNITED STATES TREASURY OBLIGATION YIELD CURVE.—For purposes of this subsection, the term 'United States Treasury obligation yield curve' means, with respect to any day, a yield curve which shall be prescribed by the Secretary for such day on interest-bearing obligations of the United States.

"(B) SHORTFALL AMORTIZATION BASE.—

"(i) PREVIOUS SHORTFALL AMORTIZATION BASES.—The shortfall amortization bases determined under subsection (c)(3) for all plan years preceding the first plan year to which the election under paragraph (1) applies (and all shortfall amortization installments determined with respect to such bases) shall be reduced to zero under rules similar to the rules of subsection (c)(6).

"(ii) NEW SHORTFALL AMORTIZATION BASE.—

Notwithstanding subsection (c)(3), the shortfall amortization base for the first plan year to which the election under paragraph (1) applies shall be the funding shortfall of such plan for such plan year (determined using the interest rates as modified under subparagraph (A)).

"(C) DETERMINATION OF SHORTFALL AMORTIZATION INSTALLMENTS.—

"(i) 30-YEAR PERIOD.—Subparagraphs (A) and (B) of subsection (c)(2) shall be applied by substituting '30-plan-year' for '7-plan-year' each place it appears.

"(ii) NO SPECIAL ELECTION.—The election under subparagraph (D) of subsection (c)(2) shall not apply to any plan year to which the election under paragraph (1) applies.

"(D) EXEMPTION FROM AT-RISK TREATMENT.—Subsection (i) shall not apply.

"(4) COMMUNITY NEWSPAPER PLAN.—For purposes of this subsection—

"(A) IN GENERAL.—The term 'community newspaper plan' means a plan to which this section applies maintained by an employer which, as of December 31, 2017—

"(i) publishes and distributes daily, either electronically or in printed form, 1 or more community newspapers in a single State,

"(ii) is not a company the stock of which is publicly traded (on a stock exchange or in an over-the-counter market), and is not controlled, directly or indirectly, by such a company,

"(iii) is controlled, directly or indirectly—

"(I) by 1 or more persons residing primarily in the State in which the community newspaper is published,

"(II) for not less than 30 years by individuals who are members of the same family,

"(III) by a trust created or organized in the State in which the community newspaper is published, the sole trustees of which are persons described in subclause (I) or (II),

"(IV) by an entity which is described in section 501(c)(3) and exempt from taxation under section 501(a), which is organized and operated in the State in which the community newspaper is published, and the primary purpose of which is to benefit communities in such State, or

"(V) by a combination of persons described in subclause (I), (III), or (IV), and

"(iv) does not control, directly or indirectly, any newspaper in any other State.

"(B) COMMUNITY NEWSPAPER.—The term 'community newspaper' means a newspaper which primarily serves a metropolitan statistical area, as determined by the Office of Management and Budget, with a population of not less than 100,000.

"(C) CONTROL.—A person shall be treated as controlled by another person if such other person possesses, directly or indirectly, the power to direct or cause the direction and management of such person (including the power to elect a majority of the members of the board of directors of such person) through the ownership of voting securities.

"(5) CONTROLLED GROUP.—For purposes of this subsection, the term 'controlled group' means all persons treated as a single employer under subsection (b), (c), (m), or (o) of section 414 as of the date of the enactment of this subsection.".

(b) AMENDMENT TO EMPLOYEE RETIREMENT INCOME SECURITY ACT OF 1974.—Section 303 of the Employee Retirement Income Security Act of 1974 (29 U.S.C. 1083) is amended by adding at the end the following new subsection:

"(m) SPECIAL RULES FOR COMMUNITY NEWSPAPER PLANS.—

"(1) IN GENERAL.—The plan sponsor of a community newspaper plan under which no participant has had the participant's accrued benefit increased (whether because of service or compensation) after December 31, 2017, may elect to have the alternative standards described in paragraph (3) apply to such plan, and any plan sponsored by any member of the same controlled group.

"(2) ELECTION.—An election under paragraph (1) shall be made at such time and in such manner as prescribed by the Secretary of the Treasury. Such election, once made with respect to a plan year, shall apply to all subsequent plan years unless revoked with the consent of the Secretary of the Treasury.

"(3) ALTERNATIVE MINIMUM FUNDING STANDARDS.—The alternative standards described in this paragraph are the following:

"(A) INTEREST RATES.—

"(i) IN GENERAL.—Notwithstanding subsection (h)(2)(C) and except as provided in clause (ii), the first, second, and third segment rates in effect for any month for purposes of this section shall be 8 percent.

"(ii) NEW BENEFIT ACCRUALS.—Notwithstanding subsection (h)(2), for purposes of determining the funding target and normal cost of a plan for any plan year, the present value of any benefits accrued or earned under the plan for a plan year with respect to which an election under paragraph (1) is in effect shall be determined on the basis of the United States Treasury obligation yield curve for the day that is the valuation date of such plan for such plan year.

"(iii) UNITED STATES TREASURY OBLIGATION YIELD CURVE.—For purposes of this subsection, the term 'United States Treasury obligation yield curve' means, with respect to any day, a yield curve which shall be prescribed by the Secretary of the Treasury for such day on interest-bearing obligations of the United States.

"(B) SHORTFALL AMORTIZATION BASE.—

"(i) PREVIOUS SHORTFALL AMORTIZATION BASES.—The shortfall amortization bases determined under subsection (c)(3) for all plan years preceding the first plan year to which the election under paragraph (1) applies (and all shortfall amortization installments determined with respect to such bases) shall be reduced to zero under rules similar to the rules of subsection (c)(6).

"(ii) NEW SHORTFALL AMORTIZATION BASE.—

Notwithstanding subsection (c)(3), the shortfall amortization base for the first plan year to which the election under paragraph (1) applies shall be the funding shortfall of such plan for such plan year (determined using the interest rates as modified under subparagraph (A)).

"(C) DETERMINATION OF SHORTFALL AMORTIZATION INSTALLMENTS.—

"(i) 30-YEAR PERIOD.—Subparagraphs (A) and (B) of subsection (c)(2) shall be applied by substituting '30-plan-year' for '7-plan-year' each place it appears.

"(ii) NO SPECIAL ELECTION.—The election under subparagraph (D) of subsection (c)(2) shall not apply to any plan year to which the election under paragraph (1) applies.

"(D) EXEMPTION FROM AT-RISK TREATMENT.—Subsection (i) shall not apply.

"(4) COMMUNITY NEWSPAPER PLAN.—For purposes of this subsection—

"(A) IN GENERAL.—The term 'community newspaper plan' means a plan to which this section applies maintained by an employer which, as of December 31, 2017—

"(i) publishes and distributes daily, either electronically or in printed form—

"(I) a community newspaper, or

"(II) 1 or more community newspapers in the same State,

"(ii) is not a company the stock of which is publicly traded (on a stock exchange or in an over-the-counter market), and is not controlled, directly or indirectly, by such a company,

"(iii) is controlled, directly or indirectly—

"(I) by 1 or more persons residing primarily in the State in which the community newspaper is published,

"(II) for not less than 30 years by individuals who are members of the same family,

"(III) by a trust created or organized in the State in which the community newspaper is published, the sole trustees of which are persons described in subclause (I) or (II),

"(IV) by an entity which is described in section 501(c)(3) of the Internal Revenue Code of 1986 and exempt from taxation under section 501(a) of such Code, which is organized and operated in the State in which the community newspaper is published, and the primary purpose of which is to benefit communities in such State, or

"(V) by a combination of persons described in subclause (I), (III), or (IV), and

"(iv) does not control, directly or indirectly, any newspaper in any other State.

"(B) COMMUNITY NEWSPAPER.—The term 'community newspaper' means a newspaper which primarily serves a metropolitan statistical area, as determined by the Office of Management and Budget, with a population of not less than 100,000.

"(C) CONTROL.—A person shall be treated as controlled by another person if such other person possesses, directly or indirectly, the power to direct or cause the direction and management of such person (including the power to elect a majority of the members of the board of directors of such person) through the ownership of voting securities.

"(5) CONTROLLED GROUP.—For purposes of this subsection, the term 'controlled group' means all persons treated as a single employer under subsection (b), (c), (m), or (o) of section 414 of the Internal Revenue Code of 1986 as of the date of the enactment of this subsection.

"(6) EFFECT ON PREMIUM RATE CALCULATION.—Notwithstanding any other provision of law or any regulation issued by the Pension Benefit Guaranty Corporation, in the case of a plan for which an election is made to apply the alternative standards described in paragraph (3), the additional premium under section 4006(a)(3)(E) shall be determined as if such election had not been made.".

(c) EFFECTIVE DATE.—The amendments made by this section shall apply to plan years ending after December 31, 2017.

[¶ 5057] SEC. 116. TREATING EXCLUDED DIFFICULTY OF CARE PAYMENTS AS COMPENSATION FOR DETERMINING RETIREMENT CONTRIBUTION LIMITATIONS.

(a) INDIVIDUAL RETIREMENT ACCOUNTS.—

(1) IN GENERAL.—Section 408(o) of the Internal Revenue Code of 1986 is amended by adding at the end the following new paragraph:

"(5) SPECIAL RULE FOR DIFFICULTY OF CARE PAYMENTS EXCLUDED FROM GROSS INCOME.—In the case of an individual who for a taxable year excludes from gross income under section 131 a qualified foster care payment which is a difficulty of care payment, if—

"(A) the deductible amount in effect for the taxable year under subsection (b), exceeds

"(B) the amount of compensation includible in the individual's gross income for the taxable year,

the individual may elect to increase the nondeductible limit under paragraph (2) for the taxable year by an amount equal to the lesser of such excess or the amount so excluded.".

"(2) EFFECTIVE DATE.—The amendments made by this subsection shall apply to contributions after the date of the enactment of this Act.

(b) DEFINED CONTRIBUTION PLANS.—

(1) IN GENERAL.—Section 415(c) of such Code is amended by adding at the end the following new paragraph:

"(8) SPECIAL RULE FOR DIFFICULTY OF CARE PAYMENTS EXCLUDED FROM GROSS INCOME.—

"(A) IN GENERAL.—For purposes of paragraph (1)(B), in the case of an individual who for a taxable year excludes from gross income under section 131 a qualified foster care payment which is a difficulty of care payment, the participant's compensation, or earned income, as the case may be, shall be increased by the amount so excluded.

"(B) CONTRIBUTIONS ALLOCABLE TO DIFFICULTY OF CARE PAYMENTS TREATED AS AFTER-TAX.—Any contribution by the participant which is allowable due to such increase—

"(i) shall be treated for purposes of this title as investment in the contract, and

"(ii) shall not cause a plan (and any arrangement which is part of such plan) to be treated as failing to meet any requirements of this chapter solely by reason of allowing any such contributions.".

(2) EFFECTIVE DATE.—The amendment made by this subsection shall apply to plan years beginning after December 31, 2015.

TITLE II—ADMINISTRATIVE IMPROVEMENTS

[¶ 5058] SEC. 201. PLAN ADOPTED BY FILING DUE DATE FOR YEAR MAY BE TREATED AS IN EFFECT AS OF CLOSE OF YEAR.

(a) IN GENERAL.—Subsection (b) of section 401 of the Internal Revenue Code of 1986 is amended—

(1) by striking "RETROACTIVE CHANGES IN PLAN.—A stock bonus" and inserting "Plan Amendments.—

"(1) CERTAIN RETROACTIVE CHANGES IN PLAN.—A stock bonus"; and

(2) by adding at the end the following new paragraph:

"(2) ADOPTION OF PLAN.—If an employer adopts a stock bonus, pension, profit-sharing, or annuity plan after the close of a taxable year but before the time prescribed by law for filing the return of the employer for the taxable year (including extensions thereof), the employer may elect to treat the plan as having been adopted as of the last day of the taxable year.".

(b) EFFECTIVE DATE.—The amendments made by this section shall apply to plans adopted for taxable years beginning after December 31, 2019.

[¶ 5059] SEC. 202. COMBINED ANNUAL REPORT FOR GROUP OF PLANS.

(a) IN GENERAL.—The Secretary of the Treasury and the Secretary of Labor shall, in cooperation, modify the returns required under section 6058 of the Internal Revenue Code of 1986 and the reports required by section 104 of the Employee Retirement Income Security Act of 1974 (29 U.S.C. 1024) so that all members of a group of plans described in subsection (c) may file a single aggregated annual return or report satisfying the requirements of both such sections.

(b) ADMINISTRATIVE REQUIREMENTS.—In developing the consolidated return or report under subsection (a), the Secretary of the Treasury and the Secretary of Labor may require such return or report to include any information regarding each plan in the group as such Secretaries determine is necessary or appropriate for the enforcement and administration of the Internal Revenue Code of 1986 and the Employee Retirement Income Security Act of 1974 and shall require such information as will enable a participant in a plan to identify any aggregated return or report filed with respect to the plan.

(c) PLANS DESCRIBED.—A group of plans is described in this subsection if all plans in the group—

(1) are individual account plans or defined contribution plans(as defined in section 3(34) of the Employee Retirement Income Security Act of 1974 (29 U.S.C. 1002(34)) or in section 414(i) of the Internal Revenue Code of 1986);

(2) have—

(A) the same trustee (as described in section 403(a) of such Act (29 U.S.C. 1103(a)));

(B) the same one or more named fiduciaries (as described in section 402(a) of such Act (29 U.S.C. 1102(a)));

(C) the same administrator (as defined in section 3(16)(A) of such Act (29 U.S.C. 1002(16)(A))) and plan administrator (as defined in section 414(g) of the Internal Revenue Code of 1986; and

(D) plan years beginning on the same date; and

(3) provide the same investments or investment options to participants and beneficiaries.

A plan not subject to title I of the Employee Retirement Income Security Act of 1974 shall be treated as meeting the requirements of paragraph (2) as part of a group of plans if the same person that performs each of the functions described in such paragraph, as applicable, for all other plans in such group performs each of such functions for such plan.

(d) CLARIFICATION RELATING TO ELECTRONIC FILING OF RETURNS FOR DEFERRED COMPENSATION PLANS.—

(1) IN GENERAL.—Section 6011(e) of the Internal Revenue Code of 1986 is amended by adding at the end the following new paragraph:

"(6) APPLICATION OF NUMERICAL LIMITATION TO RETURNS RELATING TO DEFERRED COMPENSATION PLANS.—For purposes of applying the numerical limitation under paragraph (2)(A) to any return required under section 6058, information regarding each plan for which information is provided on such return shall be treated as a separate return.".

(2) EFFECTIVE DATE.—The amendment made by paragraph (1) shall apply to returns required to be filed with respect to plan years beginning after December 31, 2019.

(e) EFFECTIVE DATE.—The modification required by subsection (a) shall be implemented not later than January 1, 2022, and shall apply to returns and reports for plan years beginning after December 31, 2021.

[¶5060] SEC. 203. DISCLOSURE REGARDING LIFETIME INCOME.

(a) IN GENERAL.—Subparagraph (B) of section 105(a)(2) of the Employee Retirement Income Security Act of 1974 (29 U.S.C. 1025(a)(2)) is amended—

(1) in clause (i), by striking "and" at the end;

(2) in clause (ii), by striking "diversification." and inserting "diversification, and"; and

(3) by inserting at the end the following:

"(iii) the lifetime income disclosure described in subparagraph (D)(i).

In the case of pension benefit statements described in clause (i) of paragraph (1)(A), a lifetime income disclosure under clause (iii) of this subparagraph shall be required to be included in only one pension benefit statement during any one 12-month period.".

(b) LIFETIME INCOME.—Paragraph (2) of section 105(a) of the Employee Retirement Income Security Act of 1974 (29 U.S.C. 1025(a)) is amended by adding at the end the following new subparagraph:

"(D) LIFETIME INCOME DISCLOSURE.—

"(i) IN GENERAL.—

"(I) DISCLOSURE.—A lifetime income disclosure shall set forth the lifetime income stream equivalent of the total benefits accrued with respect to the participant or beneficiary.

"(II) LIFETIME INCOME STREAM EQUIVALENT OF THE TOTAL BENEFITS ACCRUED.—For purposes of this subparagraph, the term 'lifetime income stream equivalent of the total benefits accrued' means the amount of monthly payments the participant or beneficiary would receive if the total accrued benefits of such participant or beneficiary were used to provide lifetime income streams described in subclause (III), based on assumptions specified in rules prescribed by the Secretary.

"(III) LIFETIME INCOME STREAMS.—The lifetime income streams described in this subclause are a qualified joint and survivor annuity (as defined in section 205(d)), based on assumptions specified in rules prescribed by the Secretary, including the assumption that the participant or beneficiary has a spouse of equal age, and a single life annuity. Such lifetime income streams may have a term certain or other features to the extent permitted under rules prescribed by the Secretary.

"(ii) MODEL DISCLOSURE.—Not later than 1 year after the date of the enactment of the Setting Every Community Up for Retirement Enhancement Act of 2019, the Secretary shall issue a model lifetime income disclosure, written in a manner so as to be understood by the average plan participant, which—

"(I) explains that the lifetime income stream equivalent is only provided as an illustration;

"(II) explains that the actual payments under the lifetime income stream described in clause (i)(III) which may be purchased with the total benefits accrued will depend on numerous factors and may vary substantially from the lifetime income stream equivalent in the disclosures;

"(III) explains the assumptions upon which the lifetime income stream equivalent was determined; and

"(IV) provides such other similar explanations as the Secretary considers appropriate.

"(iii) ASSUMPTIONS AND RULES.—Not later than 1 year after the date of the enactment of the Setting Every Community Up for Retirement Enhancement Act of 2019, the Secretary shall—

"(I) prescribe assumptions which administrators of individual account plans may use in converting total accrued benefits into lifetime income stream equivalents for purposes of this subparagraph; and

"(II) issue interim final rules under clause (i).

In prescribing assumptions under subclause (I), the Secretary may prescribe a single set of specific assumptions (in which case the Secretary may issue tables or factors which facilitate such conversions), or ranges of permissible assumptions. To the extent that an accrued benefit is or may be invested in a lifetime income stream described in clause (i)(III), the assumptions prescribed under subclause (I) shall, to the extent appropriate, permit administrators of individual account plans to use the amounts payable under such lifetime income stream as a lifetime income stream equivalent.

"(iv) LIMITATION ON LIABILITY.—No plan fiduciary, plan sponsor, or other person shall have any liability under this title solely by reason of the provision of lifetime income stream equivalents which are derived in accordance with the assumptions and rules described in clause (iii) and which include the explanations contained in the model lifetime income disclosure described in clause (ii). This clause shall apply without regard to whether the provision of such lifetime income stream equivalent is required by subparagraph (B)(iii).

"(v) EFFECTIVE DATE.—The requirement in subparagraph (B)(iii) shall apply to pension benefit statements furnished more than 12 months after the latest of the issuance by the Secretary of—

"(I) interim final rules under clause (i);

"(II) the model disclosure under clause (ii); or

"(III) the assumptions under clause (iii).".

[¶ 5061] SEC. 204. FIDUCIARY SAFE HARBOR FOR SELECTION OF LIFETIME INCOME PROVIDER.

Section 404 of the Employee Retirement Income Security Act of 1974 (29 U.S.C. 1104) is amended by adding at the end the following:

"(e) SAFE HARBOR FOR ANNUITY SELECTION.—

"(1) IN GENERAL.—With respect to the selection of an insurer for a guaranteed retirement income contract, the requirements of subsection (a)(1)(B) will be deemed to be satisfied if a fiduciary—

"(A) engages in an objective, thorough, and analytical search for the purpose of identifying insurers from which to purchase such contracts;

"(B) with respect to each insurer identified under subparagraph (A)—

"(i) considers the financial capability of such insurer to satisfy its obligations under the guaranteed retirement income contract; and "(ii) considers the cost (including fees and commissions) of the guaranteed retirement income contract offered by the insurer in relation to the benefits and product features of the contract and administrative services to be provided under such contract; and

"(C) on the basis of such consideration, concludes that—

"(i) at the time of the selection, the insurer is financially capable of satisfying its obligations under the guaranteed retirement income contract; and

"(ii) the relative cost of the selected guaranteed retirement income contract as described in subparagraph (B)(ii) is reasonable.

"(2) FINANCIAL CAPABILITY OF THE INSURER.—A fiduciary will be deemed to satisfy the requirements of paragraphs (1)(B)(i) and (1)(C)(i) if—

"(A) the fiduciary obtains written representations from the insurer that—

"(i) the insurer is licensed to offer guaranteed retirement income contracts;

"(ii) the insurer, at the time of selection and for each of the immediately preceding 7 plan years—

"(I) operates under a certificate of authority from the insurance commissioner of its domiciliary State which has not been revoked or suspended;

"(II) has filed audited financial statements in accordance with the laws of its domiciliary State under applicable statutory accounting principles;

"(III) maintains (and has maintained) reserves which satisfies all the statutory requirements of all States where the insurer does business; and

"(IV) is not operating under an order of supervision, rehabilitation, or liquidation;

"(iii) the insurer undergoes, at least every 5 years, a financial examination (within the meaning of the law of its domiciliary State) by the insurance commissioner of the domiciliary State (or representative, designee, or other party approved by such commissioner); and

"(iv) the insurer will notify the fiduciary of any change in circumstances occurring after the provision of the representations in clauses (i), (ii), and (iii) which would preclude the insurer from making such representations at the time of issuance of the guaranteed retirement income contract; and

"(B) after receiving such representations and as of the time of selection, the fiduciary has not received any notice described in subparagraph (A)(iv) and is in possession of no other information which would cause the fiduciary to question the representations provided.

"(3) NO REQUIREMENT TO SELECT LOWEST COST.—Nothing in this subsection shall be construed to require a fiduciary to select the lowest cost contract. A fiduciary may consider the value of a contract, including features and benefits of the contract and attributes of the insurer (including, without limitation, the insurer's financial strength) in conjunction with the cost of the contract.

"(4) TIME OF SELECTION.—

"(A) IN GENERAL.—For purposes of this subsection, the time of selection is—

"(i) the time that the insurer and the contract are selected for distribution of benefits to a specific participant or beneficiary; or

"(ii) if the fiduciary periodically reviews the continuing appropriateness of the conclusion described in paragraph (1)(C) with respect to a selected insurer, taking into account the considerations described in such paragraph, the time that the insurer and the contract are selected to provide benefits at future dates to participants or beneficiaries under the plan.

Nothing in the preceding sentence shall be construed to require the fiduciary to review the appropriateness of a selection after the purchase of a contract for a participant or beneficiary.

"(B) PERIODIC REVIEW.—A fiduciary will be deemed to have conducted the periodic review described in subparagraph (A)(ii) if the fiduciary obtains the written representations described in clauses (i), (ii), and (iii) of paragraph (2)(A) from the insurer on an annual basis, unless the fiduciary receives any notice described in paragraph (2)(A)(iv) or otherwise becomes aware of facts that would cause the fiduciary to question such representations.

"(5) LIMITED LIABILITY.—A fiduciary which satisfies the requirements of this subsection shall not be liable following the distribution of any benefit, or the investment by or on behalf of a participant or beneficiary pursuant to the selected guaranteed retirement income contract, for any losses that may result to the participant or beneficiary due to an insurer's inability to satisfy its financial obligations under the terms of such contract.

"(6) DEFINITIONS.—For purposes of this subsection—

"(A) INSURER.—The term 'insurer' means an insurance company, insurance service, or insurance organization, including affiliates of such companies.

"(B) GUARANTEED RETIREMENT INCOME CONTRACT.—The term 'guaranteed retirement income contract' means an annuity contract for a fixed term or a contract (or provision or feature thereof) which provides guaranteed benefits annually (or more frequently) for at least the remainder of the life of the participant or the joint lives of the participant and the participant's designated beneficiary as part of an individual account plan.".

[¶ 5062] SEC. 205. MODIFICATION OF NONDISCRIMINATION RULES TO PROTECT OLDER, LONGER SERVICE PARTICIPANTS.

(a) IN GENERAL.—Section 401 of the Internal Revenue Code of 1986 is amended—

(1) by redesignating subsection (o) as subsection (p); and

(2) by inserting after subsection (n) the following new subsection:

"(o) SPECIAL RULES FOR APPLYING NONDISCRIMINATION RULES TO PROTECT OLDER, LONGER SERVICE AND GRANDFATHERED PARTICIPANTS.—

"(1) TESTING OF DEFINED BENEFIT PLANS WITH CLOSED CLASSES OF PARTICIPANTS.—

"(A) BENEFITS, RIGHTS, OR FEATURES PROVIDED TO CLOSED CLASSES.—A defined benefit plan which provides benefits, rights, or features to a closed class of participants shall not fail to satisfy the requirements of subsection (a)(4) by reason of the composition of such closed class or the benefits, rights, or features provided to such closed class, if—

"(i) for the plan year as of which the class closes and the 2 succeeding plan years, such benefits, rights, and features satisfy the requirements of subsection (a)(4) (without regard to this subparagraph but taking into account the rules of subparagraph (I)),

"(ii) after the date as of which the class was closed, any plan amendment which modifies the closed class or the benefits, rights, and features provided to such closed class does not discriminate significantly in favor of highly compensated employees, and

"(iii) the class was closed before April 5, 2017, or the plan is described in subparagraph (C).

"(B) AGGREGATE TESTING WITH DEFINED CONTRIBUTION PLANS PERMITTED ON A BENEFITS BASIS.—

"(i) IN GENERAL.—For purposes of determining compliance with subsection (a)(4) and section 410(b), a defined benefit plan described in clause (iii) may be aggregated and tested on a benefits basis with 1 or more defined contribution plans, including with the portion of 1 or more defined contribution plans which—

"(I) provides matching contributions (as defined in subsection (m)(4)(A)),

"(II) provides annuity contracts described in section 403(b) which are purchased with matching contributions or nonelective contributions, or

"(III) consists of an employee stock ownership plan (within the meaning of section 4975(e)(7)) or a tax credit employee stock ownership plan (within the meaning of section 409(a)).

"(ii) SPECIAL RULES FOR MATCHING CONTRIBUTIONS.—For purposes of clause (i), if a defined benefit plan is aggregated with a portion of a defined contribution plan providing matching contributions—

"(I) such defined benefit plan must also be aggregated with any portion of such defined contribution plan which provides elective deferrals described in subparagraph (A) or (C) of section 402(g)(3), and

"(II) such matching contributions shall be treated in the same manner as nonelective contributions, including for purposes of applying the rules of subsection (l).

"(iii) PLANS DESCRIBED.—A defined benefit plan is described in this clause if—

"(I) the plan provides benefits to a closed class of participants,

"(II) for the plan year as of which the class closes and the 2 succeeding plan years, the plan satisfies the requirements of section 410(b) and subsection (a)(4) (without regard to this subparagraph but taking into account the rules of subparagraph (I)),

"(III) after the date as of which the class was closed, any plan amendment which modifies the closed class or the benefits provided to such closed class does not discriminate significantly in favor of highly compensated employees, and

"(IV) the class was closed before April 5, 2017, or the plan is described in subparagraph (C).

"(C) PLANS DESCRIBED.—A plan is described in this subparagraph if, taking into account any predecessor plan—

"(i) such plan has been in effect for at least 5 years as of the date the class is closed, and

"(ii) during the 5-year period preceding the date the class is closed, there has not been a substantial increase in the coverage or value of the benefits, rights, or features described in subparagraph (A) or in the coverage or benefits under the plan described in subparagraph (B)(iii) (whichever is applicable).

"(D) DETERMINATION OF SUBSTANTIAL INCREASE FOR BENEFITS, RIGHTS, AND FEATURES.—In applying subparagraph (C)(ii) for purposes of subparagraph (A)(iii), a plan shall be treated as having had a substantial increase in coverage or value of the benefits, rights, or features described in subparagraph (A) during the applicable 5-year period only if, during such period—

"(i) the number of participants covered by such benefits, rights, or features on the date such period ends is more than 50 percent greater than the number of such participants on the first day of the plan year in which such period began, or

"(ii) such benefits, rights, and features have been modified by 1 or more plan amendments in such a way that, as of the date the class is closed, the value of such benefits, rights, and features to the closed class as a whole is substantially greater than the value as of the first day of such 5-year period, solely as a result of such amendments.

"(E) DETERMINATION OF SUBSTANTIAL INCREASE FOR AGGREGATE TESTING ON BENEFITS BASIS.—In applying subparagraph (C)(ii) for purposes of subparagraph (B)(iii)(IV), a plan shall be treated as having had a substantial increase in coverage or benefits during the applicable 5-year period only if, during such period—

"(i) the number of participants benefitting under the plan on the date such period ends is more than 50 percent greater than the number of such participants on the first day of the plan year in which such period began, or

"(ii) the average benefit provided to such participants on the date such period ends is more than 50 percent greater than the average benefit provided on the first day of the plan year in which such period began.

"(F) CERTAIN EMPLOYEES DISREGARDED.—For purposes of subparagraphs (D) and (E), any increase in coverage or value or in coverage or benefits, whichever is applicable, which is attributable to such coverage and value or coverage and benefits provided to employees—

"(i) who became participants as a result of a merger, acquisition, or similar event which occurred during the 7-year period preceding the date the class is closed, or

"(ii) who became participants by reason of a merger of the plan with another plan which had been in effect for at least 5 years as of the date of the merger,

shall be disregarded, except that clause (ii) shall apply for purposes of subparagraph (D) only if, under the merger, the benefits, rights, or features under 1 plan are conformed to the benefits, rights, or features of the other plan prospectively.

"(G) RULES RELATING TO AVERAGE BENEFIT.—For purposes of subparagraph (E)—

"(i) the average benefit provided to participants under the plan will be treated as having remained the same between the 2 dates described in subparagraph (E)(ii) if the benefit formula applicable to such participants has not changed between such dates, and

"(ii) if the benefit formula applicable to 1 or more participants under the plan has changed between such 2 dates, then the average benefit under the plan shall be considered to have increased by more than 50 percent only if—

"(I) the total amount determined under section 430(b)(1)(A)(i) for all participants benefitting under the plan for the plan year in which the 5-year period described in subparagraph (E) ends, exceeds

"(II) the total amount determined under section 430(b)(1)(A)(i) for all such participants for such plan year, by using the benefit formula in effect for each such participant for the first plan year in such 5-year period,

by more than 50 percent. In the case of a CSEC plan (as defined in section 414(y)), the normal cost of the plan (as determined under section 433(j)(1)(B)) shall be used in lieu of the amount determined under section 430(b)(1)(A)(i).

"(H) TREATMENT AS SINGLE PLAN.—For purposes of subparagraphs (E) and (G), a plan described in section 413(c) shall be treated as a single plan rather than as separate plans maintained by each employer in the plan.

"(I) SPECIAL RULES.—For purposes of subparagraphs (A)(i) and (B)(iii)(II), the following rules shall apply:

"(i) In applying section 410(b)(6)(C), the closing of the class of participants shall not be treated as a significant change in coverage under section 410(b)(6)(C)(i)(II).

"(ii) 2 or more plans shall not fail to be eligible to be aggregated and treated as a single plan solely by reason of having different plan years.

"(iii) Changes in the employee population shall be disregarded to the extent attributable to individuals who become employees or cease to be employees, after the date the class is closed, by reason of a merger, acquisition, divestiture, or similar event.

"(iv) Aggregation and all other testing methodologies otherwise applicable under subsection (a)(4) and section 410(b) may be taken into account.

The rule of clause (ii) shall also apply for purposes of determining whether plans to which subparagraph (B)(i) applies may be aggregated and treated as 1 plan for purposes of determining whether such plans meet the requirements of subsection (a)(4) and section 410(b).

"(J) SPUN-OFF PLANS.—For purposes of this paragraph, if a portion of a defined benefit plan described in subparagraph (A) or (B)(iii) is spun off to another employer and the spun-off plan continues to satisfy the requirements of—

"(i) subparagraph (A)(i) or (B)(iii)(II), whichever is applicable, if the original plan was still within the 3-year period described in such subparagraph at the time of the spin off, and

"(ii) subparagraph (A)(ii) or (B)(iii)(III), whichever is applicable,

the treatment under subparagraph (A) or (B) of the spun-off plan shall continue with respect to such other employer.

"(2) TESTING OF DEFINED CONTRIBUTION PLANS.—

"(A) TESTING ON A BENEFITS BASIS.—A defined contribution plan shall be permitted to be tested on a benefits basis if—

"(i) such defined contribution plan provides make-whole contributions to a closed class of participants whose accruals under a defined benefit plan have been reduced or eliminated,

"(ii) for the plan year of the defined contribution plan as of which the class eligible to receive such make-whole contributions closes and the 2 succeeding plan years, such closed class of participants satisfies the requirements of section 410(b)(2)(A)(i) (determined by applying the rules of paragraph (1)(I)),

"(iii) after the date as of which the class was closed, any plan amendment to the defined contribution plan which modifies the closed class or the allocations, benefits, rights, and features provided to such closed class does not discriminate significantly in favor of highly compensated employees, and

"(iv) the class was closed before April 5, 2017, or the defined benefit plan under clause (i) is described in paragraph (1)(C) (as applied for purposes of paragraph (1)(B)(iii)(IV)).

"(B) AGGREGATION WITH PLANS INCLUDING MATCHING CONTRIBUTIONS.—

"(i) IN GENERAL.—With respect to 1 or more defined contribution plans described in subparagraph (A), for purposes of determining compliance with subsection (a)(4) and section 410(b), the portion of such plans which provides make-whole contributions or other nonelective contributions may be aggregated and tested on a benefits basis with the portion of 1 or more other defined contribution plans which—

"(I) provides matching contributions (as defined in subsection (m)(4)(A)),

"(II) provides annuity contracts described in section 403(b) which are purchased with matching contributions or nonelective contributions, or

"(III) consists of an employee stock ownership plan (within the meaning of section 4975(e)(7)) or a tax credit employee stock ownership plan (within the meaning of section 409(a)).

"(ii) SPECIAL RULES FOR MATCHING CONTRIBUTIONS.—Rules similar to the rules of paragraph (1)(B)(ii) shall apply for purposes of clause (i).

"(C) SPECIAL RULES FOR TESTING DEFINED CONTRIBUTION PLAN FEATURES PROVIDING MATCHING CONTRIBUTIONS TO CERTAIN OLDER, LONGER SERVICE PARTICIPANTS.—In the case of a defined contribution plan which provides benefits, rights, or features to a closed class of participants whose accruals under a defined benefit plan have been reduced or eliminated, the plan shall not fail to satisfy the requirements of subsection (a)(4) solely by reason of the composition of the closed class or the benefits, rights, or features provided to such closed class if the defined contribution plan and defined benefit plan otherwise meet the requirements of subparagraph (A) but for the fact that the make-whole contributions under the defined contribution plan are made in whole or in part through matching contributions.

"(D) SPUN-OFF PLANS.—For purposes of this paragraph, if a portion of a defined contribution plan described in subparagraph (A) or (C) is spun off to another employer, the treatment under subparagraph (A) or (C) of the spun-off plan shall continue with respect to the other employer if such plan continues to comply with the requirements of clauses (ii) (if the original plan was still within the 3-year period described in such clause at the time of the spin off) and (iii) of subparagraph (A), as determined for purposes of subparagraph (A) or (C), whichever is applicable.

"(3) DEFINITIONS AND SPECIAL RULE.—For purposes of this subsection—

"(A) MAKE-WHOLE CONTRIBUTIONS.—Except as otherwise provided in paragraph (2)(C), the term 'make-whole contributions' means nonelective allocations for each employee in the class which are reasonably calculated, in a consistent manner, to replace some or all of the retirement benefits which the employee would have received under the defined benefit plan and any other plan or qualified cash or deferred arrangement under subsection (k)(2) if no change had been made to such defined benefit plan and such other plan or arrangement. For purposes of the preceding sentence, consistency shall not be required with respect to employees who were subject to different benefit formulas under the defined benefit plan.

"(B) REFERENCES TO CLOSED CLASS OF PARTICIPANTS.—

References to a closed class of participants and similar references to a closed class shall include arrangements under which 1 or more classes of participants are closed, except that 1 or more classes of participants closed on different dates shall not be aggregated for purposes of determining the date any such class was closed.

"(C) HIGHLY COMPENSATED EMPLOYEE.—The term 'highly compensated employee' has the meaning given such term in section 414(q).".

(b) PARTICIPATION REQUIREMENTS.—Paragraph (26) of section 401(a) of the Internal Revenue Code of 1986 is amended by adding at the end the following new subparagraph:

"(I) PROTECTED PARTICIPANTS.—

"(i) IN GENERAL.—A plan shall be deemed to satisfy the requirements of subparagraph (A) if—

"(I) the plan is amended—

"(aa) to cease all benefit accruals, or

"(bb) to provide future benefit accruals only to a closed class of participants,

"(II) the plan satisfies subparagraph (A) (without regard to this subparagraph) as of the effective date of the amendment, and

"(III) the amendment was adopted before April 5, 2017, or the plan is described in clause (ii).

¶5062 SEC. 205(b)

"(ii) PLANS DESCRIBED.—A plan is described in this clause if the plan would be described in subsection (o)(1)(C), as applied for purposes of subsection (o)(1)(B)(iii)(IV) and by treating the effective date of the amendment as the date the class was closed for purposes of subsection (o)(1)(C).

"(iii) SPECIAL RULES.—For purposes of clause (i)(II), in applying section 410(b)(6)(C), the amendments described in clause (i) shall not be treated as a significant change in coverage under section 410(b)(6)(C)(i)(II).

"(iv) SPUN-OFF PLANS.—For purposes of this subparagraph, if a portion of a plan described in clause (i) is spun off to another employer, the treatment under clause (i) of the spun-off plan shall continue with respect to the other employer.".

(c) EFFECTIVE DATE.—

(1) IN GENERAL.—Except as provided in paragraph (2), the amendments made by this section shall take effect on the date of the enactment of this Act, without regard to whether any plan modifications referred to in such amendments are adopted or effective before, on, or after such date of enactment.

(2) SPECIAL RULES.—

(A) ELECTION OF EARLIER APPLICATION.—At the election of the plan sponsor, the amendments made by this section shall apply to plan years beginning after December 31, 2013.

(B) CLOSED CLASSES OF PARTICIPANTS.—For purposes of paragraphs (1)(A)(iii), (1)(B)(iii)(IV), and (2)(A)(iv) of section 401(o) of the Internal Revenue Code of 1986 (as added by this section), a closed class of participants shall be treated as being closed before April 5, 2017, if the plan sponsor's intention to create such closed class is reflected in formal written documents and communicated to participants before such date.

(C) CERTAIN POST-ENACTMENT PLAN AMENDMENTS.—A plan shall not be treated as failing to be eligible for the application of section 401(o)(1)(A), 401(o)(1)(B)(iii), or 401(a)(26) of such Code (as added by this section) to such plan solely because in the case of—

(i) such section 401(o)(1)(A), the plan was amended before the date of the enactment of this Act to eliminate 1 or more benefits, rights, or features, and is further amended after such date of enactment to provide such previously eliminated benefits, rights, or features to a closed class of participants, or

(ii) such section 401(o)(1)(B)(iii) or section 401(a)(26), the plan was amended before the date of the enactment of this Act to cease all benefit accruals, and is further amended after such date of enactment to provide benefit accruals to a closed class of participants.

Any such section shall only apply if the plan otherwise meets the requirements of such section and in applying such section, the date the class of participants is closed shall be the effective date of the later amendment.

[¶ 5063] SEC. 206. MODIFICATION OF PBGC PREMIUMS FOR CSEC PLANS.

(a) FLAT RATE PREMIUM.—Subparagraph (A) of section 4006(a)(3) of the Employee Retirement Income Security Act of 1974 (29 U.S.C. 1306(a)(3)) is amended—

(1) in clause (i), by striking "plan," and inserting "plan other than a CSEC plan (as defined in section 210(f)(1))";

(2) in clause (v), by striking "or" at the end;

(3) in clause (vi), by striking the period at the end and inserting ", or"; and

(4) by adding at the end the following new clause:

"(vii) in the case of a CSEC plan (as defined in section 210(f)(1)), for plan years beginning after December 31, 2018, for each individual who is a participant in such plan during the plan year an amount equal to the sum of—

"(I) the additional premium (if any) determined under subparagraph (E), and

"(II) $19.".

(b) VARIABLE RATE PREMIUM.—

(1) UNFUNDED VESTED BENEFITS.—

(A) IN GENERAL.—Subparagraph (E) of section 4006(a)(3) of the Employee Retirement Income Security Act of 1974 (29 U.S.C. 1306(a)(3)) is amended by adding at the end the following new clause:

"(v) For purposes of clause (ii), in the case of a CSEC plan (as defined in section 210(f)(1)), the term 'unfunded vested benefits' means, for plan years beginning after December 31, 2018, the excess (if any) of—

"(I) the funding liability of the plan as determined under section 306(j)(5)(C) for the plan year by only taking into account vested benefits, over

"(II) the fair market value of plan assets for the plan year which are held by the plan on the valuation date.".

(B) CONFORMING AMENDMENT.—Clause (iii) of section 4006(a)(3)(E) of such Act (29 U.S.C. 1306(a)(3)(E)) is amended by striking "For purposes" and inserting "Except as provided in clause (v), for purposes".

(2) APPLICABLE DOLLAR AMOUNT.—

(A) IN GENERAL.—Paragraph (8) of section 4006(a) of such Act (29 U.S.C. 1306(a)) is amended by adding at the end the following new subparagraph:

"(E) CSEC PLANS.—In the case of a CSEC plan (as defined in section 210(f)(1)), the applicable dollar amount shall be $9.".

(B) CONFORMING AMENDMENT.—Subparagraph (A) of section 4006(a)(8) of such Act (29 U.S.C. 1306(a)(8)) is amended by striking "(B) and (C)" and inserting "(B), (C), and (E)".

TITLE III—OTHER BENEFITS

[¶ 5064] SEC. 301. BENEFITS PROVIDED TO VOLUNTEER FIREFIGHTERS AND EMERGENCY MEDICAL RESPONDERS.

(a) INCREASE IN DOLLAR LIMITATION ON QUALIFIED PAYMENTS.—Subparagraph (B) of section 139B(c)(2) of the Internal Revenue Code of 1986 is amended by striking "$30" and inserting "$50".

(b) EXTENSION.—Section 139B(d) of the Internal Revenue Code of 1986 is amended by striking "beginning after December 31, 2010." and inserting "beginning—

"(1) after December 31, 2010, and before January 1, 2020, or

"(2) after December 31, 2020.".

(c) TECHNICAL CORRECTION.—Section 3121(a)(23) of such Code is amended by striking "139B(b)" and inserting "section 139B(a)".

(d) EFFECTIVE DATE.—The amendments made by this section shall apply to taxable years beginning after December 31, 2019.

[¶ 5065] SEC. 302. EXPANSION OF SECTION 529 PLANS.

(a) DISTRIBUTIONS FOR CERTAIN EXPENSES ASSOCIATED WITH REGISTERED APPRENTICESHIP PROGRAMS.—Section 529(c) of the Internal Revenue Code of 1986 is amended by adding at the end the following new paragraph:

"(8) TREATMENT OF CERTAIN EXPENSES ASSOCIATED WITH REGISTERED APPRENTICESHIP PROGRAMS.—Any reference in this subsection to the term 'qualified higher education expense' shall include a reference to expenses for fees, books, supplies, and equipment required for the participation of a designated beneficiary in an apprenticeship program registered and certified with the Secretary of Labor under section 1 of the National Apprenticeship Act (29 U.S.C. 50).".

¶ 5064   SEC. 206(b)

(b) DISTRIBUTIONS FOR QUALIFIED EDUCATION LOAN REPAYMENTS.—

(1) IN GENERAL.—Section 529(c) of such Code, as amended by subsection (a), is amended by adding at the end the following new paragraph:

"(9) TREATMENT OF QUALIFIED EDUCATION LOAN REPAYMENTS.—

"(A) IN GENERAL.—Any reference in this subsection to the term 'qualified higher education expense' shall include a reference to amounts paid as principal or interest on any qualified education loan (as defined in section 221(d)) of the designated beneficiary or a sibling of the designated beneficiary.

"(B) LIMITATION.—The amount of distributions treated as a qualified higher education expense under this paragraph with respect to the loans of any individual shall not exceed $10,000 (reduced by the amount of distributions so treated for all prior taxable years).

"(C) SPECIAL RULES FOR SIBLINGS OF THE DESIGNATED BENEFICIARY.—

"(i) SEPARATE ACCOUNTING.—For purposes of subparagraph (B) and subsection (d), amounts treated as a qualified higher education expense with respect to the loans of a sibling of the designated beneficiary shall be taken into account with respect to such sibling and not with respect to such designated beneficiary.

"(ii) SIBLING DEFINED.—For purposes of this paragraph, the term 'sibling' means an individual who bears a relationship to the designated beneficiary which is described in section 152(d)(2)(B).".

(2) COORDINATION WITH DEDUCTION FOR STUDENT LOAN INTEREST.—Section 221(e)(1) of such Code is amended by adding at the end the following: "The deduction otherwise allowable under subsection (a)(prior to the application of subsection (b)) to the taxpayer for any taxable year shall be reduced (but not below zero) by so much of the distributions treated as a qualified higher education expense under section 529(c)(9) with respect to loans of the taxpayer as would be includible in gross income under section 529(c)(3)(A) for such taxable year but for such treatment.".

(c) EFFECTIVE DATE.—The amendments made by this section shall apply to distributions made after December 31, 2018.

TITLE IV—REVENUE PROVISIONS

[¶5066] SEC. 401. MODIFICATION OF REQUIRED DISTRIBUTION RULES FOR DESIGNATED BENEFICIARIES.

(a) MODIFICATION OF RULES WHERE EMPLOYEE DIES BEFORE ENTIRE DISTRIBUTION.—

(1) IN GENERAL.—Section 401(a)(9) of the Internal Revenue Code of 1986 is amended by adding at the end the following new subparagraph:

"(H) SPECIAL RULES FOR CERTAIN DEFINED CONTRIBUTION PLANS.—In the case of a defined contribution plan, if an employee dies before the distribution of the employee's entire interest—

"(i) IN GENERAL.—Except in the case of a beneficiary who is not a designated beneficiary, subparagraph (B)(ii)—

"(I) shall be applied by substituting '10 years' for '5 years', and

"(II) shall apply whether or not distributions of the employee's interests have begun in accordance with subparagraph (A).

"(ii) EXCEPTION FOR ELIGIBLE DESIGNATED BENEFICIARIES.—Subparagraph (B)(iii) shall apply only in the case of an eligible designated beneficiary.

"(iii) RULES UPON DEATH OF ELIGIBLE DESIGNATED BENEFICIARY.—If an eligible designated beneficiary dies before the portion of the employee's interest to which this subparagraph applies is entirely distributed, the exception under clause (ii) shall not apply to any beneficiary of such eligible designated beneficiary and the remainder of such portion shall be distributed within 10 years after the death of such eligible designated beneficiary.

"(iv) SPECIAL RULE IN CASE OF CERTAIN TRUSTS FOR DISABLED OR CHRONICALLY ILL BENEFICIARIES.—In the case of an applicable multi-beneficiary trust, if under the terms of the trust—

"(I) it is to be divided immediately upon the death of the employee into separate trusts for each beneficiary, or

"(II) no individual (other than a eligible designated beneficiary described in subclause (III) or (IV) of subparagraph (E)(ii)) has any right to the employee's interest in the plan until the death of all such eligible designated beneficiaries with respect to the trust,

for purposes of a trust described in subclause (I), clause (ii) shall be applied separately with respect to the portion of the employee's interest that is payable to any eligible designated beneficiary described in subclause (III) or (IV) of subparagraph (E)(ii); and, for purposes of a trust described in subclause (II), subparagraph (B)(iii) shall apply to the distribution of the employee's interest and any beneficiary who is not such an eligible designated beneficiary shall be treated as a beneficiary of the eligible designated beneficiary upon the death of such eligible designated beneficiary.

"(v) APPLICABLE MULTI-BENEFICIARY TRUST.—For purposes of this subparagraph, the term 'applicable multi-beneficiary trust' means a trust—

"(I) which has more than one beneficiary,

"(II) all of the beneficiaries of which are treated as designated beneficiaries for purposes of determining the distribution period pursuant to this paragraph, and

"(III) at least one of the beneficiaries of which is an eligible designated beneficiary described in subclause (III) or (IV) of subparagraph (E)(ii).

"(vi) APPLICATION TO CERTAIN ELIGIBLE RETIREMENT PLANS.—For purposes of applying the provisions of this subparagraph in determining amounts required to be distributed pursuant to this paragraph, all eligible retirement plans (as defined in section 402(c)(8)(B), other than a defined benefit plan described in clause (iv) or (v) thereof or a qualified trust which is a part of a defined benefit plan) shall be treated as a defined contribution plan.".

(2) DEFINITION OF ELIGIBLE DESIGNATED BENEFICIARY.—Section 401(a)(9)(E) of such Code is amended to read as follows:

"(E) DEFINITIONS AND RULES RELATING TO DESIGNATED BENEFICIARIES.—For purposes of this paragraph—

"(i) DESIGNATED BENEFICIARY.—The term 'designated beneficiary' means any individual designated as a beneficiary by the employee.

"(ii) ELIGIBLE DESIGNATED BENEFICIARY.—The term 'eligible designated beneficiary' means, with respect to any employee, any designated beneficiary who is—

"(I) the surviving spouse of the employee,

"(II) subject to clause (iii), a child of the employee who has not reached majority (within the meaning of subparagraph (F)),

"(III) disabled (within the meaning of section 72(m)(7)),

"(IV) a chronically ill individual (within the meaning of section 7702B(c)(2), except that the requirements of subparagraph (A)(i) thereof shall only be treated as met if there is a certification that, as of such date, the period of inability described in such subparagraph with respect to the individual is an indefinite one which is reasonably expected to be lengthy in nature), or

"(V) an individual not described in any of the preceding subclauses who is not more than 10 years younger than the employee.

The determination of whether a designated beneficiary is an eligible designated beneficiary shall be made as of the date of death of the employee.

"(iii) SPECIAL RULE FOR CHILDREN.—Subject to subparagraph (F), an individual described in clause (ii)(II) shall cease to be an eligible designated beneficiary as of the date the individual reaches majority and any remainder of the portion of the individual's interest to which subparagraph (H)(ii) applies shall be distributed within 10 years after such date.".

(b) EFFECTIVE DATES.—

(1) IN GENERAL.—Except as provided in this subsection, the amendments made by this section shall apply to distributions with respect to employees who die after December 31, 2019.

¶5066 SEC. 401(a)(2)

(2) COLLECTIVE BARGAINING EXCEPTION.—In the case of a plan maintained pursuant to 1 or more collective bargaining agreements between employee representatives and 1 or more employers ratified before the date of enactment of this Act, the amendments made by this section shall apply to distributions with respect to employees who die in calendar years beginning after the earlier of—

(A) the later of—

(i) the date on which the last of such collective bargaining agreements terminates (determined without regard to any extension thereof agreed to on or after the date of the enactment of this Act), or

(ii) December 31, 2019, or

(B) December 31, 2021.

For purposes of subparagraph (A)(i), any plan amendment made pursuant to a collective bargaining agreement relating to the plan which amends the plan solely to conform to any requirement added by this section shall not be treated as a termination of such collective bargaining agreement.

(3) GOVERNMENTAL PLANS.—In the case of a governmental plan (as defined in section 414(d) of the Internal Revenue Code of 1986), paragraph (1) shall be applied by substituting "December 31, 2021" for "December 31, 2019".

(4) EXCEPTION FOR CERTAIN EXISTING ANNUITY CONTRACTS.—

(A) IN GENERAL.—The amendments made by this section shall not apply to a qualified annuity which is a binding annuity contract in effect on the date of enactment of this Act and at all times thereafter.

(B) QUALIFIED ANNUITY.—For purposes of this paragraph, the term "qualified annuity" means, with respect to an employee, an annuity—

(i) which is a commercial annuity (as defined in section 3405(e)(6) of the Internal Revenue Code of 1986);

(ii) under which the annuity payments are made over the life of the employee or over the joint lives of such employee and a designated beneficiary (or over a period not extending beyond the life expectancy of such employee or the joint life expectancy of such employee and a designated beneficiary) in accordance with the regulations described in section 401(a)(9)(A)(ii) of such Code (as in effect before such amendments) and which meets the other requirements of section 401(a)(9) of such Code (as so in effect) with respect to such payments; and

(iii) with respect to which—

(I) annuity payments to the employee have begun before the date of enactment of this Act, and the employee has made an irrevocable election before such date as to the method and amount of the annuity payments to the employee or any designated beneficiaries; or

(II) if subclause (I) does not apply, the employee has made an irrevocable election before the date of enactment of this Act as to the method and amount of the annuity payments to the employee or any designated beneficiaries.

(5) EXCEPTION FOR CERTAIN BENEFICIARIES.—

(A) IN GENERAL.—If an employee dies before the effective date, then, in applying the amendments made by this section to such employee's designated beneficiary who dies after such date—

(i) such amendments shall apply to any beneficiary of such designated beneficiary; and

(ii) the designated beneficiary shall be treated as an eligible designated beneficiary for purposes of applying section 401(a)(9)(H)(ii) of the Internal Revenue Code of 1986 (as in effect after such amendments).

SEC. 401(b)(5)(A)(ii) ¶5066

(B) EFFECTIVE DATE.—For purposes of this paragraph, the term "effective date" means the first day of the first calendar year to which the amendments made by this section apply to a plan with respect to employees dying on or after such date.

[¶ 5067] SEC. 402. INCREASE IN PENALTY FOR FAILURE TO FILE.

(a) IN GENERAL.—The second sentence of subsection (a) of section 6651 of the Internal Revenue Code of 1986 is amended by striking "$330" and inserting "$435".

(b) INFLATION ADJUSTMENT.—Section 6651(j)(1) of such Code is amended by striking "$330" and inserting "$435".

(c) EFFECTIVE DATE.—The amendments made by this section shall apply to returns the due date for which (including extensions) is after December 31, 2019.

[¶ 5068] SEC. 403. INCREASED PENALTIES FOR FAILURE TO FILE RETIREMENT PLAN RETURNS.

(a) IN GENERAL.—Subsection (e) of section 6652 of the Internal Revenue Code of 1986 is amended—

(1) by striking "$25" and inserting "$250"; and

(2) by striking "$15,000" and inserting "$150,000".

(b) ANNUAL REGISTRATION STATEMENT AND NOTIFICATION OF CHANGES.—Subsection (d) of section 6652 of the Internal Revenue Code of 1986 is amended—

(1) by striking "$1" both places it appears in paragraphs (1) and (2) and inserting "$10";

(2) by striking "$5,000" in paragraph (1) and inserting "$50,000"; and

(3) by striking "$1,000" in paragraph (2) and inserting "$10,000".

(c) FAILURE TO PROVIDE NOTICE.—Subsection (h) of section 6652 of the Internal Revenue Code of 1986 is amended—

(1) by striking "$10" and inserting "$100"; and

(2) by striking "$5,000" and inserting "$50,000".

(d) EFFECTIVE DATE.—The amendments made by this section shall apply to returns, statements, and notifications required to be filed, and notices required to be provided, after December 31, 2019.

[¶ 5069] SEC. 404. INCREASE INFORMATION SHARING TO ADMINISTER EXCISE TAXES.

(a) IN GENERAL.—Section 6103(o) of the Internal Revenue Code of 1986 is amended by adding at the end the following new paragraph:

"(3) TAXES IMPOSED BY SECTION 4481.—Returns and return information with respect to taxes imposed by section 4481 shall be open to inspection by or disclosure to officers and employees of United States Customs and Border Protection of the Department of Homeland Security whose official duties require such inspection or disclosure for purposes of administering such section.".

(b) CONFORMING AMENDMENTS.—Paragraph (4) of section 6103(p) of the Internal Revenue Code of 1986 is amended by striking "or (o)(1)(A)" each place it appears and inserting ", (o)(1)(A), or (o)(3)".

TITLE V—TAX RELIEF FOR CERTAIN CHILDREN

[¶ 5070] SEC. 501. MODIFICATION OF RULES RELATING TO THE TAXATION OF UNEARNED INCOME OF CERTAIN CHILDREN.

(a) IN GENERAL.—Section 1(j) of the Internal Revenue Code of 1986 is amended by striking paragraph (4).

(b) COORDINATION WITH ALTERNATIVE MINIMUM TAX.—Section 55(d)(4)(A) of the Internal Revenue Code of 1986 is amended by striking "and" at the end of clause (i)(II), by striking the period at the end of clause (ii)(III) and inserting ", and", and by adding at the end the following new clause:

"(iii) subsection (j) of section 59 shall not apply.".

(c) EFFECTIVE DATE.—

(1) IN GENERAL.—Except as otherwise provided in this subsection, the amendment made by subsection (a) shall apply to taxable years beginning after December 31, 2019.

(2) COORDINATION WITH ALTERNATIVE MINIMUM TAX.—The amendment made by subsection (b) shall apply to taxable years beginning after December 31, 2017.

(3) ELECTIVE RETROACTIVE APPLICATION.—A taxpayer may elect (at such time and in such manner as the Secretary of the Treasury (or the Secretary's designee) may provide) for the amendment made by subsection (a) to also apply to taxable years of the taxpayer which begin in 2018, 2019, or both (as specified by the taxpayer in such election).

TITLE VI—ADMINISTRATIVE PROVISIONS

[¶ 5071] SEC. 601. PROVISIONS RELATING TO PLAN AMENDMENTS.

(a) IN GENERAL.—If this section applies to any retirement plan or contract amendment—

(1) such retirement plan or contract shall be treated as being operated in accordance with the terms of the plan during the period described in subsection (b)(2)(A); and

(2) except as provided by the Secretary of the Treasury (or the Secretary's delegate), such retirement plan shall not fail to meet the requirements of section 411(d)(6) of the Internal Revenue Code of 1986 and section 204(g) of the Employee Retirement Income Security Act of 1974 by reason of such amendment.

(b) AMENDMENTS TO WHICH SECTION APPLIES.—

(1) IN GENERAL.—This section shall apply to any amendment to any retirement plan or annuity contract which is made—

(A) pursuant to any amendment made by this Act or pursuant to any regulation issued by the Secretary of the Treasury or the Secretary of Labor (or a delegate of either such Secretary) under this Act; and

(B) on or before the last day of the first plan year beginning on or after January 1, 2022, or such later date as the Secretary of the Treasury may prescribe.

In the case of a governmental plan (as defined in section 414(d) of the Internal Revenue Code of 1986), or an applicable collectively bargained plan in the case of section 401 (and the amendments made thereby), this paragraph shall be applied by substituting "2024" for "2022". For purposes of the preceding sentence, the term "applicable collectively bargained plan" means a plan maintained pursuant to 1 or more collective bargaining agreements between employee representatives and 1 or more employers ratified before the date of enactment of this Act.

(2) CONDITIONS.—This section shall not apply to any amendment unless—

(A) during the period—

(i) beginning on the date the legislative or regulatory amendment described in paragraph (1)(A) takes effect (or in the case of a plan or contract amendment not required by such legislative or regulatory amendment, the effective date specified by the plan); and

(ii) ending on the date described in paragraph (1)(B) (as modified by the second sentence of paragraph (1)) (or, if earlier, the date the plan or contract amendment is adopted),

the plan or contract is operated as if such plan or contract amendment were in effect; and

(B) such plan or contract amendment applies retroactively for such period.

DIVISION P—OTHER MATTER

TITLE I—PLATTE RIVER RECOVERY IMPLEMENTATION PROGRAM

[¶ 5072] SEC. 101. SHORT TITLE.

This title may be cited as the "Platte River Recovery Implementation Program Extension Act".

[¶ 5073] SEC. 102. PURPOSE.

The purpose of this Act is to authorize the Secretary of the Interior, acting through the Commissioner of Reclamation and in partnership with the States, other Federal agencies, and other non-Federal entities, to continue the cooperative effort among the Federal and non-Federal entities through the continued implementation of the Platte River Recovery Implementation Program First Increment Extension for threatened and endangered species in the Central and Lower Platte River Basin without creating Federal water rights or requiring the grant of water rights to Federal entities.

[¶ 5074] SEC. 103. DEFINITIONS.

In this Act:

(1) AGREEMENT.—The term "Agreement" means the Platte River Recovery Implementation Program Cooperative Agreement entered into by the Governors of the States and the Secretary, including an amendment or addendum to the Agreement to extend the Program.

(2) FIRST INCREMENT.—The term "First Increment" means the Program's first 13 years from January 1, 2007 through December 31, 2019.

(3) FIRST INCREMENT EXTENSION.—The term "First Increment Extension" means the extension of the Program for 13 years from January 1, 2020 through December 31, 2032.

(4) GOVERNANCE COMMITTEE.—The term "Governance Committee" means the governance committee established under the Agreement and composed of members from the States, the Federal Government, environmental interests, and water users.

(5) INTEREST IN LAND OR WATER.—The term "interest in land or water" includes fee title, short- or long-term easement, lease, or other contractual arrangement that is determined to be necessary by the Secretary to implement the land and water components of the Program.

(6) PROGRAM.—The term "Program" means the Platte River Recovery Implementation Program established under the Agreement and continued under an amendment or addendum to the Agreement.

(7) PROJECT OR ACTIVITY.—The term "project or activity" means—

(A) the planning, design, permitting, or other compliance activity, construction, construction management, operation, maintenance, and replacement of a facility;

(B) the acquisition of an interest in land or water;

(C) habitat restoration;

(D) research and monitoring;

(E) program administration; and

(F) any other activity that is determined to be necessary by the Secretary to carry out the Program.

(8) SECRETARY.—The term "Secretary" means the Secretary of the Interior, acting through the Commissioner of Reclamation.

(9) STATES.—The term "States" means the States of Colorado, Nebraska, and Wyoming.

[¶ 5075] SEC. 104. PLATTE RIVER RECOVERY IMPLEMENTATION PROGRAM.

(a) IMPLEMENTATION OF PROGRAM.—

(1) IN GENERAL.—The Secretary, in cooperation with the Governance Committee, may—

(A) participate in the Program; and

(B) carry out any projects and activities that are designated for implementation during the First Increment Extension.

(2) AUTHORITY OF THE SECRETARY.—For the purposes of carrying out this section, the Secretary, in cooperation with the Governance Committee, may—

(A) enter into agreements and contracts with Federal and non-Federal entities;

(B) acquire interests in land, water, and facilities from willing sellers without the use of eminent domain;

(C) subsequently transfer any interests acquired under subparagraph (B); and

(D) accept or provide grants.

(b) COST-SHARING CONTRIBUTIONS.—

(1) IN GENERAL.—As provided in the Agreement, the States shall contribute not less than 50 percent of the total contributions necessary to carry out the Program.

(2) NON-FEDERAL CONTRIBUTIONS.—The following contributions shall constitute the States' share of the Program:

(A) An additional $28,000,000 in non-Federal funds, with the balance of funds remaining to be contributed to be adjusted for inflation on October 1 of the year after the date of enactment of this Act and each October 1 thereafter.

(B) Additional credit for contributions of water or land for the purposes of implementing the Program, as determined to be appropriate by the Secretary.

(3) IN-KIND CONTRIBUTIONS.—The Secretary or the States may elect to provide a portion of the Federal share or non-Federal share, respectively, in the form of in-kind goods or services, if the contribution of goods or services is approved by the Governance Committee, as provided in Attachment 1 of the Agreement.

(c) AUTHORITY TO MODIFY PROGRAM.—The Program may be modified or amended before the completion of the First Increment Extension if the Secretary and the States determine that the modifications are consistent with the purposes of the Program.

(d) EFFECT.—

(1) EFFECT ON RECLAMATION LAWS.—No action carried out under this section shall, with respect to the acreage limitation provisions of the reclamation laws—

(A) be considered in determining whether a district (as the term is defined in section 202 of the Reclamation Reform Act of 1982 (43 U.S.C. 390bb)) has discharged the obligation of the district to repay the construction cost of project facilities used to make irrigation water available for delivery to land in the district;

(B) serve as the basis for reinstating acreage limitation provisions in a district that has completed payment of the construction obligations of the district; or

(C) serve as the basis for increasing the construction repayment obligation of the district, which would extend the period during which the acreage limitation provisions would apply.

(2) EFFECT ON WATER RIGHTS.—Nothing in this section—

(A) creates Federal water rights; or

(B) requires the grant of water rights to Federal entities.

(e) AUTHORIZATION OF APPROPRIATIONS.—

(1) IN GENERAL.—There is authorized to be appropriated to carry out projects and activities under this section an additional $78,000,000 as adjusted under paragraph (3).

(2) NONREIMBURSABLE FEDERAL EXPENDITURES.—Any amounts to be expended under paragraph (1) shall be considered nonreimbursable Federal expenditures.

SEC. 104(e)(2) ¶5075

(3) ADJUSTMENT.—The balance of funds remaining to be expended shall be adjusted for inflation on October 1 of the year after the date of enactment of this Act and each October 1 thereafter.

(4) AVAILABILITY OF FUNDS.—At the end of each fiscal year, any unexpended funds for projects and activities made available under paragraph (1) shall be retained for use in future fiscal years to implement projects and activities under the Program. Any unexpended funds appropriated during the First Increment shall be retained and carried over from the First Increment into the First Increment Extension.

(f) TERMINATION OF AUTHORITY.—The authority for the Secretary to implement the First Increment Extension shall terminate on September 30, 2033.

TITLE II—GREAT LAKES

[¶ 5076] SEC. 201. GREAT LAKES MONITORING, ASSESSMENT, SCIENCE, AND RESEARCH.

(a) DEFINITIONS.—In this section:

(1) DIRECTOR.—The term "Director" means the Director of the United States Geological Survey.

(2) GREAT LAKES BASIN.—The term "Great Lakes Basin" means the air, land, water, and living organisms in the United States within the drainage basin of the Saint Lawrence River at and upstream from the point at which such river and the Great Lakes become the international boundary between Canada and the United States.

(b) FINDINGS.—Congress finds the following:

(1) The Great Lakes support a diverse ecosystem, on which the vibrant and economically valuable Great Lakes fisheries depend.

(2) To continue successful fisheries management and coordination, as has occurred since signing of the Convention on Great Lakes Fisheries between the United States and Canada on September 10, 1954, management of the ecosystem and its fisheries require sound, reliable science, and the use of modern scientific technologies.

(3) Fisheries research is necessary to support multi-jurisdictional fishery management decisions and actions regarding recreational and sport fishing, commercial fisheries, tribal harvest, allocation decisions, and fish stocking activities.

(4) President Richard Nixon submitted, and the Congress approved, Reorganization Plan No. 4 (84 Stat. 2090), conferring science activities and management of marine fisheries to the National Oceanic and Atmospheric Administration.

(5) Reorganization Plan No. 4 expressly excluded fishery research activities within the Great Lakes from the transfer, retaining management and scientific research duties within the already-established jurisdictions under the 1954 Convention on Great Lakes Fisheries, including those of the Great Lakes Fishery Commission and the Department of the Interior.

(c) MONITORING, ASSESSMENT, SCIENCE, AND RESEARCH.—

(1) IN GENERAL.—The Director may conduct monitoring, assessment, science, and research, in support of the binational fisheries within the Great Lakes Basin.

(2) SPECIFIC AUTHORITIES.—The Director shall, under paragraph (1)—

(A) execute a comprehensive, multi-lake, freshwater fisheries science program;

(B) coordinate with and work cooperatively with regional, State, tribal, and local governments; and

(C) consult with other interested entities groups, including academia and relevant Canadian agencies.

(3) INCLUDED RESEARCH.—To properly serve the needs of fisheries managers, monitoring, assessment, science, and research under this section may include—

(A) deepwater ecosystem sciences;

(B) biological and food-web components;

(C) fish movement and behavior investigations;

(D) fish population structures;

(E) fish habitat investigations;

(F) invasive species science;

(G) use of existing, new, and experimental biological assessment tools, equipment, vessels, other scientific instrumentation and laboratory capabilities necessary to support fishery management decisions; and

(H) studies to assess impacts on Great Lakes Fishery resources.

(4) SAVINGS CLAUSE.—Nothing in this section is intended or shall be construed to impede, supersede, or alter the authority of the Great Lakes Fishery Commission, States, and Indian tribes under the Convention on Great Lakes Fisheries between the United States of America and Canada on September 10, 1954, and the Great Lakes Fishery Act of 1956 (16 U.S.C. 931 et seq.).

(d) AUTHORIZATION OF APPROPRIATIONS.—For each of fiscal years 2021 through 2025, there is authorized to be appropriated $15,000,000 to carry out this section.

TITLE III—MORRIS K. UDALL AND STEWART L. UDALL FOUNDATION

[¶ 5077] SEC. 301. FINDINGS.

Congress finds the following:

(1) Since 1999, the Morris K. Udall and Stewart L. Udall Foundation (referred to in this Act as the "Foundation") has operated the Parks in Focus program to provide opportunities for the youth of the United States to learn about and experience the Nation's parks and wilderness, and other outdoor areas.

(2) Since 2001, the Foundation has conducted research and provided education and training to Native American and Alaska Native professionals and leaders on Native American and Alaska Native health care issues and tribal public policy through the Native Nations Institute for Leadership, Management, and Policy.

(3) The Foundation is committed to continuing to make a substantial contribution toward public policy in the future by—

(A) playing a significant role in developing the next generation of environmental, public health, public lands, natural resource, and Native American leaders; and

(B) working with current leaders to improve collaboration and decision-making on challenging environmental, energy, public health, and related economic problems and tribal governance and economic development issues.

[¶ 5078] SEC. 302. DEFINITIONS.

(a) IN GENERAL.—Section 4 of the Morris K. Udall and Stewart L. Udall Foundation Act (20 U.S.C. 5602) is amended—

(1) in paragraph (2), by striking "the Udall Center for Studies in Public Policy established at the University of Arizona in 1987" and inserting "the Udall Center for Studies in Public Policy established in 1987 at the University of Arizona, and includes the Native Nations Institute";

(2) by striking paragraph (6);

(3) by redesignating paragraphs (3) through (5), (8), and (9) as paragraphs (4) through (6), (11), and (12), respectively;

(4) by inserting after paragraph (2) the following:

"(3) the term 'collaboration' means to work in partnership with other entities for the purpose of—

"(A) resolving disputes;

"(B) addressing issues that may cause or result in disputes; or

"(C) streamlining and enhancing Federal, State, or tribal environmental and natural resource decision-making processes or procedures that may result in a dispute or conflict;";

(5) in paragraph (7), by striking "section 1201(a)" and inserting "section 101(a)";

(6) by inserting after paragraph (7) the following:

"(8) the term 'National Center' means the John S. McCain III National Center for Environmental Conflict Resolution established pursuant to section 7(a)(1)(B);"; and

(7) by inserting after paragraph (8), as added by paragraph (6), the following:

"(9) the term 'Nation's parks and wilderness' means units of the National Park System and components of the National Wilderness Preservation System;

"(10) the term 'Native Nations Institute' means the Native Nations Institute for Leadership, Management, and Policy established at the University of Arizona in 2001;".

(b) CONFORMING AMENDMENT.—Section 3(5)(B) of the Morris K. Udall and Stewart L. Udall Foundation Act (20 U.S.C. 5601(5)(B)) is amended by striking "the United States Institute for Environmental Conflict Resolution" and inserting "the National Center (previously known as the United States Institute for Environmental Conflict Resolution)".

(c) REFERENCES TO UNITED STATES INSTITUTE FOR ENVIRONMENTAL CONFLICT RESOLUTION.—Any reference to the United States Institute for Environmental Conflict Resolution in any Federal law, Executive Order, rule, delegation of authority, or document shall be construed to refer to the John S. McCain III National Center for Environmental Conflict Resolution established under section 7(a)(1)(B) of the Morris K. Udall and Stewart L. Udall Foundation Act (20 U.S.C. 5605(a)(1)(B)).

[¶ 5079] SEC. 303. ESTABLISHMENT OF MORRIS K. UDALL AND STEWART L. UDALL FOUNDATION.

Section 5(e) of the Morris K. Udall and Stewart L. Udall Foundation Act (20 U.S.C. 5603(e)) is amended by striking "Arizona." and inserting "Arizona and the District of Columbia.".

[¶ 5080] SEC. 304. PURPOSE OF THE FOUNDATION.

Section 6 of the Morris K. Udall and Stewart L. Udall Foundation Act (20 U.S.C. 5604) is amended—

(1) in paragraph (4), by striking "establish a Program for Environmental Policy Research and Environmental Conflict Resolution and Training at the Center" and inserting "establish a program for environmental policy research at the Center and a program for environmental conflict resolution and training at the National Center";

(2) in paragraph (5), by inserting ", natural resource, conflict resolution," after "environmental";

(3) in paragraph (7)—

(A) by inserting "at the Native Nations Institute" after "develop resources"; and

(B) by inserting "providing education to and" after "policy, by"; and

(4) in paragraph (8)—

(A) by striking "United States Institute for Environmental Conflict Resolution" and inserting "John S. McCain III National Center for Environmental Conflict Resolution"; and

(B) by striking "resolve environmental" and inserting "resolve environmental issues, conflicts, and".

[¶ 5081] SEC. 305. AUTHORITY OF THE FOUNDATION.

Section 7 of the Morris K. Udall and Stewart L. Udall Foundation Act (20 U.S.C. 5605) is amended—

(1) in subsection (a)—

(A) in paragraph (1)—

(i) by striking subparagraphs (A) through (C) and inserting the following:

¶ 5079   SEC. 302(a)(5)

"(A) GENERAL PROGRAMMING AUTHORITY.—The Foundation is authorized to identify and conduct, directly or by contract, such programs, activities, and services as the Foundation considers appropriate to carry out the purposes described in section 6, which may include—

"(i) awarding scholarships, fellowships, internships, and grants, by national competition, to eligible individuals, as determined by the Foundation and in accordance with paragraphs (2), (3), and (4), for study in fields related to the environment or Native American and Alaska Native health care and tribal policy;

"(ii) funding the Center to carry out and manage other programs, activities, and services; and

"(iii) other education programs that the Board determines are consistent with the purposes for which the Foundation is established.";

(ii) by redesignating subparagraph (D) as subparagraph (B); and

(iii) in subparagraph (B), as redesignated—

(I) in the subparagraph heading, by striking "INSTITUTE FOR ENVIRONMENTAL CONFLICT RESOLUTION" and inserting "JOHN S. MCCAIN III NATIONAL CENTER FOR ENVIRONMENTAL CONFLICT RESOLUTION";

(II) in clause (i)—

(aa) in subclause (I), by striking "United States Institute for Environmental Conflict Resolution" and inserting "John S. McCain III National Center for Environmental Conflict Resolution"; and

(bb) in subclause (II)—

(AA) by inserting "collaboration," after "mediation,"; and

(BB) by striking "to resolve environmental disputes." and inserting the following: "to resolve—

"(aa) environmental disputes; and

"(bb) Federal, State, or tribal environmental or natural resource decision-making processes or procedures that may result in a dispute or conflict that may cause or result in disputes."; and

(III) in clause (ii), by inserting "collaboration," after "mediation,";

(B) by striking paragraph (5);

(C) by redesignating paragraphs (6) and (7) as paragraphs (7) and (8), respectively;

(D) by inserting after paragraph (4) the following:

"(5) PARKS IN FOCUS.—The Foundation shall—

"(A) identify and invite the participation of youth throughout the United States to enjoy the Nation's parks and wilderness and other outdoor areas, in an education program intended to carry out the purpose of paragraphs (1) and (2) of section 6; and

"(B) provide training and education programs and activities to teach Federal employees, natural resource professionals, elementary and secondary school educators, and others to work with youth to promote the use and enjoyment of the Nation's parks and wilderness and other outdoor areas.

"(6) SPECIFIC PROGRAMS.—The Foundation shall assist in the development and implementation of programs at the Center—

"(A) to provide for an annual meeting of experts to discuss contemporary environmental issues;

"(B) to conduct environmental policy research; and

"(C) to promote dialogue with visiting policymakers on environmental, natural resource, and public lands issues.";

(E) in paragraph (7), as redesignated by subparagraph (C), by striking "Morris K. Udall's papers" and inserting "the papers of Morris K. Udall and Stewart L. Udall"; and

(F) by adding at the end the following:

"(9) NATIVE NATIONS INSTITUTE.—The Foundation shall provide direct or indirect assistance to the Native Nations Institute from the annual appropriations to the Trust Fund in such amounts as Congress may direct to conduct research and provide education and training to Native American and Alaska Native professionals and leaders on Native American and Alaska Native health care issues and tribal public policy issues as provided in section 6(7).";

(2) by striking subsection (c) and inserting the following:

"(c) PROGRAM PRIORITIES.—

"(1) IN GENERAL.—The Foundation shall determine the priority of the programs to be carried out under this Act and the amount of funds to be allocated for such programs from the funds earned annually from the interest derived from the investment of the Trust Fund, subject to paragraph (2).

"(2) LIMITATIONS.—In determining the amount of funds to be allocated for programs carried out under this Act for a year—

"(A) not less than 50 percent of such annual interest earnings shall be utilized for the programs set forth in paragraphs (2), (3), (4), and (5) of subsection (a);

"(B) not more than 17.5 percent of such annual interest earnings shall be allocated for salaries and other administrative purposes; and

"(C) not less than 20 percent of such annual interest earnings shall be appropriated to the Center for activities under paragraphs (7) and (8) of subsection (a)."; and

(3) by adding at the end the following:

"(d) DONATIONS.—Any funds received by the Foundation in the form of donations or grants, as well as any unexpended earnings on interest from the Trust Fund that is carried forward from prior years—

"(1) shall not be included in the calculation of the funds available for allocations pursuant to subsection (c); and

"(2) shall be available to carry out the provisions of this Act as the Board determines to be necessary and appropriate.".

[¶ 5082] SEC. 306. ENVIRONMENTAL DISPUTE RESOLUTION FUND.

Section 10(b) of the Morris K. Udall and Stewart L. Udall Foundation Act (20 U.S.C. 5607a(b)) is amended by striking "Institute" and inserting "National Center".

[¶ 5083] SEC. 307. USE OF THE NATIONAL CENTER BY A FEDERAL AGENCY OR OTHER ENTITY.

Section 11 of the Morris K. Udall and Stewart L. Udall Foundation Act (20 U.S.C. 5607b) is amended—

(1) in the section heading, by striking "the institute" and inserting "the national center";

(2) in subsection (a)—

(A) by striking "Institute" and inserting "National Center";

(B) by inserting "collaboration," after "mediation,"; and

(C) by striking "resources." and inserting "resources, or with a Federal, State, or tribal process or procedure that may result in a dispute or conflict.";

(3) in subsection (b)(1), by striking "Institute" and inserting "National Center";

(4) in subsection (c)—

(A) in paragraph (1), by striking "Institute" and inserting "National Center";

(B) in paragraph (2)(C), by inserting "mediation, collaboration, and" after "agree to"; and

(C) in paragraph (3)(A), by striking "Institute" and inserting "National Center";

(5) in each of paragraphs (1)(A) and (2) of subsection (d), by striking "Institute" and inserting "National Center";

(6) in each of paragraphs (1) and (2) of subsection (e), by striking "Institute" and inserting "National Center"; and

(7) in subsection (f), by striking "Institute" and inserting "National Center".

[¶ 5084] SEC. 308. ADMINISTRATIVE PROVISIONS.

Section 12 of the Morris K. Udall and Stewart L. Udall Foundation Act (20 U.S.C. 5608) is amended—

(1) in subsection (a)—

(A) in paragraph (4), by striking "accept, hold, administer, and utilize gifts" and inserting "accept, hold, solicit, administer, and utilize donations, grants, and gifts"; and

(B) in paragraph (7), by striking "in the District of Columbia or its environs" and inserting "in the District of Columbia and Tucson, Arizona, or their environs"; and

(2) in subsection (b), by striking ", with the exception of paragraph (4), apply to the Institute" and inserting "apply to the National Center".

[¶ 5085] SEC. 309. AUTHORIZATION OF APPROPRIATIONS.

Section 13 of the Morris K. Udall and Stewart L. Udall Foundation Act (20 U.S.C. 5609) is amended—

(1) in subsection (a), by striking "$40,000,000" and inserting "$2,000,000 for each of fiscal years 2020 through 2023"; and

(2) in subsection (b), by striking "fiscal years 2004 through 2008" and inserting "fiscal years 2020 through 2023".

[¶ 5086] SEC. 310. AUDIT OF THE FOUNDATION.

Not later than 2 years after the date of enactment of this Act, the Inspector General of the Department of the Interior shall conduct an audit of the Morris K. Udall and Stewart L. Udall Foundation.

TITLE IV—WHITE HORSE HILL NATIONAL GAME PRESERVE

[¶ 5087] SEC. 401. SHORT TITLE.

This title may be cited as the "White Horse Hill National Game Preserve Designation Act".

[¶ 5088] SEC. 402. DESIGNATION OF WHITE HORSE HILL NATIONAL GAME PRESERVE, NORTH DAKOTA.

(a) REDESIGNATION.—The first section of the Act of March 3, 1931 (46 Stat. 1509, chapter 439; 16 U.S.C. 674a), is amended by striking "Sullys Hill National Game Preserve" and inserting "White Horse Hill National Game Preserve".

(b) CONFORMING AMENDMENT.—Section 2 of the Act of March 3, 1931 (46 Stat. 1509, chapter 439; 16 U.S.C. 674b), is amended by striking "Sullys Hill National Game Preserve" and inserting "White Horse Hill National Game Preserve".

(c) REFERENCES.—Any reference in a law, map, regulation, document, paper, or other record of the United States to the Sullys Hill National Game Preserve shall be considered to be a reference to the "White Horse Hill National Game Preserve".

TITLE V—PITTMAN-ROBERTSON FUND

[¶ 5089] SEC. 501. MODERNIZING THE PITTMAN-ROBERTSON FUND FOR TOMORROW'S NEEDS.

(a) SHORT TITLE.—This title may be cited as the "Modernizing the Pittman-Robertson Fund for Tomorrow's Needs Act".

(b) PURPOSE.—The first section of the Pittman-Robertson Wildlife Restoration Act (16 U.S.C. 669) is amended by adding at the end the following: "One of the purposes of this Act is to provide financial and technical assistance to the States for the promotion of hunting and recreational shooting.".

(c) DEFINITIONS.—Section 2 of the Pittman-Robertson Wildlife Restoration Act (16 U.S.C. 669a) is amended—

(1) by redesignating paragraphs (2) through (9) as paragraphs (4) through (11), respectively; and

(2) by inserting after paragraph (1) the following:

"(2) for the purposes of determining the number of paid hunting-license holders in a State, the term 'fiscal year' means the fiscal year or license year of the State;

"(3) the term 'hunter recruitment and recreational shooter recruitment' means any activity or project to recruit or retain hunters and recreational shooters, including by—

"(A) outreach and communications as a means—

"(i) to improve communications with hunters, recreational shooters, and the general public with respect to hunting and recreational shooting opportunities;

"(ii) to reduce barriers to participation in these activities;

"(iii) to advance the adoption of sound hunting and recreational shooting practices;

"(iv) to promote conservation and the responsible use of the wildlife resources of the United States; and

"(v) to further safety in hunting and recreational shooting;

"(B) providing education, mentoring, and field demonstrations;

"(C) enhancing access for hunting and recreational shooting, including through range construction; and

"(D) providing education to the public about the role of hunting and recreational shooting in funding wildlife conservation;".

(d) APPORTIONMENT OF AVAILABLE AMOUNTS.—

(1) APPORTIONMENT OF CERTAIN TAXES.—The first subsection (c) of section 4 of the Pittman-Robertson Wildlife Restoration Act (16 U.S.C. 669c) is amended—

(A) by inserting "APPORTIONMENT OF REVENUES FROM PISTOLS, REVOLVERS, BOWS, AND ARROWS.—"after the enumerator;

(B) by striking "One-half" and inserting the following:

"(1) IN GENERAL.—Subject to paragraph (2), $1/2$";

(C) by striking ": *Provided*, That" and inserting a period;

(D) by striking "each State shall be apportioned not more than 3 per centum and not less than 1 per centum of such revenues" and inserting the following:

"(2) CONDITION.—The amount apportioned to each State under paragraph (1) shall be not greater than 3 percent and not less than 1 percent of the revenues described in such paragraph";

(E) by striking "For the purpose" and inserting the following:

"(3) POPULATION DETERMINATION.—For the purpose"; and

(F) by adding at the end the following:

"(4) USE OF FUNDS.—In addition to other uses authorized under this Act, amounts apportioned under this subsection may be used for hunter recruitment and recreational shooter recruitment.".

(2) TECHNICAL CORRECTION.—Section 4 of the Pittman-Robertson Wildlife Restoration Act (16 U.S.C. 669c) is amended—

(A) by redesignating the second subsection (c) and subsection (d) as subsections (d) and (e), respectively; and

(B) by striking "subsection (c)" in the redesignated section 4(e)(3) and replacing it with "subsection (d), as redesignated".

(e) EXPENDITURES FOR MANAGEMENT OF WILDLIFE AREAS AND RESOURCES.—Section 8 of the Pittman-Robertson Wildlife Restoration Act (16 U.S.C. 669g) is amended—

(1) in subsection (a), in the third sentence, by striking "and public relations"; and

(2) in subsection (b), in the first sentence, by striking ", as a part of such program".

(f) FIREARM AND BOW HUNTER EDUCATION AND SAFETY PROGRAM GRANTS.—Section 10(a)(1)(A) of the Pittman-Robertson Wildlife Restoration Act (16 U.S.C. 669h-1(a)(1)(A)) is amended—

(1) in clause (iii), by striking "and" at the end; and

(2) by adding at the end the following:

"(v) the enhancement of hunter recruitment and recreational shooter recruitment; and".

(g) MULTISTATE CONSERVATION GRANT PROGRAM.—

(1) IN GENERAL.—Section 11 of the Pittman-Robertson Wildlife Restoration Act (16 U.S.C. 669h-2) is amended—

(A) in subsection (a)(1)—

(i) by striking "Not more than" and inserting the following:

"(A) IN GENERAL.—Not more than"; and

(ii) by adding at the end the following:

"(B) AVAILABILITY FOR HUNTER AND RECREATIONAL SHOOTER GRANTS.—Not more than $5,000,000 of the revenues covered into the fund from any tax imposed under section 4161(b) of the Internal Revenue Code of 1986 for a fiscal year shall be available to the Secretary exclusively for making hunter recruitment and recreational shooter recruitment grants that promote a national hunting and shooting sport recruitment program, including related communication and outreach activities.";

(B) in the matter preceding subsection (b)(3)(A), by striking "International";

(C) in the matter preceding subsection (c)(2)(A)(i), by striking "International";

(D) in subsection (c)(2)(A)(i), by inserting "or to recreational shooting activities" after "wildlife"; and

(E) in subsection (d), by inserting "or to recreational shooting activities" after "wildlife".

(2) STUDY.—Not later than 10 years after the date of enactment of this Act, the Secretary of the Interior, acting through the Director of the United States Fish and Wildlife Service, shall—

(A) review and evaluate the effects of the funds made available under subparagraph (B) of section 11(a)(1) of the Pittman-Robertson Wildlife Restoration Act (16 U.S.C. 669h-2(a)(1)) (as added by paragraph (1)(A)(ii)) on funds available for wildlife conservation; and

(B) submit a report describing the results of the review and evaluation under paragraph (1) to—

(i) the Committee on Environment and Public Works of the Senate; and

(ii) the Committee on Natural Resources of the House of Representatives.

TITLE VI—JOHN F. KENNEDY CENTER

[¶ 5090] SEC. 601. SHORT TITLE.

This title may be cited as the "John F. Kennedy Center Reauthorization Act of 2019".

[¶ 5091] SEC. 602. AUTHORIZATION OF APPROPRIATIONS.

Section 13 of the John F. Kennedy Center Act (20 U.S.C. 76r), as amended by the Department of the Interior, Environment, and Related Agencies Appropriations Act, 2020, is further amended by striking subsections (a) and (b) and inserting the following:

"(a) MAINTENANCE, REPAIR, AND SECURITY.—There are authorized to be appropriated to the Board to carry out section 4(a)(1)(H)—

"(1) $25,690,000 for fiscal year 2020;

"(2) $27,000,000 for fiscal year 2021;

"(3) $28,000,000 for fiscal year 2022;

"(4) $29,000,000 for fiscal year 2023; and

"(5) $30,000,000 for fiscal year 2024.

"(b) CAPITAL PROJECTS.—There are authorized to be appropriated to the Board to carry out subparagraphs (F) and (G) of section 4(a)(1)—

"(1) $17,800,000 for fiscal year 2020;

"(2) $18,000,000 for fiscal year 2021;

"(3) $19,000,000 for fiscal year 2022;

"(4) $20,000,000 for fiscal year 2023; and

"(5) $21,000,000 for fiscal year 2024.".

[¶ 5092] SEC. 603. COMMEMORATION OF THE JOHN F. KENNEDY CENTER FOR THE PERFORMING ARTS.

(a) SENSE OF CONGRESS.—It is the sense of Congress that the John F. Kennedy Center for the Performing Arts (referred to in this Act as the "Center")—

(1) recognize the year 2021 as the 50th anniversary of the opening of the Center;

(2) acknowledge and commemorate the mission of the Center as a national center for the performing arts and a national memorial to President John F. Kennedy; and

(3) recognize that the year 2018 is the 60th anniversary of the signing of the National Cultural Center Act (now known as the "John F. Kennedy Center Act") (20 U.S.C. 76h et seq.), signed into law by President Dwight D. Eisenhower on September 2, 1958.

(b) AUTHORIZATION FOR PLAQUE.—

(1) IN GENERAL.—The Center shall place within the Center a plaque containing an inscription to commemorate the 60th anniversary of the signing of the National Cultural Center Act (20 U.S.C. 76h et seq.) by President Dwight D. Eisenhower.

(2) SPECIFICATIONS.—The plaque shall be—

(A)(i) not less than 6 square feet in size; and

(ii) not more than 18 square feet in size;

(B) of any shape that the Trustees of the Center determine to be appropriate; and

(C) placed at a location within the Center approximate to the Eisenhower Theater that the Trustees of the Center determine to be appropriate.

(3) FUNDING.—

(A) IN GENERAL.—No Federal funds may be used to design, procure, or install the plaque.

(B) EXCEPTION.—Subparagraph (A) shall not affect the payment of salaries, expenses, and benefits otherwise authorized by law for members and employees of the Center who participate in carrying out this subsection.

(4) PRIVATE FUNDRAISING AUTHORIZED.—

(A) IN GENERAL.—The Center may solicit and accept private contributions for the design, procurement, and installation of the plaque.

(B) ACCOUNTING.—The Center may—

(i) establish an account into which any contributions received pursuant to subparagraph (A) shall be deposited; and

(ii) maintain documentation of any contributions received pursuant to subparagraph (A).

TITLE VII—PRESERVING AMERICA'S BATTLEFIELDS

[¶5093] SEC. 701. SHORT TITLE.

This title may be cited as the "Preserving America's Battlefields Act".

[¶5094] SEC. 702. AUTHORIZATION OF APPROPRIATIONS FOR BATTLEFIELD ACQUISITION GRANT PROGRAM.

Section 308103(f) of title 54, United States Code, is amended by striking "$10,000,000 for each of fiscal years 2012 and 2013" and inserting "$18,000,000 for each of fiscal years 2020 through 2028".

[¶5095] SEC. 703. ESTABLISHMENT OF BATTLEFIELD INTERPRETATION MODERNIZATION GRANT PROGRAM AND BATTLEFIELD RESTORATION GRANT PROGRAM.

(a) ESTABLISHMENT OF BATTLEFIELD GRANT PROGRAMS.—Chapter 3081 of title 54, United States Code, is amended by adding at the end the following:

"**§ 308104. Battlefield interpretation modernization grant program**

"(a) ESTABLISHMENT.—The Secretary shall establish a battlefield interpretation modernization grant program under which the Secretary may provide competitive grants to States, Tribes, local governments, and nonprofit organizations for projects and programs that deploy technology to modernize battlefield interpretation and education.

"(b) ELIGIBLE SITES.—The Secretary may make grants under this section for Revolutionary War, War of 1812, and Civil War battlefield sites eligible for assistance under the battlefield acquisition grant program established under section 308103(b).

"(c) FEDERAL SHARE.—The Federal share of the cost of a project or program funded through a grant provided under the program established under subsection (a) shall be not more than 50 percent of the total cost of the applicable project or program.

"(d) AUTHORIZATION OF APPROPRIATIONS.—There is authorized to be appropriated to the Secretary to provide grants under this section $1,000,000 for each of fiscal years 2020 through 2028.

"**§ 308105. Battlefield restoration grant program**

"(a) ESTABLISHMENT.—The Secretary shall establish a battlefield restoration grant program (referred to in this section as the 'program') under which the Secretary may provide grants to States, Tribes, local governments, and nonprofit organizations for projects that restore day-of-battle conditions on land preserved under the battlefield acquisition grant program established under section 308103(b).

"(b) ELIGIBLE SITES.—The Secretary may make grants under this section for Revolutionary War, War of 1812, and Civil War battlefield sites eligible for assistance under the battlefield acquisition grant program established under section 308103(b).

"(c) FEDERAL SHARE.—The Federal share of the cost of a restoration project funded through a grant provided under the program shall be not more than 50 percent of the total cost of the project.

"(d) RESTORATION STANDARDS.—All restoration work carried out through a grant awarded under the program shall be performed in accordance with the Secretary of the Interior's Standards for the Treatment of Historic Properties under part 68 of title 36, Code of Federal Regulations (or successor regulations).

"(e) AUTHORIZATION OF APPROPRIATIONS.—There is authorized to be appropriated to the Secretary to provide grants under this section $1,000,000 for each of fiscal years 2020 through 2028.".

(b) CLERICAL AMENDMENT.—The analysis for chapter 3081 of title 54, United States Code, is amended by adding at the end the following:

"308104. Battlefield interpretation modernization grant program.

"308105. Battlefield restoration grant program.".

TITLE VIII—VETERANS AFFAIRS REPORT ON DISABILITY COMPENSATION AND THE POSITIVE ASSOCIATION WITH EXPOSURE TO AN HERBICIDE AGENT

[¶ 5096] SEC. 801. REPORT ON EFFORTS TO DETERMINE WHETHER TO ADD TO THE LIST OF DISEASES FOR WHICH PRESUMPTION OF SERVICE-CONNECTION IS WARRANTED FOR PURPOSES OF DISABILITY COMPENSATION BY REASON OF HAVING POSITIVE ASSOCIATION WITH EXPOSURE TO AN HERBICIDE AGENT.

(a) IN GENERAL.—Not later than 30 days after the date of the enactment of this Act, the Secretary of Veterans Affairs, in consultation with the Director of the Office of Management and Budget, shall submit to the Committee on Veterans' Affairs of the Senate and the Committee on Veterans' Affairs of the House of Representatives a report setting forth the status of any efforts of the Secretary to determine whether to promulgate new regulations to add to the list of diseases for which a presumption of service-connection is warranted for purposes of section 1110 of title 38, United States Code, by reason of having positive association with exposure to an herbicide agent.

(b) CONTENTS.—The report submitted under subsection (a) shall include the following:

(1) A detailed explanation of any delays in making a determination described in such subsection.

(2) An estimate of the cost of adding to the list of diseases described in such subsection.

(3) The date the Secretary anticipates on which the Secretary will promulgate new regulations as described in such subsection.

(c) DEFINITION OF HERBICIDE AGENT.—For purposes of this section, the term "herbicide agent" has the meaning given such term in section 1116 of title 38, United States Code.

TITLE IX—DISASTER RECOVERY WORKFORCE

[¶ 5097] SEC. 901. SHORT TITLE.

This title may be cited as the "Disaster Recovery Workforce Act".

[¶ 5098] SEC. 902. CONSTRUCTION WORKER PERMITS.

Section 6(d)(3) of the Joint Resolution entitled "A Joint Resolution to approve the 'Covenant To Establish a Commonwealth of the Northern Mariana Islands in Political Union with the United States of America', and for other purposes" (48 U.S.C. 1806(d)(3)) is amended by adding at the end the following:

"(E) TYPHOON RECOVERY.—

"(i) PERMITS FOR CONSTRUCTION WORKERS.—Notwithstanding any numerical cap set forth in subparagraph (B) for each of fiscal years 2020, 2021, and 2022, the Secretary of Homeland Security shall increase by 3,000, for each such fiscal year, the total number of permits available under this subsection for Construction and Extraction Occupations (as defined by the Department of Labor as Standard Occupational Classification Group 47-0000).

"(ii) PERMIT REQUIREMENTS.—The Secretary may only issue a permit made available under clause (i) to a prospective employer if the permit is for an alien who—

"(I) is a national of a country designated eligible to participate in the program under section 101(a)(15)(H)(ii)(b) of the Immigration and Nationality Act (8 U.S.C. 1101(a)(15)(H)(ii)(b)) during calendar year 2018; and

"(II) is performing service or labor pursuant to a contract or subcontract for construction, repairs, renovations, or facility services directly connected to, or associated with recovery from a presidentially declared major disaster or emergency (as those terms are defined in section 102 of the Robert T. Stafford Disaster Relief and Emergency Assistance Act (42 U.S.C. 5122), or for preparation for a future disaster or emergency.

"(iii) EXCEPTION FOR CONSTRUCTION WORKERS.—Subparagraph (D)(v) shall not apply to a permit made available under clause (i) for any fiscal year described in such clause.".

TITLE X—TELEVISION VIEWER PROTECTION

[¶ 5099] SEC. 1001. SHORT TITLE.

This title may be cited as the "Television Viewer Protection Act of 2019".

[¶ 5100] SEC. 1002. EXTENSION OF AUTHORITY.

(a) IN GENERAL.—Section 325(b) of the Communications Act of 1934 (47 U.S.C. 325(b)) is amended—

(1) in paragraph (2)(C)—

(A) by striking "until December 31, 2019,"; and

(B) by striking "antenna," and all that follows and inserting "antenna under the statutory license of section 119 of title 17, United States Code;"; and

(2) in paragraph (3)(C), by striking "until January 1, 2020," each place it appears.

(b) CONFORMING AMENDMENT.—Section 325(b)(2) of the Communications Act of 1934 (47 U.S.C. 325(b)(2)) is amended by striking ", the term 'unserved household' has the meaning given that term under section 119(d) of such title".

[¶ 5101] SEC. 1003. SATISFACTION OF GOOD FAITH NEGOTIATION REQUIREMENT BY MULTICHANNEL VIDEO PROGRAMMING DISTRIBUTORS.

(a) SATISFACTION OF GOOD FAITH NEGOTIATION REQUIREMENT.—Section 325(b)(3)(C) of the Communications Act of 1934 (47 U.S.C. 325(b)(3)(C)) is amended—

(1) in clause (iv), by striking "; and" and inserting a semicolon;

(2) in clause (v), by striking the period at the end and inserting "; and"; and

(3) by adding at the end the following:

"(vi) not later than 90 days after the date of the enactment of the Television Viewer Protection Act of 2019, specify that—

"(I) a multichannel video programming distributor may satisfy its obligation to negotiate in good faith under clause (iii) with respect to a negotiation for retransmission consent under this section with a large station group by designating a qualified MVPD buying group to negotiate on its behalf, so long as the qualified MVPD buying group itself negotiates in good faith in accordance with such clause;

"(II) it is a violation of the obligation to negotiate in good faith under clause (iii) for the qualified MVPD buying group to disclose the prices, terms, or conditions of an ongoing negotiation or the final terms of a negotiation to a member of the qualified MVPD buying group that is not intending, or is unlikely, to enter into the final terms negotiated by the qualified MVPD buying group; and

"(III) a large station group has an obligation to negotiate in good faith under clause (ii) with respect to a negotiation for retransmission consent under this section with a qualified MVPD buying group.".

(b) DEFINITIONS.—Section 325(b)(7) of the Communications Act of 1934 (47 U.S.C. 325(b)(7)) is amended—

(1) in subparagraph (A), by striking "; and" and inserting a semicolon;

(2) in subparagraph (B), by striking the period at the end and inserting a semicolon; and

(3) by adding at the end the following:

"(C) 'qualified MVPD buying group' means an entity that, with respect to a negotiation with a large station group for retransmission consent under this section—

"(i) negotiates on behalf of two or more multichannel video programming distributors—

"(I) none of which is a multichannel video programming distributor that serves more than 500,000 subscribers nationally; and

"(II) that do not collectively serve more than 25 percent of all households served by a multichannel video programming distributor in any single local market in which the applicable large station group operates; and

"(ii) negotiates agreements for such retransmission consent—

"(I) that contain standardized contract provisions, including billing structures and technical quality standards, for each multichannel video programming distributor on behalf of which the entity negotiates; and

"(II) under which the entity assumes liability to remit to the applicable large station group all fees received from the multichannel video programming distributors on behalf of which the entity negotiates;

"(D) 'large station group' means a group of television broadcast stations that—

"(i) are directly or indirectly under common de jure control permitted by the regulations of the Commission;

"(ii) generally negotiate agreements for retransmission consent under this section as a single entity; and

"(iii) include only television broadcast stations that have a national audience reach of more than 20 percent;

"(E) 'local market' has the meaning given such term in section 122(j) of title 17, United States Code; and

"(F) 'multichannel video programming distributor' has the meaning given such term in section 602.".

(c) CONFORMING AMENDMENTS.—Section 325(b) of the Communications Act of 1934 (47 U.S.C. 325(b)) is amended—

(1) in paragraph (2), by striking ", and the term 'local market' has the meaning given that term in section 122(j) of such title"; and

(2) in paragraph (3)(C), by striking "(as defined in section 122(j) of title 17, United States Code)" each place it appears.

(d) EFFECTIVE DATE.—The amendments made by this section, and the regulations promulgated by the Federal Communications Commission under such amendments, shall not take effect before January 1 of the calendar year after the calendar year in which this Act is enacted.

[¶ 5102] SEC. 1004. REQUIREMENTS RELATING TO CHARGES FOR COVERED SERVICES.

(a) IN GENERAL.—Part IV of title VI of the Communications Act of 1934 (47 U.S.C. 551 et seq.) is amended by adding at the end the following:

"SEC. 642. REQUIREMENTS RELATING TO CHARGES FOR COVERED SERVICES.

"(a) CONSUMER RIGHTS IN SALES.—

"(1) RIGHT TO TRANSPARENCY.—Before entering into a contract with a consumer for the provision of a covered service, a provider of a covered service shall provide the consumer, by phone, in person, online, or by other reasonable means, the total monthly charge for the covered service, whether offered individually or as part of a bundled service, selected by the consumer (explicitly noting the amount of any applicable promotional discount reflected in such charge and when such discount will expire), including any related administrative fees, equipment fees, or other charges, a good faith estimate of any tax, fee, or charge imposed by the Federal Government or a State or local government (whether imposed on the provider or imposed on the consumer but collected by the provider), and a good faith estimate of any fee or charge that is used to recover any other assessment imposed on the provider by the Federal Government or a State or local government.

"(2) RIGHT TO FORMAL NOTICE.—A provider of a covered service that enters into a contract described in paragraph (1) shall, not later than 24 hours after entering into the contract, send the consumer, by email, online link, or other reasonably comparable means, a copy of the information described in such paragraph.

"(3) Right to Cancel.—A provider of a covered service that enters into a contract described in paragraph (1) shall permit the consumer to cancel the contract, without paying early cancellation fees or other disconnection fees or penalties, during the 24-hour period beginning when the provider of the covered service sends the copy required by paragraph (2).

"(b) Consumer Rights in E-Billing.—If a provider of a covered service provides a bill to a consumer in an electronic format, the provider shall include in the bill—

"(1) an itemized statement that breaks down the total amount charged for or relating to the provision of the covered service by the amount charged for the provision of the service itself and the amount of all related taxes, administrative fees, equipment fees, or other charges;

"(2) the termination date of the contract for the provision of the covered service entered into between the consumer and the provider; and

"(3) the termination date of any applicable promotional discount.

"(c) Consumer Rights to Accurate Equipment Charges.—A provider of a covered service or fixed broadband internet access service may not charge a consumer for—

"(1) using covered equipment provided by the consumer; or

"(2) renting, leasing, or otherwise providing to the consumer covered equipment if—

"(A) the provider has not provided the equipment to the consumer; or

"(B) the consumer has returned the equipment to the provider, except to the extent that the charge relates to the period beginning on the date when the provider provided the equipment to the consumer and ending on the date when the consumer returned the equipment to the provider.

"(d) Definitions.—In this section:

"(1) Broadband Internet Access Service.—The term 'broadband internet access service' has the meaning given such term in section 8.1(b) of title 47, Code of Federal Regulations, or any successor regulation.

"(2) Covered Equipment.—The term 'covered equipment' means equipment "(such as a router) employed on the premises of a person (other than a provider of a covered service or fixed broadband internet access service) to provide a covered service or to provide fixed broadband internet access service.

"(3) Covered Service.—The term 'covered service' means service provided by a multichannel video programming distributor, to the extent such distributor is acting as a multichannel video programming distributor.".

(b) Effective Date.—Section 642 of the Communications Act of 1934, as added by subsection (a) of this section, shall apply beginning on the date that is 6 months after the date of the enactment of this Act. The Federal Communications Commission may grant an additional 6-month extension if the Commission finds that good cause exists for such an additional extension.

TITLE XI—ELIGIBILITY TO RECEIVE SIGNALS UNDER A DISTANT-SIGNAL SATELLITE LICENSE

[¶ 5103] SEC. 1101. SHORT TITLE.

This title may be cited as the "Satellite Television Community Protection and Promotion Act of 2019".

[¶ 5104] SEC. 1102. ELIGIBILITY TO RECEIVE SIGNALS UNDER A DISTANT-SIGNAL SATELLITE LICENSE.

(a) In General.—Section 119 of title 17, United States Code, is amended—

(1) in subsection (a)—

(A) in paragraph (2)—

(i) in subparagraph (A)—

(I) by striking "signals, and" and inserting "signals,";

(II) by inserting ", and the carrier provides local-into-local service to all DMAs" after "receiving the secondary transmission"; and

(III) by adding at the end the following new sentence: "Failure to reach an agreement with a network station to retransmit the signals of the station shall not be construed to affect compliance with providing local-into-local service to all DMAs if the satellite carrier has the capability to retransmit such signals when an agreement is reached."; and

(ii) in subparagraph (B)—

(I) by striking clauses (ii) and (iii);

(II) by adding at the end the following:

"(ii) SHORT MARKETS.—In the case of secondary transmissions to households located in short markets, subject to clause (i), the statutory license shall be further limited to secondary transmissions of only those primary transmissions of network stations that embody the programming of networks not offered on the primary stream or the multicast stream transmitted by any network station in that market.";

(B) by striking paragraphs (3), (6)(E), (9), (10), and (13); and

(C) by redesignating paragraphs (4), (5), (6), (7), (8), (11), (12), and (14) as paragraphs (3) through (10), respectively;

(2) in subsection (c)(1)(E)—

(A) by striking the comma after "in the agreement";

(B) by striking "until December 31, 2019, or"; and

(C) by striking ", whichever is later" and inserting "until the subscriber for which the royalty is payable is no longer eligible to receive a secondary transmission pursuant to the license under this section";

(3) in subsection (d)—

(A) in paragraph (10)—

(i) in subparagraph (D), by striking "subsection (a)(11)" and inserting "subsection (a)(8)";

(ii) by striking subparagraphs (A), (B), (C), and (E);

(iii) by redesignating subparagraph (D) as subparagraph (A); and

(iv) by adding at the end the following:

"(B) is a subscriber located in a short market.";

(B) by striking paragraph (13);

(C) by redesignating paragraphs (14) and (15) as paragraphs (13) and (14), respectively; and

(D) by adding at the end the following:

"(15) LOCAL-INTO-LOCAL SERVICE TO ALL DMAS.—The term 'local-into-local service to all DMAs' has the meaning given such term in subsection (f)(7).

"(16) SHORT MARKET.—The term 'short market' means a local market in which programming of one or more of the four most widely viewed television networks nationwide is not offered on either the primary stream or multicast stream transmitted by any network station in that market or is temporarily or permanently unavailable as a result of an act of god or other force majeure event beyond the control of the carrier.";

(4) by striking subsections (e) and (h);

(5) in subsection (g)(7), by inserting ", except for designated market areas where the entity is temporarily or permanently unable to provide local service as a result of an act of god or other force majeure event beyond the control of the entity" after "section 122"; and

(6) by redesignating subsections (f) and (g) as subsections (e) and (f).

(b) PREVIOUSLY COVERED SUBSCRIBERS UNDER THE STELA REAUTHORIZATION ACT OF 2014.—

(1) IN GENERAL.—A subscriber of a satellite carrier who receives the secondary transmission of a network station under the statutory license in section 119 of title 17, United States Code, as in effect on the day before the date of the enactment of this Act, and to whom subsection (a)(2)(B) of

such section, as amended by subsection (a), does not apply, shall continue to be eligible to receive that secondary transmission from such carrier under such license, and at the royalty rate established for such license by the Copyright Royalty Board or voluntary agreement, as applicable, until the date that is the earlier of—

(A) May 31, 2020; or

(B) the date on which such carrier provides local-into-local service to all DMAs.

(2) DEFINITIONS.—In this subsection, the terms "satellite carrier", "subscriber", "secondary transmission", "network station", and "local-into-local service to all DMAs" have the meaning given those terms in section 119 of title 17, United States Code.

(c) CONFORMING AMENDMENTS.—Title 17, United States Code, is further amended—

(1) in section 119, as amended by subsection (a)—

(A) in subsection (a)—

(i) in paragraph (1), by striking "paragraphs (4), (5), and (7)" and inserting "paragraphs (3), (4), and (6)"; and

(ii) in paragraph (2), by striking "paragraphs (4), (5), (6), and (7)" and inserting "paragraphs (3), (4), (5), and (6)"; and

(B) in subsection (f), as so redesignated, by striking "subsection (a)(7)(B)" each place it appears and inserting "subsection (a)(5)(B)"; and

(2) in section 501(e), by striking "section 119(a)(5)" and inserting "section 119(a)(3)".

TITLE XII—GROUNDFISH TRAWL FISHERY

[¶ 5105] SEC. 1201. GROUNDFISH TRAWL FISHERY.

The Secretary of Commerce shall forgive the interest accrued on the Groundfish Trawl fishery sub-loan regarding fishing capacity reduction in the West Coast groundfish fishery authorized by section 212 of division B, title II, of Public Law 108-7 from December 4, 2003, through September 8, 2005, and the portion of additional interest accrued in the Groundfish Trawl fishery sub-loan since September 8, 2005, that is directly attributable to the delay in implementing a repayment system. The Secretary of the Treasury shall make available, out of any funds in the Treasury not otherwise appropriated, such sums necessary for any loan modification under this provision.

TITLE XIII—TEMPORARY RELIEF FROM CERTAIN ERISA REQUIREMENTS

[¶ 5106] SEC. 1301. SHORT TITLE.

This title may be cited as the "Temporary Relief from Certain ERISA Requirements Act of 2020".

[¶ 5107] SEC. 1302. EXEMPTION.

(a) IN GENERAL.—Section 408 of the Employee Retirement Income Security Act of 1974 (29 U.S.C. 1108) is amended by adding at the end the following:

"(h) PROVISION OF PHARMACY BENEFIT SERVICES.—

"(1) IN GENERAL.—Provided that all of the conditions described in paragraph (2) are met, the restrictions imposed by subsections (a), (b)(1), and (b)(2) of section 406 shall not apply to—

"(A) the offering of pharmacy benefit services to a group health plan that is sponsored by an entity described in section 3(37)(G)(vi) or to any other group health plan that is sponsored by a regional council, local union, or other labor organization affiliated with such entity;

"(B) the purchase of pharmacy benefit services by plan participants and beneficiaries of a group health plan that is sponsored by an entity described in section 3(37)(G)(vi) or of any other group health plan that is sponsored by a regional council, local union, or other labor organization affiliated with such entity; or

"(C) the operation or implementation of pharmacy benefit services by an entity described in section 3(37)(G)(vi) or by any other group health plan that is sponsored by a regional council, local union, or other labor organization affiliated with such entity, in any arrangement where such entity described in section 3(37)(G)(vi) or any related organization or subsidiary of such entity provides pharmacy benefit services that include prior authorization and appeals, a retail pharmacy network, pharmacy benefit administration, mail order fulfillment, formulary support, manufacturer payments, audits, and specialty pharmacy and goods, to any such group health plan.

"(2) CONDITIONS.—The conditions described in this paragraph are the following:

"(A) The terms of the arrangement are at least as favorable to the group health plan as such group health plan could obtain in a similar arm's length arrangement with an unrelated third party.

"(B) At least 50 percent of the providers participating in the pharmacy benefit services offered by the arrangement are unrelated to the contributing employers or any other party in interest with respect to the group health plan.

"(C) The group health plan retains an independent fiduciary who will be responsible for monitoring the group health plan's consultants, contractors, subcontractors, and other service providers for purposes of pharmacy benefit services described in paragraph (1) offered by such entity or any of its related organizations or subsidiaries and monitors the transactions of such entity and any of its related organizations or subsidiaries to ensure that all conditions of this exemption are satisfied during each plan year.

"(D) Any decisions regarding the provision of pharmacy benefit services described in paragraph (1) are made by the group health plan's independent fiduciary, based on objective standards developed by the independent fiduciary in reliance on information provided by the arrangement.

"(E) The independent fiduciary of the group health plan provides an annual report to the Secretary and the congressional committees of jurisdiction attesting that the conditions described in subparagraphs (C) and (D) have been met for the applicable plan year, together with a statement that use of the arrangement's services are in the best interest of the participants and beneficiaries in the aggregate for that plan year compared to other similar arrangements the group health plan could have obtained in transactions with an unrelated third party.

"(F) The arrangement is not designed to benefit any party in interest with respect to the group health plan.

"(3) VIOLATIONS.—In the event an entity described in section 3(37)(G)(vi) or any affiliate of such entity violates any of the conditions of such exemption, such exemption shall not apply with respect to such entity or affiliate and all enforcement and claims available under this Act shall apply with respect to such entity or affiliate.

"(4) RULE OF CONSTRUCTION.—Nothing in this subsection shall be construed to modify any obligation of a group health plan otherwise set forth in this Act.

"(5) GROUP HEALTH PLAN.—In this subsection, the term 'group health plan' has the meaning given such term in section 733(a).".

(b) AMENDMENT TO INTERNAL REVENUE CODE OF 1986.—Subsection (c) of section 4975 of the Internal Revenue Code of 1986 is amended by adding at the end the following new paragraph:

"(7) SPECIAL RULE FOR PROVISION OF PHARMACY BENEFIT SERVICES.—Any party to an arrangement which satisfies the requirements of section 408(h) of the Employee Retirement Income Security Act of 1974 shall be exempt from the tax imposed by this section with respect to such arrangement.".

(c) APPLICABILITY.—With respect to a group health plan subject to subsection (h) of section 408 of the Employee Retirement Income Security Act of 1974 (29 U.S.C. 1108) (as amended by subsection (a)) and subsection (c) of section 4975 of the Internal Revenue Code of 1986 (as amended by subsection (b)), beginning at the end of the fifth plan year of such group health plan that begins after the date of enactment of this Act, such subsection (h) of such section 408 and such subsection (c) of such shall have no force or effect.

TITLE XIV—LIBRARY OF CONGRESS TECHNICAL CORRECTIONS

[¶ 5108] SEC. 1401. SHORT TITLE.

This title may be cited as the "Library of Congress Technical Corrections Act of 2019".

[¶5109] **SEC. 1402. AMENDMENT TO AMERICAN FOLKLIFE PRESERVATION ACT.**

Section 4 of the American Folklife Preservation Act (20 U.S.C. 2103) is amended—

(1) in subsection (b)(1)(D)—

    (A) in the matter preceding clause (i), by striking "seven" and inserting "nine";

    (B) in clause (vi), by striking "and" after the semicolon;

    (C) in clause (vii), by striking the period at the end and inserting a semicolon; and

    (D) by adding at the end the following:

"(viii) the Secretary of Veterans Affairs; and

"(ix) the Director of the Institute of Museum and Library Services."; and

(2) in subsection (f), by striking the second sentence and inserting the following: "The rate of basic pay of the Director shall be fixed in accordance with section 5376(b) of title 5, United States Code.".

[¶5110] **SEC. 1403. NATIONAL LIBRARY SERVICE FOR THE BLIND AND PRINT DISABLED.**

(a) IN GENERAL.—The Act entitled "An Act to provide books for the adult blind", approved March 3, 1931 (2 U.S.C. 135a et seq.), is amended to read as follows:

"**SECTION 1. NATIONAL LIBRARY SERVICE FOR THE BLIND AND PRINT DISABLED.**

"(a) ACCESSIBLE MATERIALS AND REPRODUCERS.—

"(1) IN GENERAL.—The Librarian of Congress is authorized to provide to eligible persons who are residents of the United States (including residents of the several States, insular possessions, and the District of Columbia) and to eligible persons who are United States citizens residing outside the United States the following items:

"(A) Literary works published in raised characters, on sound-reproduction recordings, or in any other accessible format.

"(B) Musical scores, instructional texts, and other specialized materials used in furthering educational, vocational, and cultural opportunities in the field of music published in any accessible format.

"(C) Reproducers for such formats.

"(2) OWNERSHIP.—Any item provided under paragraph (1) shall be provided on a loan basis and shall remain the property of the Library of Congress.

"(b) LENDING PREFERENCE.—In the lending of items under subsection (a), the Librarian shall at all times give preference to—

"(1) the needs of the blind and visually disabled; and

"(2) the needs of eligible persons who have been honorably discharged from the Armed Forces of the United States.

"(c) NETWORK.—The Librarian of Congress may contract or otherwise arrange with such public or other nonprofit libraries, agencies, or organizations as the Librarian may determine appropriate to serve as local or regional centers for the circulation of items described in subsection (a)(1).

"(d) INTERNATIONAL SERVICE.—The Librarian of Congress is authorized to provide items described in subparagraphs (A) and (B) of subsection (a)(1) to authorized entities located in a country that is a party to the Marrakesh Treaty, if any such items are delivered to authorized entities through online, not physical, means. The Librarian may contract or otherwise arrange with such authorized entities to deliver such items to eligible persons located in their countries in any accessible format and consistent with section 121A of title 17, United States Code.

"(e) CONTRACTING PREFERENCE.—In the purchase and maintenance of items described in subsection (a), the Librarian of Congress, without regard to section 6101 of title 41, United States Code, shall give preference to nonprofit institutions or agencies whose activities are primarily concerned with the blind and with other physically disabled persons, in all cases where, considering all the circumstances and needs involved, the Librarian determines that the prices submitted are fair and reasonable.

"(f) REGULATIONS.—The Librarian of Congress shall prescribe regulations for services under this section, in consultation with eligible persons and authorized entities. Such regulations shall include procedures that shall be used by an individual to establish that the individual is an eligible person.

"(g) DEFINITIONS.—In this section—

"(1) the terms 'accessible format', 'authorized entity', and 'eligible person' have the meanings given those terms in section 121 of title 17, United States Code; and

"(2) the term 'Marrakesh Treaty' has the meaning given in section 121A of such title 17.

"(h) AUTHORIZATION OF APPROPRIATIONS.—There are authorized to be appropriated to carry out this section such sums as may be necessary.".

(b) CONFORMING AMENDMENT.—The Act entitled "An Act to establish in the Library of Congress a library of musical scores and other instructional materials to further educational, vocational, and cultural opportunities in the field of music for blind persons", approved October 9, 1962 (2 U.S.C. 135a-1), is repealed.

[¶ 5111] SEC. 1404. UNIFORM PAY SCALE FOR LIBRARY OF CONGRESS CAREER SENIOR EXECUTIVE POSITIONS.

(a) EXECUTIVE SCHEDULE POSITIONS.—

(1) DEPUTY LIBRARIAN OF CONGRESS.—Paragraph (2) of section 904 of the Supplemental Appropriations Act, 1983 (2 U.S.C. 136a-2) is amended to read as follows:

"(2) the Deputy Librarian of Congress shall be compensated at the greater of the rate of pay in effect for level III of the Executive Schedule under section 5314 of title 5, United States Code, or the maximum annual rate of basic pay payable under section 5376 of such title for positions at agencies with a performance appraisal system certified under section 5307(d) of such title.".

(2) DIRECTOR, CONGRESSIONAL RESEARCH SERVICE.—The second sentence of section 203(c)(1) of the Legislative Reorganization Act of 1946 (2 U.S.C. 166(c)(l)) is amended to read as follows: "The Director shall be compensated at the greater of the rate of pay in effect for level III of the Executive Schedule under section 5314 of title 5, United States Code, or the maximum annual rate of basic pay payable under section 5376 of such title for positions at agencies with a performance appraisal system certified under section 5307(d) of such title.".

(3) REGISTER OF COPYRIGHTS.—The first sentence of section 701(f) of title 17, United States Code, is amended to read as follows: "The Register of Copyrights shall be compensated at the greater of the rate of pay in effect for level III of the Executive Schedule under section 5314 of title 5 or the maximum annual rate of basic pay payable under section 5376 of such title for positions at agencies with a performance appraisal system certified under section 5307(d) of such title.".

(b) REFERENCES TO GS GRADES 16, 17, AND 18 AND SENIOR LEVEL CLASSIFICATION.—

(1) CONGRESSIONAL RESEARCH SERVICE.—Section 203(c)(2) of the Legislative Reorganization Act of 1946 (2 U.S.C. 166(c)(2)) is amended—

(A) in the second sentence of the matter preceding subparagraph (A), by deleting "subchapter III" and all that follows through "such title." and inserting "section 5376 of title 5, United States Code."; and

(B) in subparagraph (B), by striking "may be placed in GS-16, 17, and 18" and all that follows through the period at the end and inserting "may be classified above GS-15 in accordance with section 5108(c) of title 5, United States Code, and the rate of basic pay for such positions may be fixed in accordance with section 5376 of such title, subject to the prior approval of the Joint Committee on the Library.".

(2) U.S. COPYRIGHT OFFICE.—Section 701(f) of title 17, United States Code, is amended by striking the last sentence and inserting "The rate of basic pay for each Associate Register of Copyrights shall be fixed in accordance with section 5376 of title 5.".

[¶ 5112] SEC. 1405. STAFFING FOR COPYRIGHT ROYALTY JUDGES PROGRAM.

(a) REMOVAL OF CAP ON PERSONNEL.—Chapter 8 of title 17, United States Code, is amended—

(1) in section 802—

    (A) in subsection (b), by striking "3"; and

    (B) in subsection (e), by striking paragraph (2) and inserting the following:

    "(2) STAFF MEMBERS.—Staff members appointed under subsection(b) shall be compensated at a rate not more than the basic rate of pay payable for level 10 of GS-15 of the General Schedule."; and

(2) in section 803(e)(1)(A), by striking "3".

(b) EFFECTIVE DATE.—The amendments made by this section shall take effect with respect to fiscal year 2020 and each fiscal year thereafter.

TITLE XV—SENATE ENTITIES

[¶ 5112A] SEC. 1501.

Section 2(c) of chapter VIII of title I of Public Law 100-71 (2 U.S.C. 6567(c)) is amended by striking "$10,000" and inserting "$15,000".

[¶ 5112B] SEC. 1502.

Section 902 of the Emergency Supplemental Act, 2002 (2 U.S.C. 6616) is amended—

(1) in subsection (a)—

    (A) in paragraph (1)—

        (i) by striking "subsection (b)" and inserting "paragraph (3)"; and

        (ii) by striking "and" at the end;

    (B) in paragraph (2), by striking the period and inserting "; and"; and

    (C) by adding at the end the following:

    "(3) the Sergeant at Arms of the Senate may enter into a memorandum of understanding described in paragraph (1) consistent with the Senate Procurement Regulations."; and

(2) by striking subsection (b) and inserting the following:

"(b) The Sergeant at Arms of the Senate may incur obligations and make expenditures for meals, refreshments, and other support and maintenance for Members, officers, and employees of the Senate when such obligations and expenditures are necessary to respond to emergencies involving the safety of human life or the protection of property.".

TITLE XVI—LEGISLATIVE BRANCH INSPECTORS GENERAL INDEPENDENCE

[¶ 5113] SEC. 1601. SHORT TITLE.

This title may be cited as the "Legislative Branch Inspectors General Independence Act of 2019".

[¶ 5114] SEC. 1602. PAY, LIMITS ON BONUSES, COUNSEL, AND AUTHORITIES.

(a) LIBRARY OF CONGRESS.—Section 1307 of the Legislative Branch Appropriations Act, 2006 (2 U.S.C. 185) is amended—

(1) in subsection (c)—

    (A) in the subsection heading, by inserting "; PAY; LIMITS ON BONUSES; COUNSEL" after "REMOVAL";

    (B) by striking paragraph (2) and inserting the following:

    "(2) REMOVAL OR TRANSFER.—

    "(A) IN GENERAL.—The Inspector General may be removed from office, or transferred to another position within, or another location of, the Library of Congress, by the Librarian of Congress.

    "(B) NOTICE.—Not later than 30 days before the Librarian of Congress removes or transfers the Inspector General under subparagraph (A), the Librarian of Congress shall communicate in writing the reason for the removal or transfer to—

"(i) the Committee on House Administration and the Committee on Appropriations of the House of Representatives; and

"(ii) the Committee on Rules and Administration and the Committee on Appropriations of the Senate.

"(C) APPLICABILITY.—Nothing in this paragraph shall prohibit a personnel action (except for removal or transfer) that is otherwise authorized by law."; and

(C) by adding at the end the following:

"(3) PAY.—

"(A) IN GENERAL.—The position of Inspector General shall—

"(i) be classified as a position above GS-15 in accordance with section 5108 of title 5, United States Code; and

"(ii) have a rate of basic pay that is not less than the average rate of basic pay of all other employees in positions classified as above GS-15 of the Library of Congress calculated on an annual basis.

"(B) ADJUSTMENTS.—The Librarian of Congress shall establish the amount of the annual adjustment in the rate of basic pay for the Inspector General in an amount equal to the average of the annual adjustments in the rate of basic pay provided to all other employees in positions classified as above GS-15 of the Library of Congress, in a manner consistent with section 5376 of title 5, United States Code.

"(4) NO BONUSES.—The Inspector General may not receive any cash award or cash bonus, including a cash award under chapter 45 of title 5, United States Code.

"(5) COUNSEL.—The Inspector General shall, in accordance with applicable laws and regulations governing selections, appointments, and employment at the Library of Congress, obtain legal advice from a counsel reporting directly to the Inspector General or another Inspector General."; and

(2) in subsection (d)(1), by striking "Sections 4" and all that follows through "and 7" and inserting "Sections 4, 5 (other than subsection (a)(13)), 6 (other than subsection (a)(7)), and 7".

(b) OFFICE OF THE ARCHITECT OF THE CAPITOL.—Section 1301(c) of the Architect of the Capitol Inspector General Act of 2007 (2 U.S.C. 1808(c)) is amended—

(1) in the subsection heading, by inserting "; PAY; LIMITS ON BONUSES; COUNSEL" after "REMOVAL";

(2) by striking paragraph (2) and inserting the following:

"(2) REMOVAL OR TRANSFER.—

"(A) IN GENERAL.—The Inspector General may be removed from office, or transferred to another position within, or another location of, the Office of the Architect of the Capitol, by the Architect of the Capitol.

"(B) NOTICE.—Not later than 30 days before the Architect of the Capitol removes or transfers the Inspector General under subparagraph (A), the Architect of the Capitol shall communicate in writing the reason for the removal or transfer to—

"(i) the Committee on House Administration and the Committee on Appropriations of the House of Representatives; and

"(ii) the Committee on Rules and Administration and the Committee on Appropriations of the Senate.

"(C) APPLICABILITY.—Nothing in this paragraph shall prohibit a personnel action (except for removal or transfer) that is otherwise authorized by law."; and

(3) by adding at the end the following:

"(4) NO BONUSES.—The Inspector General may not receive any cash award or cash bonus, including a cash award under chapter 45 of title 5, United States Code.

"(5) COUNSEL.—The Inspector General shall, in accordance with applicable laws and regulations governing selections, appointments, and employment at the Office of the Architect of the

Capitol, obtain legal advice from a counsel reporting directly to the Inspector General or another Inspector General.".

(c) GOVERNMENT PUBLISHING OFFICE.—

(1) IN GENERAL.—Section 3902 of title 44, United States Code, is amended—

(A) in the section heading, by inserting "; **pay; limits on bonuses; counsel**" after "removal";

(B) by striking subsection (b) and inserting the following:

"(b)(1) The Inspector General may be removed from office, or transferred to another position within, or another location of, the Government Publishing Office, by the Director of the Government Publishing Office.

"(2) Not later than 30 days before the Director removes or transfers the Inspector General under paragraph (1), the Director shall communicate in writing the reason for the removal or transfer to—

"(A) the Committee on House Administration and the Committee on Appropriations of the House of Representatives; and

"(B) the Committee on Rules and Administration and the Committee on Appropriations of the Senate.

"(3) Nothing in this subsection shall prohibit a personnel action (except for removal or transfer) that is otherwise authorized by law."; and

(C) by adding at the end the following:

"(c)(1) The position of Inspector General shall be—

"(A) classified as a position as a senior level employee, in accordance with this title; and

"(B) have a rate of basic pay that is not less than the average rate of basic pay of all other senior level employees of the Government Publishing Office calculated on an annual basis.

"(2) The Director of the Government Publishing Office shall establish the amount of the annual adjustment in the rate of basic pay for the Inspector General in an amount equal to the average of the annual adjustments in the rate of basic pay provided to all other senior level employees of the Government Publishing Office, consistent with this title.

"(d) The Inspector General may not receive any cash award or cash bonus, including a cash award under chapter 45 of title 5.

"(e) The Inspector General shall, in accordance with applicable laws and regulations governing selections, appointments, and employment at the Government Publishing Office, obtain legal advice from a counsel reporting directly to the Inspector General or another Inspector General.".

(2) TECHNICAL AND CONFORMING AMENDMENT.—The table of sections for chapter 39 of title 44, United States Code, is amended by striking the item relating to section 3902 and inserting the following:

"3902. Appointment of Inspector General; supervision; removal; pay; limits on bonuses; counsel.".

[¶ 5115] SEC. 1603. LAW ENFORCEMENT AUTHORITY.

(a) LIBRARY OF CONGRESS.—Section 1307(d) of the Legislative Branch Appropriations Act, 2006 (2 U.S.C. 185(d)) is amended by adding at the end the following:

"(3) LAW ENFORCEMENT AUTHORITY.—

"(A) IN GENERAL.—Subject to subparagraph (B), any supervisory special agent under the Inspector General and any special agent supervised by such a supervisory special agent is authorized to—

"(i) make an arrest without a warrant while engaged in official duties as authorized under this section or any other statute for any offense against the United States committed in the presence of such supervisory special agent or special agent, or for any felony cognizable under the laws of the United States if such supervisory special agent or special agent has reasonable grounds to believe that the person to be arrested has committed or is committing such felony;

"(ii) seek and execute warrants for arrest, search of a premises, or seizure of evidence issued under the authority of the United States upon probable cause to believe that a violation has been committed; and

"(iii) carry a firearm while engaged in official duties as authorized under this section or any other statute.

"(B) REQUIREMENTS TO EXERCISE AUTHORITY.—

"(i) REQUIRED CERTIFICATION.—

"(I) IN GENERAL.—In order to exercise the authority under subparagraph (A), a supervisory special agent or a special agent supervised by such a supervisory special agent shall certify that he or she—

"(aa) is a citizen of the United States;

"(bb) has successfully completed a basic law enforcement training program or military or other equivalent; and

"(cc) is not prohibited from receiving a firearm under Federal law, including under section 922(g)(9) of title 18, United States Code, because of a conviction of a misdemeanor crime of domestic violence.

"(II) ADDITIONAL REQUIREMENTS.—After providing notice to the appropriate committees of Congress, the Inspector General may add requirements to the certification required under subclause (I), as determined appropriate by the Inspector General.

"(ii) MAINTENANCE OF REQUIREMENTS.—The Inspector General shall maintain firearms-related requirements (including quarterly firearms qualifications) and use of force training requirements that, except to the extent the Inspector General determines necessary to effectively carry out the duties of the Office of the Inspector General, are in accordance with the Council of the Inspectors General on Integrity and Efficiency use of force policies, which incorporate Department of Justice guidelines.

"(iii) ELIGIBILITY DETERMINATION.—

"(I) IN GENERAL.—The Inspector General shall—

"(aa) determine whether an individual meets the requirements under this paragraph; and

"(bb) revoke any authority granted to an individual under subparagraph (A) if the individual is not in compliance with the requirements of this paragraph.

"(II) REAUTHORIZATION.—The Inspector General may reauthorize an individual to exercise the authority granted under subparagraph (A) if the Inspector General determines the individual has achieved compliance with the requirements under this paragraph.

"(III) LIMITATION ON APPEAL.—A revocation of the authority granted under subparagraph (A) shall not be subject to administrative, judicial, or other review, unless the revocation results in an adverse action. Such an adverse action may, at the election of the applicable individual, be reviewed in accordance with the otherwise applicable procedures.

"(C) SEMIANNUAL CERTIFICATION OF PROGRAM.—

"(i) IN GENERAL.—Before the first grant of authority under subparagraph (A), and semiannually thereafter as part of the report under section 5 of the Inspector General Act of 1978 (5 U.S.C. App.), the Inspector General shall submit to the appropriate committees of Congress a written certification that adequate internal safeguards and management procedures exist that, except to the extent the Inspector General determines necessary to effectively carry out the duties of the Office of the Inspector General, are in compliance with standards established by the Council of the Inspectors General on Integrity and Efficiency, which incorporate Department of Justice guidelines, to ensure proper exercise of the powers authorized under this paragraph.

"(ii) SUSPENSION OF AUTHORITY.—The authority granted under this paragraph (including any grant of authority to an individual under subparagraph (A), without regard to whether the individual is in compliance with subparagraph (B)) may be suspended by the Inspector General if the Office of Inspector General fails to comply with the reporting and review requirements under clause (i) of this subparagraph or subparagraph (D). Any suspension of authority under this clause shall be reported to the appropriate committees of Congress.

"(D) PEER REVIEW.—To ensure the proper exercise of the law enforcement powers authorized under this paragraph, the Office of Inspector General shall submit to and participate in the external review process established by the Council of the Inspectors General on Integrity and Efficiency for ensuring that adequate internal safeguards and management procedures continue to exist. Under the review process, the exercise of the law enforcement powers by the Office of Inspector General shall be reviewed periodically by another Office of Inspector General or by a committee of Inspectors General. The results of each review shall be communicated in writing to the Inspector General, the Council of the Inspectors General on Integrity and Efficiency, and the appropriate committees of Congress.

"(E) ALLEGED MISCONDUCT.—Any allegation of misconduct by an individual granted authority under subparagraph (A) may be reviewed by the Integrity Committee of the Council of the Inspectors General on Integrity and Efficiency.

"(F) APPROPRIATE COMMITTEES OF CONGRESS.—In this paragraph, the term 'appropriate committees of Congress' means—

"(i) the Committee on Rules and Administration and the Committee on Appropriations of the Senate; and

"(ii) the Committee on House Administration and the Committee on Appropriations of the House of Representatives.".

(b) ARCHITECT OF THE CAPITOL.—Section 1301(d) of the Architect of the Capitol Inspector General Act of 2007 (2 U.S.C. 1808(d)) is amended by adding at the end the following:

"(3) LAW ENFORCEMENT AUTHORITY.—

"(A) IN GENERAL.—Subject to subparagraph (B), any supervisory special agent under the Inspector General and any special agent supervised by such a supervisory special agent is authorized to—

"(i) make an arrest without a warrant while engaged in official duties as authorized under this section or any other statute for any offense against the United States committed in the presence of such supervisory special agent or special agent, or for any felony cognizable under the laws of the United States if such supervisory special agent or special agent has reasonable grounds to believe that the person to be arrested has committed or is committing such felony;

"(ii) seek and execute warrants for arrest, search of a premises, or seizure of evidence issued under the authority of the United States upon probable cause to believe that a violation has been committed; and

"(iii) carry a firearm while engaged in official duties as authorized under this section or any other statute.

"(B) REQUIREMENTS TO EXERCISE AUTHORITY.—

"(i) REQUIRED CERTIFICATION.—

"(I) IN GENERAL.—In order to exercise the authority under subparagraph (A), a supervisory special agent or a special agent supervised by such a supervisory special agent shall certify that he or she—

"(aa) is a citizen of the United States;

"(bb) has successfully completed a basic law enforcement training program or military or other equivalent; and

"(cc) is not prohibited from receiving a firearm under Federal law, including under section 922(g)(9) of title 18, United States Code, because of a conviction of a misdemeanor crime of domestic violence.

"(II) ADDITIONAL REQUIREMENTS.—After providing notice to the appropriate committees of Congress, the Inspector General may add requirements to the certification required under subclause (I), as determined appropriate by the Inspector General.

"(ii) MAINTENANCE OF REQUIREMENTS.—The Inspector General shall maintain firearms-related requirements (including quarterly firearms qualifications) and use of force training requirements that, except to the extent the Inspector General determines necessary to effectively carry out the duties of the Office of the Inspector General, are in accordance with the Council of the Inspectors General on Integrity and Efficiency use of force policies, which incorporate Department of Justice guidelines.

"(iii) ELIGIBILITY DETERMINATION.—

"(I) IN GENERAL.—The Inspector General shall—

"(aa) determine whether an individual meets the requirements under this paragraph; and "(bb) revoke any authority granted to an individual under subparagraph (A) if the individual is not in compliance with the requirements of this paragraph.

"(II) REAUTHORIZATION.—The Inspector General may reauthorize an individual to exercise the authority granted under subparagraph (A) if the Inspector General determines the individual has achieved compliance with the requirements under this paragraph.

"(III) LIMITATION ON APPEAL.—A revocation of the authority granted under subparagraph (A) shall not be subject to administrative, judicial, or other review, unless the revocation results in an adverse action. Such an adverse action may, at the election of the applicable individual, be reviewed in accordance with the otherwise applicable procedures.

"(C) SEMIANNUAL CERTIFICATION OF PROGRAM.—

"(i) IN GENERAL.—Before the first grant of authority under subparagraph (A), and semiannually thereafter as part of the report under section 5 of the Inspector General Act of 1978 (5 U.S.C. App.), the Inspector General shall submit to the appropriate committees of Congress a written certification that adequate internal safeguards and management procedures exist that, except to the extent the Inspector General determines necessary to effectively carry out the duties of the Office of the Inspector General, are in compliance with standards established by the Council of the Inspectors General on Integrity and Efficiency, which incorporate Department of Justice guidelines, to ensure proper exercise of the powers authorized under this paragraph.

"(ii) SUSPENSION OF AUTHORITY.—The authority granted under this paragraph (including any grant of authority to an individual under subparagraph (A), without regard to whether the individual is in compliance with subparagraph (B)) may be suspended by the Inspector General if the Office of Inspector General fails to comply with the reporting and review requirements under clause (i) of this subparagraph or subparagraph (D). Any suspension of authority under this clause shall be reported to the appropriate committees of Congress.

"(D) PEER REVIEW.—To ensure the proper exercise of the law enforcement powers authorized under this paragraph, the Office of Inspector General shall submit to and participate in the external review process established by the Council of the Inspectors General on Integrity and Efficiency for ensuring that adequate internal safeguards and management procedures continue to exist. Under the review process, the exercise of the law enforcement powers by the Office of Inspector General shall be reviewed periodically by another Office of Inspector General or by a committee of Inspectors General. The results of each review shall be communicated in writing to the Inspector General, the Council of the Inspectors General on Integrity and Efficiency, and the appropriate committees of Congress.

"(E) ALLEGED MISCONDUCT.—Any allegation of misconduct by an individual granted authority under subparagraph (A) may be reviewed by the Integrity Committee of the Council of the Inspectors General on Integrity and Efficiency.

"(F) APPROPRIATE COMMITTEES OF CONGRESS.—In this paragraph, the term 'appropriate committees of Congress' means—

"(i) the Committee on Rules and Administration and the Committee on Appropriations of the Senate; and

"(ii) the Committee on House Administration and the Committee on Appropriations of the House of Representatives.".

(c) GOVERNMENT PUBLISHING OFFICE.—Section 3903 of title 44, United States Code, is amended is amended by adding at the end the following:

"(c)(1) Subject to paragraph (2), any supervisory special agent under the Inspector General and any special agent supervised by such a supervisory special agent is authorized to—

"(A) make an arrest without a warrant while engaged in official duties as authorized under this chapter or any other statute for any offense against the United States committed in the presence of such supervisory special agent or special agent, or for any felony cognizable under the laws of the United States if such supervisory special agent or special agent has reasonable grounds to believe that the person to be arrested has committed or is committing such felony;

"(B) seek and execute warrants for arrest, search of a premises, or seizure of evidence issued under the authority of the United States upon probable cause to believe that a violation has been committed; and

¶5115   SEC. 1603(c)

"(C) carry a firearm while engaged in official duties as authorized under this chapter or any other statute.

"(2)(A)(i) In order to exercise the authority under paragraph (1), a supervisory special agent or a special agent supervised by such a supervisory special agent shall certify that he or she—

"(I) is a citizen of the United States;

"(II) has successfully completed a basic law enforcement training program or military or other equivalent; and

"(III) is not prohibited from receiving a firearm under Federal law, including under section 922(g)(9) of title 18, United States Code, because of a conviction of a misdemeanor crime of domestic violence.

"(ii) After providing notice to the appropriate committees of Congress, the Inspector General may add requirements to the certification required under clause (i), as determined appropriate by the Inspector General.

"(B) The Inspector General shall maintain firearms-related requirements (including quarterly firearms qualifications) and use of force training requirements that, except to the extent the Inspector General determines necessary to effectively carry out the duties of the Office of the Inspector General, are in accordance with the Council of the Inspectors General on Integrity and Efficiency use of force policies, which incorporate Department of Justice guidelines.

"(C)(i) The Inspector General shall—

"(I) determine whether an individual meets the requirements under this subsection; and

"(II) revoke any authority granted to an individual under paragraph (1) if the individual is not in compliance with the requirements of this subsection.

"(ii) The Inspector General may reauthorize an individual to exercise the authority granted under paragraph (1) if the Inspector General determines the individual has achieved compliance with the requirements under this subsection.

"(iii) A revocation of the authority granted under paragraph (1) shall not be subject to administrative, judicial, or other review, unless the revocation results in an adverse action. Such an adverse action may, at the election of the applicable individual, be reviewed in accordance with the otherwise applicable procedures.

"(3)(A) Before the first grant of authority under paragraph (1), and semiannually thereafter as part of the report under section 5 of the Inspector General Act of 1978 (5 U.S.C. App.), the Inspector General shall submit to the appropriate committees of Congress a written certification that adequate internal safeguards and management procedures exist that, except to the extent the Inspector General determines necessary to effectively carry out the duties of the Office of the Inspector General, are in compliance with standards established by the Council of the Inspectors General on Integrity and Efficiency, which incorporate Department of Justice guidelines, to ensure proper exercise of the powers authorized under this subsection.

"(B) The authority granted under this subsection (including any grant of authority to an individual under paragraph (1), without regard to whether the individual is in compliance with paragraph (2)) may be suspended by the Inspector General if the Office of Inspector General fails to comply with the reporting and review requirements under subparagraph (A) of this paragraph or paragraph (4). Any suspension of authority under this subparagraph shall be reported to the appropriate committees of Congress.

"(4) To ensure the proper exercise of the law enforcement powers authorized under this subsection, the Office of Inspector General shall submit to and participate in the external review process established by the Council of the Inspectors General on Integrity and Efficiency for ensuring that adequate internal safeguards and management procedures continue to exist. Under the review process, the exercise of the law enforcement powers by the Office of Inspector General shall be reviewed periodically by another Office of Inspector General or by a committee of Inspectors General. The results of each review shall be communicated in writing to the Inspector General, the Council of the Inspectors General on Integrity and Efficiency, and the appropriate committees of Congress.

"(5) Any allegation of misconduct by an individual granted authority under paragraph (1) may be reviewed by the Integrity Committee of the Council of the Inspectors General on Integrity and Efficiency.

"(6) In this subsection, the term 'appropriate committees of Congress' means—

"(A) the Committee on Rules and Administration and the Committee on Appropriations of the Senate; and

"(B) the Committee on House Administration and the Committee on Appropriations of the House of Representatives.".

[¶ 5116] **SEC. 1604. BUDGET INDEPENDENCE.**

(a) LIBRARY OF CONGRESS.—

(1) AUTHORITY.—Section 1307(d) of the Legislative Branch Appropriations Act, 2006 (2 U.S.C. 185(d)), as amended by section 1603 of this Act, is amended by adding at the end the following:

"(4) BUDGET INDEPENDENCE.—The Librarian of Congress shall include the annual budget request of the Inspector General in the budget of the Library of Congress without change.".

(b) OFFICE OF THE ARCHITECT OF THE CAPITOL.—Section 1301(d) of the Architect of the Capitol Inspector General Act of 2007 (2 U.S.C. 1808(d)), as amended by section 1603 of this Act, is amended by adding at the end the following:

"(4) BUDGET INDEPENDENCE.—The Architect of the Capitol shall include the annual budget request of the Inspector General in the budget of the Office of the Architect of the Capitol without change.".

(c) GOVERNMENT PUBLISHING OFFICE.—Section 3903 of title 44, United States Code, as amended by section 1603 of this Act, is amended by adding at the end the following:

"(d) The Director of the Government Publishing Office shall include the annual budget request of the Inspector General in the budget of the Government Publishing Office without change.".

(d) SEPARATE ALLOCATIONS.—

(1) LEGISLATIVE BRANCH INSTRUMENTALITY DEFINED.—In this subsection, the term "legislative branch instrumentality" means the Library of Congress, the Office of the Architect of the Capitol, or the Government Publishing Office.

(2) ALLOCATION.—For fiscal year 2021, and each fiscal year thereafter, Congress shall provide, within the amounts made available for salaries and expenses of each legislative branch instrumentality, a separate allocation of amounts for salaries and expenses of the Office of the Inspector General of the covered legislative branch instrumentality.

[¶ 5117] **SEC. 1605. HIRING AUTHORITY.**

(a) LIBRARY OF CONGRESS.—Section 1307(d)(2) of the Legislative Branch Appropriations Act, 2006 (2 U.S.C. 185(d)(2)) is amended—

(1) by striking "The Inspector" and inserting the following:

"(A) IN GENERAL.—The Inspector";

(2) in subparagraph (A), as so designated, by inserting ", without the supervision or approval of any other employee, office, or other entity within the Library of Congress," after "is authorized"; and

(3) by adding at the end the following:

"(B) SECURITY AND SUITABILITY.—Appointments under the authority under subparagraph (A) shall be made consistent with personnel security and suitability requirements.

"(C) CONSULTANTS.—Any appointment of a consultant under the authority under subparagraph (A) shall be made consistent with section 6(a)(8) of the Inspector General Act of 1978 (5 U.S.C. App.).".

(b) OFFICE OF THE ARCHITECT OF THE CAPITOL.—Section 1301(d)(2) of the Architect of the Capitol Inspector General Act of 2007 (2 U.S.C. 1808(d)(2)) is amended—

(1) by striking "The Inspector" and inserting the following:

"(A) IN GENERAL.—The Inspector";

(2) in subparagraph (A), as so designated, by inserting ", without the supervision or approval of any other employee, office, or other entity within the Office of the Architect of the Capitol," after "is authorized"; and

(3) by adding at the end the following:

"(B) SECURITY AND SUITABILITY.—Appointments under the authority under subparagraph (A) shall be made consistent with personnel security and suitability requirements.

"(C) CONSULTANTS.—Any appointment of a consultant under the authority under subparagraph (A) shall be made consistent with section 6(a)(8) of the Inspector General Act of 1978 (5 U.S.C. App.).".

(c) GOVERNMENT PUBLISHING OFFICE.—Section 3903(b) of title 44, United States Code, is amended—

(1) by inserting "(1)" before "The Inspector";

(2) in paragraph (1), as so designated, by inserting ", without the supervision or approval of any other employee, office, or other entity within the Government Publishing Office," after "is authorized"; and

(3) by adding at the end the following:

"(2) Appointments under the authority under paragraph (1) shall be made consistent with personnel security and suitability requirements.

"(3) Any appointment of a consultant under the authority under paragraph (1) shall be made consistent with section 6(a)(8) of the Inspector General Act of 1978 (5 U.S.C. App.).".

TITLE XVII—MANAGING POLITICAL FUND ACTIVITY

[¶5118] SEC. 1701. MANAGING POLITICAL FUND ACTIVITY.

The Majority Leader and the Minority Leader may each designate up to 2 employees of their respective leadership office staff as designees referred to in the second sentence of paragraph 1 of rule XLI of the Standing Rules of the Senate.

TITLE XVIII—KENTUCKY WILDLANDS NATIONAL HERITAGE AREA STUDY

[¶5119] SEC. 1801. SHORT TITLE.

This title may be cited as the "Kentucky Wildlands National Heritage Area Study Act".

[¶5120] SEC. 1802. DEFINITIONS.

In this Act:

(1) HERITAGE AREA.—The term "Heritage Area" means the Kentucky Wildlands National Heritage Area.

(2) SECRETARY.—The term "Secretary" means the Secretary of the Interior.

(3) STATE.—The term "State" means the State of Kentucky.

(4) STUDY AREA.—The term "study area" means—

(A) Adair, Bath, Bell, Boyd, Breathitt, Carter, Casey, Clay, Clinton, Cumberland, Elliott, Floyd, Green, Harlan, Jackson, Johnson, Knott, Knox, Laurel, Lawrence, Lee, Leslie, Letcher, Lincoln, Magoffin, Martin, McCreary, Menifee, Metcalfe, Monroe, Morgan, Owsley, Perry, Pike, Pulaski, Rockcastle, Rowan, Russell, Wayne, Whitley, and Wolfe Counties in the State; and

(B) any other areas in the State that—

(i) have heritage aspects that are similar to the heritage aspects of the areas described in subparagraph (A); and

(ii) are adjacent to, or in the vicinity of, the areas described in that subparagraph.

[¶ 5121] SEC. 1803. STUDY.

(a) IN GENERAL.—The Secretary, in consultation with State and local historic preservation officers, State and local historical societies, State and local tourism offices, and other appropriate organizations and governmental agencies, shall conduct a study to assess the suitability and feasibility of designating the study area as a National Heritage Area, to be known as the "Kentucky Wildlands National Heritage Area".

(b) REQUIREMENTS.—The study shall include analysis, documentation, and determinations on whether the study area—

(1) has an assemblage of natural, historic, and cultural resources that—

(A) represent distinctive aspects of the heritage of the United States;

(B) are worthy of recognition, conservation, interpretation, and continuing use; and

(C) would be best managed—

(i) through partnerships among public and private entities; and

(ii) by linking diverse and sometimes noncontiguous resources and active communities;

(2) reflects traditions, customs, beliefs, and folklife that are a valuable part of the story of the United States;

(3) provides outstanding opportunities—

(A) to conserve natural, historic, cultural, or scenic features; and

(B) for recreation and education;

(4) contains resources that—

(A) are important to any identified themes of the study area; and

(B) retain a degree of integrity capable of supporting interpretation;

(5) includes residents, business interests, nonprofit organizations, and State and local governments that—

(A) are involved in the planning of the Heritage Area;

(B) have developed a conceptual financial plan that outlines the roles of all participants in the Heritage Area, including the Federal Government; and

(C) have demonstrated support for the designation of the Heritage Area;

(6) has a potential management entity to work in partnership with the individuals and entities described in paragraph (5) to develop the Heritage Area while encouraging State and local economic activity;

(7) could impact the rights of private property owners with respect to private property; and

(8) has a conceptual boundary map that is supported by the public.

[¶ 5122] SEC. 1804. REPORT.

Not later than 3 years after the date on which funds are first made available to carry out this Act, the Secretary shall submit to the Committee on Energy and Natural Resources of the Senate and the Committee on Natural Resources of the House of Representatives a report that describes—

(1) the findings of the study under section 1803; and

(2) any conclusions and recommendations of the Secretary.

TITLE XIX—INTERNATIONAL BANK FOR RECONSTRUCTION AND DEVELOPMENT

[¶ 5123] SEC. 1901. INTERNATIONAL BANK FOR RECONSTRUCTION AND DEVELOPMENT.

The Bretton Woods Agreements Act (22 U.S.C. 286 et seq.) is amended by adding at the end the following new section:

"SEC. 73. CAPITAL STOCK INCREASES.

"(a) INCREASES AUTHORIZED.—The United States Governor of the Bank is authorized—

"(1)(A) to vote in favor of a resolution to increase the capital stock of the Bank on a selective basis by 245,773 shares; and

"(B) to subscribe on behalf of the United States to 42,298 additional shares of the capital stock of the Bank, as part of the selective increase in the capital stock of the Bank, except that any subscription to such additional shares shall be effective only to the extent or in such amounts as are provided in advance in appropriations Acts; and

"(2)(A) to vote in favor of a resolution to increase the capital stock of the Bank on a general basis by 230,500 shares; and

"(B) to subscribe on behalf of the United States to 38,662 additional shares of the capital stock of the Bank, as part of the general increase in the capital stock of the Bank, except that any subscription to such additional shares shall be effective only to the extent or in such amounts as are provided in advance in appropriations Acts.

"(b) LIMITATIONS ON AUTHORIZATION OF APPROPRIATIONS.—(1) In order to pay for the increase in the United States subscription to the Bank under subsection (a)(2)(B), there are authorized to be appropriated, without fiscal year limitation, $4,663,990,370 for payment by the Secretary of the Treasury.

"(2) Of the amount authorized to be appropriated under paragraph (1), $932,798,074 shall be for paid in shares of the Bank, and $3,731,192,296 shall be for callable shares of the Bank.

"(3) In order to pay for the increase in the United States subscription to the Bank under subsection (a)(1)(B), there are authorized to be appropriated, without fiscal year limitation $5,102,619,230 for payment by the Secretary of the Treasury.

"(4) Of the amount authorized to be appropriated under paragraph (3), $306,157,153.80 shall be for paid in shares of the Bank, and $4,796,462,076.20 shall be for callable shares of the Bank.".

TITLE XX—EUROPEAN ENERGY SECURITY AND DIVERSIFICATION ACT OF 2019

[¶5124] SEC. 2001. SHORT TITLE.

This title may be cited as the "European Energy Security and Diversification Act of 2019".

[¶5125] SEC. 2002. DEFINITIONS.

In this title:

(1) EARLY-STAGE PROJECT SUPPORT.—The term "early-stage project support" includes—

(A) feasibility studies;

(B) resource evaluations;

(C) project appraisal and costing;

(D) pilot projects;

(E) commercial support, such as trade missions, reverse trade missions, technical workshops, international buyer programs, and international partner searchers to link suppliers to projects;

(F) technical assistance and other guidance to improve the local regulatory environment and market frameworks to encourage transparent competition and enhance energy security; and

(G) long-term energy sector planning.

(2) LATE-STAGE PROJECT SUPPORT.—The term "late-stage project support" includes debt financing, insurance, and transaction advisory services.

[¶5126] SEC. 2003. STATEMENT OF POLICY.

(a) SENSE OF CONGRESS.—It is the sense of Congress that the United States has economic and national security interests in assisting European and Eurasian countries achieve energy security through diversification of their energy sources and supply routes.

(b) STATEMENT OF POLICY.—It is the policy of the United States—

(1) to advance United States foreign policy and development goals by assisting European and Eurasian countries to reduce their dependence on energy resources from countries that use energy dependence for undue political influence, such as the Russian Federation, which has used natural gas to coerce, intimidate, and influence other countries;

(2) to promote the energy security of allies and partners of the United States by encouraging the development of accessible, transparent, and competitive energy markets that provide diversified sources, types, and routes of energy;

(3) to encourage United States public and private sector investment in European energy infrastructure projects to bridge the gap between energy security requirements and commercial demand in a way that is consistent with the region's absorptive capacity; and

(4) to help facilitate the export of United States energy resources, technology, and expertise to global markets in a way that benefits the energy security of allies and partners of the United States, including in Europe and Eurasia.

[¶ 5127] SEC. 2004. PRIORITIZATION OF EFFORTS AND ASSISTANCE FOR ENERGY INFRASTRUCTURE PROJECTS IN EUROPE AND EURASIA.

(a) IN GENERAL.—In pursuing the policy described in section 2003, the Secretary of State, in consultation with the Secretary of Energy and the heads of other relevant United States agencies, shall, as appropriate, prioritize and expedite the efforts of the Department of State and those agencies in supporting the efforts of the European Commission and the governments of European and Eurasian countries to increase their energy security, including through—

(1) providing diplomatic and political support to the European Commission and those governments, as necessary—

(A) to facilitate international negotiations concerning cross-border infrastructure;

(B) to enhance Europe's regulatory environment with respect to energy; and

(C) to develop accessible, transparent, and competitive energy markets supplied by diverse sources, types, and routes of energy; and

(2) providing support to improve European and Eurasian energy markets, including early-stage project support and late-stage project support for the construction or improvement of energy and related infrastructure, as necessary—

(A) to diversify the energy sources and supply routes of European and Eurasian countries;

(B) to enhance energy market integration across the region; and

(C) to increase competition within energy markets.

(b) PROJECT SELECTION.—

(1) IN GENERAL.—The agencies described in subsection (a) shall identify energy infrastructure projects that would be appropriate for United States assistance under this section.

(2) PROJECT ELIGIBILITY.—A project is eligible for United States assistance under this section if the project—

(A)(i) improves electricity transmission infrastructure, power generation through the use of a broad power mix (including fossil fuel and renewable energy), or energy efficiency; or

(ii) advances electricity storage projects, smart grid projects, distributed generation models, or other technological innovations, as appropriate; and

(B) is located in a European or Eurasian country.

(3) PREFERENCE.—In selecting among projects that are eligible under paragraph (2), the agencies described in subsection (a) shall give preference to projects that—

(A) link the energy systems of 2 or more European or Eurasian countries;

(B) have already been identified by the European Commission as being integral for the energy security of European countries;

(C) are expected to enhance energy market integration;

(D) can attract funding from the private sector, an international financial institution, the government of the country in which the project will be carried out, or the European Commission; or

(E) have the potential to use United States goods and services during project implementation.

(c) TYPES OF ASSISTANCE.—

(1) DIPLOMATIC AND POLITICAL SUPPORT.—The Secretary of State shall provide diplomatic and political support to the European Commission and the governments of European and Eurasian countries, as necessary, including by using the diplomatic and political influence and expertise of the Department of State to build the capacity of those countries to resolve any impediments to the development of projects selected under subsection (b).

(2) EARLY-STAGE PROJECT SUPPORT.—The Director of the Trade and Development Agency shall provide early-stage project support with respect to projects selected under subsection (b), as necessary.

(3) LATE-STAGE PROJECT SUPPORT.—Agencies described in subsection (a) that provide late-stage project support shall do so with respect to projects selected under subsection (b), as necessary.

(d) FUNDING.—

(1) TRADE AND DEVELOPMENT AGENCY.—Section 661(f)(1)(A) of the Foreign Assistance Act of 1961 (22 U.S.C. 2421(f)(1)(A)) is amended by striking "$48,000,000 for fiscal year 2000" and inserting "$79,500,000 for fiscal year 2020".

(2) COUNTERING RUSSIAN INFLUENCE FUND.—Section 254 of the Countering Russian Influence in Europe and Eurasia Act of 2017 (22 U.S.C. 9543) is amended—

(A) in subsection (a), by striking "fiscal years 2018 and 2019" and inserting "fiscal years 2020, 2021, 2022, and 2023"; and

(B) in subsection (b), by adding at the end the following new paragraph:

"(7) To assist United States agencies that operate under the foreign policy guidance of the Secretary of State in providing assistance under section 2004 of the European Energy Security and Diversification Act of 2019.".

(e) EXCEPTION FROM CERTAIN LIMITATION UNDER BUILD ACT.—

(1) IN GENERAL.—For purposes of providing support for projects under this section—

(A) the United States International Development Finance Corporation may provide support for projects in countries with upper-middle-income economies or high-income economies (as those terms are defined by the World Bank);

(B) the restriction under section 1412(c)(2) of the Better Utilization of Investments Leading to Development Act of 2018 (22 U.S.C. 9612(c)(2)) shall not apply; and

(C) the Corporation shall restrict the provision of such support in a country described in subparagraph (A) unless—

(i) the President certifies to the appropriate congressional committees that such support furthers the national economic or foreign policy interests of the United States; and

(ii) such support is—

(I) designed to produce significant developmental outcomes or provide developmental benefits to the poorest population of that country; or

(II) necessary to preempt or counter efforts by a strategic competitor of the United States to secure significant political or economic leverage or acquire national security-sensitive technologies or infrastructure in a country that is an ally or partner of the United States.

(2) DEFINITIONS.—In this subsection, the terms "appropriate congressional committees" and "less developed country" have the meanings given those terms in section 1402 of the Better Utilization of Investments Leading to Development Act of 2018 (22 U.S.C. 9601).

[¶ 5128] SEC. 2005. PROGRESS REPORTS.

Not later than one year after the date of the enactment of this Act, and annually thereafter, the President shall submit to the Committee on Foreign Relations of the Senate and the Committee on Foreign Affairs of the House of Representatives a report on progress made in providing assistance for projects under section 2004 that includes—

(1) a description of the energy infrastructure projects the United States has identified for such assistance; and

(2) for each such project—

(A) a description of the role of the United States in the project, including in early-stage project support and late-stage project support;

(B) the amount and form of any debt financing and insurance provided by the United States Government for the project;

(C) the amount and form of any early-stage project support; and

(D) an update on the progress made on the project as of the date of the report.

DIVISION Q—REVENUE PROVISIONS

[¶ 5129] SEC. 1. SHORT TITLE; ETC.

(a) SHORT TITLE.—This division may be cited as the "Taxpayer Certainty and Disaster Tax Relief Act of 2019".

(b) TABLE OF CONTENTS.—The table of contents for this division is as follows:

Sec. 1. Short title; etc.

TITLE I—EXTENSION OF CERTAIN EXPIRING PROVISIONS

Subtitle A—Tax Relief and Support for Families and Individuals

Sec. 101. Exclusion from gross income of discharge of qualified principal residence indebtedness.

Sec. 102. Treatment of mortgage insurance premiums as qualified residence interest.

Sec. 103. Reduction in medical expense deduction floor.

Sec. 104. Deduction of qualified tuition and related expenses.

Sec. 105. Black lung disability trust fund excise tax.

Subtitle B—Incentives for Employment, Economic Growth, and Community Development

Sec. 111. Indian employment credit.

Sec. 112. Railroad track maintenance credit.

Sec. 113. Mine rescue team training credit.

Sec. 114. Classification of certain race horses as 3-year property.

Sec. 115. 7-year recovery period for motorsports entertainment complexes.

Sec. 116. Accelerated depreciation for business property on Indian reservations.

Sec. 117. Expensing rules for certain productions.

Sec. 118. Empowerment zone tax incentives.

Sec. 119. American Samoa economic development credit.

Subtitle C—Incentives for Energy Production, Efficiency, and Green Economy Jobs

Sec. 121. Biodiesel and renewable diesel.

Sec. 122. Second generation biofuel producer credit.

Sec. 123. Nonbusiness energy property.

Sec. 124. Qualified fuel cell motor vehicles.

Sec. 125. Alternative fuel refueling property credit.
Sec. 126. 2-wheeled plug-in electric vehicle credit.
Sec. 127. Credit for electricity produced from certain renewable resources.
Sec. 128. Production credit for Indian coal facilities.
Sec. 129. Energy efficient homes credit.
Sec. 130. Special allowance for second generation biofuel plant property.
Sec. 131. Energy efficient commercial buildings deduction.
Sec. 132. Special rule for sales or dispositions to implement FERC or State electric restructuring policy for qualified electric utilities.
Sec. 133. Extension and clarification of excise tax credits relating to alternative fuels.
Sec. 134. Oil spill liability trust fund rate.

Subtitle D—Certain Provisions Expiring at the End of 2019

Sec. 141. New markets tax credit.
Sec. 142. Employer credit for paid family and medical leave.
Sec. 143. Work opportunity credit.
Sec. 144. Certain provisions related to beer, wine, and distilled spirits.
Sec. 145. Look-thru rule for related controlled foreign corporations.
Sec. 146. Credit for health insurance costs of eligible individuals.

TITLE II—DISASTER TAX RELIEF

Sec. 201. Definitions.
Sec. 202. Special disaster-related rules for use of retirement funds.
Sec. 203. Employee retention credit for employers affected by qualified disasters.
Sec. 204. Other disaster-related tax relief provisions.
Sec. 205. Automatic extension of filing deadlines in case of certain taxpayers affected by Federally declared disasters.
Sec. 206. Modification of the tax rate for the excise tax on investment income of private foundations.
Sec. 207. Additional low-income housing credit allocations for qualified 2017 and 2018 California disaster areas.
Sec. 208. Treatment of certain possessions.

TITLE III—OTHER PROVISIONS

Sec. 301. Modification of income for purposes of determining tax-exempt status of certain mutual or cooperative telephone or electric companies.
Sec. 302. Repeal of increase in unrelated business taxable income for certain fringe benefit expenses.

(c) AMENDMENT OF 1986 CODE.—Except as otherwise expressly provided, whenever in this division an amendment or repeal is expressed in terms of an amendment to, or repeal of, a section or other provision, the reference shall be considered to be made to a section or other provision of the Internal Revenue Code of 1986.

TITLE I—EXTENSION OF CERTAIN EXPIRING PROVISIONS

Subtitle A—Tax Relief and Support for Families and Individuals

[¶5130] SEC. 101. EXCLUSION FROM GROSS INCOME OF DISCHARGE OF QUALIFIED PRINCIPAL RESIDENCE INDEBTEDNESS.

(a) IN GENERAL.—Section 108(a)(1)(E) is amended by striking "January 1, 2018" each place it appears and inserting "January 1, 2021".

(b) CONFORMING AMENDMENT.—Section 108(h)(2) is amended by inserting "and determined without regard to the substitution described in section 163(h)(3)(F)(i)(II)" after "clause (ii) thereof".

(c) EFFECTIVE DATE.—The amendments made by this section shall apply to discharges of indebtedness after December 31, 2017.

[¶ 5131] SEC. 102. TREATMENT OF MORTGAGE INSURANCE PREMIUMS AS QUALIFIED RESIDENCE INTEREST.

(a) IN GENERAL.—Section 163(h)(3)(E)(iv)(I) is amended by striking "December 31, 2017" and inserting "December 31, 2020".

(b) EFFECTIVE DATE.—The amendment made by this section shall apply to amounts paid or accrued after December 31, 2017.

[¶ 5132] SEC. 103. REDUCTION IN MEDICAL EXPENSE DEDUCTION FLOOR.

(a) IN GENERAL.—Section 213(f) is amended to read as follows:

"(f) TEMPORARY SPECIAL RULE.—In the case of taxable years beginning before January 1, 2021, subsection (a) shall be applied with respect to a taxpayer by substituting '7.5 percent' for '10 percent'.".

(b) ALTERNATIVE MINIMUM TAX.—Section 56(b)(1) is amended by striking subparagraph (B) and by redesignating subparagraphs (C), (D), (E), and (F), as subparagraphs (B), (C), (D), and (E), respectively.

(c) EFFECTIVE DATE.—The amendments made by this section shall apply to taxable years ending after December 31, 2018.

[¶ 5133] SEC. 104. DEDUCTION OF QUALIFIED TUITION AND RELATED EXPENSES.

(a) IN GENERAL.—Section 222(e) is amended by striking "December 31, 2017" and inserting "December 31, 2020".

(b) EFFECTIVE DATE.—The amendment made by this section shall apply to taxable years beginning after December 31, 2017.

[¶ 5134] SEC. 105. BLACK LUNG DISABILITY TRUST FUND EXCISE TAX.

(a) IN GENERAL.—Section 4121(e)(2)(A) is amended by striking "December 31, 2018" and inserting "December 31, 2020".

(b) EFFECTIVE DATE.—The amendment made by this section shall apply on and after the first day of the first calendar month beginning after the date of the enactment of this Act.

Subtitle B—Incentives for Employment, Economic Growth, and Community Development

[¶ 5135] SEC. 111. INDIAN EMPLOYMENT CREDIT.

(a) IN GENERAL.—Section 45A(f) is amended by striking "December 31, 2017" and inserting "December 31, 2020".

(b) EFFECTIVE DATE.—The amendment made by this section shall apply to taxable years beginning after December 31, 2017.

[¶ 5136] SEC. 112. RAILROAD TRACK MAINTENANCE CREDIT.

(a) IN GENERAL.—Section 45G(f) is amended by striking "January 1, 2018" and inserting "January 1, 2023".

(b) SAFE HARBOR ASSIGNMENTS.—Any assignment, including related expenditures paid or incurred, under section 45G(b)(2) of the Internal Revenue Code of 1986 for a taxable year beginning on or after January 1, 2018, and ending before January 1, 2020, shall be treated as effective as of the close of such taxable year if made pursuant to a written agreement entered into no later than 90 days following the date of the enactment of this Act.

(c) EFFECTIVE DATE.—The amendment made by this section shall apply to expenditures paid or incurred during taxable years beginning after December 31, 2017.

[¶5137] SEC. 113. MINE RESCUE TEAM TRAINING CREDIT.

(a) IN GENERAL.—Section 45N(e) is amended by striking "December 31, 2017" and inserting "December 31, 2020".

(b) EFFECTIVE DATE.—The amendment made by this section shall apply to taxable years beginning after December 31, 2017.

[¶5138] SEC. 114. CLASSIFICATION OF CERTAIN RACE HORSES AS 3-YEAR PROPERTY.

(a) IN GENERAL.—Section 168(e)(3)(A)(i) is amended—

(1) by striking "January 1, 2018" in subclause (I) and inserting "January 1, 2021", and

(2) by striking "December 31, 2017" in subclause (II) and inserting "December 31, 2020".

(b) EFFECTIVE DATE.—The amendments made by this section shall apply to property placed in service after December 31, 2017.

[¶5139] SEC. 115. 7-YEAR RECOVERY PERIOD FOR MOTORSPORTS ENTERTAINMENT COMPLEXES.

(a) IN GENERAL.—Section 168(i)(15)(D) is amended by striking "December 31, 2017" and inserting "December 31, 2020".

(b) EFFECTIVE DATE.—The amendment made by this section shall apply to property placed in service after December 31, 2017.

[¶5140] SEC. 116. ACCELERATED DEPRECIATION FOR BUSINESS PROPERTY ON INDIAN RESERVATIONS.

(a) IN GENERAL.—Section 168(j)(9) is amended by striking "December 31, 2017" and inserting "December 31, 2020".

(b) EFFECTIVE DATE.—The amendment made by this section shall apply to property placed in service after December 31, 2017.

[¶5141] SEC. 117. EXPENSING RULES FOR CERTAIN PRODUCTIONS.

(a) IN GENERAL.—Section 181(g) is amended by striking "December 31, 2017" and inserting "December 31, 2020".

(b) EFFECTIVE DATE.—The amendment made by this section shall apply to productions commencing after December 31, 2017.

[¶5142] SEC. 118. EMPOWERMENT ZONE TAX INCENTIVES.

(a) IN GENERAL.—Section 1391(d)(1)(A)(i) is amended by striking "December 31, 2017" and inserting "December 31, 2020".

(b) TREATMENT OF CERTAIN TERMINATION DATES SPECIFIED IN NOMINATIONS.—In the case of a designation of an empowerment zone the nomination for which included a termination date which is contemporaneous with the date specified in subparagraph (A)(i) of section 1391(d)(1) of the Internal Revenue Code of 1986 (as in effect before the enactment of this Act), subparagraph (B) of such section shall not apply with respect to such designation if, after the date of the enactment of this section, the entity which made such nomination amends the nomination to provide for a new termination date in such manner as the Secretary of the Treasury (or the Secretary's designee) may provide.

SEC. 118(b) ¶5142

(c) EFFECTIVE DATE.—The amendment made by subsection (a) shall apply to taxable years beginning after December 31, 2017.

[¶ 5143] SEC. 119. AMERICAN SAMOA ECONOMIC DEVELOPMENT CREDIT.

(a) IN GENERAL.—Section 119(d) of division A of the Tax Relief and Health Care Act of 2006 is amended—

(1) by striking "January 1, 2018" each place it appears and inserting "January 1, 2021",

(2) by striking "first 12 taxable years" in paragraph (1) and inserting "first 15 taxable years",

(3) by striking "first 6 taxable years" in paragraph (2) and inserting "first 9 taxable years", and

(4) by adding at the end the following flush sentence:

"In the case of a corporation described in subsection (a)(2), the Internal Revenue Code of 1986 shall be applied and administered without regard to the amendments made by section 401(d)(1) of the Tax Technical Corrections Act of 2018.".

(b) CONFORMING AMENDMENT.—Section 119(e) of division A of the Tax Relief and Health Care Act of 2006 is amended by inserting "(as in effect before its repeal)" after "section 199 of the Internal Revenue Code of 1986".

(c) EFFECTIVE DATE.—The amendments made by this section shall apply to taxable years beginning after December 31, 2017.

Subtitle C—Incentives for Energy Production, Efficiency, and Green Economy Jobs

[¶ 5144] SEC. 121. BIODIESEL AND RENEWABLE DIESEL.

(a) INCOME TAX CREDIT.—

(1) IN GENERAL.—Section 40A(g) is amended by striking "December 31, 2017" and inserting "December 31, 2022".

(2) EFFECTIVE DATE.—The amendment made by this subsection shall apply to fuel sold or used after December 31, 2017.

(b) EXCISE TAX INCENTIVES.—

(1) TERMINATION.—

(A) IN GENERAL.—Section 6426(c)(6) is amended by striking "December 31, 2017" and inserting "December 31, 2022".

(B) PAYMENTS.—Section 6427(e)(6)(B) is amended by striking "December 31, 2017" and inserting "December 31, 2022".

(2) EFFECTIVE DATE.—The amendments made by this subsection shall apply to fuel sold or used after December 31, 2017.

(3) SPECIAL RULE.—Notwithstanding any other provision of law, in the case of any biodiesel mixture credit properly determined under section 6426(c) of the Internal Revenue Code of 1986 for the period beginning on January 1, 2018, and ending with the close of the last calendar quarter beginning before the date of the enactment of this Act, such credit shall be allowed, and any refund or payment attributable to such credit (including any payment under section 6427(e) of such Code) shall be made, only in such manner as the Secretary of the Treasury (or the Secretary's delegate) shall provide. Such Secretary shall issue guidance within 30 days after the date of the enactment of this Act providing for a one-time submission of claims covering periods described in the preceding sentence. Such guidance shall provide for a 180-day period for the submission of such claims (in such manner as prescribed by such Secretary) to begin not later than 30 days after such guidance is issued. Such claims shall be paid by such Secretary not later than 60 days after receipt. If such Secretary has not paid pursuant to a claim filed under this subsection within 60 days after the date of the filing of such claim, the claim shall be paid with

interest from such date determined by using the overpayment rate and method under section 6621 of such Code.

[¶5145] SEC. 122. SECOND GENERATION BIOFUEL PRODUCER CREDIT.

(a) IN GENERAL.—Section 40(b)(6)(J)(i) is amended by striking "January 1, 2018" and inserting "January 1, 2021".

(b) EFFECTIVE DATE.—The amendment made by this section shall apply to qualified second generation biofuel production after December 31, 2017.

[¶5146] SEC. 123. NONBUSINESS ENERGY PROPERTY.

(a) IN GENERAL.—Section 25C(g)(2) is amended by striking "December 31, 2017" and inserting "December 31, 2020".

(b) TECHNICAL AMENDMENT.—Section 25C(d)(3) is amended—

(1) by striking "an energy factor of at least 2.0" in subparagraph (A) and inserting "a Uniform Energy Factor of at least 2.2", and

(2) by striking "an energy factor" in subparagraph (D) and inserting "a Uniform Energy Factor".

(c) EFFECTIVE DATE.—The amendments made by this section shall apply to property placed in service after December 31, 2017.

[¶5147] SEC. 124. QUALIFIED FUEL CELL MOTOR VEHICLES.

(a) IN GENERAL.—Section 30B(k)(1) is amended by striking "December 31, 2017" and inserting "December 31, 2020".

(b) EFFECTIVE DATE.—The amendment made by this section shall apply to property purchased after December 31, 2017.

[¶5148] SEC. 125. ALTERNATIVE FUEL REFUELING PROPERTY CREDIT.

(a) IN GENERAL.—Section 30C(g) is amended by striking "December 31, 2017" and inserting "December 31, 2020".

(b) EFFECTIVE DATE.—The amendment made by this section shall apply to property placed in service after December 31, 2017.

[¶5149] SEC. 126. 2-WHEELED PLUG-IN ELECTRIC VEHICLE CREDIT.

(a) IN GENERAL.—Section 30D(g)(3)(E)(ii) is amended by striking "January 1, 2018" and inserting "January 1, 2021".

(b) EFFECTIVE DATE.—The amendment made by this section shall apply to vehicles acquired after December 31, 2017.

[¶5150] SEC. 127. CREDIT FOR ELECTRICITY PRODUCED FROM CERTAIN RENEWABLE RESOURCES.

(a) IN GENERAL.—The following provisions of section 45(d) are each amended by striking "January 1, 2018" each place it appears and inserting "January 1, 2021":

(1) Paragraph (2)(A).

(2) Paragraph (3)(A).

(3) Paragraph (4)(B).

(4) Paragraph (6).

(5) Paragraph (7).

(6) Paragraph (9).

(7) Paragraph (11)(B).

(b) EXTENSION OF ELECTION TO TREAT QUALIFIED FACILITIES AS ENERGY PROPERTY.—Section 48(a)(5)(C)(ii) is amended by striking "January 1, 2018 (January 1, 2020, in the case of any facility which is described in paragraph (1) of section 45(d))" and inserting "January 1, 2021".

(c) APPLICATION OF EXTENSION TO WIND FACILITIES.—

(1) IN GENERAL.—Section 45(d)(1) is amended by striking "January 1, 2020" and inserting "January 1, 2021".

(2) APPLICATION OF PHASEOUT PERCENTAGE.—

(A) IN GENERAL.—Section 45(b)(5) is amended by striking "and" at the end of subparagraph (B), by striking the period at the end of subparagraph (C) and inserting ", and", and by adding at the end the following new subparagraph:

"(D) in the case of any facility the construction of which begins after December 31, 2019, and before January 1, 2021, 40 percent.".

(B) TREATMENT AS ENERGY PROPERTY.—Section 48(a)(5)(E) is amended by striking "and" at the end of clause (ii), by striking the period at the end of clause (iii) and inserting ", and", and by adding at the end the following new clause:

"(iv) in the case of any facility the construction of which begins after December 31, 2019, and before January 1, 2021, 40 percent.".

(d) EFFECTIVE DATE.—The amendments made by this section shall take effect on January 1, 2018.

[¶ 5151] SEC. 128. PRODUCTION CREDIT FOR INDIAN COAL FACILITIES.

(a) IN GENERAL.—Section 45(e)(10)(A) is amended by striking "12-year period" each place it appears and inserting "15-year period".

(b) EFFECTIVE DATE.—The amendment made by this section shall apply to coal produced after December 31, 2017.

[¶ 5152] SEC. 129. ENERGY EFFICIENT HOMES CREDIT.

(a) IN GENERAL.—Section 45L(g) is amended by striking "December 31, 2017" and inserting "December 31, 2020".

(b) EFFECTIVE DATE.—The amendment made by this section shall apply to homes acquired after December 31, 2017.

[¶ 5153] SEC. 130. SPECIAL ALLOWANCE FOR SECOND GENERATION BIOFUEL PLANT PROPERTY.

(a) IN GENERAL.—Section 168(l)(2)(D) is amended by striking "January 1, 2018" and inserting "January 1, 2021".

(b) EFFECTIVE DATE.—The amendment made by this section shall apply to property placed in service after December 31, 2017.

[¶ 5154] SEC. 131. ENERGY EFFICIENT COMMERCIAL BUILDINGS DEDUCTION.

(a) IN GENERAL.—Section 179D(h) is amended by striking "December 31, 2017" and inserting "December 31, 2020".

(b) EFFECTIVE DATES.—The amendment made by subsection (a) shall apply to property placed in service after December 31, 2017.

[¶ 5155] SEC. 132. SPECIAL RULE FOR SALES OR DISPOSITIONS TO IMPLEMENT FERC OR STATE ELECTRIC RESTRUCTURING POLICY FOR QUALIFIED ELECTRIC UTILITIES.

(a) IN GENERAL.—Section 451(k)(3) is amended by striking "January 1, 2018" and inserting "January 1, 2021".

(b) EFFECTIVE DATE.—The amendment made by this section shall apply to dispositions after December 31, 2017.

[¶5156] SEC. 133. EXTENSION AND CLARIFICATION OF EXCISE TAX CREDITS RELATING TO ALTERNATIVE FUELS.

(a) EXTENSION.—

(1) IN GENERAL.—Sections 6426(d)(5) and 6426(e)(3) are each amended by striking "December 31, 2017" and inserting "December 31, 2020".

(2) OUTLAY PAYMENTS FOR ALTERNATIVE FUELS.—Section 6427(e)(6)(C) is amended by striking "December 31, 2017" and inserting "December 31, 2020".

(3) SPECIAL RULE.—Notwithstanding any other provision of law, in the case of any alternative fuel credit properly determined under section 6426(d) of the Internal Revenue Code of 1986 for the period beginning on January 1, 2018, and ending with the close of the last calendar quarter beginning before the date of the enactment of this Act, such credit shall be allowed, and any refund or payment attributable to such credit (including any payment under section 6427(e) of such Code) shall be made, only in such manner as the Secretary of the Treasury (or the Secretary's delegate) shall provide. Such Secretary shall issue guidance within 30 days after the date of the enactment of this Act providing for a one-time submission of claims covering periods described in the preceding sentence. Such guidance shall provide for a 180-day period for the submission of such claims (in such manner as prescribed by such Secretary) to begin not later than 30 days after such guidance is issued. Such claims shall be paid by such Secretary not later than 60 days after receipt. If such Secretary has not paid pursuant to a claim filed under this subsection within 60 days after the date of the filing of such claim, the claim shall be paid with interest from such date determined by using the overpayment rate and method under section 6621 of such Code.

(4) EFFECTIVE DATE.—The amendments made by this subsection shall apply to fuel sold or used after December 31, 2017.

(b) CLARIFICATION OF RULES REGARDING ALTERNATIVE FUEL MIXTURE CREDIT.—

(1) IN GENERAL.—Paragraph (2) of section 6426(e) is amended by striking "mixture of alternative fuel" and inserting "mixture of alternative fuel (other than a fuel described in subparagraph (A),(C), or (F) of subsection (d)(2))".

(2) EFFECTIVE DATE.—The amendment made by this subsection shall apply to—

(A) fuel sold or used on or after the date of the enactment of this Act, and

(B) fuel sold or used before such date of enactment, but only to the extent that claims for the credit under section 6426(e) of the Internal Revenue Code of 1986 with respect to such sale or use—

(i) have not been paid or allowed as of such date, and

(ii) were made on or after January 8, 2018.

(3) NO INFERENCE.—Nothing contained in this subsection or the amendments made by this subsection shall be construed to create any inference as to a change in law or guidance in effect prior to enactment of this subsection.

[¶5157] SEC. 134. OIL SPILL LIABILITY TRUST FUND RATE.

(a) IN GENERAL.—Section 4611(f)(2) is amended by striking "December 31, 2018" and inserting "December 31, 2020".

(b) EFFECTIVE DATE.—The amendment made by this section shall apply on and after the first day of the first calendar month beginning after the date of the enactment of this Act.

Subtitle D—Certain Provisions Expiring at the End of 2019

[¶ 5158] SEC. 141. NEW MARKETS TAX CREDIT.

(a) IN GENERAL.—Section 45D(f)(1) is amended by striking "and" at the end of subparagraph (F), by striking the period at the end of subparagraph (G) and inserting ", and", and by adding at the end the following new subparagraph:

"(H) $5,000,000,000 for 2020.".

(b) CARRYOVER OF UNUSED LIMITATION.—Section 45D(f)(3) is amended by striking "2024" and inserting "2025".

(c) EFFECTIVE DATE.—The amendments made by this section shall apply to calendar years beginning after December 31, 2019.

[¶ 5159] SEC. 142. EMPLOYER CREDIT FOR PAID FAMILY AND MEDICAL LEAVE.

(a) IN GENERAL.—Section 45S(i) is amended by striking "December 31, 2019" and inserting "December 31, 2020".

(b) EFFECTIVE DATE.—The amendment made by this section shall apply to wages paid in taxable years beginning after December 31, 2019.

[¶ 5160] SEC. 143. WORK OPPORTUNITY CREDIT.

(a) IN GENERAL.—Section 51(c)(4) is amended by striking "December 31, 2019" and inserting "December 31, 2020".

(b) EFFECTIVE DATE.—The amendment made by this section shall apply to individuals who begin work for the employer after December 31, 2019.

[¶ 5161] SEC. 144. CERTAIN PROVISIONS RELATED TO BEER, WINE, AND DISTILLED SPIRITS.

(a) EXEMPTION FOR AGING PROCESS OF BEER, WINE, AND DISTILLED SPIRITS.—

(1) IN GENERAL.—Section 263A(f)(4)(B) is amended by striking "December 31, 2019" and inserting "December 31, 2020".

(2) EFFECTIVE DATE.—The amendment made by this subsection shall apply to interest costs paid or accrued after December 31, 2019.

(b) REDUCED RATE OF EXCISE TAX ON BEER.—

(1) IN GENERAL.—Paragraphs (1)(C) and (2)(A) of section 5051(a) are each amended by striking "January 1, 2020" and inserting "January 1, 2021".

(2) EFFECTIVE DATE.—The amendments made by this subsection shall apply to beer removed after December 31, 2019.

(c) TRANSFER OF BEER BETWEEN BONDED FACILITIES.—

(1) IN GENERAL.—Section 5414(b)(3) is amended by striking "December 31, 2019" and inserting "December 31, 2020".

(2) EFFECTIVE DATE.—The amendment made by this subsection shall apply to calendar quarters beginning after December 31, 2019.

(d) REDUCED RATE OF EXCISE TAX ON CERTAIN WINE.—

(1) IN GENERAL.—Section 5041(c)(8)(A) is amended by striking "January 1, 2020" and inserting "January 1, 2021".

(2) CONFORMING AMENDMENT.—The heading of section 5041(c)(8) is amended by striking "SPECIAL RULE FOR 2018 AND 2019" and inserting "TEMPORARY SPECIAL RULE".

(3) EFFECTIVE DATE.—The amendments made by this subsection shall apply to wine removed after December 31, 2019.

(e) ADJUSTMENT OF ALCOHOL CONTENT LEVEL FOR APPLICATION OF EXCISE TAXES.—

(1) IN GENERAL.—Paragraphs (1) and (2) of section 5041(b) are each amended by striking "January 1, 2020" and inserting "January 1, 2021".

(2) EFFECTIVE DATE.—The amendments made by this subsection shall apply to wine removed after December 31, 2019.

(f) DEFINITION OF MEAD AND LOW ALCOHOL BY VOLUME WINE.—

(1) IN GENERAL.—Section 5041(h)(3) is amended by striking "December 31, 2019" and inserting "December 31, 2020".

(2) EFFECTIVE DATE.—The amendment made by this subsection shall apply to wine removed after December 31, 2019.

(g) REDUCED RATE OF EXCISE TAX ON CERTAIN DISTILLED SPIRITS.—

(1) IN GENERAL.—Section 5001(c)(4) is amended by striking "December 31, 2019" and inserting "December 31, 2020".

(2) CONFORMING AMENDMENT.—The heading of section 5001(c) is amended by striking "REDUCED RATE FOR 2018 AND 2019" and inserting "TEMPORARY REDUCED RATE".

(3) EFFECTIVE DATE.—The amendments made by this subsection shall apply to distilled spirits removed after December 31, 2019.

(h) BULK DISTILLED SPIRITS.—

(1) IN GENERAL.—Section 5212 is amended by striking "January 1, 2020" and inserting "January 1, 2021".

(2) EFFECTIVE DATE.—The amendment made by this subsection shall apply to distilled spirits transferred in bond after December 31, 2019.

(i) SIMPLIFICATION OF RULES REGARDING RECORDS, STATEMENTS, AND RETURNS.—

(1) IN GENERAL.—Section 5555(a) is amended by striking "January 1, 2020" and inserting "January 1, 2021".

(2) EFFECTIVE DATE.—The amendment made by this subsection shall apply to calendar quarters beginning after December 31, 2019.

(j) TECHNICAL CORRECTION.—

(1) IN GENERAL.—Section 5041(c)(8) is amended by adding at the end the following new subparagraph:

"(C) APPLICATION OF CERTAIN RULES.—Paragraphs (3) and (6) shall be applied by substituting 'paragraph (1) or (8)' for 'paragraph (1)' each place it appears therein.".

(2) EFFECTIVE DATE.—The amendment made by this subsection shall take effect as if included in section 13804 of Public Law 115-97.

[¶ 5162] SEC. 145. LOOK-THRU RULE FOR RELATED CONTROLLED FOREIGN CORPORATIONS.

(a) IN GENERAL.—Section 954(c)(6)(C) is amended by striking "January 1, 2020" and inserting "January 1, 2021".

(b) EFFECTIVE DATE.—The amendment made by this section shall apply to taxable years of foreign corporations beginning after December 31, 2019, and to taxable years of United States shareholders with or within which such taxable years of foreign corporations end.

[¶ 5163] **SEC. 146. CREDIT FOR HEALTH INSURANCE COSTS OF ELIGIBLE INDIVIDUALS.**

(a) IN GENERAL.—Section 35(b)(1)(B) is amended by striking "January 1, 2020" and inserting "January 1, 2021".

(b) EFFECTIVE DATE.—The amendment made by this section shall apply to months beginning after December 31, 2019.

TITLE II—DISASTER TAX RELIEF

[¶ 5164] **SEC. 201. DEFINITIONS.**

For purposes of this title—

(1) QUALIFIED DISASTER AREA.—

(A) IN GENERAL.—The term "qualified disaster area" means any area with respect to which a major disaster was declared, during the period beginning on January 1, 2018, and ending on the date which is 60 days after the date of the enactment of this Act, by the President under section 401 of the Robert T. Stafford Disaster Relief and Emergency Assistance Act if the incident period of the disaster with respect to which such declaration is made begins on or before the date of the enactment of this Act.

(B) DENIAL OF DOUBLE BENEFIT.—Such term shall not include the California wildfire disaster area (as defined in section 20101 of subdivision 2 of division B of the Bipartisan Budget Act of 2018).

(2) QUALIFIED DISASTER ZONE.—The term "qualified disaster zone" means that portion of any qualified disaster area which was determined by the President, during the period beginning on January 1, 2018, and ending on the date which is 60 days after the date of the enactment of this Act, to warrant individual or individual and public assistance from the Federal Government under the Robert T. Stafford Disaster Relief and Emergency Assistance Act by reason of the qualified disaster with respect to such disaster area.

(3) QUALIFIED DISASTER.—The term "qualified disaster" means, with respect to any qualified disaster area, the disaster by reason of which a major disaster was declared with respect to such area.

(4) INCIDENT PERIOD.—The term "incident period" means, with respect to any qualified disaster, the period specified by the Federal Emergency Management Agency as the period during which such disaster occurred (except that for purposes of this title such period shall not be treated as beginning before January 1, 2018, or ending after the date which is 30 days after the date of the enactment of this Act).

[¶ 5165] **SEC. 202. SPECIAL DISASTER-RELATED RULES FOR USE OF RETIREMENT FUNDS.**

(a) TAX-FAVORED WITHDRAWALS FROM RETIREMENT PLANS.—

(1) IN GENERAL.—Section 72(t) of the Internal Revenue Code of 1986 shall not apply to any qualified disaster distribution.

(2) AGGREGATE DOLLAR LIMITATION.—

(A) IN GENERAL.—For purposes of this subsection, the aggregate amount of distributions received by an individual which may be treated as qualified disaster distributions for any taxable year shall not exceed the excess (if any) of—

(i) $100,000, over

(ii) the aggregate amounts treated as qualified disaster distributions received by such individual for all prior taxable years.

(B) TREATMENT OF PLAN DISTRIBUTIONS.—If a distribution to an individual would (without regard to subparagraph (A)) be a qualified disaster distribution, a plan shall not be treated as violating any requirement of the Internal Revenue Code of 1986 merely because the plan treats such distribution as a qualified disaster distribution, unless the aggregate amount of such distributions from all plans maintained by the employer (and any member of any controlled group which includes the employer) to such individual exceeds $100,000.

(C) CONTROLLED GROUP.—For purposes of subparagraph (B), the term "controlled group" means any group treated as a single employer under subsection (b), (c), (m), or (o) of section 414 of the Internal Revenue Code of 1986.

(D) SPECIAL RULE FOR INDIVIDUALS AFFECTED BY MORE THAN ONE DISASTER.—The limitation of subparagraph (A) shall be applied separately with respect to distributions made with respect to each qualified disaster.

(3) AMOUNT DISTRIBUTED MAY BE REPAID.—

(A) IN GENERAL.—Any individual who receives a qualified disaster distribution may, at any time during the 3-year period beginning on the day after the date on which such distribution was received, make 1 or more contributions in an aggregate amount not to exceed the amount of such distribution to an eligible retirement plan of which such individual is a beneficiary and to which a rollover contribution of such distribution could be made under section 402(c), 403(a)(4), 403(b)(8), 408(d)(3), or 457(e)(16), of the Internal Revenue Code of 1986, as the case may be.

(B) TREATMENT OF REPAYMENTS OF DISTRIBUTIONS FROM ELIGIBLE RETIREMENT PLANS OTHER THAN IRAS.—For purposes of the Internal Revenue Code of 1986, if a contribution is made pursuant to subparagraph (A) with respect to a qualified disaster distribution from an eligible retirement plan other than an individual retirement plan, then the taxpayer shall, to the extent of the amount of the contribution, be treated as having received the qualified disaster distribution in an eligible rollover distribution (as defined in section 402(c)(4) of such Code) and as having transferred the amount to the eligible retirement plan in a direct trustee to trustee transfer within 60 days of the distribution.

(C) TREATMENT OF REPAYMENTS OF DISTRIBUTIONS FROM IRAS.—

For purposes of the Internal Revenue Code of 1986, if a contribution is made pursuant to subparagraph (A) with respect to a qualified disaster distribution from an individual retirement plan (as defined by section 7701(a)(37) of such Code), then, to the extent of the amount of the contribution, the qualified disaster distribution shall be treated as a distribution described in section 408(d)(3) of such Code and as having been transferred to the eligible retirement plan in a direct trustee to trustee transfer within 60 days of the distribution.

(4) DEFINITIONS.—For purposes of this subsection—

(A) QUALIFIED DISASTER DISTRIBUTION.—Except as provided in paragraph (2), the term "qualified disaster distribution" means any distribution from an eligible retirement plan made—

(i) on or after the first day of the incident period of a qualified disaster and before the date which is 180 days after the date of the enactment of this Act, and

(ii) to an individual whose principal place of abode at any time during the incident period of such qualified disaster is located in the qualified disaster area with respect to such qualified disaster and who has sustained an economic loss by reason of such qualified disaster.

(B) ELIGIBLE RETIREMENT PLAN.—The term "eligible retirement plan" shall have the meaning given such term by section 402(c)(8)(B) of the Internal Revenue Code of 1986.

(5) INCOME INCLUSION SPREAD OVER 3-YEAR PERIOD.—

(A) IN GENERAL.—In the case of any qualified disaster distribution, unless the taxpayer elects not to have this paragraph apply for any taxable year, any amount required to be included in gross income for such taxable year shall be so included ratably over the 3-taxable-year period beginning with such taxable year.

SEC. 202(a)(5)(A) ¶5165

(B) SPECIAL RULE.—For purposes of subparagraph (A), rules similar to the rules of subparagraph (E) of section 408A(d)(3) of the Internal Revenue Code of 1986 shall apply.

(6) SPECIAL RULES.—

(A) EXEMPTION OF DISTRIBUTIONS FROM TRUSTEE TO TRUSTEE TRANSFER AND WITHHOLDING RULES.—For purposes of sections 401(a)(31), 402(f), and 3405 of the Internal Revenue Code of 1986, qualified disaster distributions shall not be treated as eligible rollover distributions.

(B) QUALIFIED DISASTER DISTRIBUTIONS TREATED AS MEETING PLAN DISTRIBUTION REQUIREMENTS.—For purposes the Internal Revenue Code of 1986, a qualified disaster distribution shall be treated as meeting the requirements of sections 401(k)(2)(B)(i), 403(b)(7)(A)(ii), 403(b)(11), and 457(d)(1)(A) of such Code.

(b) RECONTRIBUTIONS OF WITHDRAWALS FOR HOME PURCHASES.—

(1) RECONTRIBUTIONS.—

(A) IN GENERAL.—Any individual who received a qualified distribution may, during the applicable period, make 1 or more contributions in an aggregate amount not to exceed the amount of such qualified distribution to an eligible retirement plan (as defined in section 402(c)(8)(B) of the Internal Revenue Code of 1986) of which such individual is a beneficiary and to which a rollover contribution of such distribution could be made under section 402(c), 403(a)(4), 403(b)(8), or 408(d)(3), of such Code, as the case may be.

(B) TREATMENT OF REPAYMENTS.—Rules similar to the rules of subparagraphs (B) and (C) of subsection (a)(3) shall apply for purposes of this subsection.

(2) QUALIFIED DISTRIBUTION.—For purposes of this subsection, the term "qualified distribution" means any distribution—

(A) described in section 401(k)(2)(B)(i)(IV), 403(b)(7)(A)(ii) (but only to the extent such distribution relates to financial hardship), 403(b)(11)(B), or 72(t)(2)(F), of the Internal Revenue Code of 1986,

(B) which was to be used to purchase or construct a principal residence in a qualified disaster area, but which was not so used on account of the qualified disaster with respect to such area, and

(C) which was received during the period beginning on the date which is 180 days before the first day of the incident period of such qualified disaster and ending on the date which is 30 days after the last day of such incident period.

(3) APPLICABLE PERIOD.—For purposes of this subsection, the term "applicable period" means, in the case of a principal residence in a qualified disaster area with respect to any qualified disaster, the period beginning on the first day of the incident period of such qualified disaster and ending on the date which is 180 days after the date of the enactment of this Act.

(c) LOANS FROM QUALIFIED PLANS.—

(1) INCREASE IN LIMIT ON LOANS NOT TREATED AS DISTRIBUTIONS.—

In the case of any loan from a qualified employer plan (as defined under section 72(p)(4) of the Internal Revenue Code of 1986) to a qualified individual made during the 180-day period beginning on the date of the enactment of this Act—

(A) clause (i) of section 72(p)(2)(A) of such Code shall be applied by substituting "$100,000" for "$50,000", and

(B) clause (ii) of such section shall be applied by substituting "the present value of the nonforfeitable accrued benefit of the employee under the plan" for "one-half of the present value of the nonforfeitable accrued benefit of the employee under the plan".

(2) DELAY OF REPAYMENT.—In the case of a qualified individual(with respect to any qualified disaster) with an outstanding loan (on or after the first day of the incident period of such qualified disaster) from a qualified employer plan (as defined in section 72(p)(4) of the Internal Revenue Code of 1986)—

(A) if the due date pursuant to subparagraph (B) or (C) of section 72(p)(2) of such Code for any repayment with respect to such loan occurs during the period beginning on the first day of the incident period of such qualified disaster and ending on the date which is 180 days after the last day of such incident period, such due date shall be delayed for 1 year (or, if later, until the date which is 180 days after the date of the enactment of this Act),

(B) any subsequent repayments with respect to any such loan shall be appropriately adjusted to reflect the delay in the due date under subparagraph (A) and any interest accruing during such delay, and

(C) in determining the 5-year period and the term of a loan under subparagraph (B) or (C) of section 72(p)(2) of such Code, the period described in subparagraph (A) of this paragraph shall be disregarded.

(3) QUALIFIED INDIVIDUAL.—For purposes of this subsection, the term "qualified individual" means any individual—

(A) whose principal place of abode at any time during the incident period of any qualified disaster is located in the qualified disaster area with respect to such qualified disaster, and

(B) who has sustained an economic loss by reason of such qualified disaster.

(d) PROVISIONS RELATING TO PLAN AMENDMENTS.—

(1) IN GENERAL.—If this subsection applies to any amendment to any plan or annuity contract, such plan or contract shall be treated as being operated in accordance with the terms of the plan during the period described in paragraph (2)(B)(i).

(2) AMENDMENTS TO WHICH SUBSECTION APPLIES.—

(A) IN GENERAL.—This subsection shall apply to any amendment to any plan or annuity contract which is made—

(i) pursuant to any provision of this section, or pursuant to any regulation issued by the Secretary or the Secretary of Labor under any provision of this section, and

(ii) on or before the last day of the first plan year beginning on or after January 1, 2020, or such later date as the Secretary may prescribe.

In the case of a governmental plan (as defined in section 414(d) of the Internal Revenue Code of 1986), clause (ii) shall be applied by substituting the date which is 2 years after the date otherwise applied under clause (ii).

(B) CONDITIONS.—This subsection shall not apply to any amendment unless—

(i) during the period—

(I) beginning on the date that this section or the regulation described in subparagraph (A)(i) takes effect (or in the case of a plan or contract amendment not required by this section or such regulation, the effective date specified by the plan), and

(II) ending on the date described in subparagraph (A)(ii) (or, if earlier, the date the plan or contract amendment is adopted),

the plan or contract is operated as if such plan or contract amendment were in effect, and

(ii) such plan or contract amendment applies retroactively for such period.

[¶5166] SEC. 203. EMPLOYEE RETENTION CREDIT FOR EMPLOYERS AFFECTED BY QUALIFIED DISASTERS.

(a) IN GENERAL.—For purposes of section 38 of the Internal Revenue Code of 1986, in the case of an eligible employer, the 2018 through 2019 qualified disaster employee retention credit shall be treated as a credit listed at the end of subsection (b) of such section. For purposes of this subsection, the 2018 through 2019 qualified disaster employee retention credit for any taxable year is an amount equal to 40 percent of the qualified wages with respect to each eligible employee of such employer for such taxable year. The amount of qualified wages with respect to any employee which may be taken into account under this subsection by the employer for any taxable year shall not exceed $6,000 (reduced by the amount of qualified wages with respect to such employee which may be so taken into account for any prior taxable year).

(b) DEFINITIONS.—For purposes of this section—

(1) ELIGIBLE EMPLOYER.—The term "eligible employer" means any employer—

(A) which conducted an active trade or business in a qualified disaster zone at any time during the incident period of the qualified disaster with respect to such qualified disaster zone, and

(B) with respect to whom the trade or business described in subparagraph (A) is inoperable at any time during the period beginning on the first day of the incident period of such qualified disaster and ending on the date of the enactment of this Act, as a result of damage sustained by reason of such qualified disaster.

(2) ELIGIBLE EMPLOYEE.—The term "eligible employee" means with respect to an eligible employer an employee whose principal place of employment with such eligible employer (determined immediately before the qualified disaster referred to in paragraph (1)) was in the qualified disaster zone referred to in such paragraph.

(3) QUALIFIED WAGES.—The term "qualified wages" means wages (as defined in section 51(c)(1) of the Internal Revenue Code of 1986, but without regard to section 3306(b)(2)(B) of such Code) paid or incurred by an eligible employer with respect to an eligible employee at any time on or after the date on which the trade or business described in paragraph (1) first became inoperable at the principal place of employment of the employee (determined immediately before the qualified disaster referred to in such paragraph) and before the earlier of—

(A) the date on which such trade or business has resumed significant operations at such principal place of employment, or

(B) the date which 150 days after the last day of the incident period of the qualified disaster referred to in paragraph (1).

Such term shall include wages paid without regard to whether the employee performs no services, performs services at a different place of employment than such principal place of employment, or performs services at such principal place of employment before significant operations have resumed.

(c) CERTAIN RULES TO APPLY.—For purposes of this section, rules similar to the rules of sections 51(i)(1), 52, and 280C(a), of the Internal Revenue Code of 1986, shall apply.

(d) EMPLOYEE NOT TAKEN INTO ACCOUNT MORE THAN ONCE.—An employee shall not be treated as an eligible employee for purposes of this section for any period with respect to any employer if such employer is allowed a credit under section 51 of the Internal Revenue Code of 1986 with respect to such employee for such period.

[¶ 5167] SEC. 204. OTHER DISASTER-RELATED TAX RELIEF PROVISIONS.

(a) TEMPORARY INCREASE IN LIMITATION ON QUALIFIED CONTRIBUTIONS.—

(1) SUSPENSION OF CURRENT LIMITATION.—Except as otherwise provided in paragraph (2), qualified contributions shall be disregarded in applying subsections (b) and (d) of section 170 of the Internal Revenue Code of 1986.

(2) APPLICATION OF INCREASED LIMITATION.—For purposes of section 170 of the Internal Revenue Code of 1986—

(A) INDIVIDUALS.—In the case of an individual—

(i) LIMITATION.—Any qualified contribution shall be allowed as a deduction only to the extent that the aggregate of such contributions does not exceed the excess of the taxpayer's contribution base (as defined in subparagraph (H) of section 170(b)(1) of such Code) over the amount of all other charitable contributions allowed under section 170(b)(1) of such Code.

(ii) CARRYOVER.—If the aggregate amount of qualified contributions made in the contribution year (within the meaning of section 170(d)(1) of such Code) exceeds the limitation of clause (i), such excess shall be added to the excess described in section 170(b)(1)(G)(ii).

(B) CORPORATIONS.—In the case of a corporation—

(i) LIMITATION.—Any qualified contribution shall be allowed as a deduction only to the extent that the aggregate of such contributions does not exceed the excess of the taxpayer's taxable income (as determined under paragraph (2) of section 170(b) of such Code) over the amount of all other charitable contributions allowed under such paragraph.

(ii) CARRYOVER.—If the aggregate amount of qualified contributions made in the contribution year (within the meaning of section 170(d)(2) of such Code) exceeds the limitation of clause (i), such excess shall be appropriately taken into account under section 170(d)(2) subject to the limitations thereof.

(3) QUALIFIED CONTRIBUTIONS.—

(A) IN GENERAL.—For purposes of this subsection, the term "qualified contribution" means any charitable contribution (as defined in section 170(c) of the Internal Revenue Code of 1986) if—

(i) such contribution—

(I) is paid, during the period beginning on January 1, 2018, and ending on the date which is 60 days after the date of the enactment of this Act, in cash to an organization described in section 170(b)(1)(A) of such Code, and

(II) is made for relief efforts in one or more qualified disaster areas,

(ii) the taxpayer obtains from such organization contemporaneous written acknowledgment (within the meaning of section 170(f)(8) of such Code) that such contribution was used (or is to be used) for relief efforts described in clause (i)(II), and

(iii) the taxpayer has elected the application of this subsection with respect to such contribution.

(B) EXCEPTION.—Such term shall not include a contribution by a donor if the contribution is—

(i) to an organization described in section 509(a)(3) of the Internal Revenue Code of 1986, or

(ii) for the establishment of a new, or maintenance of an existing, donor advised fund (as defined in section 4966(d)(2) of such Code).

(C) APPLICATION OF ELECTION TO PARTNERSHIPS AND S CORPORATIONS.—In the case of a partnership or S corporation, the election under subparagraph (A)(iii) shall be made separately by each partner or shareholder.

(b) SPECIAL RULES FOR QUALIFIED DISASTER-RELATED PERSONAL CASUALTY LOSSES.—

(1) IN GENERAL.—If an individual has a net disaster loss for any taxable year—

(A) the amount determined under section 165(h)(2)(A)(ii) of the Internal Revenue Code of 1986 shall be equal to the sum of—

(i) such net disaster loss, and

(ii) so much of the excess referred to in the matter preceding clause (i) of section 165(h)(2)(A) of such Code (reduced by the amount in clause (i) of this subparagraph) as exceeds 10 percent of the adjusted gross income of the individual,

(B) section 165(h)(1) of such Code shall be applied by substituting "$500" for "$500 ($100 for taxable years beginning after December 31, 2009)",

(C) the standard deduction determined under section 63(c) of such Code shall be increased by the net disaster loss, and

(D) section 56(b)(1)(E) of such Code (section 56(b)(1)(D) of such Code in the case of taxable years ending after December 31, 2018) shall not apply to so much of the standard deduction as is attributable to the increase under subparagraph (C) of this paragraph.

(2) NET DISASTER LOSS.—For purposes of this subsection, the term "net disaster loss" means the excess of qualified disaster-related personal casualty losses over personal casualty gains (as defined in section 165(h)(3)(A) of the Internal Revenue Code of 1986).

(3) QUALIFIED DISASTER-RELATED PERSONAL CASUALTY LOSSES.—For purposes of this subsection, the term "qualified disaster-related personal casualty losses" means losses described in section 165(c)(3) of the Internal Revenue Code of 1986 which arise in a qualified disaster area on or after the first day of the incident period of the qualified disaster to which such area relates, and which are attributable to such qualified disaster.

(c) SPECIAL RULE FOR DETERMINING EARNED INCOME.—

(1) IN GENERAL.—In the case of a qualified individual, if the earned income of the taxpayer for the applicable taxable year is less than the earned income of the taxpayer for the preceding taxable year, the credits allowed under sections 24(d) and 32 of the Internal Revenue Code of 1986 may, at the election of the taxpayer, be determined by substituting—

(A) such earned income for the preceding taxable year, for

(B) such earned income for the applicable taxable year.

(2) QUALIFIED INDIVIDUAL.—For purposes of this subsection, the term "qualified individual" means any individual whose principal place of abode at any time during the incident period of any qualified disaster was located—

(A) in the qualified disaster zone with respect to such qualified disaster, or

(B) in the qualified disaster area with respect to such qualified disaster (but outside the qualified disaster zone with respect to such qualified disaster) and such individual was displaced from such principal place of abode by reason of such qualified disaster.

(3) APPLICABLE TAXABLE YEAR.—For purposes of this subsection, the term "applicable taxable year" means—

(A) in the case of a qualified individual other than an individual described in subparagraph (B), any taxable year which includes any portion of the incident period of the qualified disaster to which the qualified disaster area referred to in paragraph (2)(A) relates, or

(B) in the case of a qualified individual described in subparagraph (B) of paragraph (2), any taxable year which includes any portion of the period described in such subparagraph.

(4) EARNED INCOME.—For purposes of this subsection, the term "earned income" has the meaning given such term under section 32(c) of the Internal Revenue Code of 1986.

(5) SPECIAL RULES.—

(A) APPLICATION TO JOINT RETURNS.—For purposes of paragraph (1), in the case of a joint return for an applicable taxable year—

(i) such paragraph shall apply if either spouse is a qualified individual, and

(ii) the earned income of the taxpayer for the preceding taxable year shall be the sum of the earned income of each spouse for such preceding taxable year.

(B) UNIFORM APPLICATION OF ELECTION.—Any election made under paragraph (1) shall apply with respect to both sections 24(d) and 32 of the Internal Revenue Code of 1986.

(C) ERRORS TREATED AS MATHEMATICAL ERROR.—For purposes of section 6213 of the Internal Revenue Code of 1986, an incorrect use on a return of earned income pursuant to paragraph (1) shall be treated as a mathematical or clerical error.

(D) NO EFFECT ON DETERMINATION OF GROSS INCOME, ETC.—Except as otherwise provided in this subsection, the Internal Revenue Code of 1986 shall be applied without regard to any substitution under paragraph (1).

[¶ 5168] SEC. 205. AUTOMATIC EXTENSION OF FILING DEADLINES IN CASE OF CERTAIN TAXPAYERS AFFECTED BY FEDERALLY DECLARED DISASTERS.

(a) IN GENERAL.—Section 7508A is amended by adding at the end the following new subsection:

"(d) MANDATORY 60-DAY EXTENSION.—

"(1) IN GENERAL.—In the case of any qualified taxpayer, the period—

"(A) beginning on the earliest incident date specified in the declaration to which the disaster area referred to in paragraph (2) relates, and

"(B) ending on the date which is 60 days after the latest incident date so specified,

shall be disregarded in the same manner as a period specified under subsection (a).

"(2) QUALIFIED TAXPAYER.—For purposes of this subsection, the term 'qualified taxpayer' means—

"(A) any individual whose principal residence (for purposes of section 1033(h)(4)) is located in a disaster area,

"(B) any taxpayer if the taxpayer's principal place of business (other than the business of performing services as an employee) is located in a disaster area,

"(C) any individual who is a relief worker affiliated with a recognized government or philanthropic organization and who is assisting in a disaster area,

"(D) any taxpayer whose records necessary to meet a deadline for an act described in section 7508(a)(1) are maintained in a disaster area,

"(E) any individual visiting a disaster area who was killed or injured as a result of the disaster, and

"(F) solely with respect to a joint return, any spouse of an individual described in any preceding subparagraph of this paragraph.

"(3) DISASTER AREA.—For purposes of this subsection, the term 'disaster area' has the meaning given such term under subparagraph (B) of section 165(i)(5) with respect to a Federally declared disaster (as defined in subparagraph (A) of such section).

"(4) APPLICATION TO RULES REGARDING PENSIONS.—In the case of any person described in subsection (b), a rule similar to the rule of paragraph (1) shall apply for purposes of subsection (b) with respect to—

"(A) making contributions to a qualified retirement plan (within the meaning of section 4974(c)) under section 219(f)(3), 404(a)(6), 404(h)(1)(B), or 404(m)(2),

"(B) making distributions under section 408(d)(4),

"(C) recharacterizing contributions under section 408A(d)(6), and

"(D) making a rollover under section 402(c), 403(a)(4), 403(b)(8), or 408(d)(3).

"(5) COORDINATION WITH PERIODS SPECIFIED BY THE SECRETARY.—

Any period described in paragraph (1) with respect to any person (including by reason of the application of paragraph (4)) shall be in addition to (or concurrent with, as the case may be) any period specified under subsection (a) or (b) with respect to such person.".

(b) EFFECTIVE DATE.—The amendment made by this section shall apply to federally declared disasters declared after the date of the enactment of this Act.

[¶ 5169] SEC. 206. MODIFICATION OF THE TAX RATE FOR THE EXCISE TAX ON INVESTMENT INCOME OF PRIVATE FOUNDATIONS.

(a) IN GENERAL.—Section 4940(a) is amended by striking "2 percent" and inserting "1.39 percent".

(b) ELIMINATION OF REDUCED TAX WHERE FOUNDATION MEETS CERTAIN DISTRIBUTION REQUIREMENTS.—Section 4940 is amended by striking subsection (e).

(c) EFFECTIVE DATE.—The amendments made by this section shall apply to taxable years beginning after the date of the enactment of this Act.

[¶ 5170] **SEC. 207. ADDITIONAL LOW-INCOME HOUSING CREDIT ALLOCATIONS FOR QUALIFIED 2017 AND 2018 CALIFORNIA DISASTER AREAS.**

(a) IN GENERAL.—For purposes of section 42 of the Internal Revenue Code of 1986, the State housing credit ceiling for California for calendar year 2020 shall be increased by the lesser of—

(1) the aggregate housing credit dollar amount allocated by the State housing credit agencies of California for such calendar year to buildings located in qualified 2017 and 2018 California disaster areas, or

(2) 50 percent of the sum of the State housing credit ceilings for California for calendar years 2017 and 2018.

(b) ALLOCATIONS TREATED AS MADE FIRST FROM ADDITIONAL ALLOCATION FOR PURPOSES OF DETERMINING CARRYOVER.—For purposes of determining the unused State housing credit ceiling for any calendar year under section 42(h)(3)(C) of the Internal Revenue Code of 1986, any increase in the State housing credit ceiling under subsection (a) shall be treated as an amount described in clause (ii) of such section.

(c) DEFINITIONS.—For purposes of this section—

(1) QUALIFIED 2017 AND 2018 CALIFORNIA DISASTER AREAS.—The term "qualified 2017 and 2018 California disaster areas" means any area in California which was determined by the President(before January 1, 2019) to warrant individual or individual and public assistance from the Federal Government under the Robert T. Stafford Disaster Relief and Emergency Assistance Act by reason of a major disaster the incident period of which begins or ends in calendar year 2017 or 2018. Notwithstanding section 201, for purposes of the preceding sentence, the term "incident period" means the period specified by the Federal Emergency Management Agency as the period during which the disaster occurred.

(2) OTHER DEFINITIONS.—Terms used in this section which are also used in section 42 of the Internal Revenue Code of 1986 shall have the same meaning in this section as in such section 42.

[¶ 5171] **SEC. 208. TREATMENT OF CERTAIN POSSESSIONS.**

(a) PAYMENTS TO POSSESSIONS WITH MIRROR CODE TAX SYSTEMS.—The Secretary of the Treasury shall pay to each possession of the United States which has a mirror code tax system amounts equal to the loss (if any) to that possession by reason of the application of the provisions of this title. Such amounts shall be determined by the Secretary of the Treasury based on information provided by the government of the respective possession.

(b) PAYMENTS TO OTHER POSSESSIONS.—The Secretary of the Treasury shall pay to each possession of the United States which does not have a mirror code tax system amounts estimated by the Secretary of the Treasury as being equal to the aggregate benefits (if any) that would have been provided to residents of such possession by reason of the provisions of this title if a mirror code tax system had been in effect in such possession. The preceding sentence shall not apply unless the respective possession has a plan, which has been approved by the Secretary of the Treasury, under which such possession will promptly distribute such payments to its residents.

(c) MIRROR CODE TAX SYSTEM.—For purposes of this section, the term "mirror code tax system" means, with respect to any possession of the United States, the income tax system of such possession if the income tax liability of the residents of such possession under such system is determined by reference to the income tax laws of the United States as if such possession were the United States.

(d) TREATMENT OF PAYMENTS.—For purposes of section 1324 of title 31, United States Code, the payments under this section shall be treated in the same manner as a refund due from a credit provision referred to in subsection (b)(2) of such section.

TITLE III—OTHER PROVISIONS

[¶ 5172] SEC. 301. MODIFICATION OF INCOME FOR PURPOSES OF DETERMINING TAX-EXEMPT STATUS OF CERTAIN MUTUAL OR COOPERATIVE TELEPHONE OR ELECTRIC COMPANIES.

(a) IN GENERAL.—Section 501(c)(12) is amended by adding at the end the following new subparagraph:

"(J) In the case of a mutual or cooperative telephone or electric company described in this paragraph, subparagraph (A) shall be applied without taking into account any income received or accrued from—

"(i) any grant, contribution, or assistance provided pursuant to the Robert T. Stafford Disaster Relief and Emergency Assistance Act or any similar grant, contribution, or assistance by any local, State, or regional governmental entity for the purpose of relief, recovery, or restoration from, or preparation for, a disaster or emergency, or

"(ii) any grant or contribution by any governmental entity (other than a contribution in aid of construction or any other contribution as a customer or potential customer) the purpose of which is substantially related to providing, constructing, restoring, or relocating electric, communication, broadband, internet, or other utility facilities or services.".

(b) EFFECTIVE DATE.—The amendment made by this section shall apply to taxable years beginning after December 31, 2017.

[¶ 5173] SEC. 302. REPEAL OF INCREASE IN UNRELATED BUSINESS TAXABLE INCOME FOR CERTAIN FRINGE BENEFIT EXPENSES.

(a) IN GENERAL.—Section 512(a) is amended by striking paragraph (7).

(b) EFFECTIVE DATE.—The amendment made by this section shall take effect as if included in the amendments made by section 13703 of Public Law 115-97.

Internal Revenue Code Sections Added, Amended or Repealed

[¶ 6000]
INTRODUCTION

Select Internal Revenue Code provisions amended by the Further Consolidated Appropriations Act, 2020 (P.L. 116-94) are shown in the following paragraphs. Deleted Code material or the text of the Code Section prior to amendment appears in the amendment notes following each amended Code provision. *Any changed or added material is set out in italics.*

[¶ 6001] CODE SEC. 35. HEALTH INSURANCE COSTS OF ELIGIBLE INDIVIDUALS.

* * *

(b) ELIGIBLE COVERAGE MONTH.—For purposes of this section—

(1) IN GENERAL.—The term "eligible coverage month" means any month if—

* * *

(B) such month begins more than 90 days after the date of the enactment of the Trade Act of 2002, and before *January 1, 2021.*

* * *

[Explanation at ¶ 545.]
Amendments
• **Further Consolidated Appropriations Act, 2020** (P.L. 116-94)

P.L. 116-94, § 146(a), Div. Q:

Amended Code Sec. 35(b)(1)(B) by striking "January 1, 2020" and inserting "January 1, 2021". **Effective** for months beginning after 12-31-2019.

[¶ 6005] CODE SEC. 38. GENERAL BUSINESS CREDIT.

* * *

(b) CURRENT YEAR BUSINESS CREDIT.—

* * *

(31) the small employer health insurance credit determined under section 45R,

(32) in the case of an eligible employer (as defined in section 45S(c)), the paid family and medical leave credit determined under section 45S(a), *plus*

(33) in the case of an eligible employer (as defined in section 45T(c)), the retirement auto-enrollment credit determined under section 45T(a).

[Explanation at ¶ 135.]
Amendments
• **Further Consolidated Appropriations Act, 2020** (P.L. 116-94)

P.L. 116-94, § 105(b), Div. O:

Amended Code Sec. 38(b) by striking "plus" at the end of paragraph (31), by striking the period at the end of paragraph (32) and inserting ", plus", and by adding at the end a new paragraph (33). **Effective** for tax years beginning after 12-31-2019.

Code Sec. 38(b)(33) ¶ 6005

[¶6010] CODE SEC. 45E. SMALL EMPLOYER PENSION PLAN STARTUP COSTS.

* * *

(b) DOLLAR LIMITATION.—The amount of the credit determined under this section for any taxable year shall not exceed—

(1) for the first credit year and each of the 2 taxable years immediately following the first credit year, the greater of—

(A) $500, or

(B) the lesser of—

(i) $250 for each employee of the eligible employer who is not a highly compensated employee (as defined in section 414(q)) and who is eligible to participate in the eligible employer plan maintained by the eligible employer, or

(ii) $5,000, and

[Explanation at ¶130.]

Amendments

• **Further Consolidated Appropriations Act, 2020 (P.L. 116-94)**

P.L. 116-94, §104(a), Div. O:

Amended Code Sec. 45E(b)(1). **Effective** for tax years beginning after 12-31-2019. Prior to amendment, Code Sec. 45E(b)(1) read as follows:

(1) $500 for the first credit year and each of the 2 taxable years immediately following the first credit year, and

[¶6015] CODE SEC. 45S. EMPLOYER CREDIT FOR PAID FAMILY AND MEDICAL LEAVE.

* * *

(i) TERMINATION.—This section shall not apply to wages paid in taxable years beginning after December 31, 2020.

[Explanation at ¶520.]

Amendments

• **Further Consolidated Appropriations Act, 2020 (P.L. 116-94)**

P.L. 116-94, §142(a), Div. Q:

Amended Code Sec. 45S(i) by striking "December 31, 2019" and inserting "December 31, 2020". **Effective** for wages paid in tax years beginning after 12-31-2019.

[¶6020] CODE SEC. 45T. AUTO-ENROLLMENT OPTION FOR RETIREMENT SAVINGS OPTIONS PROVIDED BY SMALL EMPLOYERS.

(a) IN GENERAL.—For purposes of section 38, in the case of an eligible employer, the retirement auto-enrollment credit determined under this section for any taxable year is an amount equal to—

(1) $500 for any taxable year occurring during the credit period, and

(2) zero for any other taxable year.

(b) CREDIT PERIOD.—For purposes of subsection (a)—

(1) IN GENERAL.—The credit period with respect to any eligible employer is the 3-taxable-year period beginning with the first taxable year for which the employer includes an eligible automatic contribution arrangement (as defined in section 414(w)(3)) in a qualified employer plan (as defined in section 4972(d)) sponsored by the employer.

(2) MAINTENANCE OF ARRANGEMENT.—No taxable year with respect to an employer shall be treated as occurring within the credit period unless the arrangement described in paragraph (1) is included in the plan for such year.

(c) ELIGIBLE EMPLOYER.—*For purposes of this section, the term "eligible employer" has the meaning given such term in section 408(p)(2)(C)(i).*

[Explanation at ¶ 135.]
Amendments
• **Further Consolidated Appropriations Act, 2020 (P.L. 116-94)**

P.L. 116-94, § 105(a), Div. O:

Amended subpart D of part IV of subchapter A of chapter 1 by adding at the end a new Code Sec. 45T. **Effective** for tax years beginning after 12-31-2019.

[¶ 6025] CODE SEC. 72. ANNUITIES; CERTAIN PROCEEDS OF ENDOWMENT AND LIFE INSURANCE CONTRACTS.

* * *

(p) LOANS TREATED AS DISTRIBUTIONS.—For purposes of this section—

* * *

(2) EXCEPTION FOR CERTAIN LOANS.—

* * *

(D) PROHIBITION OF LOANS THROUGH CREDIT CARDS AND OTHER SIMILAR ARRANGEMENTS.—*Subparagraph (A) shall not apply to any loan which is made through the use of any credit card or any other similar arrangement.*

(E) RELATED EMPLOYERS AND RELATED PLANS.—For purposes of this paragraph—

(i) the rules of subsections (b), (c), and (m) of section 414 shall apply, and

(ii) all plans of an employer (determined after the application of such subsections) shall be treated as 1 plan.

* * *

[Explanation at ¶ 155.]
Amendments
• **Further Consolidated Appropriations Act, 2020 (P.L. 116-94)**

P.L. 116-94, § 108(a), Div. O:

Amended Code Sec. 72(p)(2) by redesignating subparagraph (D) as subparagraph (E) and by inserting after subparagraph (C) a new subparagraph (D). **Effective** for loans made after 12-20-2019.

P.L. 116-94, § 202(c), Div. Q, provides:

For a special rule, see Act Sec. 202(c), Div. Q, in the amendment notes for Code Sec. 1400Q.

(t) 10-PERCENT ADDITIONAL TAX ON EARLY DISTRIBUTIONS FROM QUALIFIED RETIREMENT PLANS.—

* * *

(2) SUBSECTION NOT TO APPLY TO CERTAIN DISTRIBUTIONS.—Except as provided in paragraphs (3) and (4), paragraph (1) shall not apply to any of the following distributions:

* * *

(H) DISTRIBUTIONS FROM RETIREMENT PLANS IN CASE OF BIRTH OF CHILD OR ADOPTION.—

(i) IN GENERAL.—*Any qualified birth or adoption distribution.*

(ii) LIMITATION.—*The aggregate amount which may be treated as qualified birth or adoption distributions by any individual with respect to any birth or adoption shall not exceed $5,000.*

(iii) QUALIFIED BIRTH OR ADOPTION DISTRIBUTION.—*For purposes of this subparagraph—*

(I) IN GENERAL.—*The term "qualified birth or adoption distribution" means any distribution from an applicable eligible retirement plan to an individual if made during the*

1-year period beginning on the date on which a child of the individual is born or on which the legal adoption by the individual of an eligible adoptee is finalized.

(II) ELIGIBLE ADOPTEE.—The term "eligible adoptee" means any individual (other than a child of the taxpayer's spouse) who has not attained age 18 or is physically or mentally incapable of self-support.

(iv) TREATMENT OF PLAN DISTRIBUTIONS.—

(I) IN GENERAL.—If a distribution to an individual would (without regard to clause (ii)) be a qualified birth or adoption distribution, a plan shall not be treated as failing to meet any requirement of this title merely because the plan treats the distribution as a qualified birth or adoption distribution, unless the aggregate amount of such distributions from all plans maintained by the employer (and any member of any controlled group which includes the employer) to such individual exceeds $5,000.

(II) CONTROLLED GROUP.—For purposes of subclause (I), the term "controlled group" means any group treated as a single employer under subsection (b), (c), (m), or (o) of section 414.

(v) AMOUNT DISTRIBUTED MAY BE REPAID.—

(I) IN GENERAL.—Any individual who receives a qualified birth or adoption distribution may make one or more contributions in an aggregate amount not to exceed the amount of such distribution to an applicable eligible retirement plan of which such individual is a beneficiary and to which a rollover contribution of such distribution could be made under section 402(c), 403(a)(4), 403(b)(8), 408(d)(3), or 457(e)(16), as the case may be.

(II) LIMITATION ON CONTRIBUTIONS TO APPLICABLE ELIGIBLE RETIREMENT PLANS OTHER THAN IRAS.—The aggregate amount of contributions made by an individual under subclause (I) to any applicable eligible retirement plan which is not an individual retirement plan shall not exceed the aggregate amount of qualified birth or adoption distributions which are made from such plan to such individual. Subclause (I) shall not apply to contributions to any applicable eligible retirement plan which is not an individual retirement plan unless the individual is eligible to make contributions (other than those described in subclause (I)) to such applicable eligible retirement plan.

(III) TREATMENT OF REPAYMENTS OF DISTRIBUTIONS FROM APPLICABLE ELIGIBLE RETIREMENT PLANS OTHER THAN IRAS.—If a contribution is made under subclause (I) with respect to a qualified birth or adoption distribution from an applicable eligible retirement plan other than an individual retirement plan, then the taxpayer shall, to the extent of the amount of the contribution, be treated as having received such distribution in an eligible rollover distribution (as defined in section 402(c)(4)) and as having transferred the amount to the applicable eligible retirement plan in a direct trustee to trustee transfer within 60 days of the distribution.

(IV) TREATMENT OF REPAYMENTS FOR DISTRIBUTIONS FROM IRAS.—If a contribution is made under subclause (I) with respect to a qualified birth or adoption distribution from an individual retirement plan, then, to the extent of the amount of the contribution, such distribution shall be treated as a distribution described in section 408(d)(3) and as having been transferred to the applicable eligible retirement plan in a direct trustee to trustee transfer within 60 days of the distribution.

(vi) DEFINITION AND SPECIAL RULES.—For purposes of this subparagraph—

(I) APPLICABLE ELIGIBLE RETIREMENT PLAN.—The term "applicable eligible retirement plan" means an eligible retirement plan (as defined in section 402(c)(8)(B)) other than a defined benefit plan.

(II) EXEMPTION OF DISTRIBUTIONS FROM TRUSTEE TO TRUSTEE TRANSFER AND WITHHOLDING RULES.—For purposes of sections 401(a)(31), 402(f), and 3405, a qualified birth or adoption distribution shall not be treated as an eligible rollover distribution.

¶6025 Code Sec. 72(t)(2)(H)(iii)(II)

(III) TAXPAYER MUST INCLUDE TIN.—A distribution shall not be treated as a qualified birth or adoption distribution with respect to any child or eligible adoptee unless the taxpayer includes the name, age, and TIN of such child or eligible adoptee on the taxpayer's return of tax for the taxable year.

(IV) DISTRIBUTIONS TREATED AS MEETING PLAN DISTRIBUTION REQUIREMENTS.—Any qualified birth or adoption distribution shall be treated as meeting the requirements of sections 401(k)(2)(B)(i), 403(b)(7)(A)(ii), 403(b)(11), and 457(d)(1)(A).

* * *

[Explanation at ¶ 160.]

Amendments

• **Further Consolidated Appropriations Act, 2020 (P.L. 116-94)**

P.L. 116-94, § 113(a), Div. O:

Amended Code Sec. 72(t)(2) by adding at the end a new subparagraph (H). **Effective** for distributions made after 12-31-2019.

P.L. 116-94, § 202(a), Div. Q, provides:

For a special rule, see Act Sec. 202(a), Div. Q, in the amendment notes for Code Sec. 1400Q.

[¶ 6030] CODE SEC. 139B. BENEFITS PROVIDED TO VOLUNTEER FIREFIGHTERS AND EMERGENCY MEDICAL RESPONDERS.

* * *

(c) DEFINITIONS.—For purposes of this section—

* * *

(2) QUALIFIED PAYMENT.—

* * *

(B) APPLICABLE DOLLAR LIMITATION.—The amount determined under subparagraph (A) for any taxable year shall not exceed *$50* multiplied by the number of months during such year that the taxpayer performs such services.

[Explanation at ¶ 525.]

Amendments

• **Further Consolidated Appropriations Act, 2020 (P.L. 116-94)**

P.L. 116-94, § 301(a), Div. O:

Amended Code Sec. 139B(c)(2)(B) by striking "$30" and inserting "$50". **Effective** for tax years beginning after 12-31-2019.

(d) TERMINATION.—This section shall not apply with respect to taxable years *beginning—*

(1) after December 31, 2010, and before January 1, 2020, or

(2) after December 31, 2020.

[Explanation at ¶ 525.]

Amendments

• **Further Consolidated Appropriations Act, 2020 (P.L. 116-94)**

P.L. 116-94, § 301(b), Div. O:

Amended Code Sec. 139B(d) by striking "beginning after December 31, 2010." and inserting "beginning—"

"(1) after December 31, 2010, and before January 1, 2020, or"

"(2) after December 31, 2020.".

Effective for tax years beginning after 12-31-2019.

[¶ 6035] CODE SEC. 213. MEDICAL, DENTAL, ETC., EXPENSES.

* * *

(f) Temporary Special Rule.—*In the case of taxable years beginning before January 1, 2021, subsection (a) shall be applied with respect to a taxpayer by substituting "7.5 percent" for "10 percent".*

Amendments

• **Further Consolidated Appropriations Act, 2020 (P.L. 116-94)**

P.L. 116-94, § 103(a), Div. Q:

Amended Code Sec. 213(f). **Effective** for tax years ending after 12-31-2018. Prior to amendment, Code Sec. 213(f) read as follows:

(f) Special Rules for 2013 Through 2018.—In the case of any taxable year—

(1) beginning after December 31, 2012, and ending before January 1, 2017, in the case of a taxpayer if such taxpayer or such taxpayer's spouse has attained age 65 before the close of such taxable year, and

(2) beginning after December 31, 2016, and ending before January 1, 2019, in the case of any taxpayer,

subsection (a) shall be applied with respect to a taxpayer by substituting "7.5 percent" for "10 percent".

[¶ 6040] CODE SEC. 219. RETIREMENT SAVINGS.

* * *

(d) Other Limitations and Restrictions.—

(1) [Repealed.]

* * *

[Explanation at ¶ 145.]

Amendments

• **Further Consolidated Appropriations Act, 2020 (P.L. 116-94)**

P.L. 116-94, § 107(a), Div. O:

Repealed Code Sec. 219(d)(1). **Effective** for contributions made for tax years beginning after 12-31-2019. Prior to repeal, Code Sec. 219(d)(1) read as follows:

(1) Beneficiary Must Be Under Age $70^1/_2$.—No deduction shall be allowed under this section with respect to any qualified retirement contribution for the benefit of an individual if such individual has attained age $70^1/_2$ before the close of such individual's taxable year for which the contribution was made.

(f) Other Definitions and Special Rules.—

(1) Compensation.—For purposes of this section, the term "compensation" includes earned income (as defined in section 401(c)(2)). The term "compensation" does not include any amount received as a pension or annuity and does not include any amount received as deferred compensation. For purposes of this paragraph, section 401(c)(2) shall be applied as if the term trade or business for purposes of section 1402 included service described in subsection (c)(6). The term "compensation" includes any differential wage payment (as defined in section 3401(h)(2)). *The term "compensation" shall include any amount which is included in the individual's gross income and paid to the individual to aid the individual in the pursuit of graduate or postdoctoral study.*

* * *

[Explanation at ¶ 140.]

Amendments

• **Further Consolidated Appropriations Act, 2020 (P.L. 116-94)**

P.L. 116-94, § 106(a), Div. O:

Amended Code Sec. 219(f)(1) by adding at the end a new sentence. **Effective** for tax years beginning after 12-31-2019.

[¶ 6045] CODE SEC. 221. INTEREST ON EDUCATION LOANS.

* * *

(e) Special Rules.—

(1) Denial of double benefit.—No deduction shall be allowed under this section for any amount for which a deduction is allowable under any other provision of this chapter. *The deduction otherwise allowable under subsection (a) (prior to the application of subsection (b)) to the taxpayer for any taxable year shall be reduced (but not below zero) by so much of the distributions treated as a qualified higher education expense under section 529(c)(9) with respect to loans of the taxpayer as*

would be includible in gross income under section 529(c)(3)(A) for such taxable year but for such treatment.

* * *

[Explanation at ¶540.]

Amendments

• **Further Consolidated Appropriations Act, 2020 (P.L. 116-94)**

P.L. 116-94, §302(b)(2), Div. O:

Amended Code Sec. 221(e)(1) by adding at the end a new sentence. **Effective** for distributions made after 12-31-2018.

[¶6050] CODE SEC. 401. QUALIFIED PENSION, PROFIT-SHARING, AND STOCK BONUS PLANS.

(a) REQUIREMENTS FOR QUALIFICATION.—A trust created or organized in the United States and forming part of a stock bonus, pension, or profit-sharing plan of an employer for the exclusive benefit of his employees or their beneficiaries shall constitute a qualified trust under this section—

* * *

(9) REQUIRED DISTRIBUTIONS.—

* * *

(B) REQUIRED DISTRIBUTION WHERE EMPLOYEE DIES BEFORE ENTIRE INTEREST IS DISTRIBUTED.—

* * *

(iv) SPECIAL RULE FOR SURVIVING SPOUSE OF EMPLOYEE.—If the designated beneficiary referred to in clause (iii)(I) is the surviving spouse of the employee—

(I) the date on which the distributions are required to begin under clause (iii)(III) shall not be earlier than the date on which the employee would have attained *age 72*, and

(C) REQUIRED BEGINNING DATE.—For purposes of this paragraph—

(i) IN GENERAL.—The term "required beginning date" means April 1 of the calendar year following the later of—

(I) the calendar year in which the employee attains *age 72*, or

(ii) EXCEPTION.—Subclause (II) of clause (i) shall not apply—

(I) except as provided in section 409(d), in the case of an employee who is a 5-percent owner (as defined in section 416) with respect to the plan year ending in the calendar year in which the employee attains *age 72*, or

* * *

(E) DEFINITIONS AND RULES RELATING TO DESIGNATED BENEFICIARIES.—*For purposes of this paragraph—*

(i) DESIGNATED BENEFICIARY.—The term "designated beneficiary" means any individual designated as a beneficiary by the employee.

(ii) ELIGIBLE DESIGNATED BENEFICIARY.—The term "eligible designated beneficiary" means, with respect to any employee, any designated beneficiary who is—

(I) the surviving spouse of the employee,

(II) subject to clause (iii), a child of the employee who has not reached majority (within the meaning of subparagraph (F)),

(III) disabled (within the meaning of section 72(m)(7)),

(IV) a chronically ill individual (within the meaning of section 7702B(c)(2), except that the requirements of subparagraph (A)(i) thereof shall only be treated as met if there is a certification that, as of such date, the period of inability described in such subparagraph with respect to the individual is an indefinite one which is reasonably expected to be lengthy in nature), or

(V) an individual not described in any of the preceding subclauses who is not more than 10 years younger than the employee.

The determination of whether a designated beneficiary is an eligible designated beneficiary shall be made as of the date of death of the employee.

(iii) SPECIAL RULE FOR CHILDREN.—Subject to subparagraph (F), an individual described in clause (ii)(II) shall cease to be an eligible designated beneficiary as of the date the individual reaches majority and any remainder of the portion of the individual's interest to which subparagraph (H)(ii) applies shall be distributed within 10 years after such date.

* * *

(H) SPECIAL RULES FOR CERTAIN DEFINED CONTRIBUTION PLANS.—In the case of a defined contribution plan, if an employee dies before the distribution of the employee's entire interest—

(i) IN GENERAL.—Except in the case of a beneficiary who is not a designated beneficiary, subparagraph (B)(ii)—

(I) shall be applied by substituting "10 years" for "5 years", and

(II) shall apply whether or not distributions of the employee's interests have begun in accordance with subparagraph (A).

(ii) EXCEPTION FOR ELIGIBLE DESIGNATED BENEFICIARIES.—Subparagraph (B)(iii) shall apply only in the case of an eligible designated beneficiary.

(iii) RULES UPON DEATH OF ELIGIBLE DESIGNATED BENEFICIARY.—If an eligible designated beneficiary dies before the portion of the employee's interest to which this subparagraph applies is entirely distributed, the exception under clause (ii) shall not apply to any beneficiary of such eligible designated beneficiary and the remainder of such portion shall be distributed within 10 years after the death of such eligible designated beneficiary.

(iv) SPECIAL RULE IN CASE OF CERTAIN TRUSTS FOR DISABLED OR CHRONICALLY ILL BENEFICIARIES.—In the case of an applicable multi-beneficiary trust, if under the terms of the trust—

(I) it is to be divided immediately upon the death of the employee into separate trusts for each beneficiary, or

(II) no individual (other than a eligible designated beneficiary described in subclause (III) or (IV) of subparagraph (E)(ii)) has any right to the employee's interest in the plan until the death of all such eligible designated beneficiaries with respect to the trust,

for purposes of a trust described in subclause (I), clause (ii) shall be applied separately with respect to the portion of the employee's interest that is payable to any eligible designated beneficiary described in subclause (III) or (IV) of subparagraph (E)(ii); and, for purposes of a trust described in subclause (II), subparagraph (B)(iii) shall apply to the distribution of the employee's interest and any beneficiary who is not such an eligible designated beneficiary shall be treated as a beneficiary of the eligible designated beneficiary upon the death of such eligible designated beneficiary.

(v) APPLICABLE MULTI-BENEFICIARY TRUST.—For purposes of this subparagraph, the term "applicable multi-beneficiary trust" means a trust—

(I) which has more than one beneficiary,

(II) all of the beneficiaries of which are treated as designated beneficiaries for purposes of determining the distribution period pursuant to this paragraph, and

(III) at least one of the beneficiaries of which is an eligible designated beneficiary described in subclause (III) or (IV) of subparagraph (E)(ii).

(vi) APPLICATION TO CERTAIN ELIGIBLE RETIREMENT PLANS.—For purposes of applying the provisions of this subparagraph in determining amounts required to be distributed pursuant to this paragraph, all eligible retirement plans (as defined in section 402(c)(8)(B), other than a defined benefit plan described in clause (iv) or (v) thereof or a qualified trust which is a part of a defined benefit plan) shall be treated as a defined contribution plan.

* * *

(26) ADDITIONAL PARTICIPATION REQUIREMENTS.—

* * *

(I) PROTECTED PARTICIPANTS.—

(i) IN GENERAL.—A plan shall be deemed to satisfy the requirements of subparagraph (A) if—

(I) the plan is amended—

(aa) to cease all benefit accruals, or

(bb) to provide future benefit accruals only to a closed class of participants,

(II) the plan satisfies subparagraph (A) (without regard to this subparagraph) as of the effective date of the amendment, and

(III) the amendment was adopted before April 5, 2017, or the plan is described in clause (ii).

(ii) PLANS DESCRIBED.—A plan is described in this clause if the plan would be described in subsection (o)(1)(C), as applied for purposes of subsection (o)(1)(B)(iii)(IV) and by treating the effective date of the amendment as the date the class was closed for purposes of subsection (o)(1)(C).

(iii) SPECIAL RULES.—For purposes of clause (i)(II), in applying section 410(b)(6)(C), the amendments described in clause (i) shall not be treated as a significant change in coverage under section 410(b)(6)(C)(i)(II).

(iv) SPUN-OFF PLANS.—For purposes of this subparagraph, if a portion of a plan described in clause (i) is spun off to another employer, the treatment under clause (i) of the spun-off plan shall continue with respect to the other employer.

* * *

(36) DISTRIBUTIONS DURING WORKING RETIREMENT.—A trust forming part of a pension plan shall not be treated as failing to constitute a qualified trust under this section solely because the plan provides that a distribution may be made from such trust to an employee who has attained *age 59½* and who is not separated from employment at the time of such distribution.

* * *

(38) PORTABILITY OF LIFETIME INCOME.—

(A) IN GENERAL.—Except as may be otherwise provided by regulations, a trust forming part of a defined contribution plan shall not be treated as failing to constitute a qualified trust under this section solely by reason of allowing—

(i) qualified distributions of a lifetime income investment, or

(ii) distributions of a lifetime income investment in the form of a qualified plan distribution annuity contract,

on or after the date that is 90 days prior to the date on which such lifetime income investment is no longer authorized to be held as an investment option under the plan.

(B) DEFINITIONS.—For purposes of this subsection—

(i) the term "qualified distribution" means a direct trustee-to-trustee transfer described in paragraph (31)(A) to an eligible retirement plan (as defined in section 402(c)(8)(B)),

(ii) the term "lifetime income investment" means an investment option which is designed to provide an employee with election rights—

(I) which are not uniformly available with respect to other investment options under the plan, and

(II) which are to a lifetime income feature available through a contract or other arrangement offered under the plan (or under another eligible retirement plan (as so defined), if paid by means of a direct trustee-to-trustee transfer described in paragraph (31)(A) to such other eligible retirement plan),

(iii) the term "lifetime income feature" means—

(I) a feature which guarantees a minimum level of income annually (or more frequently) for at least the remainder of the life of the employee or the joint lives of the employee and the employee's designated beneficiary, or

(II) an annuity payable on behalf of the employee under which payments are made in substantially equal periodic payments (not less frequently than annually) over the life of the employee or the joint lives of the employee and the employee's designated beneficiary, and

(iv) the term "qualified plan distribution annuity contract" means an annuity contract purchased for a participant and distributed to the participant by a plan or contract described in subparagraph (B) of section 402(c)(8) (without regard to clauses (i) and (ii) thereof).

Paragraphs (11), (12), (13), (14), (15), (19), and (20) shall apply only in the case of a plan to which section 411 (relating to minimum vesting standards) applies without regard to subsection (e)(2) of such section.

[Explanation at ¶165, ¶180, ¶225, ¶300 and ¶410.]

Amendments

- **Further Consolidated Appropriations Act, 2020 (P.L. 116-94)**

P.L. 116-94, §104(a), Div. M:

Amended Code Sec. 401(a)(36) by striking "age 62" and inserting "age 59½". **Effective** for plan years beginning after 12-31-2019.

P.L. 116-94, §109(a), Div. O:

Amended Code Sec. 401(a) by inserting after paragraph (37) a new paragraph (38). **Effective** for plan years beginning after 12-31-2019.

P.L. 116-94, §114(a), Div. O:

Amended Code Sec. 401(a)(9)(C)(i)(I) by striking "age 70½" and inserting "age 72". **Effective** for distributions required to be made after 12-31-2019, with respect to individuals who attain age 70½ after such date.

P.L. 116-94, §114(b), Div. O:

Amended Code Sec. 401(a)(9)(B)(iv)(I) and (C)(ii)(I) by striking "age 70½" and inserting "age 72". **Effective** for distributions required to be made after 12-31-2019, with respect to individuals who attain age 70½ after such date.

P.L. 116-94, §205(b), Div. O:

Amended Code Sec. 401(a)(26) by adding at the end a new subparagraph (I). For the **effective** date and special rules, see Act Sec. 205(c)(1)-(2), Div. O, below.

P.L. 116-94, §401(a)(1), Div. O:

Amended Code Sec. 401(a)(9) by adding at the end a new subparagraph (H). For the **effective** date, see Act Sec. 401(b), Div. O, below.

P.L. 116-94, §401(a)(2), Div. O:

Amended Code Sec. 401(a)(9)(E). For the **effective** date, see Act Sec. 401(b), Div. O, below. Prior to amendment, Code Sec. 401(a)(9)(E) read as follows:

(E) Designated beneficiary.—For purposes of this paragraph, the term "designated beneficiary" means any individual designated as a beneficiary by the employee.

P.L. 116-94, §401(b), Div. O, provides:

(b) Effective Dates.—

(1) In General.—Except as provided in this subsection, the amendments made by this section shall apply to distributions with respect to employees who die after December 31, 2019.

(2) Collective bargaining exception.—In the case of a plan maintained pursuant to 1 or more collective bargaining agreements between employee representatives and 1 or more employers ratified before the date of enactment of this Act, the amendments made by this section shall apply to distributions with respect to employees who die in calendar years beginning after the earlier of—

(A) the later of—

(i) the date on which the last of such collective bargaining agreements terminates (determined without regard to any extension thereof agreed to on or after the date of the enactment of this Act), or

(ii) December 31, 2019, or

(B) December 31, 2021.

For purposes of subparagraph (A)(i), any plan amendment made pursuant to a collective bargaining agreement relating to the plan which amends the plan solely to conform to any requirement added by this section shall not be treated as a termination of such collective bargaining agreement.

(3) Governmental plans.—In the case of a governmental plan (as defined in section 414(d) of the Internal Revenue Code of 1986), paragraph (1) shall be applied by substituting "December 31, 2021" for "December 31, 2019".

(4) Exception for certain existing annuity contracts.—

(A) In general.—The amendments made by this section shall not apply to a qualified annuity which is a binding annuity contract in effect on the date of enactment of this Act and at all times thereafter.

(B) Qualified annuity.—For purposes of this paragraph, the term "qualified annuity" means, with respect to an employee, an annuity—

(i) which is a commercial annuity (as defined in section 3405(e)(6) of the Internal Revenue Code of 1986);

(ii) under which the annuity payments are made over the life of the employee or over the joint lives of such employee and a designated beneficiary (or over a period not extending beyond the life expectancy of such employee or the joint life expectancy of such employee and a designated beneficiary) in accordance with the regulations described in section 401(a)(9)(A)(ii) of such Code (as in effect before such amendments) and which meets the other requirements of section 401(a)(9) of such Code (as so in effect) with respect to such payments; and

(iii) with respect to which—

(I) annuity payments to the employee have begun before the date of enactment of this Act, and the employee has made an irrevocable election before such date as to the method and amount of the annuity payments to the employee or any designated beneficiaries; or

(II) if subclause (I) does not apply, the employee has made an irrevocable election before the date of enactment of this Act as to the method and amount of the annuity payments to the employee or any designated beneficiaries.

(5) EXCEPTION FOR CERTAIN BENEFICIARIES.—

(A) IN GENERAL.—If an employee dies before the effective date, then, in applying the amendments made by this section to such employee's designated beneficiary who dies after such date—

(i) such amendments shall apply to any beneficiary of such designated beneficiary; and

(ii) the designated beneficiary shall be treated as an eligible designated beneficiary for purposes of applying section 401(a)(9)(H)(ii) of the Internal Revenue Code of 1986 (as in effect after such amendments).

(B) EFFECTIVE DATE.—For purposes of this paragraph, the term "effective date" means the first day of the first calendar year to which the amendments made by this section apply to a plan with respect to employees dying on or after such date.

P.L. 116-94, §202(a), Div. Q, provides:

For a special rule, see Act Sec. 202(a), Div. Q, in the amendment notes for Code Sec. 1400Q.

(b) CERTAIN PLAN AMENDMENTS.—

(1) CERTAIN PLAN AMENDMENTS.—Pension, profit-sharing, or annuity plan shall be considered as satisfying the requirements of subsection (a) for the period beginning with the date on which it was put into effect, or for the period beginning with the earlier of the date on which there was adopted or put into effect any amendment which caused the plan to fail to satisfy such requirements, and ending with the time prescribed by law for filing the return of the employer for his taxable year in which such plan or amendment was adopted (including extensions thereof) or such later time as the Secretary may designate, if all provisions of the plan which are necessary to satisfy such requirements are in effect by the end of such period and have been made effective for all purposes for the whole of such period.

(2) ADOPTION OF PLAN.—*If an employer adopts a stock bonus, pension, profit-sharing, or annuity plan after the close of a taxable year but before the time prescribed by law for filing the return of the employer for the taxable year (including extensions thereof), the employer may elect to treat the plan as having been adopted as of the last day of the taxable year.*

[Explanation at ¶ 200.]

Amendments

• **Further Consolidated Appropriations Act, 2020 (P.L. 116-94)**

P.L. 116-94, §201(a)(1)-(2), Div. O:

Amended Code Sec. 401(b) by striking "RETROACTIVE CHANGES IN PLAN.—A stock bonus" and inserting "PLAN AMENDMENTS.—",

"(1) CERTAIN RETROACTIVE CHANGES IN PLAN.—A stock bonus",

and by adding at the end a new paragraph (2). **Effective** for plans adopted for tax years beginning after 12-31-2019. Prior to amendment, Code Sec. 401(b) read as follows:

(b) CERTAIN RETROACTIVE CHANGES IN PLAN.—A stock bonus, pension, profit-sharing, or annuity plan shall be considered as satisfying the requirements of subsection (a) for the period beginning with the date on which it was put into effect, or for the period beginning with the earlier of the date on which there was adopted or put into effect any amendment which caused the plan to fail to satisfy such requirements, and ending with the time prescribed by law for filing the return of the employer for his taxable year in which such plan or amendment was adopted (including extensions thereof) or such later time as the Secretary may designate, if all provisions of the plan which are necessary to satisfy such requirements are in effect by the end of such period and have been made effective for all purposes for the whole of such period.

(k) CASH OR DEFERRED ARRANGEMENTS.—

* * *

(2) QUALIFIED CASH OR DEFERRED ARRANGEMENT.—A qualified cash or deferred arrangement is any arrangement which is part of a profit-sharing or stock bonus plan, a pre-ERISA money purchase plan, or a rural cooperative plan which meets the requirements of subsection (a)—

* * *

(B) under which amounts held by the trust which are attributable to employer contributions made pursuant to the employee's election—

(i) may not be distributable to participants or other beneficiaries earlier than—

Code Sec. 401(k)(2)(B)(i) ¶6050

(I) severance from employment, death, or disability,

(II) an event described in paragraph (10),

(III) in the case of a profit-sharing or stock bonus plan, the attainment of age 59$\frac{1}{2}$,

(IV) subject to the provisions of paragraph (14), upon hardship of the employee,

(V) in the case of a qualified reservist distribution (as defined in section 72(t)(2)(G)(iii)), the date on which a period referred to in subclause (III) of such section begins, *or*

(VI) except as may be otherwise provided by regulations, with respect to amounts invested in a lifetime income investment (as defined in subsection (a)(38)(B)(ii)), the date that is 90 days prior to the date that such lifetime income investment may no longer be held as an investment option under the arrangement,

(ii) will not be distributable merely by reason of the completion of a stated period of participation or the lapse of a fixed number of years, *and*

(iii) except as may be otherwise provided by regulations, in the case of amounts described in clause (i)(VI), will be distributed only in the form of a qualified distribution (as defined in subsection (a)(38)(B)(i)) or a qualified plan distribution annuity contract (as defined in subsection (a)(38)(B)(iv)),

(D) which does not require, as a condition of participation in the arrangement, that an employee complete a period of service with the employer (or employers) maintaining the plan extending beyond the close of the earlier of—

(i) the period permitted under section 410(a)(1) (determined without regard to subparagraph (B)(i) thereof), *or*

(ii) subject to the provisions of paragraph (15), the first period of 3 consecutive 12-month periods during each of which the employee has at least 500 hours of service.

* * *

(12) ALTERNATIVE METHODS OF MEETING NONDISCRIMINATION REQUIREMENTS.—

(A) IN GENERAL.—A cash or deferred arrangement shall be treated as meeting the requirements of paragraph (3)(A)(ii) *if such arrangement*—

(i) *meets the contribution requirements of subparagraph (B) and the notice requirements of subparagraph (D), or*

(ii) *meets the contribution requirements of subparagraph (C).*

* * *

(F) TIMING OF PLAN AMENDMENT FOR EMPLOYER MAKING NONELECTIVE CONTRIBUTIONS.—

(i) IN GENERAL.—*Except as provided in clause (ii), a plan may be amended after the beginning of a plan year to provide that the requirements of subparagraph (C) shall apply to the arrangement for the plan year, but only if the amendment is adopted*—

(I) *at any time before the 30th day before the close of the plan year, or*

(II) *at any time before the last day under paragraph (8)(A) for distributing excess contributions for the plan year.*

(ii) EXCEPTION WHERE PLAN PROVIDED FOR MATCHING CONTRIBUTIONS.—*Clause (i) shall not apply to any plan year if the plan provided at any time during the plan year that the requirements of subparagraph (B) or paragraph (13)(D)(i)(I) applied to the plan year.*

(iii) 4-PERCENT CONTRIBUTION REQUIREMENT.—*Clause (i)(II) shall not apply to an arrangement unless the amount of the contributions described in subparagraph (C) which the employer is required to make under the arrangement for the plan year with respect to any employee is an amount equal to at least 4 percent of the employee's compensation.*

(G) OTHER PLANS.—An arrangement shall be treated as meeting the requirements under subparagraph (A)(i) if any other plan maintained by the employer meets such requirements with respect to employees eligible under the arrangement.

(13) ALTERNATIVE METHOD FOR AUTOMATIC CONTRIBUTION ARRANGEMENTS TO MEET NONDISCRIMINATION REQUIREMENTS.—

* * *

(B) QUALIFIED AUTOMATIC CONTRIBUTION ARRANGEMENT.—For purposes of this paragraph, the term "qualified automatic contribution arrangement" *means a cash or deferred arrangement—*

(i) which is described in subparagraph (D)(i)(I) and meets the applicable requirements of subparagraphs (C) through (E), or

(ii) which is described in subparagraph (D)(i)(II) and meets the applicable requirements of subparagraphs (C) and (D).

(C) AUTOMATIC DEFERRAL.—

* * *

(iii) QUALIFIED PERCENTAGE.—For purposes of this subparagraph, the term "qualified percentage" means, with respect to any employee, any percentage determined under the arrangement if such percentage is applied uniformly, *does not exceed 15 percent (10 percent during the period described in subclause (I)), and is at least—*

(I) 3 percent during the period ending on the last day of the first plan year which begins after the date on which the first elective contribution described in clause (i) is made with respect to such employee,

(II) 4 percent during the first plan year following the plan year described in subclause (I),

(III) 5 percent during the second plan year following the plan year described in subclause (I), and

(IV) 6 percent during any subsequent plan year.

* * *

(F) TIMING OF PLAN AMENDMENT FOR EMPLOYER MAKING NONELECTIVE CONTRIBUTIONS.—

(i) IN GENERAL.—*Except as provided in clause (ii), a plan may be amended after the beginning of a plan year to provide that the requirements of subparagraph (D)(i)(II) shall apply to the arrangement for the plan year, but only if the amendment is adopted—*

(I) at any time before the 30th day before the close of the plan year, or

(II) at any time before the last day under paragraph (8)(A) for distributing excess contributions for the plan year.

(ii) EXCEPTION WHERE PLAN PROVIDED FOR MATCHING CONTRIBUTIONS.—*Clause (i) shall not apply to any plan year if the plan provided at any time during the plan year that the requirements of subparagraph (D)(i)(I) or paragraph (12)(B) applied to the plan year.*

(iii) 4-PERCENT CONTRIBUTION REQUIREMENT.—*Clause (i)(II) shall not apply to an arrangement unless the amount of the contributions described in subparagraph (D)(i)(II) which the employer is required to make under the arrangement for the plan year with respect to any employee is an amount equal to at least 4 percent of the employee's compensation.*

* * *

(15) SPECIAL RULES FOR PARTICIPATION REQUIREMENT FOR LONG-TERM, PART-TIME WORKERS.—For purposes of paragraph (2)(D)(ii)—

(A) AGE REQUIREMENT MUST BE MET.—*Paragraph (2)(D)(ii) shall not apply to an employee unless the employee has met the requirement of section 410(a)(1)(A)(i) by the close of the last of the 12-month periods described in such paragraph.*

(B) NONDISCRIMINATION AND TOP-HEAVY RULES NOT TO APPLY.—

(i) NONDISCRIMINATION RULES.—*In the case of employees who are eligible to participate in the arrangement solely by reason of paragraph (2)(D)(ii)—*

(I) notwithstanding subsection (a)(4), an employer shall not be required to make nonelective or matching contributions on behalf of such employees even if such contributions are made on behalf of other employees eligible to participate in the arrangement, and

(II) an employer may elect to exclude such employees from the application of subsection (a)(4), paragraphs (3), (12), and (13), subsection (m)(2), and section 410(b).

(ii) TOP-HEAVY RULES.—*An employer may elect to exclude all employees who are eligible to participate in a plan maintained by the employer solely by reason of paragraph (2)(D)(ii) from the application of the vesting and benefit requirements under subsections (b) and (c) of section 416.*

(iii) VESTING.—*For purposes of determining whether an employee described in clause (i) has a nonforfeitable right to employer contributions (other than contributions described in paragraph (3)(D)(i)) under the arrangement, each 12-month period for which the employee has at least 500 hours of service shall be treated as a year of service, and section 411(a)(6) shall be applied by substituting "at least 500 hours of service" for "more than 500 hours of service" in subparagraph (A) thereof.*

(iv) EMPLOYEES WHO BECOME FULL-TIME EMPLOYEES.—*This subparagraph (other than clause (iii)) shall cease to apply to any employee as of the first plan year beginning after the plan year in which the employee meets the requirements of section 410(a)(1)(A)(ii) without regard to paragraph (2)(D)(ii).*

(C) EXCEPTION FOR EMPLOYEES UNDER COLLECTIVELY BARGAINED PLANS, ETC.—*Paragraph (2)(D)(ii) shall not apply to employees described in section 410(b)(3).*

(D) SPECIAL RULES.—

(i) TIME OF PARTICIPATION.—*The rules of section 410(a)(4) shall apply to an employee eligible to participate in an arrangement solely by reason of paragraph (2)(D)(ii).*

(ii) 12-MONTH PERIODS.—*12-month periods shall be determined in the same manner as under the last sentence of section 410(a)(3)(A).*

[Explanation at ¶110, ¶115, ¶120, ¶125 and ¶180.]

Amendments

• **Further Consolidated Appropriations Act, 2020 (P.L. 116-94)**

P.L. 116-94, §102(a), Div. O:

Amended Code Sec. 401(k)(13)(C)(iii) by striking "does not exceed 10 percent" and inserting "does not exceed 15 percent (10 percent during the period described in subclause (I))". **Effective** for plan years beginning after 12-31-2019.

P.L. 116-94, §103(a)(1), Div. O:

Amended Code Sec. 401(k)(12)(A) by striking "if such arrangement" and all that follows and inserting "if such arrangement—"and new clauses (i)-(ii). **Effective** for plan years beginning after 12-31-2019. Prior to amendment, Code Sec. 401(k)(12)(A) read as follows:

(A) IN GENERAL.—A cash or deferred arrangement shall be treated as meeting the requirements of paragraph (3)(A)(ii) if such arrangement—

(i) meets the contribution requirements of subparagraph (B) or (C), and

(ii) meets the notice requirements of subparagraph (D).

P.L. 116-94, §103(a)(2), Div. O:

Amended Code Sec. 401(k)(13)(B) by striking "means" and all that follows and inserting "means a cash or deferred arrangement—"and new clauses (i)-(ii). **Effective** for plan years beginning after 12-31-2019. Prior to amendment, Code Sec. 401(k)(13)(B) read as follows:

(B) QUALIFIED AUTOMATIC CONTRIBUTION ARRANGEMENT.—For purposes of this paragraph, the term "qualified automatic contribution arrangement" means any cash or deferred arrangement which meets the requirements of subparagraphs (C) through (E).

P.L. 116-94, §103(b), Div. O:

Amended Code Sec. 401(k)(12) by redesignating subparagraph (F) as subparagraph (G), and by inserting after subparagraph (E) a new subparagraph (F). **Effective** for plan years beginning after 12-31-2019.

P.L. 116-94, §103(c), Div. O:

Amended Code Sec. 401(k)(13) by adding at the end a new subparagraph (F). **Effective** for plan years beginning after 12-31-2019.

P.L. 116-94, §109(b)(1), Div. O:

Amended Code Sec. 401(k)(2)(B)(i) by striking "or" at the end of subclause (IV), by striking "and" at the end of subclause (V) and inserting "or", and by adding at the end a new subclause (VI). **Effective** for plan years beginning after 12-31-2019.

Code Sections Added, Amended or Repealed 257

P.L. 116-94, § 109(b)(2), Div. O:

Amended Code Sec. 401(k)(2)(B), as amended by Act Sec. 109(b)(1), Div. O, by striking "and" at the end of clause (i), by striking the semicolon at the end of clause (ii) and inserting ", and", and by adding at the end a new clause (iii). **Effective** for plan years beginning after 12-31-2019.

P.L. 116-94, § 112(a)(1), Div. O:

Amended Code Sec. 401(k)(2)(D). **Effective** for plan years beginning after 12-31-2020, except that, for purposes of Code Sec. 401(k)(2)(D)(ii) (as added by Act Sec. 112), 12-month periods beginning before 1-1-2021, shall not be taken into account. Prior to amendment, Code Sec. 401(k)(2)(D) read as follows:

(D) which does not require, as a condition of participation in the arrangement, that an employee complete a period of service with the employer (or employers) maintaining the plan extending beyond the period permitted under section 410(a)(1) (determined without regard to subparagraph (B)(i) thereof).

P.L. 116-94, § 112(a)(2), Div. O:

Amended Code Sec. 401(k) by adding at the end a new paragraph (15). **Effective** for plan years beginning after 12-31-2020, except that, for purposes of Code Sec. 401(k)(2)(D)(ii) (as added by Act Sec. 112), 12-month periods beginning before 1-1-2021, shall not be taken into account.

P.L. 116-94, § 202(a), Div. Q, provides:

For a special rule, see Act Sec. 202(a), Div. Q, in the amendment notes for Code Sec. 1400Q.

(o) SPECIAL RULES FOR APPLYING NONDISCRIMINATION RULES TO PROTECT OLDER, LONGER SERVICE AND GRANDFATHERED PARTICIPANTS.—

(1) TESTING OF DEFINED BENEFIT PLANS WITH CLOSED CLASSES OF PARTICIPANTS.—

(A) BENEFITS, RIGHTS, OR FEATURES PROVIDED TO CLOSED CLASSES.—A defined benefit plan which provides benefits, rights, or features to a closed class of participants shall not fail to satisfy the requirements of subsection (a)(4) by reason of the composition of such closed class or the benefits, rights, or features provided to such closed class, if—

(i) for the plan year as of which the class closes and the 2 succeeding plan years, such benefits, rights, and features satisfy the requirements of subsection (a)(4) (without regard to this subparagraph but taking into account the rules of subparagraph (I)),

(ii) after the date as of which the class was closed, any plan amendment which modifies the closed class or the benefits, rights, and features provided to such closed class does not discriminate significantly in favor of highly compensated employees, and

(iii) the class was closed before April 5, 2017, or the plan is described in subparagraph (C).

(B) AGGREGATE TESTING WITH DEFINED CONTRIBUTION PLANS PERMITTED ON A BENEFITS BASIS.—

(i) IN GENERAL.—For purposes of determining compliance with subsection (a)(4) and section 410(b), a defined benefit plan described in clause (iii) may be aggregated and tested on a benefits basis with 1 or more defined contribution plans, including with the portion of 1 or more defined contribution plans which—

(I) provides matching contributions (as defined in subsection (m)(4)(A)),

(II) provides annuity contracts described in section 403(b) which are purchased with matching contributions or nonelective contributions, or

(III) consists of an employee stock ownership plan (within the meaning of section 4975(e)(7)) or a tax credit employee stock ownership plan (within the meaning of section 409(a)).

(ii) SPECIAL RULES FOR MATCHING CONTRIBUTIONS.—For purposes of clause (i), if a defined benefit plan is aggregated with a portion of a defined contribution plan providing matching contributions—

(I) such defined benefit plan must also be aggregated with any portion of such defined contribution plan which provides elective deferrals described in subparagraph (A) or (C) of section 402(g)(3), and

(II) such matching contributions shall be treated in the same manner as nonelective contributions, including for purposes of applying the rules of subsection (l).

(iii) PLANS DESCRIBED.—A defined benefit plan is described in this clause if—

(I) the plan provides benefits to a closed class of participants,

(II) for the plan year as of which the class closes and the 2 succeeding plan years, the plan satisfies the requirements of section 410(b) and subsection (a)(4) (without regard to this subparagraph but taking into account the rules of subparagraph (I)),

Code Sec. 401(o)(1)(B)(iii)(II) ¶6050

(III) after the date as of which the class was closed, any plan amendment which modifies the closed class or the benefits provided to such closed class does not discriminate significantly in favor of highly compensated employees, and

(IV) the class was closed before April 5, 2017, or the plan is described in subparagraph (C).

(C) PLANS DESCRIBED.—A plan is described in this subparagraph if, taking into account any predecessor plan—

(i) such plan has been in effect for at least 5 years as of the date the class is closed, and

(ii) during the 5-year period preceding the date the class is closed, there has not been a substantial increase in the coverage or value of the benefits, rights, or features described in subparagraph (A) or in the coverage or benefits under the plan described in subparagraph (B)(iii) (whichever is applicable).

(D) DETERMINATION OF SUBSTANTIAL INCREASE FOR BENEFITS, RIGHTS, AND FEATURES.—In applying subparagraph (C)(ii) for purposes of subparagraph (A)(iii), a plan shall be treated as having had a substantial increase in coverage or value of the benefits, rights, or features described in subparagraph (A) during the applicable 5-year period only if, during such period—

(i) the number of participants covered by such benefits, rights, or features on the date such period ends is more than 50 percent greater than the number of such participants on the first day of the plan year in which such period began, or

(ii) such benefits, rights, and features have been modified by 1 or more plan amendments in such a way that, as of the date the class is closed, the value of such benefits, rights, and features to the closed class as a whole is substantially greater than the value as of the first day of such 5-year period, solely as a result of such amendments.

(E) DETERMINATION OF SUBSTANTIAL INCREASE FOR AGGREGATE TESTING ON BENEFITS BASIS.—In applying subparagraph (C)(ii) for purposes of subparagraph (B)(iii)(IV), a plan shall be treated as having had a substantial increase in coverage or benefits during the applicable 5-year period only if, during such period—

(i) the number of participants benefitting under the plan on the date such period ends is more than 50 percent greater than the number of such participants on the first day of the plan year in which such period began, or

(ii) the average benefit provided to such participants on the date such period ends is more than 50 percent greater than the average benefit provided on the first day of the plan year in which such period began.

(F) CERTAIN EMPLOYEES DISREGARDED.—For purposes of subparagraphs (D) and (E), any increase in coverage or value or in coverage or benefits, whichever is applicable, which is attributable to such coverage and value or coverage and benefits provided to employees—

(i) who became participants as a result of a merger, acquisition, or similar event which occurred during the 7-year period preceding the date the class is closed, or

(ii) who became participants by reason of a merger of the plan with another plan which had been in effect for at least 5 years as of the date of the merger,

shall be disregarded, except that clause (ii) shall apply for purposes of subparagraph (D) only if, under the merger, the benefits, rights, or features under 1 plan are conformed to the benefits, rights, or features of the other plan prospectively.

(G) RULES RELATING TO AVERAGE BENEFIT.—For purposes of subparagraph (E)—

(i) the average benefit provided to participants under the plan will be treated as having remained the same between the 2 dates described in subparagraph (E)(ii) if the benefit formula applicable to such participants has not changed between such dates, and

(ii) if the benefit formula applicable to 1 or more participants under the plan has changed between such 2 dates, then the average benefit under the plan shall be considered to have increased by more than 50 percent only if—

(I) the total amount determined under section 430(b)(1)(A)(i) for all participants benefitting under the plan for the plan year in which the 5-year period described in subparagraph (E) ends, exceeds

(II) the total amount determined under section 430(b)(1)(A)(i) for all such participants for such plan year, by using the benefit formula in effect for each such participant for the first plan year in such 5-year period,

by more than 50 percent. In the case of a CSEC plan (as defined in section 414(y)), the normal cost of the plan (as determined under section 433(j)(1)(B)) shall be used in lieu of the amount determined under section 430(b)(1)(A)(i).

(H) TREATMENT AS SINGLE PLAN.—For purposes of subparagraphs (E) and (G), a plan described in section 413(c) shall be treated as a single plan rather than as separate plans maintained by each employer in the plan.

(I) SPECIAL RULES.—For purposes of subparagraphs (A)(i) and (B)(iii)(II), the following rules shall apply:

(i) In applying section 410(b)(6)(C), the closing of the class of participants shall not be treated as a significant change in coverage under section 410(b)(6)(C)(i)(II).

(ii) 2 or more plans shall not fail to be eligible to be aggregated and treated as a single plan solely by reason of having different plan years.

(iii) Changes in the employee population shall be disregarded to the extent attributable to individuals who become employees or cease to be employees, after the date the class is closed, by reason of a merger, acquisition, divestiture, or similar event.

(iv) Aggregation and all other testing methodologies otherwise applicable under subsection (a)(4) and section 410(b) may be taken into account.

The rule of clause (ii) shall also apply for purposes of determining whether plans to which subparagraph (B)(i) applies may be aggregated and treated as 1 plan for purposes of determining whether such plans meet the requirements of subsection (a)(4) and section 410(b).

(J) SPUN-OFF PLANS.—For purposes of this paragraph, if a portion of a defined benefit plan described in subparagraph (A) or (B)(iii) is spun off to another employer and the spun-off plan continues to satisfy the requirements of—

(i) subparagraph (A)(i) or (B)(iii)(II), whichever is applicable, if the original plan was still within the 3-year period described in such subparagraph at the time of the spin off, and

(ii) subparagraph (A)(ii) or (B)(iii)(III), whichever is applicable,

the treatment under subparagraph (A) or (B) of the spun-off plan shall continue with respect to such other employer.

(2) TESTING OF DEFINED CONTRIBUTION PLANS.—

(A) TESTING ON A BENEFITS BASIS.—A defined contribution plan shall be permitted to be tested on a benefits basis if—

(i) such defined contribution plan provides make-whole contributions to a closed class of participants whose accruals under a defined benefit plan have been reduced or eliminated,

(ii) for the plan year of the defined contribution plan as of which the class eligible to receive such make-whole contributions closes and the 2 succeeding plan years, such closed class of participants satisfies the requirements of section 410(b)(2)(A)(i) (determined by applying the rules of paragraph (1)(I)),

(iii) after the date as of which the class was closed, any plan amendment to the defined contribution plan which modifies the closed class or the allocations, benefits, rights, and features provided to such closed class does not discriminate significantly in favor of highly compensated employees, and

(iv) the class was closed before April 5, 2017, or the defined benefit plan under clause (i) is described in paragraph (1)(C) (as applied for purposes of paragraph (1)(B)(iii)(IV)).

(B) AGGREGATION WITH PLANS INCLUDING MATCHING CONTRIBUTIONS.—

(i) IN GENERAL.—With respect to 1 or more defined contribution plans described in subparagraph (A), for purposes of determining compliance with subsection (a)(4) and section 410(b), the portion of such plans which provides make-whole contributions or other nonelective contributions may be aggregated and tested on a benefits basis with the portion of 1 or more other defined contribution plans which—

(I) provides matching contributions (as defined in subsection (m)(4)(A)),

(II) provides annuity contracts described in section 403(b) which are purchased with matching contributions or nonelective contributions, or

(III) consists of an employee stock ownership plan (within the meaning of section 4975(e)(7)) or a tax credit employee stock ownership plan (within the meaning of section 409(a)).

(ii) SPECIAL RULES FOR MATCHING CONTRIBUTIONS.—Rules similar to the rules of paragraph (1)(B)(ii) shall apply for purposes of clause (i).

(C) SPECIAL RULES FOR TESTING DEFINED CONTRIBUTION PLAN FEATURES PROVIDING MATCHING CONTRIBUTIONS TO CERTAIN OLDER, LONGER SERVICE PARTICIPANTS.—In the case of a defined contribution plan which provides benefits, rights, or features to a closed class of participants whose accruals under a defined benefit plan have been reduced or eliminated, the plan shall not fail to satisfy the requirements of subsection (a)(4) solely by reason of the composition of the closed class or the benefits, rights, or features provided to such closed class if the defined contribution plan and defined benefit plan otherwise meet the requirements of subparagraph (A) but for the fact that the make-whole contributions under the defined contribution plan are made in whole or in part through matching contributions.

(D) SPUN-OFF PLANS.—For purposes of this paragraph, if a portion of a defined contribution plan described in subparagraph (A) or (C) is spun off to another employer, the treatment under subparagraph (A) or (C) of the spun-off plan shall continue with respect to the other employer if such plan continues to comply with the requirements of clauses (ii) (if the original plan was still within the 3-year period described in such clause at the time of the spin off) and (iii) of subparagraph (A), as determined for purposes of subparagraph (A) or (C), whichever is applicable.

(3) DEFINITIONS AND SPECIAL RULE.—For purposes of this subsection—

(A) MAKE-WHOLE CONTRIBUTIONS.—Except as otherwise provided in paragraph (2)(C), the term "make-whole contributions" means snonelective allocations for each employee in the class which are reasonably calculated, in a consistent manner, to replace some or all of the retirement benefits which the employee would have received under the defined benefit plan and any other plan or qualified cash or deferred arrangement under subsection (k)(2) if no change had been made to such defined benefit plan and such other plan or arrangement. For purposes of the preceding sentence, consistency shall not be required with respect to employees who were subject to different benefit formulas under the defined benefit plan.

(B) REFERENCES TO CLOSED CLASS OF PARTICIPANTS.—References to a closed class of participants and similar references to a closed class shall include arrangements under which 1 or more classes of participants are closed, except that 1 or more classes of participants closed on different dates shall not be aggregated for purposes of determining the date any such class was closed.

(C) HIGHLY COMPENSATED EMPLOYEE.—The term "highly compensated employee" has the meaning given such term in section 414(q).

[Explanation at ¶ 225.]

Amendments

• Further Consolidated Appropriations Act, 2020 (P.L. 116-94)

P.L. 116-94, § 205(a)(1)-(2), Div. O:

Amended Code Sec. 401 by redesignating subsection (o) as subsection (p), and by inserting after subsection (n) a new subsection (o). For the **effective** date and special rules, see Act Sec. 205(c)(1)-(2), Div. O, below.

P.L. 116-94, § 205(c)(1)-(2), Div. O, provides:

(c) EFFECTIVE DATE.—

(1) IN GENERAL.—Except as provided in paragraph (2), the amendments made by this section shall take effect on the

date of the enactment of this Act, without regard to whether any plan modifications referred to in such amendments are adopted or effective before, on, or after such date of enactment.

(2) SPECIAL RULES.—

(A) ELECTION OF EARLIER APPLICATION.—At the election of the plan sponsor, the amendments made by this section shall apply to plan years beginning after December 31, 2013.

(B) CLOSED CLASSES OF PARTICIPANTS.—For purposes of paragraphs (1)(A)(iii), (1)(B)(iii)(IV), and (2)(A)(iv) of section 401(o) of the Internal Revenue Code of 1986 (as added by this section), a closed class of participants shall be treated as being closed before April 5, 2017, if the plan sponsor's intention to create such closed class is reflected in formal written documents and communicated to participants before such date.

(C) CERTAIN POST-ENACTMENT PLAN AMENDMENTS.—A plan shall not be treated as failing to be eligible for the application of section 401(o)(1)(A), 401(o)(1)(B)(iii), or 401(a)(26) of such Code (as added by this section) to such plan solely because in the case of—

(i) such section 401(o)(1)(A), the plan was amended before the date of the enactment of this Act to eliminate 1 or more benefits, rights, or features, and is further amended after such date of enactment to provide such previously eliminated benefits, rights, or features to a closed class of participants, or

(ii) such section 401(o)(1)(B)(iii) or section 401(a)(26), the plan was amended before the date of the enactment of this Act to cease all benefit accruals, and is further amended after such date of enactment to provide benefit accruals to a closed class of participants.

Any such section shall only apply if the plan otherwise meets the requirements of such section and in applying such section, the date the class of participants is closed shall be the effective date of the later amendment.

(p) CROSS REFERENCE.—

For exemption from tax of a trust qualified under this section, see section 501(a).

[Explanation at ¶ 225.]

Amendments

• **Further Consolidated Appropriations Act, 2020** (P.L. 116-94)

P.L. 116-94, §205(a)(1)-(2), Div. O:

Amended Code Sec. 401 by redesignating subsection (o) as subsection (p). For the **effective** date and special rules, see Act Sec. 205(c)(1)-(2), Div. O, below.

P.L. 116-94, §205(c)(1)-(2), Div. O, provides:

(c) EFFECTIVE DATE.—

(1) IN GENERAL.—Except as provided in paragraph (2), the amendments made by this section shall take effect on the date of the enactment of this Act, without regard to whether any plan modifications referred to in such amendments are adopted or effective before, on, or after such date of enactment.

(2) SPECIAL RULES.—

(A) ELECTION OF EARLIER APPLICATION.—At the election of the plan sponsor, the amendments made by this section shall apply to plan years beginning after December 31, 2013.

(B) CLOSED CLASSES OF PARTICIPANTS.—For purposes of paragraphs (1)(A)(iii), (1)(B)(iii)(IV), and (2)(A)(iv) of section 401(o) of the Internal Revenue Code of 1986 (as added by this section), a closed class of participants shall be treated as being closed before April 5, 2017, if the plan sponsor's intention to create such closed class is reflected in formal written documents and communicated to participants before such date.

(C) CERTAIN POST-ENACTMENT PLAN AMENDMENTS.—A plan shall not be treated as failing to be eligible for the application of section 401(o)(1)(A), 401(o)(1)(B)(iii), or 401(a)(26) of such Code (as added by this section) to such plan solely because in the case of—

(i) such section 401(o)(1)(A), the plan was amended before the date of the enactment of this Act to eliminate 1 or more benefits, rights, or features, and is further amended after such date of enactment to provide such previously eliminated benefits, rights, or features to a closed class of participants, or

(ii) such section 401(o)(1)(B)(iii) or section 401(a)(26), the plan was amended before the date of the enactment of this Act to cease all benefit accruals, and is further amended after such date of enactment to provide benefit accruals to a closed class of participants.

Any such section shall only apply if the plan otherwise meets the requirements of such section and in applying such section, the date the class of participants is closed shall be the effective date of the later amendment.

[¶ 6055] CODE SEC. 403. TAXATION OF EMPLOYEE ANNUITIES.

* * *

(b) TAXABILITY OF BENEFICIARY UNDER ANNUITY PURCHASED BY A SECTION 501(c)(3) ORGANIZATION OR PUBLIC SCHOOL.—

* * *

(7) CUSTODIAL ACCOUNTS FOR REGULATED INVESTMENT COMPANY STOCK.—

(A) AMOUNTS PAID TREATED AS CONTRIBUTIONS.—For purposes of this title, amounts paid by an employer described in paragraph (1)(A) to a custodial account which satisfies the requirements of section 401(f)(2) shall be treated as amounts contributed by him for an annuity contract for his employee *if the amounts are to be invested in regulated investment company stock to be held in that custodial account, and under the custodial account*—

(i) no such amounts may be paid or made available to any distributee (unless such amount is a distribution to which section 72(t)(2)(G) applies) before—

(I) the employee dies,

(II) the employee attains age 59½,

(III) the employee has a severance from employment,

(IV) the employee becomes disabled (within the meaning of section 72(m)(7)),

(V) in the case of contributions made pursuant to a salary reduction agreement (within the meaning of section 3121(a)(5)(D)), the employee encounters financial hardship, or

(VI) except as may be otherwise provided by regulations, with respect to amounts invested in a lifetime income investment (as defined in section 401(a)(38)(B)(ii)), the date that is 90 days prior to the date that such lifetime income investment may no longer be held as an investment option under the contract, and

(ii) in the case of amounts described in clause (i)(VI), such amounts will be distributed only in the form of a qualified distribution (as defined in section 401(a)(38)(B)(i)) or a qualified plan distribution annuity contract (as defined in section 401(a)(38)(B)(iv)).

* * *

(9) RETIREMENT INCOME ACCOUNTS PROVIDED BY CHURCHES, ETC.—

* * *

(B) RETIREMENT INCOME ACCOUNT.—For purposes of this paragraph, the term "retirement income account" means a defined contribution program established or maintained by a church, or a convention or association of churches, including an organization described in section 414(e)(3)(A), to provide benefits under section 403(b) for an employee described in paragraph (1) *(including an employee described in section 414(e)(3)(B))*.

(11) REQUIREMENT THAT DISTRIBUTIONS NOT BEGIN BEFORE AGE 59½, SEVERANCE FROM EMPLOYMENT, DEATH, OR DISABILITY.—This subsection shall not apply to any annuity contract unless under such contract distributions attributable to contributions made pursuant to a salary reduction agreement (within the meaning of section 402(g)(3)(C)) may be paid only—

* * *

(B) in the case of hardship,

(C) for distributions to which section 72(t)(2)(G) applies, *or*

(D) except as may be otherwise provided by regulations, with respect to amounts invested in a lifetime income investment (as defined in section 401(a)(38)(B)(ii))—

(i) on or after the date that is 90 days prior to the date that such lifetime income investment may no longer be held as an investment option under the contract, and

(ii) in the form of a qualified distribution (as defined in section 401(a)(38)(B)(i)) or a qualified plan distribution annuity contract (as defined in section 401(a)(38)(B)(iv)).

Such contract may not provide for the distribution of any income attributable to such contributions in the case of hardship.

[Explanation at ¶ 180 and ¶ 190.]

Amendments

• **Further Consolidated Appropriations Act, 2020** (P.L. 116-94)

P.L. 116-94, § 109(c)(1), Div. O:

Amended Code Sec. 403(b)(11) by striking "or" at the end of subparagraph (B), by striking the period at the end of subparagraph (C) and inserting ", or", and by inserting after subparagraph (C) a new subparagraph (D). **Effective** for plan years beginning after 12-31-2019.

P.L. 116-94, § 109(c)(2), Div. O:

Amended Code Sec. 403(b)(7)(A) by striking "if—"and all that follows and inserting "if the amounts are to be invested in regulated investment company stock to be held in that custodial account, and under the custodial account—"and new clauses (i) and (ii). **Effective** for plan years beginning after 12-31-2019. Prior to amendment, Code Sec. 403(b)(7)(A) read as follows:

(A) AMOUNTS PAID TREATED AS CONTRIBUTIONS.—For purposes of this title, amounts paid by an employer described in paragraph (1)(A) to a custodial account which satisfies the requirements of section 401(f)(2) shall be treated as amounts contributed by him for an annuity contract for his employee if—

(i) the amounts are to be invested in regulated investment company stock to be held in that custodial account, and

(ii) under the custodial account no such amounts may be paid or made available to any distributee (unless such amount is a distribution to which section 72(t)(2)(G) applies) before the employee dies, attains age 59½, has a severance

¶6055 Code Sec. 403(b)(7)(A)(i)(I)

from employment, becomes disabled (within the meaning of section 72(m)(7)), or in the case of contributions made pursuant to a salary reduction agreement (within the meaning of section 3121(a)(5)(D)), encounters financial hardship.

P.L. 116-94, §110, Div. O, provides:

SEC. 110. TREATMENT OF CUSTODIAL ACCOUNTS ON TERMINATION OF SECTION 403(b) PLANS.

Not later than six months after the date of enactment of this Act, the Secretary of the Treasury shall issue guidance to provide that, if an employer terminates the plan under which amounts are contributed to a custodial account under subparagraph (A) of section 403(b)(7), the plan administrator or custodian may distribute an individual custodial account in kind to a participant or beneficiary of the plan and the distributed custodial account shall be maintained by the custodian on a tax-deferred basis as a section 403(b)(7) custodial account, similar to the treatment of fully-paid individual annuity contracts under Revenue Ruling 2011-7, until amounts are actually paid to the participant or beneficiary. The guidance shall provide further (i) that the section 403(b)(7) status of the distributed custodial account is generally maintained if the custodial account thereafter adheres to the requirements of section 403(b) that are in effect at the time of the distribution of the account and (ii) that a custodial account would not be considered distributed to the participant or beneficiary if the employer has any material retained rights under the account (but the employer would not be treated as retaining material rights simply because the custodial account was originally opened under a group contract). Such guidance shall be retroactively effective for taxable years beginning after December 31, 2008.

P.L. 116-94, §111(a), Div. O:

Amended Code Sec. 403(b)(9)(B) by inserting "(including an employee described in section 414(e)(3)(B))" after "employee described in paragraph (1)". **Effective** for years beginning before, on, or after 12-20-2019.

P.L. 116-94, §202(a)-(b), Div. Q, provides:

For a special rule, see Act Sec. 202(a)-(b), Div. Q, in the amendment notes for Code Sec. 1400Q.

[¶6060] CODE SEC. 408. INDIVIDUAL RETIREMENT ACCOUNTS.

* * *

(b) INDIVIDUAL RETIREMENT ANNUITY.—For purposes of this section, the term "individual retirement annuity" means an annuity contract, or an endowment contract (as determined under regulations prescribed by the Secretary), issued by an insurance company which meets the following requirements:

(1) The contract is not transferable by the owner.

(2) Under the contract—

(A) the premiums are not fixed,

(B) the annual premium on behalf of any individual will not exceed the dollar amount in effect under section 219(b)(1)(A), and

(C) any refund of premiums will be applied before the close of the calendar year following the year of the refund toward the payment of future premiums or the purchase of additional benefits.

(3) Under regulations prescribed by the Secretary, rules similar to the rules of section 401(a)(9) and the incidental death benefit requirements of section 401(a) shall apply to the distribution of the entire interest of the owner.

(4) The entire interest of the owner is nonforfeitable.

Such term does not include such an annuity contract for any taxable year of the owner in which it is disqualified on the application of subsection (e) or for any subsequent taxable year. For purposes of this subsection, no contract shall be treated as an endowment contract if it matures later than the taxable year in which the individual in whose name such contract is purchased attains age 72; if it is not for the exclusive benefit of the individual in whose name it is purchased or his beneficiaries; or if the aggregate annual premiums under all such contracts purchased in the name of such individual for any taxable year exceed the dollar amount in effect under section 219(b)(1)(A).

Amendments

• **Further Consolidated Appropriations Act, 2020 (P.L. 116-94)**

P.L. 116-94, §114(c), Div. O:

Amended the last sentence of Code Sec. 408(b) by striking "age 70½" and inserting "age 72". **Effective** for distributions required to be made after 12-31-2019, with respect to individuals who attain age 70½ after such date.

(c) ACCOUNTS ESTABLISHED BY EMPLOYERS AND CERTAIN ASSOCIATIONS OF EMPLOYEES.—A trust created or organized in the United States by an employer for the exclusive benefit of his employees or their beneficiaries, or by an association of employees (which may include employees within the meaning of section 401(c)(1)) for the exclusive benefit of its members or their beneficiaries, shall be treated as an individual retirement account (described in subsection (a)), but only if the written governing instrument creating the trust meets the following requirements:

* * *

(3) There is a separate accounting for any interest of an employee or member (or spouse of an employee or member) in a Roth IRA.

The assets of the trust may be held in a common fund for the account of all individuals who have an interest in the trust.

Amendments

• **Further Consolidated Appropriations Act, 2020** (P.L. 116-94)

P.L. 116-94, §101(a)(3), Div. O:

Amended Code Sec. 408(c) by inserting after paragraph (2) a new paragraph (3). **Effective** for plan years beginning after 12-31-2020. For a special rule, see Act Sec. 101(e)(2), Div. O.

P.L. 116-94, §101(e)(2), Div. O, provides:

(2) RULE OF CONSTRUCTION.—Nothing in the amendments made by subsection (a) shall be construed as limiting the authority of the Secretary of the Treasury or the Secretary's delegate (determined without regard to such amendment) to provide for the proper treatment of a failure to meet any requirement applicable under the Internal Revenue Code of 1986 with respect to one employer (and its employees) in a multiple employer plan.

(d) TAX TREATMENT OF DISTRIBUTIONS.—

* * *

(8) DISTRIBUTIONS FOR CHARITABLE PURPOSES.—

(A) IN GENERAL.—So much of the aggregate amount of qualified charitable distributions with respect to a taxpayer made during any taxable year which does not exceed $100,000 shall not be includible in gross income of such taxpayer for such taxable year. *The amount of distributions not includible in gross income by reason of the preceding sentence for a taxable year (determined without regard to this sentence) shall be reduced (but not below zero) by an amount equal to the excess of—*

(i) the aggregate amount of deductions allowed to the taxpayer under section 219 for all taxable years ending on or after the date the taxpayer attains age 70½, over

(ii) the aggregate amount of reductions under this sentence for all taxable years preceding the current taxable year.

[Explanation at ¶145.]

Amendments

• **Further Consolidated Appropriations Act, 2020** (P.L. 116-94)

P.L. 116-94, §107(b), Div. O:

Amended Code Sec. 408(d)(8)(A) by adding at the end a new sentence and new clauses (i)-(ii). **Effective** for distributions made for tax years beginning after 12-31-2019.

P.L. 116-94, §202(b), Div. Q, provides:

For a special rule, see Act Sec. 202(b), Div. Q, in the amendment notes for Code Sec. 1400Q.

(o) DEFINITIONS AND RULES RELATING TO NONDEDUCTIBLE CONTRIBUTIONS TO INDIVIDUAL RETIREMENT PLANS.—

* * *

(5) SPECIAL RULE FOR DIFFICULTY OF CARE PAYMENTS EXCLUDED FROM GROSS INCOME.—*In the case of an individual who for a taxable year excludes from gross income under section 131 a qualified foster care payment which is a difficulty of care payment, if—*

(A) the deductible amount in effect for the taxable year under subsection (b), exceeds

(B) the amount of compensation includible in the individual's gross income for the taxable year,

the individual may elect to increase the nondeductible limit under paragraph (2) for the taxable year by an amount equal to the lesser of such excess or the amount so excluded.

¶6060   Code Sec. 408(c)(3)

[Explanation at ¶ 150.]

Amendments

• **Further Consolidated Appropriations Act, 2020** (P.L. 116-94)

P.L. 116-94, §116(a)(1), Div. O:

Amended Code Sec. 408(o) by adding at the end a new paragraph (5). **Effective** for contributions after 12-20-2019.

[¶ 6065] CODE SEC. 408A. ROTH IRAs.

* * *

(c) Treatment of Contributions.—

* * *

(4) Mandatory distribution rules not to apply before death.—Notwithstanding subsections (a)(6) and (b)(3) of section 408 (relating to required distributions), the following provisions shall not apply to any Roth IRA:

(A) Section 401(a)(9)(A).

(B) The incidental death benefit requirements of section 401(a).

(5) Rollover contributions.—

(A) In general.—No rollover contribution may be made to a Roth IRA unless it is a qualified rollover contribution.

(B) Coordination with limit.—A qualified rollover contribution shall not be taken into account for purposes of paragraph (2).

(6) Time when contributions made.—For purposes of this section, the rule of section 219(f)(3) shall apply.

[Explanation at ¶ 145.]

Amendments

• **Further Consolidated Appropriations Act, 2020** (P.L. 116-94)

P.L. 116-94, §107(c), Div. O:

Amended Code Sec. 408A(c) by striking paragraph (4) and by redesignating paragraphs (5), (6), and (7) as paragraphs (4), (5), and (6), respectively. **Effective** for contributions made for tax years beginning after 12-31-2019. Prior to being stricken, Code Sec. 408A(c)(4) read as follows:

(4) Contributions permitted after age 70 $1/2$.—Contributions to a Roth IRA may be made even after the individual for whom the account is maintained has attained age $70^{1}/_{2}$.

[¶ 6070] CODE SEC. 413. COLLECTIVELY BARGAINED PLANS, ETC.

* * *

(c) Plans Maintained by More Than One Employer.—In the case of a plan maintained by more than one employer—

* * *

(2) Exclusive benefit.—For purposes of *sections 401(a) and 408(c)*, in determining whether the plan of an employer is for the exclusive benefit of his employees and their beneficiaries all plan participants shall be considered to be his employees.

Amendments

• **Further Consolidated Appropriations Act, 2020** (P.L. 116-94)

P.L. 116-94, §101(a)(2), Div. O:

Amended Code Sec. 413(c)(2) by striking "section 401(a)" and inserting "sections 401(a) and 408(c)". **Effective** for plan years beginning after 12-31-2020. For a special rule, see Act Sec. 101(e)(2), Div. O, below.

P.L. 116-94, §101(e)(2), Div. O, provides:

(2) Rule of construction.—Nothing in the amendments made by subsection (a) shall be construed as limiting the authority of the Secretary of the Treasury or the Secretary's delegate (determined without regard to such amendment) to provide for the proper treatment of a failure to meet any requirement applicable under the Internal Revenue Code of 1986 with respect to one employer (and its employees) in a multiple employer plan.

(e) APPLICATION OF QUALIFICATION REQUIREMENTS FOR CERTAIN MULTIPLE EMPLOYER PLANS WITH POOLED PLAN PROVIDERS.—

(1) IN GENERAL.—*Except as provided in paragraph (2), if a defined contribution plan to which subsection (c) applies—*

(A) *is maintained by employers which have a common interest other than having adopted the plan, or*

(B) *in the case of a plan not described in subparagraph (A), has a pooled plan provider,*

then the plan shall not be treated as failing to meet the requirements under this title applicable to a plan described in section 401(a) or to a plan that consists of individual retirement accounts described in section 408 (including by reason of subsection (c) thereof), whichever is applicable, merely because one or more employers of employees covered by the plan fail to take such actions as are required of such employers for the plan to meet such requirements.

(2) LIMITATIONS.—

(A) IN GENERAL.—*Paragraph (1) shall not apply to any plan unless the terms of the plan provide that in the case of any employer in the plan failing to take the actions described in paragraph (1)—*

(i) *the assets of the plan attributable to employees of such employer (or beneficiaries of such employees) will be transferred to a plan maintained only by such employer (or its successor), to an eligible retirement plan as defined in section 402(c)(8)(B) for each individual whose account is transferred, or to any other arrangement that the Secretary determines is appropriate, unless the Secretary determines it is in the best interests of the employees of such employer (and the beneficiaries of such employees) to retain the assets in the plan, and*

(ii) *such employer (and not the plan with respect to which the failure occurred or any other employer in such plan) shall, except to the extent provided by the Secretary, be liable for any liabilities with respect to such plan attributable to employees of such employer (or beneficiaries of such employees).*

(B) FAILURES BY POOLED PLAN PROVIDERS.—*If the pooled plan provider of a plan described in paragraph (1)(B) does not perform substantially all of the administrative duties which are required of the provider under paragraph (3)(A)(i) for any plan year, the Secretary may provide that the determination as to whether the plan meets the requirements under this title applicable to a plan described in section 401(a) or to a plan that consists of individual retirement accounts described in section 408 (including by reason of subsection (c) thereof), whichever is applicable, shall be made in the same manner as would be made without regard to paragraph (1).*

(3) POOLED PLAN PROVIDER.—

(A) IN GENERAL.—*For purposes of this subsection, the term "pooled plan provider" means, with respect to any plan, a person who—*

(i) *is designated by the terms of the plan as a named fiduciary (within the meaning of section 402(a)(2) of the Employee Retirement Income Security Act of 1974), as the plan administrator, and as the person responsible to perform all administrative duties (including conducting proper testing with respect to the plan and the employees of each employer in the plan) which are reasonably necessary to ensure that—*

(I) *the plan meets any requirement applicable under the Employee Retirement Income Security Act of 1974 or this title to a plan described in section 401(a) or to a plan that consists of individual retirement accounts described in section 408 (including by reason of subsection (c) thereof), whichever is applicable, and*

(II) *each employer in the plan takes such actions as the Secretary or such person determines are necessary for the plan to meet the requirements described in subclause (I), including providing to such person any disclosures or other information which the Secretary may require or which such person otherwise determines are necessary to administer the plan or to allow the plan to meet such requirements,*

(ii) *registers as a pooled plan provider with the Secretary, and provides such other information to the Secretary as the Secretary may require, before beginning operations as a pooled plan provider,*

(iii) acknowledges in writing that such person is a named fiduciary (within the meaning of section 402(a)(2) of the Employee Retirement Income Security Act of 1974), and the plan administrator, with respect to the plan, and

(iv) is responsible for ensuring that all persons who handle assets of, or who are fiduciaries of, the plan are bonded in accordance with section 412 of the Employee Retirement Income Security Act of 1974.

(B) AUDITS, EXAMINATIONS AND INVESTIGATIONS.—The Secretary may perform audits, examinations, and investigations of pooled plan providers as may be necessary to enforce and carry out the purposes of this subsection.

(C) AGGREGATION RULES.—For purposes of this paragraph, in determining whether a person meets the requirements of this paragraph to be a pooled plan provider with respect to any plan, all persons who perform services for the plan and who are treated as a single employer under subsection (b), (c), (m), or (o) of section 414 shall be treated as one person.

(D) TREATMENT OF EMPLOYERS AS PLAN SPONSORS.—Except with respect to the administrative duties of the pooled plan provider described in subparagraph (A)(i), each employer in a plan which has a pooled plan provider shall be treated as the plan sponsor with respect to the portion of the plan attributable to employees of such employer (or beneficiaries of such employees).

(4) GUIDANCE.—

(A) IN GENERAL.—The Secretary shall issue such guidance as the Secretary determines appropriate to carry out this subsection, including guidance—

(i) to identify the administrative duties and other actions required to be performed by a pooled plan provider under this subsection,

(ii) which describes the procedures to be taken to terminate a plan which fails to meet the requirements to be a plan described in paragraph (1), including the proper treatment of, and actions needed to be taken by, any employer in the plan and the assets and liabilities of the plan attributable to employees of such employer (or beneficiaries of such employees), and

(iii) identifying appropriate cases to which the rules of paragraph (2)(A) will apply to employers in the plan failing to take the actions described in paragraph (1).

The Secretary shall take into account under clause (iii) whether the failure of an employer or pooled plan provider to provide any disclosures or other information, or to take any other action, necessary to administer a plan or to allow a plan to meet requirements applicable to the plan under section 401(a) or 408, whichever is applicable, has continued over a period of time that demonstrates a lack of commitment to compliance.

(B) GOOD FAITH COMPLIANCE WITH LAW BEFORE GUIDANCE.—An employer or pooled plan provider shall not be treated as failing to meet a requirement of guidance issued by the Secretary under this paragraph if, before the issuance of such guidance, the employer or pooled plan provider complies in good faith with a reasonable interpretation of the provisions of this subsection to which such guidance relates.

(5) MODEL PLAN.—The Secretary shall publish model plan language which meets the requirements of this subsection and of paragraphs (43) and (44) of section 3 of the Employee Retirement Income Security Act of 1974 and which may be adopted in order for a plan to be treated as a plan described in paragraph (1)(B).

[Explanation at ¶100.]

Amendments

• **Further Consolidated Appropriations Act, 2020 (P.L. 116-94)**

P.L. 116-94, §101(a)(1), Div. O:

Amended Code Sec. 413 by adding at the end a new subsection (e). **Effective** for plan years beginning after 12-31-2020. For a special rule, see Act Sec. 101(e)(2), Div. O, below.

P.L. 116-94, §101(e)(2), Div. O, provides:

(2) RULE OF CONSTRUCTION.—Nothing in the amendments made by subsection (a) shall be construed as limiting the authority of the Secretary of the Treasury or the Secretary's delegate (determined without regard to such amendment) to provide for the proper treatment of a failure to meet any requirement applicable under the Internal Revenue Code of 1986 with respect to one employer (and its employees) in a multiple employer plan.

[¶ 6075] **CODE SEC. 415. LIMITATIONS ON BENEFITS AND CONTRIBUTION UNDER QUALIFIED PLANS.**

* * *

(c) LIMITATION FOR DEFINED CONTRIBUTION PLANS.—

* * *

(8) SPECIAL RULE FOR DIFFICULTY OF CARE PAYMENTS EXCLUDED FROM GROSS INCOME.—

(A) IN GENERAL.—For purposes of paragraph (1)(B), in the case of an individual who for a taxable year excludes from gross income under section 131 a qualified foster care payment which is a difficulty of care payment, the participant's compensation, or earned income, as the case may be, shall be increased by the amount so excluded.

(B) CONTRIBUTIONS ALLOCABLE TO DIFFICULTY OF CARE PAYMENTS TREATED AS AFTER-TAX.—Any contribution by the participant which is allowable due to such increase—

(i) shall be treated for purposes of this title as investment in the contract, and

(ii) shall not cause a plan (and any arrangement which is part of such plan) to be treated as failing to meet any requirements of this chapter solely by reason of allowing any such contributions.

[Explanation at ¶ 150.]

Amendments

• **Further Consolidated Appropriations Act, 2020 (P.L. 116-94)**

P.L. 116-94, §116(b)(1), Div. O:

Amended Code Sec. 415(c) by adding at the end a new paragraph (8). **Effective** for plan years beginning after 12-31-2015.

[¶ 6080] **CODE SEC. 430. MINIMUM FUNDING STANDARDS FOR SINGLE-EMPLOYER DEFINED BENEFIT PENSION PLANS.**

* * *

(m) SPECIAL RULES FOR COMMUNITY NEWSPAPER PLANS.—

(1) IN GENERAL.—The plan sponsor of a community newspaper plan under which no participant has had the participant's accrued benefit increased (whether because of service or compensation) after December 31, 2017, may elect to have the alternative standards described in paragraph (3) apply to such plan, and any plan sponsored by any member of the same controlled group.

(2) ELECTION.—An election under paragraph (1) shall be made at such time and in such manner as prescribed by the Secretary. Such election, once made with respect to a plan year, shall apply to all subsequent plan years unless revoked with the consent of the Secretary.

(3) ALTERNATIVE MINIMUM FUNDING STANDARDS.—The alternative standards described in this paragraph are the following:

(A) INTEREST RATES.—

(i) IN GENERAL.—Notwithstanding subsection (h)(2)(C) and except as provided in clause (ii), the first, second, and third segment rates in effect for any month for purposes of this section shall be 8 percent.

(ii) NEW BENEFIT ACCRUALS.—Notwithstanding subsection (h)(2), for purposes of determining the funding target and normal cost of a plan for any plan year, the present value of any benefits accrued or earned under the plan for a plan year with respect to which an election under paragraph (1) is in effect shall be determined on the basis of the United States Treasury obligation yield curve for the day that is the valuation date of such plan for such plan year.

(iii) UNITED STATES TREASURY OBLIGATION YIELD CURVE.—*For purposes of this subsection, the term "United States Treasury obligation yield curve" means, with respect to any day, a yield curve which shall be prescribed by the Secretary for such day on interest-bearing obligations of the United States.*

(B) SHORTFALL AMORTIZATION BASE.—

(i) PREVIOUS SHORTFALL AMORTIZATION BASES.—*The shortfall amortization bases determined under subsection (c)(3) for all plan years preceding the first plan year to which the election under paragraph (1) applies (and all shortfall amortization installments determined with respect to such bases) shall be reduced to zero under rules similar to the rules of subsection (c)(6).*

(ii) NEW SHORTFALL AMORTIZATION BASE.—*Notwithstanding subsection (c)(3), the shortfall amortization base for the first plan year to which the election under paragraph (1) applies shall be the funding shortfall of such plan for such plan year (determined using the interest rates as modified under subparagraph (A)).*

(C) DETERMINATION OF SHORTFALL AMORTIZATION INSTALLMENTS.—

(i) 30-YEAR PERIOD.—*Subparagraphs (A) and (B) of subsection (c)(2) shall be applied by substituting "30-plan-year" for "7-plan-year" each place it appears.*

(ii) NO SPECIAL ELECTION.—*The election under subparagraph (D) of subsection (c)(2) shall not apply to any plan year to which the election under paragraph (1) applies.*

(D) EXEMPTION FROM AT-RISK TREATMENT.—*Subsection (i) shall not apply.*

(4) COMMUNITY NEWSPAPER PLAN.—*For purposes of this subsection—*

(A) IN GENERAL.—*The term "community newspaper plan" means a plan to which this section applies maintained by an employer which, as of December 31, 2017—*

(i) *publishes and distributes daily, either electronically or in printed form, 1 or more community newspapers in a single State,*

(ii) *is not a company the stock of which is publicly traded (on a stock exchange or in an over-the-counter market), and is not controlled, directly or indirectly, by such a company,*

(iii) *is controlled, directly or indirectly—*

(I) *by 1 or more persons residing primarily in the State in which the community newspaper is published,*

(II) *for not less than 30 years by individuals who are members of the same family,*

(III) *by a trust created or organized in the State in which the community newspaper is published, the sole trustees of which are persons described in subclause (I) or (II),*

(IV) *by an entity which is described in section 501(c)(3) and exempt from taxation under section 501(a), which is organized and operated in the State in which the community newspaper is published, and the primary purpose of which is to benefit communities in such State, or*

(V) *by a combination of persons described in subclause (I), (III), or (IV), and*

(iv) *does not control, directly or indirectly, any newspaper in any other State.*

(B) COMMUNITY NEWSPAPER.—*The term "community newspaper" means a newspaper which primarily serves a metropolitan statistical area, as determined by the Office of Management and Budget, with a population of not less than 100,000.*

(C) CONTROL.—*A person shall be treated as controlled by another person if such other person possesses, directly or indirectly, the power to direct or cause the direction and management of such person (including the power to elect a majority of the members of the board of directors of such person) through the ownership of voting securities.*

(5) CONTROLLED GROUP.—*For purposes of this subsection, the term "controlled group" means all persons treated as a single employer under subsection (b), (c), (m), or (o) of section 414 as of the date of the enactment of this subsection.*

[Explanation at ¶ 195.]

Amendments

- **Further Consolidated Appropriations Act, 2020 (P.L. 116-94)**

P.L. 116-94, §115(a), Div. O:

Amended Code Sec. 430 by adding at the end a new subsection (m). **Effective** for plan years ending after 12-31-2017.

[¶ 6085] CODE SEC. 457. DEFERRED COMPENSATION PLANS OF STATE AND LOCAL GOVERNMENTS AND TAX-EXEMPT ORGANIZATIONS.

* * *

(d) DISTRIBUTION REQUIREMENTS.—

(1) IN GENERAL.—For purposes of subsection (b)(5), a plan meets the distribution requirements of this subsection if—

(A) under the plan amounts will not be made available to participants or beneficiaries earlier than—

(i) the calendar year in which the participant attains age $70^{1}/_{2}$ *(in the case of a plan maintained by an employer described in subsection (e)(1)(A), age $59^{1}/_{2}$)*,

(ii) when the participant has a severance from employment with the employer,

(iii) when the participant is faced with an unforeseeable emergency (determined in the manner prescribed by the Secretary in regulations), *or*

(iv) except as may be otherwise provided by regulations, in the case of a plan maintained by an employer described in subsection (e)(1)(A), with respect to amounts invested in a lifetime income investment (as defined in section 401(a)(38)(B)(ii)), the date that is 90 days prior to the date that such lifetime income investment may no longer be held as an investment option under the plan,

(B) the plan meets the minimum distribution requirements of paragraph (2),

(C) in the case of a plan maintained by an employer described in subsection (e)(1)(A), the plan meets requirements similar to the requirements of section 401(a)(31), *and*

(D) except as may be otherwise provided by regulations, in the case of amounts described in subparagraph (A)(iv), such amounts will be distributed only in the form of a qualified distribution (as defined in section 401(a)(38)(B)(i)) or a qualified plan distribution annuity contract (as defined in section 401(a)(38)(B)(iv)).

Any amount transferred in a direct trustee-to-trustee transfer in accordance with section 401(a)(31) shall not be includible in gross income for the taxable year of transfer.

[Explanation at ¶ 180 and ¶ 410.]

Amendments

- **Further Consolidated Appropriations Act, 2020 (P.L. 116-94)**

P.L. 116-94, §104(b), Div. M:

Amended Code Sec. 457(d)(1)(A)(i) by inserting "(in the case of a plan maintained by an employer described in subsection (e)(1)(A), age $59^{1}/_{2}$)" before the comma at the end. **Effective** for plan years beginning after 12-31-2019.

P.L. 116-94, §109(d)(1), Div. O:

Amended Code Sec. 457(d)(1)(A) by striking "or" at the end of clause (ii), by inserting "or" at the end of clause (iii), and by adding after clause (iii) a new clause (iv). **Effective** for plan years beginning after 12-31-2019.

P.L. 116-94, §109(d)(2), Div. O:

Amended Code Sec. 457(d)(1) by striking "and" at the end of subparagraph (B), by striking the period at the end of subparagraph (C) and inserting ", and", and by inserting after subparagraph (C) a new subparagraph (D). **Effective** for plan years beginning after 12-31-2019.

P.L. 116-94, §202(a), Div. Q, provides:

For a special rule, see Act Sec. 202(a), Div. Q, in the amendment notes for Code Sec. 1400Q.

[¶ 6090] CODE SEC. 501. EXEMPTION FROM TAX ON CORPORATIONS, CERTAIN TRUSTS, ETC.

* * *

(c) LIST OF EXEMPT ORGANIZATIONS.—The following organizations are referred to in subsection (a):

* * *

(12)

* * *

(J) In the case of a mutual or cooperative telephone or electric company described in this paragraph, subparagraph (A) shall be applied without taking into account any income received or accrued from—

(i) any grant, contribution, or assistance provided pursuant to the Robert T. Stafford Disaster Relief and Emergency Assistance Act or any similar grant, contribution, or assistance by any local, State, or regional governmental entity for the purpose of relief, recovery, or restoration from, or preparation for, a disaster or emergency, or

(ii) any grant or contribution by any governmental entity (other than a contribution in aid of construction or any other contribution as a customer or potential customer) the purpose of which is substantially related to providing, constructing, restoring, or relocating electric, communication, broadband, internet, or other utility facilities or services.

* * *

Amendments

• **Further Consolidated Appropriations Act, 2020** (P.L. 116-94)

P.L. 116-94, §301(a), Div. Q:

Amended Code Sec. 501(c)(12) by adding at the end a new subparagraph (J). **Effective** for tax years beginning after 12-31-2017.

[¶6095] CODE SEC. 529. QUALIFIED TUITION PROGRAMS.

* * *

(c) TAX TREATMENT OF DESIGNATED BENEFICIARIES AND CONTRIBUTORS.—

* * *

(8) TREATMENT OF CERTAIN EXPENSES ASSOCIATED WITH REGISTERED APPRENTICESHIP PROGRAMS.—Any reference in this subsection to the term "qualified higher education expense" shall include a reference to expenses for fees, books, supplies, and equipment required for the participation of a designated beneficiary in an apprenticeship program registered and certified with the Secretary of Labor under section 1 of the National Apprenticeship Act (29 U.S.C. 50).

(9) TREATMENT OF QUALIFIED EDUCATION LOAN REPAYMENTS.—

(A) IN GENERAL.—Any reference in this subsection to the term "qualified higher education expense" shall include a reference to amounts paid as principal or interest on any qualified education loan (as defined in section 221(d)) of the designated beneficiary or a sibling of the designated beneficiary.

(B) LIMITATION.—The amount of distributions treated as a qualified higher education expense under this paragraph with respect to the loans of any individual shall not exceed $10,000 (reduced by the amount of distributions so treated for all prior taxable years).

(C) SPECIAL RULES FOR SIBLINGS OF THE DESIGNATED BENEFICIARY.—

(i) SEPARATE ACCOUNTING.—For purposes of subparagraph (B) and subsection (d), amounts treated as a qualified higher education expense with respect to the loans of a sibling of the designated beneficiary shall be taken into account with respect to such sibling and not with respect to such designated beneficiary.

(ii) SIBLING DEFINED.—For purposes of this paragraph, the term "sibling" means an individual who bears a relationship to the designated beneficiary which is described in section 152(d)(2)(B).

[Explanation at ¶ 540.]

Amendments

• Further Consolidated Appropriations Act, 2020 (P.L. 116-94)

P.L. 116-94, § 302(a), Div. O:

Amended Code Sec. 529(c) by adding at the end a new paragraph (8). **Effective** for distributions made after 12-31-2018.

P.L. 116-94, § 302(b)(1), Div. O:

Amended Code Sec. 529(c), as amended by Act Sec. 302(a), by adding at the end a new paragraph (9). **Effective** for distributions made after 12-31-2018.

[¶ 6100] CODE SEC. 3121. DEFINITIONS.

(a) WAGES.—For purposes of this chapter, the term "wages" means all remuneration for employment, including the cash value of all remuneration (including benefits) paid in any medium other than cash; except that such term shall not include—

* * *

(23) any benefit or payment which is excludable from the gross income of the employee under section [sic]*section 139B(a)*.

* * *

[Explanation at ¶ 525.]

Amendments

• Further Consolidated Appropriations Act, 2020 (P.L. 116-94)

P.L. 116-94, § 301(c), Div. O:

Amended Code Sec. 3121(a)(23) by striking "139B(b)" and inserting "section 139B(a)". **Effective** for tax years beginning after 12-31-2019.

[¶ 6105] CODE SEC. 4191 STRICKEN.—

[Code Sec. 4191—Stricken]

[Explanation at ¶ 500.]

Amendments

• 2019, Further Consolidated Appropriations Act, 2020 (P.L. 116-94)

P.L. 116-94, § 501(a), Div. N:

Amended chapter 32 by striking subchapter E (Code Sec. 4191). **Effective** for sales after 12-31-2019. Prior to being stricken, Code Sec. 4191 read as follows:

SEC. 4191. MEDICAL DEVICES.

[Sec. 4191(a)]

(a) IN GENERAL.—There is hereby imposed on the sale of any taxable medical device by the manufacturer, producer, or importer a tax equal to 2.3 percent of the price for which so sold.

[Sec. 4191(b)]

(b) TAXABLE MEDICAL DEVICE.—For purposes of this section—

(1) IN GENERAL.—The term "taxable medical device" means any device (as defined in section 201(h) of the Federal Food, Drug, and Cosmetic Act) intended for humans.

(2) EXEMPTIONS.—Such term shall not include—

(A) eyeglasses,

(B) contact lenses,

(C) hearing aids, and

(D) any other medical device determined by the Secretary to be of a type which is generally purchased by the general public at retail for individual use.

Amendments

• 2010, Health Care and Education Reconciliation Act of 2010 (P.L. 111-152)

P.L. 111-152, § 1405(a)(1):

Amended chapter 32 by inserting after subchapter D a new subchapter E (Code Sec. 4191). **Effective** for sales after 12-31-2012.

[Sec. 4191(c)]

(c) MORATORIUM.—The tax imposed under subsection (a) shall not apply to sales during the period beginning on January 1, 2016, and ending on December 31, 2019.

Amendments

• 2018 (P.L. 115-120)

P.L. 115-120, § 4001(a), Div. D:

Amended Code Sec. 4191(c) by striking "December 31, 2017" and inserting "December 31, 2019". **Effective** for sales after 12-31-2017.

• 2015, Protecting Americans from Tax Hikes Act of 2015 (P.L. 114-113)

P.L. 114-113, § 174(a), Div. Q:

Amended Code Sec. 4191 by adding at the end a new subsection (c). **Effective** for sales after 12-31-2015.

[¶6110] CODE SEC. 4221. CERTAIN TAX-FREE SALES.

(a) GENERAL RULE.—Under regulations prescribed by the Secretary, no tax shall be imposed under this chapter (other than under section 4121 or 4081) on the sale by the manufacturer (or under subchapter C of chapter 31 on the first retail sale) of an article—

* * *

[Explanation at ¶500.]

Amendments

- **2019, Further Consolidated Appropriations Act, 2020 (P.L. 116-94)**

P.L. 116-94, §501(b)(1), Div. N:

Amended Code Sec. 4221(a) by striking the last sentence. Effective for sales after 12-31-2019. Prior to being stricken, the last sentence of Code Sec. 4221(a) read as follows:

In the case of the tax imposed by section 4191, paragraphs (3), (4), (5), and (6) shall not apply.

[¶6115] CODE SEC. 4375. HEALTH INSURANCE.

* * *

(e) TERMINATION.—This section shall not apply to policy years ending after September 30, 2029.

Amendments

- **Further Consolidated Appropriations Act, 2020 (P.L. 116-94)**

P.L. 116-94, §104(b), Div. N:

Amended Code Sec. 4375(e) by striking "2019" and inserting "2029". Effective 12-20-2019.

[¶6120] CODE SEC. 4376. SELF-INSURED HEALTH PLANS.

* * *

(e) TERMINATION.—This section shall not apply to plan years ending after September 30, 2029.

Amendments

- **Further Consolidated Appropriations Act, 2020 (P.L. 116-94)**

P.L. 116-94, §104(c), Div. N:

Amended Code Sec. 4376(e) by striking "2019" and inserting "2029". Effective 12-20-2019.

[¶6125] CODE SEC. 4975. TAX ON PROHIBITED TRANSACTIONS.

* * *

(c) PROHIBITED TRANSACTION.—

* * *

(7) SPECIAL RULE FOR PROVISION OF PHARMACY BENEFIT SERVICES.—Any party to an arrangement which satisfies the requirements of section 408(h) of the Employee Retirement Income Security Act of 1974 shall be exempt from the tax imposed by this section with respect to such arrangement.

[Explanation at ¶515.]

Amendments

- **Further Consolidated Appropriations Act, 2020 (P.L. 116-94)**

P.L. 116-94, §1302(b), Div. P:

Amended Code Sec. 4975(c) by adding at the end a new paragraph (7). Effective 12-20-2019. For a special rule, see Act Sec. 1302(c), Div. P.

P.L. 116-94, §1302(c), Div. P, provides:

(c) APPLICABILITY.—With respect to a group health plan subject to subsection (h) of section 408 of the Employee Retirement Income Security Act of 1974 (29 U.S.C. 1108) (as amended by subsection (a)) and subsection (c) of section 4975 of the Internal Revenue Code of 1986 (as amended by subsection (b)), beginning at the end of the fifth plan year of such group health plan that begins after the date of enactment of this Act, such subsection (h) of such section 408 and such subsection (c) of such [section 4975] shall have no force or effect.

[¶ 6130] CODE SEC. 4980I. STRICKEN.—

[Code Sec. 4980I—Stricken]

[Explanation at ¶ 510.]

Amendments

- **Further Consolidated Appropriations Act, 2020 (P.L. 116-94)**

P.L. 116-94, § 503(a), Div. N:

Amended chapter 43 by striking Code Sec. 4980I. Effective for tax years beginning after 12-31-2019. Prior to being stricken, Code Sec. 4980I read as follows:

SEC. 4980I. EXCISE TAX ON HIGH COST EMPLOYER-SPONSORED HEALTH COVERAGE.

[Sec. 4980I(a)]

(a) IMPOSITION OF TAX.—If—

(1) an employee is covered under any applicable employer-sponsored coverage of an employer at any time during a taxable period, and

(2) there is any excess benefit with respect to the coverage,

there is hereby imposed a tax equal to 40 percent of the excess benefit.

[Sec. 4980I(b)]

(b) EXCESS BENEFIT.—For purposes of this section—

(1) IN GENERAL.—The term "excess benefit" means, with respect to any applicable employer-sponsored coverage made available by an employer to an employee during any taxable period, the sum of the excess amounts determined under paragraph (2) for months during the taxable period.

(2) MONTHLY EXCESS AMOUNT.—The excess amount determined under this paragraph for any month is the excess (if any) of—

(A) the aggregate cost of the applicable employer-sponsored coverage of the employee for the month, over

(B) an amount equal to 1/12 of the annual limitation under paragraph (3) for the calendar year in which the month occurs.

(3) ANNUAL LIMITATION.—For purposes of this subsection—

(A) IN GENERAL.—The annual limitation under this paragraph for any calendar year is the dollar limit determined under subparagraph (C) for the calendar year.

(B) APPLICABLE ANNUAL LIMITATION.—

(i) IN GENERAL.—Except as provided in clause (ii), the annual limitation which applies for any month shall be determined on the basis of the type of coverage (as determined under subsection (f)(1)) provided to the employee by the employer as of the beginning of the month.

(ii) MULTIEMPLOYER PLAN COVERAGE.—Any coverage provided under a multiemployer plan (as defined in section 414(f)) shall be treated as coverage other than self-only coverage.

(C) APPLICABLE DOLLAR LIMIT.—

(i) 2018.—In the case of 2018, the dollar limit under this subparagraph is—

(I) in the case of an employee with self-only coverage, $10,200 multiplied by the health cost adjustment percentage (determined by only taking into account self-only coverage), and

(II) in the case of an employee with coverage other than self-only coverage, $27,500 multiplied by the health cost adjustment percentage (determined by only taking into account coverage other than self-only coverage).

(ii) HEALTH COST ADJUSTMENT PERCENTAGE.—For purposes of clause (i), the health cost adjustment percentage is equal to 100 percent plus the excess (if any) of—

(I) the percentage by which the per employee cost for providing coverage under the Blue Cross/Blue Shield standard benefit option under the Federal Employees Health Benefits Plan for plan year 2018 (determined by using the benefit package for such coverage in 2010) exceeds such cost for plan year 2010, over

(II) 55 percent.

(iii) AGE AND GENDER ADJUSTMENT.—

(I) IN GENERAL.—The amount determined under subclause (I) or (II) of clause (i), whichever is applicable, for any taxable period shall be increased by the amount determined under subclause (II).

(II) AMOUNT DETERMINED.—The amount determined under this subclause is an amount equal to the excess (if any) of—

(aa) the premium cost of the Blue Cross/Blue Shield standard benefit option under the Federal Employees Health Benefits Plan for the type of coverage provided such individual in such taxable period if priced for the age and gender characteristics of all employees of the individual's employer, over

(bb) that premium cost for the provision of such coverage under such option in such taxable period if priced for the age and gender characteristics of the national workforce.

(iv) EXCEPTION FOR CERTAIN INDIVIDUALS.—In the case of an individual who is a qualified retiree or who participates in a plan sponsored by an employer the majority of whose employees covered by the plan are engaged in a high-risk profession or employed to repair or install electrical or telecommunications lines—

(I) the dollar amount in clause (i)(I) shall be increased by $1,650, and

(II) the dollar amount in clause (i)(II) shall be increased by $3,450.

(v) SUBSEQUENT YEARS.—In the case of any calendar year after 2018, each of the dollar amounts under clauses (i) (after the application of clause (ii)) and (iv) shall be increased to the amount equal to such amount as determined for the calendar year preceding such year, increased by an amount equal to the product of—

(I) such amount as so determined, multiplied by

(II) the cost-of-living adjustment determined under section 1(f)(3) for such year (determined by substituting the calendar year that is 2 years before such year for "2016" in subparagraph (A)(ii) thereof), increased by 1 percentage point in the case of determinations for calendar years beginning before 2020.

If any amount determined under this clause is not a multiple of $50, such amount shall be rounded to the nearest multiple of $50.

[Sec. 4980I(c)]

(c) LIABILITY TO PAY TAX.—

(1) IN GENERAL.—Each coverage provider shall pay the tax imposed by subsection (a) on its applicable share of the excess benefit with respect to an employee for any taxable period.

(2) COVERAGE PROVIDER.—For purposes of this subsection, the term "coverage provider" means each of the following:

(A) HEALTH INSURANCE COVERAGE.—If the applicable employer-sponsored coverage consists of coverage under a group health plan which provides health insurance coverage, the health insurance issuer.

(B) HSA AND MSA CONTRIBUTIONS.—If the applicable employer-sponsored coverage consists of coverage under an arrangement under which the employer makes contributions described in subsection (b) or (d) of section 106, the employer.

(C) OTHER COVERAGE.—In the case of any other applicable employer-sponsored coverage, the person that administers the plan benefits.

(3) APPLICABLE SHARE.—For purposes of this subsection, a coverage provider's applicable share of an excess benefit for any taxable period is the amount which bears the same ratio to the amount of such excess benefit as—

(A) the cost of the applicable employer-sponsored coverage provided by the provider to the employee during such period, bears to

(B) the aggregate cost of all applicable employer-sponsored coverage provided to the employee by all coverage providers during such period.

(4) RESPONSIBILITY TO CALCULATE TAX AND APPLICABLE SHARES.—

(A) IN GENERAL.—Each employer shall—

(i) calculate for each taxable period the amount of the excess benefit subject to the tax imposed by subsection (a) and the applicable share of such excess benefit for each coverage provider, and

(ii) notify, at such time and in such manner as the Secretary may prescribe, the Secretary and each coverage provider of the amount so determined for the provider.

(B) SPECIAL RULE FOR MULTIEMPLOYER PLANS.—In the case of applicable employer-sponsored coverage made available to employees through a multiemployer plan (as defined in section 414(f)), the plan sponsor shall make the calculations, and provide the notice, required under subparagraph (A).

[Sec. 4980I(d)]

(d) APPLICABLE EMPLOYER-SPONSORED COVERAGE; COST.—For purposes of this section—

(1) APPLICABLE EMPLOYER-SPONSORED COVERAGE.—

(A) IN GENERAL.—The term "applicable employer-sponsored coverage" means, with respect to any employee, coverage under any group health plan made available to the employee by an employer which is excludable from the employee's gross income under section 106, or would be so excludable if it were employer-provided coverage (within the meaning of such section 106).

(B) EXCEPTIONS.—The term "applicable employer-sponsored coverage" shall not include—

(i) any coverage (whether through insurance or otherwise) described in section 9832(c)(1) (other than subparagraph (G) thereof) or for long-term care, or

(ii) any coverage under a separate policy, certificate, or contract of insurance which provides benefits substantially all of which are for treatment of the mouth (including any organ or structure within the mouth) or for treatment of the eye, or

(iii) any coverage described in section 9832(c)(3) the payment for which is not excludable from gross income and for which a deduction under section 162(l) is not allowable.

(C) COVERAGE INCLUDES EMPLOYEE PAID PORTION.—Coverage shall be treated as applicable employer-sponsored coverage without regard to whether the employer or employee pays for the coverage.

(D) SELF-EMPLOYED INDIVIDUAL.—In the case of an individual who is an employee within the meaning of section 401(c)(1), coverage under any group health plan providing health insurance coverage shall be treated as applicable employer-sponsored coverage if a deduction is allowable under section 162(l) with respect to all or any portion of the cost of the coverage.

(E) GOVERNMENTAL PLANS INCLUDED.—Applicable employer-sponsored coverage shall include coverage under any group health plan established and maintained primarily for its civilian employees by the Government of the United States, by the government of any State or political subdivision thereof, or by any agency or instrumentality of any such government.

(2) DETERMINATION OF COST.—

(A) IN GENERAL.—The cost of applicable employer-sponsored coverage shall be determined under rules similar to the rules of section 4980B(f)(4), except that in determining such cost, any portion of the cost of such coverage which is attributable to the tax imposed under this section shall not be taken into account and the amount of such cost shall be calculated separately for self-only coverage and other coverage. In the case of applicable employer-sponsored coverage which provides coverage to retired employees, the plan may elect to treat a retired employee who has not attained the age of 65 and a retired employee who has attained the age of 65 as similarly situated beneficiaries.

(B) HEALTH FSAS.—In the case of applicable employer-sponsored coverage consisting of coverage under a flexible spending arrangement (as defined in section 106(c)(2)), the cost of the coverage shall be equal to the sum of—

(i) the amount of employer contributions under any salary reduction election under the arrangement, plus

(ii) the amount determined under subparagraph (A) with respect to any reimbursement under the arrangement in excess of the contributions described in clause (i).

(C) ARCHER MSAS AND HSAS.—In the case of applicable employer-sponsored coverage consisting of coverage under an arrangement under which the employer makes contributions described in subsection (b) or (d) of section 106, the cost of the coverage shall be equal to the amount of employer contributions under the arrangement.

(D) QUALIFIED SMALL EMPLOYER HEALTH REIMBURSEMENT ARRANGEMENTS.—In the case of applicable employer-sponsored coverage consisting of coverage under any qualified small employer health reimbursement arrangement (as defined in section 9831(d)(2)), the cost of coverage shall be equal to the amount described in section 6051(a)(15).

(E) ALLOCATION ON A MONTHLY BASIS.—If cost is determined on other than a monthly basis, the cost shall be allocated to months in a taxable period on such basis as the Secretary may prescribe.

(3) EMPLOYEE.—The term "employee" includes any former employee, surviving spouse, or other primary insured individual.

Amendments

P.L. 114-255, § 18001(a)(4)(B):

Amended Code Sec. 4980I(d)(2) by redesignating subparagraph (D) as subparagraph (E) and by inserting after subparagraph (C) a new subparagraph (D). **Effective** for years beginning after 12-31-2016.

P.L. 111-152, § 1401(a)(4)-(5):

Amended Code Sec. 4980I, as added by section 9001 of the Patient Protection and Affordable Care Act (P.L. 111-148), and amended by section 10901 of such Act, by redesignating clause (ii) as clause (iii) in subsection (d)(1)(B), and by inserting after clause (i) a new clause (ii); and by adding at the end of subsection (d) a new paragraph (3). **Effective** 3-30-2010.

P.L. 111-148, § 10901(b):

Amended Code Sec. 4980I(d)(1)(B)(i), as added by Act Sec. 9001, by striking "section 9832(c)(1)(A)" and inserting "section 9832(c)(1) (other than subparagraph (G) thereof)". **Effective** for tax years beginning after 12-31-2019 [effective date changed by P.L. 111-152, § 1401(b)(2), and P.L. 114-113, § 101(a), Div. P].

[Sec. 4980I(e)]

(e) PENALTY FOR FAILURE TO PROPERLY CALCULATE EXCESS BENEFIT.—

(1) IN GENERAL.—If, for any taxable period, the tax imposed by subsection (a) exceeds the tax determined under such subsection with respect to the total excess benefit calculated by the employer or plan sponsor under subsection (c)(4)—

(A) each coverage provider shall pay the tax on its applicable share (determined in the same manner as under subsection (c)(4)) of the excess, but no penalty shall be imposed on the provider with respect to such amount, and

(B) the employer or plan sponsor shall, in addition to any tax imposed by subsection (a), pay a penalty in an amount equal to such excess, plus interest at the underpayment rate determined under section 6621 for the period beginning on the due date for the payment of tax imposed by subsection (a) to which the excess relates and ending on the date of payment of the penalty.

(2) LIMITATIONS ON PENALTY.—

(A) PENALTY NOT TO APPLY WHERE FAILURE NOT DISCOVERED EXERCISING REASONABLE DILIGENCE.—No penalty shall be imposed by paragraph (1)(B) on any failure to properly calculate the excess benefit during any period for which it is established to the satisfaction of the Secretary that the employer or plan sponsor neither knew, nor exercising reasonable diligence would have known, that such failure existed.

(B) PENALTY NOT TO APPLY TO FAILURES CORRECTED WITHIN 30 DAYS.—No penalty shall be imposed by paragraph (1)(B) on any such failure if—

(i) such failure was due to reasonable cause and not to willful neglect, and

(ii) such failure is corrected during the 30-day period beginning on the 1st date that the employer knew, or exercising reasonable diligence would have known, that such failure existed.

(C) WAIVER BY SECRETARY.—In the case of any such failure which is due to reasonable cause and not to willful neglect, the Secretary may waive part or all of the penalty imposed by paragraph (1), to the extent that the payment of such penalty would be excessive or otherwise inequitable relative to the failure involved.

[Sec. 4980I(f)]

(f) OTHER DEFINITIONS AND SPECIAL RULES.—For purposes of this section—

(1) COVERAGE DETERMINATIONS.—

(A) IN GENERAL.—Except as provided in subparagraph (B), an employee shall be treated as having self-only coverage with respect to any applicable employer-sponsored coverage of an employer.

(B) MINIMUM ESSENTIAL COVERAGE.—An employee shall be treated as having coverage other than self-only coverage only if the employee is enrolled in coverage other than self-only coverage in a group health plan which provides minimum essential coverage (as defined in section 5000A(f)) to the employee and at least one other beneficiary, and the benefits provided under such minimum essential coverage do not vary based on whether any individual covered under such coverage is the employee or another beneficiary.

(2) QUALIFIED RETIREE.—The term "qualified retiree" means any individual who—

(A) is receiving coverage by reason of being a retiree,

(B) has attained age 55, and

(C) is not entitled to benefits or eligible for enrollment under the Medicare program under title XVIII of the Social Security Act.

(3) EMPLOYEES ENGAGED IN HIGH-RISK PROFESSION.—The term "employees engaged in a high-risk profession" means law enforcement officers (as such term is defined in section 1204 of the Omnibus Crime Control and Safe Streets Act of 1968), employees in fire protection activities (as such term is defined in section 3(y) of the Fair Labor Standards Act of 1938), individuals who provide out-of-hospital emergency medical care (including emergency medical technicians, paramedics, and first-responders), individuals whose primary work is longshore work (as defined in section 258(b) of the Immigration and Nationality Act (8 U.S.C. 1288(b)), determined without regard to paragraph (2) thereof), and individuals engaged in the construction, mining, agriculture (not including food processing), forestry, and fishing industries. Such term includes an employee who is retired from a high-risk profession described in the preceding sentence, if such employee satisfied the requirements of such sentence for a period of not less than 20 years during the employee's employment.

(4) GROUP HEALTH PLAN.—The term "group health plan" has the meaning given such term by section 5000(b)(1). Section 9831(d)(1) shall not apply for purposes of this section.

(5) HEALTH INSURANCE COVERAGE; HEALTH INSURANCE ISSUER.—

(A) HEALTH INSURANCE COVERAGE.—The term "health insurance coverage" has the meaning given such term by section 9832(b)(1) (applied without regard to subparagraph (B) thereof, except as provided by the Secretary in regulations).

(B) HEALTH INSURANCE ISSUER.—The term "health insurance issuer" has the meaning given such term by section 9832(b)(2).

(6) PERSON THAT ADMINISTERS THE PLAN BENEFITS.—The term "person that administers the plan benefits" shall include the plan sponsor if the plan sponsor administers benefits under the plan.

(7) PLAN SPONSOR.—The term "plan sponsor" has the meaning given such term in section 3(16)(B) of the Employee Retirement Income Security Act of 1974.

(8) TAXABLE PERIOD.—The term "taxable period" means the calendar year or such shorter period as the Secretary may prescribe. The Secretary may have different taxable periods for employers of varying sizes.

(9) AGGREGATION RULES.—All employers treated as a single employer under subsection (b), (c), (m), or (o) of section 414 shall be treated as a single employer.

(10) DEDUCTIBILITY OF TAX.—Section 275(a)(6) shall not apply to the tax imposed by subsection (a).

Amendments

P.L. 114-255, § 18001(a)(4)(A):

Amended Code Sec. 4980I(f)(4) by adding at the end a new sentence. **Effective** for years beginning after 12-31-2016.

P.L. 114-113, § 102, Div. P:

Amended Code Sec. 4980I(f)(10). **Effective** 12-18-2015. Prior to amendment, Code Sec. 4980I(f)(10) read as follows:

(10) DENIAL OF DEDUCTION.—For denial of a deduction for the tax imposed by this section, see section 275(a)(6).

P.L. 111-148, §10901(a):

Amended Code Sec. 4980I(f)(3), as added by Act Sec. 9001, by inserting "individuals whose primary work is longshore work (as defined in section 258(b) of the Immigration and Nationality Act (8 U.S.C. 1288(b)), determined without regard to paragraph (2) thereof)," before "and individuals engaged in the construction, mining". **Effective** for tax years beginning after 12-31-2019 [**effective** date changed by P.L. 111-152, § 1401(b)(2), and P.L. 114-113, § 101(a), Div. P].

[Sec. 4980I(g)]

(g) REGULATIONS.—The Secretary shall prescribe such regulations as may be necessary to carry out this section.

Amendments

P.L. 111-148, §9001(a):

Amended chapter 43, as amended by Act Sec. 1513, by adding at the end a new Code Sec. 4980I. **Effective** for tax years beginning after 12-31-2021 [**effective** date changed by P.L. 111-152, § 1401(b)(1), P.L. 114-113, § 101(a), Div. P, and P.L. 115-120, § 4002, Div. D].

[¶6135] CODE SEC. 6011. GENERAL REQUIREMENT OF RETURN, STATEMENT, OR LIST.

* * *

(e) REGULATIONS REQUIRING RETURNS ON MAGNETIC MEDIA, ETC.—

* * *

(6)[(7)] APPLICATION OF NUMERICAL LIMITATION TO RETURNS RELATING TO DEFERRED COMPENSATION PLANS.—For purposes of applying the numerical limitation under paragraph (2)(A) to any return required under section 6058, information regarding each plan for which information is provided on such return shall be treated as a separate return.

[Explanation at ¶205.]

Amendments

• **Further Consolidated Appropriations Act, 2020 (P.L. 116-94)**

P.L. 116-94, §202(d)(1), Div. O:

Amended Code Sec. 6011(e) by adding at the end a new paragraph (6)[(7)]. **Effective** for returns required be filed with respect to plan years beginning after 12-31-2019.

[¶6140] CODE SEC. 6051. RECEIPTS FOR EMPLOYEES.

(a) REQUIREMENT.—Every person required to deduct and withhold from an employee a tax under section 3101 or 3402, or who would have been required to deduct and withhold a tax under section 3402 (determined without regard to subsection (n)) if the employee had claimed no more than one withholding exemption, or every employer engaged in a trade or business who pays remuneration for services performed by an employee, including the cash value of such remuneration paid in any medium other than cash, shall furnish to each such employee in respect of the remuneration paid by such person to such employee during the calendar year, on or before January 31 of the succeeding year, or, if his employment is terminated before the close of such calendar year, within 30 days after the date of receipt of a written request from the employee if such 30-day period ends before January 31, a written statement showing the following:

* * *

(14) the aggregate cost (determined under rules similar to the rules of section 4980B(f)(4)) of applicable employer-sponsored coverage (as defined in *subsection (g)*), except that this paragraph shall not apply to—

(A) coverage to which paragraphs (11) and (12) apply, or

(B) the amount of any salary reduction contributions to a flexible spending arrangement (within the meaning of section 125),

* * *

[Explanation at ¶ 510.]

Amendments

• **Further Consolidated Appropriations Act, 2020 (P.L. 116-94)**

P.L. 116-94, § 503(b)(1)(A), Div. N:

Amended Code Sec. 6051(a)(14) by striking "section 4980I(d)(1)" and inserting "subsection (g)". **Effective** for tax years beginning after 12-31-2019.

(g) APPLICABLE EMPLOYER-SPONSORED COVERAGE.—*For purposes of subsection (a)(14)*—

(1) IN GENERAL.—*The term "applicable employer-sponsored coverage" means, with respect to any employee, coverage under any group health plan made available to the employee by an employer which is excludable from the employee's gross income under section 106, or would be so excludable if it were employer-provided coverage (within the meaning of such section 106).*

(2) EXCEPTIONS.—*The term "applicable employer-sponsored coverage" shall not include—*

(A) *any coverage (whether through insurance or otherwise) described in section 9832(c)(1) (other than subparagraph (G) thereof) or for long-term care,*

(B) *any coverage under a separate policy, certificate, or contract of insurance which provides benefits substantially all of which are for treatment of the mouth (including any organ or structure within the mouth) or for treatment of the eye, or*

(C) *any coverage described in section 9832(c)(3) the payment for which is not excludable from gross income and for which a deduction under section 162(l) is not allowable.*

(3) COVERAGE INCLUDES EMPLOYEE PAID PORTION.—*Coverage shall be treated as applicable employer-sponsored coverage without regard to whether the employer or employee pays for the coverage.*

(4) GOVERNMENTAL PLANS INCLUDED.—*Applicable employer-sponsored coverage shall include coverage under any group health plan established and maintained primarily for its civilian employees by the Government of the United States, by the government of any State or political subdivision thereof, or by any agency or instrumentality of any such government.*

[Explanation at ¶ 510.]

Amendments

• **Further Consolidated Appropriations Act, 2020 (P.L. 116-94)**

P.L. 116-94, § 503(b)(1)(B), Div. N:

Amended Code Sec. 6051 by adding at the end a new subsection (g). **Effective** for tax years beginning after 12-31-2019.

[¶ 6145] CODE SEC. 6416. CERTAIN TAXES ON SALES AND SERVICES.

* * *

(b) SPECIAL CASES IN WHICH TAX PAYMENTS CONSIDERED OVERPAYMENTS.—Under regulations prescribed by the Secretary, credit or refund (without interest) shall be allowed or made in respect of the overpayments determined under the following paragraphs:

* * *

(2) SPECIFIED USES AND RESALES.—The tax paid under chapter 32 (or under subsection (a) or (d) of section 4041 in respect of sales or under section 4051) in respect of any article shall be deemed to be an overpayment if such article was, by any person—

* * *

[Explanation at ¶ 500.]

Amendments

• **2019, Further Consolidated Appropriations Act, 2020 (P.L. 116-94)**

P.L. 116-94, §501(b)(2), Div. N:

Amended Code Sec. 6416(b)(2) by striking the last sentence. **Effective** for sales after 12-31-2019. Prior to being stricken, the last sentence of Code Sec. 6416(b)(2) read as follows:

In the case of the tax imposed by section 4191, subparagraphs (B), (C), (D), and (E) shall not apply.

[¶ 6150] CODE SEC. 6651. FAILURE TO FILE TAX RETURN OR TO PAY TAX.

(a) ADDITION TO THE TAX.—In case of failure—

(1) to file any return required under authority of subchapter A of chapter 61 (other than part III thereof), subchapter A of chapter 51 (relating to distilled spirits, wines, and beer), or of subchapter A of chapter 52 (relating to tobacco, cigars, cigarettes, and cigarette papers and tubes) or of subchapter A of chapter 53 (relating to machine guns and certain other firearms), on the date prescribed therefor (determined with regard to any extension of time for filing), unless it is shown that such failure is due to reasonable cause and not due to willful neglect, there shall be added to the amount required to be shown as tax on such return 5 percent of the amount of such tax if the failure is for not more than 1 month, with an additional 5 percent for each additional month or fraction thereof during which such failure continues, not exceeding 25 percent in the aggregate;

(2) to pay the amount shown as tax on any return specified in paragraph (1) on or before the date prescribed for payment of such tax (determined with regard to any extension of time for payment), unless it is shown that such failure is due to reasonable cause and not due to willful neglect, there shall be added to the amount shown as tax on such return 0.5 percent of the amount of such tax if the failure is for not more than 1 month, with an additional 0.5 percent for each additional month or fraction thereof during which such failure continues, not exceeding 25 percent in the aggregate; or

(3) to pay any amount in respect of any tax required to be shown on a return specified in paragraph (1) which is not so shown (including an assessment made pursuant to section 6213(b)) within 21 calendar days from the date of notice and demand therefor (10 business days if the amount for which such notice and demand is made equals or exceeds $100,000), unless it is shown that such failure is due to reasonable cause and not due to willful neglect, there shall be added to the amount of tax stated in such notice and demand 0.5 percent of the amount of such tax if the failure is for not more than 1 month, with an additional 0.5 percent for each additional month or fraction thereof during which such failure continues, not exceeding 25 percent in the aggregate.

In the case of a failure to file a return of tax imposed by chapter 1 within 60 days of the date prescribed for filing of such return (determined with regard to any extensions of time for filing), unless it is shown that such failure is due to reasonable cause and not due to willful neglect, the addition to tax under paragraph (1) shall not be less than the lesser of *$435* or 100 percent of the amount required to be shown as tax on such return.

[Explanation at ¶ 305.]

Amendments

• **Further Consolidated Appropriations Act, 2020 (P.L. 116-94)**

P.L. 116-94, §402(a), Div. O:

Amended the second sentence of Code Sec. 6651(a) by striking "$330" and inserting "$435". **Effective** for returns the due date for which (including extensions) is after 12-31-2019.

(j) ADJUSTMENT FOR INFLATION.—

(1) IN GENERAL.—In the case of any return required to be filed in a calendar year beginning after 2020, the *$435* dollar amount under subsection (a) shall be increased by an amount equal to such dollar amount multiplied by the cost-of-living adjustment determined under section 1(f)(3) for the calendar year determined by substituting "calendar year 2019" for "calendar year 2016" in subparagraph (A)(ii) thereof.

***

[Explanation at ¶ 305.]

Amendments

• **Further Consolidated Appropriations Act, 2020 (P.L. 116-94)**

P.L. 116-94, § 402(b), Div. O:

Amended Code Sec. 6651(j)(1) by striking "$330" and inserting "$435". **Effective** for returns the due date for which (including extensions) is after 12-31-2019.

[¶ 6155] CODE SEC. 6652. FAILURE TO FILE CERTAIN INFORMATION RETURNS, REGISTRATION STATEMENTS, ETC.

***

(d) ANNUAL REGISTRATION AND OTHER NOTIFICATION BY PENSION PLAN.—

(1) REGISTRATION.—In the case of any failure to file a registration statement required under section 6057(a) (relating to annual registration of certain plans) which includes all participants required to be included in such statement, on the date prescribed therefor (determined without regard to any extension of time for filing), unless it is shown that such failure is due to reasonable cause, there shall be paid (on notice and demand by the Secretary and in the same manner as tax) by the person failing so to file, an amount equal to *$10* for each participant with respect to whom there is a failure to file, multiplied by the number of days during which such failure continues, but the total amount imposed under this paragraph on any person for any failure to file with respect to any plan year shall not exceed *$50,000*.

(2) NOTIFICATION OF CHANGE OF STATUS.—In the case of failure to file a notification required under section 6057(b) (relating to notification of change of status) on the date prescribed therefor (determined without regard to any extension of time for filing), unless it is shown that such failure is due to reasonable cause, there shall be paid (on notice and demand by the Secretary and in the same manner as tax) by the person failing so to file, *$10* for each day during which such failure continues, but the total amounts imposed under this paragraph on any person for failure to file any notification shall not exceed *$10,000*.

[Explanation at ¶ 310.]

Amendments

• **Further Consolidated Appropriations Act, 2020 (P.L. 116-94)**

P.L. 116-94, § 403(b)(1)-(3), Div. O:

Amended Code Sec. 6652(d) by striking "$1" both places it appears in paragraphs (1) and (2) and inserting "$10"; by striking "$5,000" in paragraph (1) and inserting "$50,000"; and by striking "$1,000" in paragraph (2) and inserting "$10,000". **Effective** for returns, statements, and notifications required to be filed, and notices required to be provided, after 12-31-2019.

(e) INFORMATION REQUIRED IN CONNECTION WITH CERTAIN PLANS OF DEFERRED COMPENSATION; ETC.—In the case of failure to file a return or statement required under section 6058 (relating to information required in connection with certain plans of deferred compensation), 6047 (relating to information relating to certain trusts and annuity and bond purchase plans), or 6039D (relating to returns and records with respect to certain fringe benefit plans) on the date and in the manner prescribed therefor (determined with regard to any extension of time for filing), unless it is shown that such failure is due to reasonable cause, there shall be paid (on notice and demand by the Secretary and in the same manner as tax) by the person failing so to file, *$250* for each day during which such failure continues, but the total amount imposed under this subsection on any person for failure to file any return shall not exceed *$150,000*. This subsection shall not apply to any return or statement which is an information return described in section 6724(d)(1)(C)(ii) or a payee statement described in section 6724(d)(2)(AA).

[Explanation at ¶ 310.]

Amendments

• **Further Consolidated Appropriations Act, 2020** (P.L. 116-94)

P.L. 116-94, § 403(a)(1)-(2), Div. O:

Amended Code Sec. 6652(e) by striking "$25" and inserting "$250"; and by striking "$15,000" and inserting "$150,000". **Effective** for returns, statements, and notifications required to be filed, and notices required to be provided, after 12-31-2019.

(h) FAILURE TO GIVE NOTICE TO RECIPIENTS OF CERTAIN PENSION, ETC., DISTRIBUTIONS.—In the case of each failure to provide notice as required by section 3405(e)(10)(B), at the time prescribed therefor, unless it is shown that such failure is due to reasonable cause and not to willful neglect, there shall be paid, on notice and demand of the Secretary and in the same manner as tax, by the person failing to provide such notice, an amount equal to *$100* for each such failure, but the total amount imposed on such person for all such failures during any calendar year shall not exceed *$50,000*.

[Explanation at ¶ 310.]

Amendments

• **Further Consolidated Appropriations Act, 2020** (P.L. 116-94)

P.L. 116-94, § 403(c)(1)-(2), Div. O:

Amended Code Sec. 6652(h) by striking "$10" and inserting "$100"; and by striking "$5,000" and inserting "$50,000". **Effective** for returns, statements, and notifications required to be filed, and notices required to be provided, after 12-31-2019.

[¶ 6160] CODE SEC. 7508A. AUTHORITY TO POSTPONE CERTAIN DEADLINES BY REASON OF PRESIDENTIALLY DECLARED DISASTER OR TERRORISTIC OR MILITARY ACTIONS.

* * *

(d) MANDATORY 60-DAY EXTENSION.—

(1) IN GENERAL.—*In the case of any qualified taxpayer, the period—*

(A) beginning on the earliest incident date specified in the declaration to which the disaster area referred to in paragraph (2) relates, and

(B) ending on the date which is 60 days after the latest incident date so specified,

shall be disregarded in the same manner as a period specified under subsection (a).

(2) QUALIFIED TAXPAYER.—*For purposes of this subsection, the term "qualified taxpayer" means—*

(A) any individual whose principal residence (for purposes of section 1033(h)(4)) is located in a disaster area,

(B) any taxpayer if the taxpayer's principal place of business (other than the business of performing services as an employee) is located in a disaster area,

(C) any individual who is a relief worker affiliated with a recognized government or philanthropic organization and who is assisting in a disaster area,

(D) any taxpayer whose records necessary to meet a deadline for an act described in section 7508(a)(1) are maintained in a disaster area,

(E) any individual visiting a disaster area who was killed or injured as a result of the disaster, and

(F) solely with respect to a joint return, any spouse of an individual described in any preceding subparagraph of this paragraph.

(3) DISASTER AREA.—*For purposes of this subsection, the term "disaster area" has the meaning given such term under subparagraph (B) of section 165(i)(5) with respect to a Federally declared disaster (as defined in subparagraph (A) of such section).*

(4) APPLICATION TO RULES REGARDING PENSIONS.—*In the case of any person described in subsection (b), a rule similar to the rule of paragraph (1) shall apply for purposes of subsection (b) with respect to—*

(A) *making contributions to a qualified retirement plan (within the meaning of section 4974(c)) under section 219(f)(3), 404(a)(6), 404(h)(1)(B), or 404(m)(2),*

(B) *making distributions under section 408(d)(4),*

(C) *recharacterizing contributions under section 408A(d)(6), and*

(D) *making a rollover under section 402(c), 403(a)(4), 403(b)(8), or 408(d)(3).*

(5) COORDINATION WITH PERIODS SPECIFIED BY THE SECRETARY.—*Any period described in paragraph (1) with respect to any person (including by reason of the application of paragraph (4) shall be in addition to (or concurrent with, as the case may be) any period specified under subsection (a) or (b) with respect to such person.*

Amendments

• **Further Consolidated Appropriations Act, 2020 (P.L. 116-94)**

P.L. 116-94, § 205(a), Div. Q:

Amended Code Sec. 7508A by adding at the end a new subsection (d). **Effective** for federally declared disasters declared after 12-20-2019.

[¶ 6165] CODE SEC. 9831. GENERAL EXCEPTIONS.

* * *

(d) EXCEPTION FOR QUALIFIED SMALL EMPLOYER HEALTH REIMBURSEMENT ARRANGEMENTS.—

(1) IN GENERAL.—For purposes of this title (and notwithstanding any other provision of this title), the term "group health plan" shall not include any qualified small employer health reimbursement arrangement.

Amendments

• **Further Consolidated Appropriations Act, 2020 (P.L. 116-94)**

P.L. 116-94, § 503(b)(2), Div. N:

Amended Code Sec. 9831(d)(1) by striking "except as provided in section 4980I(f)(4)" before "and notwithstanding any other provision". **Effective** for tax years beginning after 12-31-2019.

ERISA Sections Added, Amended Or Repealed

[¶ 7000]

INTRODUCTION

All Employee Retirement Income Security Act (ERISA) provisions amended by the Further Consolidated Appropriations Act, 2020 (P.L. 116-94) are shown in the following paragraphs. Deleted ERISA material or the text of the ERISA Section prior to amendment appears in the amendment notes following each amended ERISA provision. *Any changed or added material is set out in italics.*

[¶ 7001] ERISA SEC. 3. DEFINITIONS

* * *

* * *

(2)(C) *A pooled employer plan shall be treated as—*

(i) a single employee pension benefit plan or single pension plan; and

(ii) a plan to which section 210(a) applies.

* * *

* * *

(16)(B) The term "plan sponsor" means (i) the employer in the case of an employee benefit plan established or maintained by a single employer, (ii) the employee organization in the case of a plan established or maintained by an employee organization, (iii) in the case of a plan established or maintained by two or more employers or jointly by one or more employers and one or more employee organizations, the association, committee, joint board of trustees, or other similar group of representatives of the parties who establish or maintain the plan or, *(iv) in the case of a pooled employer plan, the pooled plan provider.*

* * *

(41) SINGLE-EMPLOYER PLAN.—The term "single-employer plan" means an employee benefit plan other than a multiemployer plan.

* * *

(43) POOLED EMPLOYER PLAN.—

(A) IN GENERAL.—

The term 'pooled employer plan' means a plan—

(i) which is an individual account plan established or maintained for the purpose of providing benefits to the employees of 2 or more employers;

(ii) which is a plan described in section 431(a) of the Internal Revenue Code of 1986 which includes a trust exempt from tax under section 501(a) of such Code or a plan that consists of individual retirement accounts described in section 438 of such Code (including by reason of subsection (c) thereof); and

(iii) the terms of which meet the requirements of subparagraph (B).

Such term shall not include a plan maintained by employers which have a common interest other than having adopted the plan.

(B) REQUIREMENTS FOR PLAN TERMS.—

The requirements of this subparagraph are met with respect to any plan if the terms of the plan—

(i) designate a pooled plan provider and provide that the pooled plan provider is a named fiduciary of the plan;

(ii) designate one or more trustees meeting the requirements of section 408(a)(2) of the Internal Revenue Code of 1986 (other than an employer in the plan) to be responsible for collecting contributions to, and holding the assets of, the plan and require such trustees to implement written contribution collection procedures that are reasonable, diligent, and systematic;

(iii) provide that each employer in the plan retains fiduciary responsibility for—

(I) the selection and monitoring in accordance with section 404(a) of the person designated as the pooled plan provider and any other person who, in addition to the pooled plan provider, is designated as a named fiduciary of the plan; and

(II) to the extent not otherwise delegated to another fiduciary by the pooled plan provider and subject to the provisions of section 404(c), the investment and management of the portion of the plan's assets attributable to the employees of the employer (or beneficiaries of such employees);

(iv) provide that employers in the plan, and participants and beneficiaries, are not subject to unreasonable restrictions, fees, or penalties with regard to ceasing participation, receipt of distributions, or otherwise transferring assets of the plan in accordance with section 208 or paragraph (44)(C)(i)(II);

(v) require—

(I) the pooled plan provider to provide to employers in the plan any disclosures or other information which the Secretary may require, including any disclosures or other information to facilitate the selection or any monitoring of the pooled plan provider by employers in the plan; and

(II) each employer in the plan to take such actions as the Secretary or the pooled plan provider determines are necessary to administer the plan or for the plan to meet any requirement applicable under this Act or the Internal Revenue Code of 1986 to a plan described in section 401(a) of such Code or to a plan that consists of individual retirement accounts described in section 408 of such Code (including by reason of subsection (c) thereof), whichever is applicable, including providing any disclosures or other information which the Secretary may require or which the pooled plan provider otherwise determines are necessary to administer the plan or to allow the plan to meet such requirements; and

(vi) provide that any disclosure or other information required to be provided under clause (v) may be provided in electronic form and will be designed to ensure only reasonable costs are imposed on pooled plan providers and employers in the plan.

(C) EXCEPTIONS.—

The term 'pooled employer plan' does not include—

(i) a multiemployer plan; or

(ii) a plan established before the date of the enactment of the Setting Every Community Up for Retirement Enhancement Act of 2019 unless the plan administrator elects that the plan will be treated as a pooled employer plan and the plan meets the requirements of this title applicable to a pooled employer plan established on or after such date.

(D) TREATMENT OF EMPLOYERS AS PLAN SPONSORS.—

Except with respect to the administrative duties of the pooled plan provider described in paragraph (44)(A)(i), each employer in a pooled employer plan shall be treated as the plan sponsor with respect to the portion of the plan attributable to employees of such employer (or beneficiaries of such employees).

(44) POOLED PLAN PROVIDER.—

(A) IN GENERAL.—

The term 'pooled plan provider' means a person who—

(i) is designated by the terms of a pooled employer plan as a named fiduciary, as the plan administrator, and as the person responsible for the performance of all administrative duties (including conducting proper testing with respect to the plan and the employees of each employer in the plan) which are reasonably necessary to ensure that—

(I) the plan meets any requirement applicable under this Act or the Internal Revenue Code of 1986 to a plan described in section 401(a) of such Code or to a plan that consists of individual retirement accounts described in section 408 of such Code (including by reason of subsection (c) thereof), whichever is applicable; and

(II) each employer in the plan takes such actions as the Secretary or pooled plan provider determines are necessary for the plan to meet the requirements described in subclause (I), including providing the disclosures and information described in paragraph (43)(B)(v)(II);

(ii) registers as a pooled plan provider with the Secretary, and provides to the Secretary such other information as the Secretary may require, before beginning operations as a pooled plan provider;

(iii) acknowledges in writing that such person is a named fiduciary, and the plan administrator, with respect to the pooled employer plan; and

(iv) is responsible for ensuring that all persons who handle assets of, or who are fiduciaries of, the pooled employer plan are bonded in accordance with section 412.

(B) AUDITS, EXAMINATIONS AND INVESTIGATIONS.—

The Secretary may perform audits, examinations, and investigations of pooled plan providers as may be necessary to enforce and carry out the purposes of this paragraph and paragraph (43).

(C) GUIDANCE.—

The Secretary shall issue such guidance as the Secretary determines appropriate to carry out this paragraph and paragraph (43), including guidance—

(i) to identify the administrative duties and other actions required to be performed by a pooled plan provider under either such paragraph; and

(ii) Which requires in appropriate cases that if an employer in the plan fails to take the actions required under subparagraph (A)(i)(II)—

(I) the assets of the plan attributable to employees of such employer (or beneficiaries of such employees) are transferred to a plan maintained only by such employer (or its successor), to an eligible retirement plan as defined in section 402(c)(8)(B) of the Internal Revenue Code of 1986 for each individual whose account is transferred, or to any other arrangement that the Secretary determines is appropriate in such guidance; and

(II) such employer (and not the plan with respect to which the failure occurred or any other employer in such plan) shall, except to the extent provided in such guidance, be liable for any liabilities with respect to such plan attributable to employees of such employer (or beneficiaries of such employees).

The Secretary shall take into account under clause (ii) whether the failure of an employer or pooled plan provider to provide any disclosures or other information, or to take any other action, necessary to administer a plan or to allow a plan to meet requirements described in subparagraph (A)(i)(II) has continued over a period of time that demonstrates a lack of commitment to compliance. The Secretary may waive the requirements of subclause (ii)(I) in appropriate circumstances if the Secretary determines it is in the best interests of the employees of the employer referred to in such clause (and the beneficiaries of such employees) to retain the assets in the plan with respect to which the employer's failure occurred.

(D) GOOD FAITH COMPLIANCE WITH LAW BEFORE GUIDANCE.—

An employer or pooled plan provider shall not be treated as failing to meet a requirement of guidance issued by the Secretary under subparagraph (C) if, before the issuance of such guidance, the employer or pooled plan provider complies in good faith with a reasonable interpretation of the provisions of this paragraph, or paragraph (43), to which such guidance relates.

(E) AGGREGATION RULES.—

For purposes of this paragraph, in determining whether a person meets the requirements of this paragraph to be a pooled plan provider with respect to any plan, all persons who perform services for the plan and who are treated as a single employer under subsection (b), (c), (m), or (o) of section 414 of the Internal Revenue Code of 1986 shall be treated as one person.

[Explanation at ¶ 100.]

Amendments

• Further Consolidated Appropriations Act, 2020 (P.L. 116-94)

P.L. 116-94, Div. O, § 101(b):

Amended ERISA Sec. 3(2) by adding new subparagraph (C) to read as above.

The above amendment shall apply to plan years beginning after December 31, 2020.

P.L. 116-94, Div. O, § 101(c)(3)(A):

Amended ERISA Sec. 3(16)(B) by striking "or" at the end of clause (ii) and by striking the period at the end and inserting ", or (iv) in the case of a pooled employer plan, the pooled plan provider."

The above amendment shall apply to plan years beginning after December 31, 2020.

P.L. 116-94, Div. O, § 101(c)(3)(B):

Amended ERISA Sec. 3(41) by striking the second paragraph (41).

The above amendment shall apply to plan years beginning after December 31, 2020.

P.L. 116-94, Div. O, § 101(c)(1):

Amended ERISA Sec. 3 by adding at the end new paragraphs (43) and (44) to read as above.

The above amendment shall apply to plan years beginning after December 31, 2020.

P.L. 116-94, Div. O, § 101(e)(2) provides:

The amendments made by this section shall apply to plan years beginning after December 31, 2020.

[¶ 7002] ERISA SEC. 103. ANNUAL REPORTS

(a) PUBLICATION AND FILING.—

* * *

(1)(B) The annual report shall include the information described in subsections (b) and (c) and where *applicable subsections (d), (e), (f), and (g)* and shall also include—

(i) a financial statement and opinion, as required by paragraph (3) of this subsection, and

(ii) an actuarial statement and opinion, as required by paragraph (4) of this subsection.

* * *

(g) ADDITIONAL INFORMATION WITH RESPECT TO POOLED EMPLOYER AND MULTIPLE EMPLOYER PLANS.—An annual report under this section for a plan year shall include—

(1) with respect to any plan to which section 210(a) applies (including a pooled employer plan), a list of employers in the plan and a good faith estimate the percentage of total contributions made by such employers during the plan year and the aggregate account balances attributable to each employer in the plan (determined as the sum of the account balances of the employees of such employer (and the beneficiaries of such employees)); and

(2) with respect to a pooled employer plan, the identifying information for the person designated under the terms of the plan as the pooled plan provider.

[Explanation at ¶ 100.]

Amendments

• Further Consolidated Appropriations Act, 2020 (P.L. 116-94)

P.L. 116-94, Div. O, § 101(d)(1)(A):

Amended ERISA Sec. 103(a)(1)(B) by striking "applicable subsections (d), (e), and (f)" and inserting "applicable subsections (d), (e), (f), and (g)".

The above amendment shall apply to plan years beginning after December 31, 2020.

P.L. 116-94, Div. O, § 101(d)(1)(B):

Amended ERISA Sec. 103(g) to read as above. Prior to amendment, Sec. 103(g) read as follows:

(g) ADDITIONAL INFORMATION WITH RESPECT TO MULTIPLE EMPLOYER PLANS.—With respect to any multiple employer plan, an annual report under this section for a plan year shall include a list of participating employers and a good faith estimate of the percentage of total contributions made by such participating employers during the plan year.

The above amendment shall apply to plan years beginning after December 31, 2020.

P.L. 116-94, Div. O, § 101(e)(2) provides:

(2) RULE OF CONSTRUCTION.—Nothing in the amendments made by subsection (a) shall be construed as limiting the authority of the Secretary of the Treasury or the Secretary's delegate (determined without regard to such amendment) to provide for the proper treatment of a failure to meet any requirement applicable under the Internal Revenue Code of 1986 with respect to one employer (and its employees) in a multiple employer plan.

The above amendment shall apply to plan years beginning after December 31, 2020.

[¶ 7003] ERISA SEC. 104. FILING WITH SECRETARY AND FURNISHING INFORMATION TO PARTICIPANTS AND CERTAIN EMPLOYERS

(a) FILING OF ANNUAL REPORT WITH SECRETARY.—

* * *

(2)(A) With respect to annual reports required to be filed with the Secretary under this part, the Secretary may by regulation prescribe simplified annual reports for any pension plan that—

(i) covers fewer than 100 participants; or

(ii) is a plan described in section 210(a) that covers fewer than 1,000 participants, but only if no single employer in the plan has 100 or more participants covered by the plan.

* * *

[Explanation at ¶ 100.]
Amendments

• Further Consolidated Appropriations Act, 2020 (P.L. 116-94)

P.L. 116-94, Div. O, § 101(d)(2):

Amended ERISA Sec. 104(a) by striking paragraph (2)(A) to read as above. Prior to amendment, paragraph (2)(A) read as follows:

(2)(A) With respect to annual reports required to be filed with the Secretary under this part, he may by regulation prescribe simplified annual reports for any pension plan which covers less than 100 participants.

The above amendment applies to plan years beginning after December 31, 2020.

P.L. 116-94, Div. O, § 101(e)(2) provides:

(2) RULE OF CONSTRUCTION.—Nothing in the amendments made by subsection (a) shall be construed as limiting the authority of the Secretary of the Treasury or the Secretary's delegate (determined without regard to such amendment) to provide for the proper treatment of a failure to meet any requirement applicable under the Internal Revenue Code of 1986 with respect to one employer (and its employees) in a multiple employer plan.

[¶ 7004] ERISA SEC. 105. REPORTING OF PARTICIPANT'S BENEFIT RIGHTS

(a) REQUIREMENTS TO PROVIDE PENSION BENEFIT STATEMENTS.—

* * *

(2) STATEMENTS.—

* * *

(B) ADDITIONAL INFORMATION.—In the case of an individual account plan, any pension benefit statement under clause (i) or (ii) of paragraph (1)(A) shall include—

(i) the value of each investment to which assets in the individual account have been allocated, determined as of the most recent valuation date under the plan, including the value of any assets held in the form of employer securities, without regard to whether such securities were contributed by the plan sponsor or acquired at the direction of the plan or of the participant or beneficiary,

(ii) in the case of a pension benefit statement under paragraph (1)(A)(i)—

(I) an explanation of any limitations or restrictions on any right of the participant or beneficiary under the plan to direct an investment,

(II) an explanation, written in a manner calculated to be understood by the average plan participant, of the importance, for the long-term retirement security of participants and beneficiaries, of a well-balanced and diversified investment portfolio, including a statement of the risk that holding more than 20 percent of a portfolio in the security of one entity (such as employer securities) may not be adequately diversified, and

(III) a notice directing the participant or beneficiary to the Internet website of the Department of Labor for sources of information on individual investing and diversification, and

(iii) the lifetime income disclosure described in subparagraph (D)(i).

In the case of pension benefit statements described in clause (i) of paragraph (1)(A), a lifetime income disclosure under clause (iii) of this subparagraph shall be required to be included in only one pension benefit statement during any one 12-month period.

* * *

(D) Lifetime Income Disclosure.—

(i) In General.—

(I) Disclosure.—

A lifetime income disclosure shall set forth the lifetime income stream equivalent of the total benefits accrued with respect to the participant or beneficiary.

(II) Lifetime Income Stream Equivalent of The Total Benefits Accrued.—

For purposes of this subparagraph, the term 'lifetime income stream equivalent of the total benefits accrued' means the amount of monthly payments the participant or beneficiary would receive if the total accrued benefits of such participant or beneficiary were used to provide lifetime income streams described in subclause (III), based on assumptions specified in rules prescribed by the Secretary.

(III) Lifetime Income Streams.—

The lifetime income streams described in this subclause are a qualified joint and survivor annuity (as defined in section 205(d)), based on assumptions specified in rules prescribed by the Secretary, including the assumption that the participant or beneficiary has a spouse of equal age, and a single life annuity. Such lifetime income streams may have a term certain or other features to the extent permitted under rules prescribed by the Secretary.

(ii) Model Disclosure.—

Not later than 1 year after the date of the enactment of the Setting Every Community Up for Retirement Enhancement Act of 2019, the Secretary shall issue a model lifetime income disclosure, written in a manner so as to be understood by the average plan participant, which—

(I) explains that the lifetime income stream equivalent is only provided as an illustration;

(II) explains that the actual payments under the lifetime income stream described in clause (i)(III) which may be purchased with the total benefits accrued will depend on numerous factors and may vary substantially from the lifetime income stream equivalent in the disclosures;

(III) explains the assumptions upon which the lifetime income stream equivalent was determined; and

(IV) provides such other similar explanations as the Secretary considers appropriate.

(iii) Assumptions and Rules.—

Not later than 1 year after the date of the enactment of the Setting Every Community Up for Retirement Enhancement Act of 2019, the Secretary shall—

(I) prescribe assumptions which administrators of individual account plans may use in converting total accrued benefits into lifetime income stream equivalents for purposes of this subparagraph; and

(II) issue interim final rules under clause (i). In prescribing assumptions under subclause (I), the Secretary may prescribe a single set of specific assumptions (in which case the Secretary may issue tables or factors which facilitate such conversions), or ranges of permissible assumptions. To the extent that an accrued benefit is or may be invested in a lifetime income stream described in clause (i)(III), the assumptions prescribed under subclause (I) shall, to the extent appropriate, permit administrators of individual account plans to use the amounts payable under such lifetime income stream as a lifetime income stream equivalent.

(iv) Limitation on Liability.—

No plan fiduciary, plan sponsor, or other person shall have any liability under this title solely by reason of the provision of lifetime income stream equivalents which are derived in accordance with the assumptions and rules described in clause (iii) and which include the explanations contained in the model lifetime income disclosure described in clause (ii). This clause shall apply without regard to whether the provision of such lifetime income stream equivalent is required by subparagraph (B)(iii).

(v) EFFECTIVE DATE.—

The requirement in subparagraph (B)(iii) shall apply to pension benefit statements furnished more than 12 months after the latest of the issuance by the Secretary of—

(I) interim final rules under clause (i);

(II) the model disclosure under clause (ii); or

(III) the assumptions under clause (iii).

* * *

[Explanation at ¶ 210.]

Amendments

• Further Consolidated Appropriations Act, 2020 (P.L. 116-94)

P.L. 116-94, Div. O, § 203(a)(1):

Amended ERISA Sec. 105(a)(2)(B) in clause (i) by striking "and" at the end.

The above amendment is effective as of December 20, 2019 (date of enactment).

P.L. 116-94, Div. O, § 203(a)(2):

Amended ERISA Sec. 105(a)(2)(B) in clause (ii) by striking "diversification." and inserting "diversification, and".

The above amendment is effective on December 20, 2019 (date of enactment).

P.L. 116-94, Div. O, § 203(a)(3):

Amended ERISA Sec. 105(a)(2)(B) by adding a new clause (iii) to read as above.

The above amendment is effective on December 20, 2019 (date of enactment).

P.L. 116-94, Div. O, § 203(b):

Amended ERISA Sec. 105(a)(2) by adding a new subparagraph (D) to read as above.

The above amendment is effective on December 20, 2019 (date of enactment).

[¶ 7005] ERISA SEC. 303. MINIMUM FUNDING STANDARDS FOR SINGLE-EMPLOYER DEFINED BENEFIT PENSION PLANS

* * *

(m) SPECIAL RULES FOR COMMUNITY NEWSPAPER PLANS.—

(1) IN GENERAL.——The plan sponsor of a community newspaper plan under which no participant has had the participant's accrued benefit increased (whether because of service or compensation) after December 31, 2017, may elect to have the alternative standards described in paragraph (3) apply to such plan, and any plan sponsored by any member of the same controlled group.

(2) ELECTION.——An election under paragraph (1) shall be made at such time and in such manner as prescribed by the Secretary of the Treasury. Such election, once made with respect to a plan year, shall apply to all subsequent plan years unless revoked with the consent of the Secretary of the Treasury.

(3) ALTERNATIVE MINIMUM FUNDING STANDARDS.——The alternative standards described in this paragraph are the following:

(A) INTEREST RATES.—

(i) IN GENERAL.——Notwithstanding subsection (h)(2)(C) and except as provided in clause (ii), the first, second, and third segment rates in effect for any month for purposes of this section shall be 8 percent.

(ii) NEW BENEFIT ACCRUALS.——Notwithstanding subsection (h)(2), for purposes of determining the funding target and normal cost of a plan for any plan year, the present value of any benefits accrued or earned under the plan for a plan year with respect to which an election under paragraph (1) is in effect shall be determined on the basis of the United States Treasury obligation yield curve for the day that is the valuation date of such plan for such plan year.

(iii) UNITED STATES TREASURY OBLIGATION YIELD CURVE.——For purposes of this subsection, the term 'United States Treasury obligation yield curve' means, with respect to any day, a yield curve which shall be prescribed by the Secretary of the Treasury for such day on interest-bearing obligations of the United States.

(B) SHORTFALL AMORTIZATION BASE.—

(i) PREVIOUS SHORTFALL AMORTIZATION BASES.——The shortfall amortization bases determined under subsection (c)(3) for all plan years preceding the first plan year to which the election under paragraph (1) applies (and all shortfall amortization installments determined with respect to such bases) shall be reduced to zero under rules similar to the rules of subsection (c)(6).

(ii) NEW SHORTFALL AMORTIZATION BASE.——Notwithstanding subsection (c)(3), the shortfall amortization base for the first plan year to which the election under paragraph (1) applies shall be the funding shortfall of such plan for such plan year (determined using the interest rates as modified under subparagraph (A)).

(C) DETERMINATION OF SHORTFALL AMORTIZATION INSTALLMENTS.——

(i) 30-YEAR PERIOD.——Subparagraphs (A) and (B) of subsection (c)(2) shall be applied by substituting '30-plan-year' for '7-plan-year' each place it appears.

(ii) NO SPECIAL ELECTION.——The election under subparagraph (D) of subsection (c)(2) shall not apply to any plan year to which the election under paragraph (1) applies.

(D) EXEMPTION FROM AT-RISK TREATMENT.——Subsection (i) shall not apply.

(4) COMMUNITY NEWSPAPER PLAN.——For purposes of this subsection—

(A) IN GENERAL.——The term 'community newspaper plan' means a plan to which this section applies maintained by an employer which, as of December 31, 2017—

(i) publishes and distributes daily, either electronically or in printed form—

(I) a community newspaper, or

(II) 1 or more community newspapers in the same State,

(ii) is not a company the stock of which is publicly traded (on a stock exchange or in an over-the-counter market), and is not controlled, directly or indirectly, by such a company,

(iii) is controlled, directly or indirectly—

(I) by 1 or more persons residing primarily in the State in which the community newspaper is published,

(II) for not less than 30 years by individuals who are members of the same family,

(III) by a trust created or organized in the State in which the community newspaper is published, the sole trustees of which are persons described in subclause (I) or (II),

(IV) by an entity which is described in section 501(c)(3) of the Internal Revenue Code of 1986 and exempt from taxation under section 501(a) of such Code, which is organized and operated in the State in which the community newspaper is published, and the primary purpose of which is to benefit communities in such State, or

(V) by a combination of persons described in subclause (I), (III), or (IV), and

(iv) does not control, directly or indirectly, any newspaper in any other State.

(B) COMMUNITY NEWSPAPER.——The term 'community newspaper' means a newspaper which primarily serves a metropolitan statistical area, as determined by the Office of Management and Budget, with a population of not less than 100,000.

(C) CONTROL.——A person shall be treated as controlled by another person if such other person possesses, directly or indirectly, the power to direct or cause the direction and management of such person (including the power to elect a majority of the members of the board of directors of such person) through the ownership of voting securities.

(5) CONTROLLED GROUP.——For purposes of this subsection, the term 'controlled group' means all persons treated as a single employer under subsection (b), (c), (m), or (o) of section 414 of the Internal Revenue Code of 1986 as of the date of the enactment of this subsection.

(6) EFFECT ON PREMIUM RATE CALCULATION.——Notwithstanding any other provision of law or any regulation issued by the Pension Benefit Guaranty Corporation, in the case of a plan for which an election

¶7005   ERISA Sec. 303(m)(3)(B)

is made to apply the alternative standards described in paragraph (3), the additional premium under section 4006(a)(3)(E) shall be determined as if such election had not been made.

[Explanation at ¶195.]

Amendments

• Further Consolidated Appropriations Act, 2020 (P.L. 116-94)

P.L. 116-94, Div. O, Sec. 115(b):

Amended ERISA Sec. 303 by adding at the end a new subsection (m) to read as above.

The above amendment shall apply to plan years ending after December 31, 2017.

P.L. 116-94, Div. O, Sec. 115(c):

(c) EFFECTIVE DATE.—The amendments made by this section shall apply to plan years ending after December 31, 2017.

[¶7006] ERISA SEC. 404. FIDUCIARY DUTIES

* * *

(e) SAFE HARBOR FOR ANNUITY SELECTION.—

(1) *In general.*—With respect to the selection of an insurer for a guaranteed retirement income contract, the requirements of subsection (a)(1)(B) will be deemed to be satisfied if a fiduciary—

(A) engages in an objective, thorough, and analytical search for the purpose of identifying insurers from which to purchase such contracts;

(B) with respect to each insurer identified under subparagraph (A)—

(i) considers the financial capability of such insurer to satisfy its obligations under the guaranteed retirement income contract; and

(ii) considers the cost (including fees and commissions) of the guaranteed retirement income contract offered by the insurer in relation to the benefits and product features of the contract and administrative services to be provided under such contract; and

(C) on the basis of such consideration, concludes that—

(i) at the time of the selection, the insurer is financially capable of satisfying its obligations under the guaranteed retirement income contract; and

(ii) the relative cost of the selected guaranteed retirement income contract as described in subparagraph (B)(ii) is reasonable.

(2) *Financial capability of the insurer.*—A fiduciary will be deemed to satisfy the requirements of paragraphs (1)(B)(i) and(1)(C)(i) if—

(A) the fiduciary obtains written representations from the insurer that—

(i) the insurer is licensed to offer guaranteed retirement income contracts;

(ii) the insurer, at the time of selection and for each of the immediately preceding 7 plan years—

(I) operates under a certificate of authority from the insurance commissioner of its domiciliary State which has not been revoked or suspended;

(II) has filed audited financial statements in accordance with the laws of its domiciliary State under applicable statutory accounting principles;

(III) maintains (and has maintained) reserves which satisfies all the statutory requirements of all States where the insurer does business; and

(IV) is not operating under an order of supervision, rehabilitation, or liquidation;

(iii) the insurer undergoes, at least every 5 years, a financial examination (within the meaning of the law of its domiciliary State) by the insurance commissioner of the domiciliary State (or representative, designee, or other party approved by such commissioner); and

(iv) the insurer will notify the fiduciary of any change in circumstances occurring after the provision of the representations in clauses (i), (ii), and (iii) which would preclude the insurer from making such representations at the time of issuance of the guaranteed retirement income contract; and

(B) after receiving such representations and as of the time of selection, the fiduciary has not received any notice described in subparagraph (A)(iv) and is in possession of no other information which would cause the fiduciary to question the representations provided.

(3) No requirement to select lowest cost.—Nothing in this subsection shall be construed to require a fiduciary to select the lowest cost contract. A fiduciary may consider the value of a contract, including features and benefits of the contract and attributes of the insurer (including, without limitation, the insurer's financial strength) in conjunction with the cost of the contract.

(4) TIME OF SELECTION.—

(A) In general.—For purposes of this subsection, the time of selection is—

(i) the time that the insurer and the contract are selected for distribution of benefits to a specific participant or beneficiary; or

(ii) if the fiduciary periodically reviews the continuing appropriateness of the conclusion described in paragraph (1)(C) with respect to a selected insurer, taking into account the considerations described in such paragraph, the time that the insurer and the contract are selected to provide benefits at future dates to participants or beneficiaries under the plan.

Nothing in the preceding sentence shall be construed to require the fiduciary to review the appropriateness of a selection after the purchase of a contract for a participant or beneficiary.

(B) Periodic review.—A fiduciary will be deemed to have conducted the periodic review described in subparagraph (A)(ii) if the fiduciary obtains the written representations described in clauses (i), (ii), and (iii) of paragraph (2)(A) from the insurer on an annual basis, unless the fiduciary receives any notice described in paragraph (2)(A)(iv) or otherwise becomes aware of facts that would cause the fiduciary to question such representations.

(5) Limited liability.—A fiduciary which satisfies the requirements of this subsection shall not be liable following the distribution of any benefit, or the investment by or on behalf of a participant or beneficiary pursuant to the selected guaranteed retirement income contract, for any losses that may result to the participant or beneficiary due to an insurer's inability to satisfy its financial obligations under the terms of such contract.

(6) Definitions.—For purposes of this subsection—

(A) Insurer.—The term 'insurer' means an insurance company, insurance service, or insurance organization, including affiliates of such companies.

(B) Guaranteed retirement income contract.—The term 'guaranteed retirement income contract' means an annuity contract for a fixed term or a contract (or provision or feature thereof) which provides guaranteed benefits annually (or more frequently) for at least the remainder of the life of the participant or the joint lives of the participant and the participant's designated beneficiary as part of an individual account plan.

[Explanation at ¶ 220.]

Amendments

• Further Consolidated Appropriations Act, 2020 (P.L. 116-94)

The above amendment is effective as of December 20, 2019 (date of enactment).

P.L. 116-94, Div. O, Sec. 204:

Amended ERISA Sec. 404 by adding at the end a new subsection (e) to read as above.

[¶ 7007] ERISA SEC. 408. EXEMPTIONS FROM PROHIBITED TRANSACTIONS

* * *

(h) PROVISION OF PHARMACY BENEFIT SERVICES.—

(1) IN GENERAL.——Provided that all of the conditions described in paragraph (2) are met, the restrictions imposed by subsections (a), (b)(1), and (b)(2) of section 406 shall not apply to—

(A) the offering of pharmacy benefit services to a group health plan that is sponsored by an entity described in section 3(37)(G)(vi) or to any other group health plan that is sponsored by a regional council, local union, or other labor organization affiliated with such entity;

(B) the purchase of pharmacy benefit services by plan participants and beneficiaries of a group health plan that is sponsored by an entity described in section 3(37)(G)(vi) or of any other group health plan that is sponsored by a regional council, local union, or other labor organization affiliated with such entity; or

(C) the operation or implementation of pharmacy benefit services by an entity described in section 3(37)(G)(vi) or by any other group health plan that is sponsored by a regional council, local union, or other labor organization affiliated with such entity,

in any arrangement where such entity described in section 3(37)(G)(vi) or any related organization or subsidiary of such entity provides pharmacy benefit services that include prior authorization and appeals, a retail pharmacy network, pharmacy benefit administration, mail order fulfillment, formulary support, manufacturer payments, audits, and specialty pharmacy and goods, to any such group health plan.

(2) CONDITIONS.—The conditions described in this paragraph are the following:

(A) The terms of the arrangement are at least as favorable to the group health plan as such group health plan could obtain in a similar arm's length arrangement with an unrelated third party.

(B) At least 50 percent of the providers participating in the pharmacy benefit services offered by the arrangement are unrelated to the contributing employers or any other party in interest with respect to the group health plan.

(C) The group health plan retains an independent fiduciary who will be responsible for monitoring the group health plan's consultants, contractors, subcontractors, and other service providers for purposes of pharmacy benefit services described in paragraph (1) offered by such entity or any of its related organizations or subsidiaries and monitors the transactions of such entity and any of its related organizations or subsidiaries to ensure that all conditions of this exemption are satisfied during each plan year.

(D) Any decisions regarding the provision of pharmacy benefit services described in paragraph (1) are made by the group health plan's independent fiduciary, based on objective standards developed by the independent fiduciary in reliance on information provided by the arrangement.

(E) The independent fiduciary of the group health plan provides an annual report to the Secretary and the congressional committees of jurisdiction attesting that the conditions described in subparagraphs (C) and (D) have been met for the applicable plan year, together with a statement that use of the arrangement's services are in the best interest of the participants and beneficiaries in the aggregate for that plan year compared to other similar arrangements the group health plan could have obtained in transactions with an unrelated third party.

(F) The arrangement is not designed to benefit any party in interest with respect to the group health plan.

(3) VIOLATIONS.—In the event an entity described in section 3(37)(G)(vi) or any affiliate of such entity violates any of the conditions of such exemption, such exemption shall not apply with respect to such entity or affiliate and all enforcement and claims available under this Act shall apply with respect to such entity or affiliate.

(4) RULE OF CONSTRUCTION.—Nothing in this subsection shall be construed to modify any obligation of a group health plan otherwise set forth in this Act.

(5) GROUP HEALTH PLAN.—In this subsection, the term 'group health plan' has the meaning given such term in section 733(a).

[Explanation at ¶ 515.]

Amendments

• **Further Consolidated Appropriations Act, 2020** (P.L. 116-94)

P.L. 116-94, Div. P, Sec. 1302(a):

Amended ERISA Sec. 408 by adding at the end a new subsection (h) to read as above.

The above amendment is effective as of December 20, 2019 (date of enactment).

P.L. 116-94, Div. P, Sec. 1302(c), provides:

(c) APPLICABILITY.—With respect to a group health plan subject to subsection (h) of section 408 of the Employee Retirement Income Security Act of 1974 (29 U.S.C. 1108) (as amended by subsection (a)) and subsection (c) of section 4975 of the Internal Revenue Code of 1986 (as amended by subsection (b)), beginning at the end of the fifth plan year of such group health plan that begins after the date of enactment of this Act, such subsection (h) of such section 408 and such subsection (c) of such shall have no force or effect.

[¶ 7008] ERISA SEC. 412. BONDING

(a) REQUISITE BONDING OF PLAN OFFICIALS.—Every fiduciary of an employee benefit plan and every person who handles funds or other property of such a plan (hereafter in this section referred to as "plan official") shall be bonded as provided in this section; except that—

(1) where such plan is one under which the only assets from which benefits are paid are the general assets of a union or of an employer, the administrator, officers, and employees of such plan shall be exempt from the bonding requirements of this section,

(2) no bond shall be required of any entity which is registered as a broker or a dealer under section 15(b) of the Securities Exchange Act of 1934 (15 U.S.C. 78o(b)) if the broker or dealer is subject to the fidelity bond requirements of a self-regulatory organization (within the meaning of section 3(a)(26) of such Act (15 U.S.C. 78c(a)(26)).

(3) no bond shall be required of a fiduciary (or of any director, officer, or employee of such fiduciary) if such fiduciary—

(A) is a corporation organized and doing business under the laws of the United States or of any State;

(B) is authorized under such laws to exercise trust powers or to conduct an insurance business;

(C) is subject to supervision or examination by Federal or State authority; and

(D) has at all times a combined capital and surplus in excess of such a minimum amount as may be established by regulations issued by the Secretary, which amount shall be at least $1,000,000.

Paragraph (2) shall apply to a bank or other financial institution which is authorized to exercise trust powers and the deposits of which are not insured by the Federal Deposit Insurance Corporation, only if such bank or institution meets bonding or similar requirements under State law which the Secretary determines are at least equivalent to those imposed on banks by Federal law.

The amount of such bond shall be fixed at the beginning of each fiscal year of the plan. Such amount shall be not less than 10 per centum of the amount of funds handled. In no case shall such bond be less than $1,000 nor more than $500,000, except that the Secretary, after due notice and opportunity for hearing to all interested parties, and after consideration of the record, may prescribe an amount in excess of $500,000, subject to the 10 per centum limitation of the preceding sentence. For purposes of fixing the amount of such bond, the amount of funds handled shall be determined by the funds handled by the person, group, or class to be covered by such bond and by their predecessor or predecessors, if any, during the preceding reporting year, or if the plan has no preceding reporting year, the amount of funds to be handled during the current reporting year by such person, group, or class, estimated as provided in regulations of the Secretary. Such bond shall provide protection to the plan against loss by reason of acts of fraud or dishonesty on the part of the plan official, directly or through connivance with others. Any bond shall have as surety thereon a corporate surety company which is an acceptable surety on Federal bonds under authority granted by the Secretary of the Treasury pursuant to sections 9304-9308 of title 31. Any bond shall be in a form or of a type approved by the Secretary, including individual bonds or schedule or blanket forms of bonds which cover a group or class. In the case of a plan that holds employer securities (within the meaning of section 407(d)(1)) *or in the case of a pooled employer plan (as defined in section 3(43))*, this subsection shall be applied by substituting "$1,000,000" for "$500,000" each place it appears.

* * *

[Explanation at ¶ 100.]
Amendment:

• **Further Consolidated Appropriations Act, 2020 (P.L. 116-94)**

P.L. 116-94, Div. O, Sec. 101(c)(2):

Amended ERISA Sec. 412(a) by inserting in the last sentence "or in the case of a pooled employer plan (as defined in section 3(43))" after "section 407(d)(1)".

The above amendment shall apply to plan years beginning after December 31, 2020.

P.L. 116-94, Div. O, Sec. 101(e), provides:

(e) EFFECTIVE DATE.—

(1) IN GENERAL.—The amendments made by this section shall apply to plan years beginning after December 31, 2020.

(2) RULE OF CONSTRUCTION.—Nothing in the amendments made by subsection (a) shall be construed as limiting the authority of the Secretary of the Treasury or the Secretary's delegate (determined without regard to such amendment) to provide for the proper treatment of a failure to meet any requirement applicable under the Internal Revenue Code of 1986 with respect to one employer (and its employees) in a multiple employer plan.

¶7008   ERISA Sec. 412(a)(1)

[¶7009] **ERISA SEC. 4006. PREMIUM RATES**

* * *

(a)(3)(A) Except as provided in subparagraph (C), the annual premium rate payable to the corporation by all plans for basic benefits guaranteed under this title is—

(i) in the case of a single-employer *plan other than a CSEC plan (as defined in section 210(f)(1))* an amount for each individual who is a participant in such plan during the plan year equal to the sum of the additional premium (if any) determined under subparagraph (E) and—

(I) for plan years beginning after December 31, 2005, and before January 1, 2013, $30;

(II) for plan years beginning after December 31, 2012, and before January 1, 2014, $42;

(III) for plan years beginning after December 31, 2013, and before January 1, 2015, $49;

(IV) for plan years beginning after December 31, 2014, and before January 1, 2016, $57; and

(V) for plan years beginning after December 31, 2015, and before January 1, 2017, $64;

(VI) for plan years beginning after December 31, 2016, and before January 1, 2018, $69;

(VII) for plan years beginning after December 31, 2017, and before January 1, 2019, $74; and

(VIII) for plan years beginning after December 31, 2018, $80.

* * *

(v) in the case of a multiemployer plan, for plan years beginning after December 31, 2012, and before January 1, 2015, $12.00 for each individual who is a participant in such plan during the applicable plan year,

(vi) in the case of a multiemployer plan, for plan years beginning after December 31, 2014, $26 for each individual who is a participant in such plan during the applicable plan year, *or*

(vii) in the case of a CSEC plan (as defined in section 210(f)(1)), for plan years beginning after December 31, 2018, for each individual who is a participant in such plan during the plan year an amount equal to the sum of—

(I) the additional premium (if any) determined under subparagraph (E), and

(II) $19.

* * *

(E)(iii) *Except as provided in clause (v), for purposes* of clause (ii), the term "unfunded vested benefits" means, for a plan year, the excess (if any) of—

(I) the funding target of the plan as determined under section 303(d) for the plan year by only taking into account vested benefits and by using the interest rate described in clause (iv), over

(II) the fair market value of plan assets for the plan year which are held by the plan on the valuation date.

* * *

(v) For purposes of clause (ii), in the case of a CSEC plan (as defined in section 210(f)(1)), the term 'unfunded vested benefits' means, for plan years beginning after December 31, 2018, the excess (if any) of—

(I) the funding liability of the plan as determined under section 306(j)(5)(C) for the plan year by only taking into account vested benefits, over

(II) the fair market value of plan assets for the plan year which are held by the plan on the valuation date.

(8) APPLICABLE DOLLAR AMOUNT FOR VARIABLE RATE PREMIUM.—For purposes of paragraph (3)(E)(ii)—

(A) IN GENERAL.—Except as provided in subparagraphs (B), (C) and (E) the applicable dollar amount shall be—

(i) $9 for plan years beginning in a calendar year before 2015;

(ii) for plan years beginning in calendar year 2015, the amount in effect for plan years beginning in 2014 (determined after application of subparagraph (C));

(iii) for plan years beginning after calendar year 2015, the amount in effect for plan years beginning in 2015 (determined after application of subparagraph (C));

(iv) for plan years beginning after calendar year 2016, the amount in effect for plan years beginning in 2016 (determined after application of subparagraph (C));

(v) for plan years beginning after calendar year 2017, the amount in effect for plan years beginning in 2017 (determined after application of subparagraph (C));

(vi) for plan years beginning after calendar year 2018, the amount in effect for plan years beginning in 2018 (determined after application of subparagraph (C)); and

(vii) for plan years beginning after calendar year 2019, the amount in effect for plan years beginning in 2019 (determined after application of subparagraph (C)).

(E) CSEC PLANS.——In the case of a CSEC plan (as defined in section 210(f)(1)), the applicable dollar amount shall be $9.

[Explanation at ¶ 230.]

Amendments

• **Further Consolidated Appropriations Act, 2020 (P.L. 116-94)**

P.L. 116-94, Div. O, Sec. 206(a)(1):

Amended ERISA Sec. 4006(a)(3)(A) by, in clause (i), striking "plan," and inserting "plan other than a CSEC plan (as defined in section 210(f)(1))".

The above amendment is effective as of December 20, 2019 (date of enactment).

P.L. 116-94, Div. O, Sec. 206(a)(2):

Amended ERISA Sec. 4006(a)(3)(A) by, in clause (v), by striking "or" at the end.

The above amendment is effective as of December 20, 2019 (date of enactment).

P.L. 116-94, Div. O, Sec. 206(a)(3):

Amended ERISA Sec. 4006(a)(3)(A) by, in clause (vi), striking the period at the end and inserting ",or".

The above amendment is effective as of December 20, 2019 (date of enactment).

P.L. 116-94, Div. O, Sec. 206(a)(4):

Amended ERISA Sec. 4006(a)(3)(A) by adding at the end a new clause (vii) to read as above.

The above amendment is effective as of December 20, 2019 (date of enactment).

P.L. 116-94, Div. O, Sec. 206(b)(1)(A):

Amended ERISA Sec. 4006(a)(3)(E) by adding at the end a new clause (v) to read as above.

The above amendment is effective as of December 20, 2019 (date of enactment).

P.L. 116-94, Div. O, Sec. 206(b)(1)(B):

Amended ERISA Sec. 4006(a)(3)(E)(iii) by striking "For purposes" and inserting "except as provided in clause (v), for purposes".

The above amendment is effective as of December 20, 2019 (date of enactment).

P.L. 116-94, Div. O, Sec. 206(b)(2)(A):

Amended ERISA Sec. 4006(a)(8) by adding at the end a new subparagraph (E) to read as above.

The above amendment is effective as of December 20, 2019 (date of enactment).

P.L. 116-94, Div. O, Sec. 206(b)(2)(B):

Amended ERISA Sec. 4006(a)(8)(A) by striking "(B) and (C)" and inserting "(B), (C), and (E)".

The above amendment is effective as of December 20, 2019 (date of enactment).

¶7009 ERISA Sec. 4006(a)(8)

¶10,001 Internal Revenue Code Section to Explanation Table

Code Sec.	Explanation
35(b)(1)(B)	¶545
38(b)(33)	¶135
45E(b)(1)	¶130
45S(i)	¶520
45T	¶135
72(p)(2)(D)	¶155
72(t)(2)(H)	¶160
139B(c)(2)(B)	¶525
139B(d)	¶525
219(d)(1)	¶145
219(f)(1)	¶140
221(e)(1)	¶540
401(a)(9)(B)(iv)(I)	¶165
401(a)(9)(C)(i)(I)	¶165
401(a)(9)(C)(ii)(I)	¶165
401(a)(9)(E)	¶300
401(a)(9)(H)	¶300
401(a)(26)(I)	¶225
401(a)(36)	¶410
401(a)(38)	¶180
401(b)	¶200
401(b)(2)	¶200
401(k)(2)(B)(i)(VI)	¶180
401(k)(2)(D)	¶125
401(k)(12)(A)	¶115
401(k)(12)(F)	¶120
401(k)(12)(F)(iii)	¶120
401(k)(13)(C)(iii)	¶110
401(k)(13)(F)	¶120
401(k)(15)(A)	¶125
401(k)(15)(B)	¶125

Code Sec.	Explanation
401(k)(15)(C)	¶125
401(k)(15)(D)	¶125
401(o)	¶225
403(b)(9)(B)	¶190
403(b)(11)(D)	¶180
408(d)(8)(A)	¶145
408(o)(5)	¶150
408A(c)(4)	¶145
413(e)	¶100
415(c)(8)	¶150
430(m)	¶195
457(d)(1)(A)(i)	¶410
457(d)(1)(A)(iv)	¶180
512(a)(7)	¶530
529(c)(8)	¶540
529(c)(9)	¶540
3121(a)(23)	¶525
4191	¶500
4221(a)	¶500
4975(c)(7)	¶515
4980I	¶510
6051(a)(14)	¶510
6051(g)	¶510
6416(b)(2)	¶500
6651(a)	¶305
6651(j)(1)	¶305
6652(d)	¶310
6652(e)	¶310
6652(h)	¶310

¶10,005 Internal Revenue Code Sections Added, Amended or Repealed

The list below notes all the Code Sections or subsections of the Internal Revenue Code that were added, amended or repealed by Divisions M through Q, including the SECURE Act provisions of the Further Consolidated Appropriations Act, 2020 (P.L. 116-94), enacted December 20, 2019. The first column indicates the Code Section added, amended or repealed, and the second column indicates the Act Section.

SECURE Act and Selected Provisions of the Further Consolidated Appropriations Act, 2020

Code Sec.	Act Sec.	Code Sec.	Act Sec.
35(b)(1)(B)	146(a), Div. Q	408(b)	114(c), Div. O
38(b)(31)-(33)	105(b), Div. O	408(c)(3)	101(a)(3), Div. O
45E(b)(1)	104(a), Div. O	408(d)(8)(A)	107(b), Div. O
45S(i)	142(a), Div. Q	408(o)(5)	116(a)(1), Div. O
45T	105(a), Div. O	408A(c)(4)-(7)	107(c), Div. O
72(p)(2)(D)-(E)	108(a), Div. O	413(c)(2)	101(a)(2), Div. O
72(t)(2)(H)	113(a), Div. O	413(e)	101(a)(1), Div. O
139B(c)(2)(B)	301(a), Div. O	415(c)(8)	116(b)(1), Div. O
139B(d)	301(b), Div. O	430(m)	115(a), Div. O
213(f)	103(a), Div. Q	457(d)(1)(A)(i)	104(b), Div. M
219(d)(1)	107(a), Div. O	457(d)(1)(A)(ii)-(iv)	109(d)(1), Div. O
219(f)(1)	106(a), Div. O	457(d)(1)(B)-(D)	109(d)(2), Div. O
221(e)(1)	302(b)(2), Div. O	501(c)(12)(J)	301(a), Div. Q
401(a)(9)(B)(iv)(I)	114(b), Div. O	529(c)(8)	302(a), Div. O
401(a)(9)(C)(i)(I)	114(a), Div. O	529(c)(9)	302(b)(1), Div. O
401(a)(9)(C)(ii)(I)	114(b), Div. O	3121(a)(23)	301(c), Div. O
401(a)(9)(E)	401(a)(2), Div. O	4191	501(a), Div. N
401(a)(9)(H)	401(a)(1), Div. O	4221(a)	501(b)(1), Div. N
401(a)(26)(I)	205(b), Div. O	4375(e)	104(b), Div. N
401(a)(36)	104(a), Div. M	4376(e)	104(c), Div. N
401(a)(38)	109(a), Div. O	4975(c)(7)	1302(b), Div. P
401(b)	201(a)(1)-(2), Div. O	4980I	503(a), Div. N
401(k)(2)(B)(i)-(iii)	109(b)(2), Div. O	6011(e)(6)	202(d)(1), Div. O
401(k)(2)(B)(i)(IV)-(VI)	109(b)(1), Div. O	6051(a)(14)	503(b)(1)(A), Div. N
401(k)(2)(D)	112(a)(1), Div. O	6051(g)	503(b)(1)(B), Div. N
401(k)(12)(A)	103(a)(1), Div. O	6416(b)(2)	501(b)(2), Div. N
401(k)(12)(F)-(G)	103(b), Div. O	6651(a)	402(a), Div. O
401(k)(13)(B)	103(a)(2), Div. O	6651(j)(1)	401(b), Div. O
401(k)(13)(C)(iii)	102(a), Div. O	6652(d)	403(b)(1)-(3), Div. O
401(k)(13)(F)	103(c), Div. O	6652(e)	403(a)(1)-(2), Div. O
401(k)(15)	112(a)(2), Div. O	6652(h)	403(c)(1)-(2), Div. O
401(o)-(p)	205(a)(1)-(2), Div. O	7508A(d)	205(a), Div. Q
403(b)(7)(A)	109(c)(2), Div. O	9831(d)(1)	503(b)(2), Div. N
403(b)(9)(B)	111(a), Div. O		
403(b)(11)(B)-(D)	109(c)(1), Div. O		

¶10,010 Act Sections Amending Internal Revenue Code Sections

SECURE Act and Selected Provisions of the Further Consolidated Appropriations Act, 2020

Act Sec.	Code Sec.	Act Sec.	Code Sec.
104(a), Div. M	401(a)(36)	112(a)(1), Div. O	401(k)(2)(D)
104(b), Div. M	457(d)(1)(A)(i)	112(a)(2), Div. O	401(k)(15)
104(b), Div. N	4375(e)	113(a), Div. O	72(t)(2)(H)
104(c), Div. N	4376(e)	114(a), Div. O	401(a)(9)(C)(i)(I)
501(a), Div. N	4191	114(b), Div. O	401(a)(9)(B)(iv)(I)
501(b)(1), Div. N	4221(a)	114(b), Div. O	401(a)(9)(C)(ii)(I)
501(b)(2), Div. N	6416(b)(2)	114(c), Div. O	408(b)
503(a), Div. N	4980I	115(a), Div. O	430(m)
503(b)(1)(A), Div. N	6051(a)(14)	116(a)(1), Div. O	408(o)(5)
503(b)(1)(B), Div. N	6051(g)	116(b)(1), Div. O	415(c)(8)
503(b)(2), Div. N	9831(d)(1)	201(a)(1)-(2), Div. O	401(b)
101(a)(1), Div. O	413(e)	202(d)(1), Div. O	6011(e)(6)
101(a)(2), Div. O	413(c)(2)	205(a)(1)-(2), Div. O	401(o)-(p)
101(a)(3), Div. O	408(c)(3)	205(b), Div. O	401(a)(26)(I)
102(a), Div. O	401(k)(13)(C)(iii)	301(a), Div. O	139B(c)(2)(B)
103(a)(1), Div. O	401(k)(12)(A)	301(b), Div. O	139B(d)
103(a)(2), Div. O	401(k)(13)(B)	301(c), Div. O	3121(a)(23)
103(b), Div. O	401(k)(12)(F)-(G)	302(a), Div. O	529(c)(8)
103(c), Div. O	401(k)(13)(F)	302(b)(1), Div. O	529(c)(9)
104(a), Div. O	45E(b)(1)	302(b)(2), Div. O	221(e)(1)
105(a), Div. O	45T	401(a)(1), Div. O	401(a)(9)(H)
105(b), Div. O	38(b)(31)-(33)	401(a)(2), Div. O	401(a)(9)(E)
106(a), Div. O	219(f)(1)	402(a), Div. O	6651(a)
107(a), Div. O	219(d)(1)	402(b), Div. O	6651(j)(1)
107(b), Div. O	408(d)(8)(A)	403(a)(1)-(2), Div. O	6652(e)
107(c), Div. O	408A(c)(4)-(7)	403(b)(1)-(3), Div. O	6652(d)
108(a), Div. O	72(p)(2)(D)-(E)	403(c)(1)-(2), Div. O	6652(h)
109(a), Div. O	401(a)(38)	1302(b), Div. P	4975(c)(7)
109(b)(1), Div. O	401(k)(2)(B)(i)(IV)-(VI)	103(a), Div. Q	213(f)
109(b)(2), Div. O	401(k)(2)(B)(i)-(iii)	142(a), Div. Q	45S(i)
109(c)(1), Div. O	403(b)(11)(B)-(D)	146(a), Div. Q	35(b)(1)(B)
109(c)(2), Div. O	403(b)(7)(A)	205(a), Div. Q	7508A(d)
109(d)(1), Div. O	457(d)(1)(A)(ii)-(iv)	301(a), Div. Q	501(c)(12)(J)
109(d)(2), Div. O	457(d)(1)(B)-(D)		
111(a), Div. O	403(b)(9)(B)		

¶10,010

¶10,015 ERISA Sections to Explanation Table

ERISA Sec.	Explanation	ERISA Sec.	Explanation
3(43)	¶100	408(h)	¶515
3(44)	¶100	412(a)	¶100
103(g)	¶100	4006(a)(3)(A)(i)	¶230
104(a)(2)(A)	¶100	4006(a)(3)(A)(vii)	¶230
105(a)(2)(B)(iii)	¶210	4006(a)(3)(E)(iii)	¶230
105(a)(2)(D)	¶210	4006(a)(3)(E)(v)	¶230
303(m)	¶195	4006(a)(8)(E)	¶230
404(e)	¶220		

¶10,020 ERISA Sections Added, Amended or Repealed

The list below notes all the ERISA Sections or subsections that were added, amended or repealed by Divisions M through Q, including the SECURE Act provisions of the Further Consolidated Appropriations Act, 2020 (P.L. 116-94), enacted December 20, 2019. The first column indicates the ERISA Section added, amended or repealed, and the second column indicates the Act Section.

SECURE Act and Selected Provisions of the Further Consolidated Appropriations Act, 2020

ERISA Sec.	Act Sec.	ERISA Sec.	Act Sec.
3(2)	Div. O, Sec. 101(b)	303(m)	Div. O, Sec. 115(c)
3(16)(B)	Div. O, Sec. 101(c)(3)(A)	404(e)	Div. O, Sec. 204
3(41)	Div. O, Sec. 101(c)(3)(B)	408(h)	Div. P, Sec. 1302(a)
3(43), (44)	Div. O, Sec. 101(c)(1)	408(h)	Div. P, Sec. 1302(c)
103(a)(1)(B)	Div. O, Sec. 101(d)(1)(A)	412(a)	Div. O, Sec. 101(c)(2)
103(g)	Div. O, Sec. 101(d)(1)(B)	4006(a)(3)(A)(i)	Div. O, Sec. 206(a)(1)
104(a)(2)(A)	Div. O, Sec. 101(d)(2)	4006(a)(3)(A)(v)	Div. O, Sec. 206(a)(2)
104(a)(2)(A)	Div. O, Sec. 101(e)(1)	4006(a)(3)(A)(vi)	Div. O, Sec. 206(a)(3)
104(a)(2)(A)	Div. O, Sec. 101(e)(2)	4006(a)(3)(A)(vii)	Div. O, Sec. 206(a)(4)
105(a)(2)(B)(i)	Div. O, Sec. 203(a)(1)	4006(a)(3)(E)(iii)	Div. O, Sec. 206(b)(1)(B)
105(a)(2)(B)(ii)	Div. O, Sec. 203(a)(2)	4006(a)(3)(E)(v)	Div. O, Sec. 206(b)(1)(A)
105(a)(2)(B)(iii)	Div. O, Sec. 203(a)(3)	4006(a)(8)(A)	Div. O, Sec 206(b)(2)(B)
105(a)(2)(D)	Div. O, Sec. 203(b)	4006(a)(8)(E)	Div. O, Sec 206(b)(2)(A)
303(m)	Div. O, Sec. 115(b)		

¶10,025 Act Sections Amending ERISA Sections

SECURE Act and Selected Provisions of the Further Consolidated Appropriations Act, 2020

Act Sec.	ERISA Sec.	Act Sec.	ERISA Sec.
Div. O, Sec. 101(b)	3(2)	Div. O, Sec. 203(a)(3)	105(a)(2)(B)(iii)
Div. O, Sec. 101(c)(1)	3(43), (44)	Div. O, Sec. 203(b)	105(a)(2)(D)
Div. O, Sec. 101(c)(2)	412(a)	Div. O, Sec. 204	404(e)
Div. O, Sec. 101(c)(3)(A)	3(16)(B)	Div. O, Sec. 206(a)(1)	4006(a)(3)(A)(i)
Div. O, Sec. 101(c)(3)(B)	3(41)	Div. O, Sec. 206(a)(2)	4006(a)(3)(A)(v)
Div. O, Sec. 101(d)(1)(A)	103(a)(1)(B)	Div. O, Sec. 206(a)(3)	4006(a)(3)(A)(vi)
Div. O, Sec. 101(d)(1)(B)	103(g)	Div. O, Sec. 206(a)(4)	4006(a)(3)(A)(vii)
Div. O, Sec. 101(d)(2)	104(a)(2)(A)	Div. O, Sec. 206(b)(1)(A)	4006(a)(3)(E)(v)
Div. O, Sec. 101(e)(1)	104(a)(2)(A)	Div. O, Sec. 206(b)(1)(B)	4006(a)(3)(E)(iii)
Div. O, Sec. 101(e)(2)	104(a)(2)(A)	Div. O, Sec 206(b)(2)(A)	4006(a)(8)(E)
Div. O, Sec. 115(b)	303(m)	Div. O, Sec 206(b)(2)(B)	4006(a)(8)(A)
Div. O, Sec. 115(c)	303(m)	Div. P, Sec. 1302(a)	408(h)
Div. O, Sec. 203(a)(1)	105(a)(2)(B)(i)	Div. P, Sec. 1302(c)	408(h)
Div. O, Sec. 203(a)(2)	105(a)(2)(B)(ii)		

Topical Index

A

Automatic contribution arrangements
. safe harbor contributions
.. default maximum contribution . . . 110

Automatic enrollment
. start-up costs
.. tax credit . . . 135

B

Bipartisan American Miners Act
. funding multiemployer health plans
.. eligible employees . . . 405
.. employer bankruptcy . . . 405
.. related coal wage agreement . . . 405
.. transfer of surplus funds . . . 405
. Treasury transfers to UMWA Pension Plan
.. annual reporting requirements . . . 400
.. cap on amount of transfer . . . 400
.. compliance with rehabilitation plan . . . 400
.. critical status maintained . . . 400
.. employer contribution . . . 400
.. period of transfer . . . 400
.. withdrawal liability . . . 400

C

Cooperative and Small Employer Charity (CSEC) plans
. PBGC premiums
.. flat rate premium . . . 230
.. variable rate premium . . . 230

D

Disaster relief
. qualified disaster distributions
.. economic loss requirement . . . 175
.. hardship withdrawal, recontribution . . . 175
.. income tax applied ratably over three years . . . 175
.. limit on distribution amount . . . 175
.. loan relief . . . 175
.. qualified disaster area . . . 175
.. recontribution of distribution . . . 175
.. withholding exemption . . . 175

Disclosure requirements
. lifetime income disclosure
.. assumptions and rules . . . 210
.. fiduciary liability limitation . . . 210
.. lifetime income stream of equivalent of total benefits accrued . . . 210
.. model disclosure . . . 210

Distributions
. early distribution penalty
.. qualified disaster distribution . . . 175
. hardship withdrawal
.. recontribution following qualified disaster . . . 175
. in-service distributions
.. reduction in minimum age . . . 410
. qualified birth or adoption distributions
.. eligible adoptee . . . 160
.. eligible plans . . . 160

Distributions—continued
. qualified birth or adoption distributions—continued
.. maximum aggregate amount . . . 160
.. recontribution of distributions . . . 160

E

Establishing a plan
. adoption date
.. plan adopted by filing due date . . . 200
. start-up costs
.. automatic enrollment . . . 135
.. tax credit . . . 130

Excise taxes
. high cost coverage ("Cadillac") tax
.. repealed . . . 510
. medical device tax
.. repealed . . . 500

F

Family and medical leave
. employer credit
.. extended through 2020 . . . 520

Fiduciary liability
. lifetime income provider, selection
.. determination of financial capability of insurer . . . 220
.. guaranteed retirement income contract . . . 220
.. liability limitation . . . 220
.. lowest cost contract . . . 220
.. representation by insurer . . . 220
.. time of selection of insurer and contract . . . 220

Form 5500
. combined annual report for group of plans . . . 205
. failure to file penalty . . . 310
. multiple employer plans (MEPs) . . . 100

401(k) plans
. automatic enrollment
.. safe harbor maximum default contribution . . . 110
.. small employer tax credit . . . 135
. eligibility requirements
.. long-term part-time employees . . . 125
. loans
.. credit card loan, prohibition . . . 155
.. qualified disaster relief . . . 175
. nonelective safe harbor plan
.. notice requirement, repealed . . . 115
.. amendment deadline extended . . . 120
. required minimum distributions
.. required beginning date, increased . . . 165
... ten-year default distribution rule . . . 300

403(b) plans
. automatic enrollment
.. small employer tax credit . . . 135
. church retirement accounts
.. church-controlled organization . . . 190
.. covered employees . . . 190
. required minimum distributions
.. ten-year default distribution rule . . . 300
. termination of custodial account
.. in-kind distribution of account . . . 185

403

457(b) plans
. in-service distributions
. . reduced minimum age . . . 410
. required minimum distributions
. . ten-year default rule . . . 300

529 plans
. qualified distributions
. . qualified education loan repayments . . . 540
. . registered apprenticeship programs . . . 540
. . student loan interest . . . 540

Funding standards
. interest rate
. . frozen community newspaper plan . . . 195
. shortfall amortization
. . frozen community newspaper plan . . . 195

H

Hardship distributions
. qualified disaster
. . recontribution of distribution . . . 175

Health coverage tax credit
. expiration date extended . . . 545

Health insurance providers
. annual fee on covered entities
. . repealed . . . 505

I

Individual retirement arrangements (IRAs)
. compensation
. . non-tuition fellowship and stipend payments . . . 140
. . difficulty of care payments . . . 150
. contributions
. . maximum age limit repealed . . . 145
. required minimum distributions
. . required beginning date . . . 165
. . ten-year default rule . . . 300

In-service distributions
. minimum age
. . 457(b) plans . . . 410
. . reduced to age 59 1/2 . . . 410

L

Lifetime income
. defined . . . 180
. disclosure requirements
. . benefit statements . . . 210
. fiduciary safe harbor
. . selection of lifetime income provider . . . 220
. portability of lifetime income options
. . eligible plans . . . 180
. . lifetime income investments . . . 180
. . trustee-to-trustee transfer . . . 180

Loans from qualified plans
. credit card loans, prohibited . . . 155
. qualified disaster loan
. . increased loan limit . . . 175
. . delayed date of repayment . . . 175

M

Multiple employer plans
. Form 5500 reporting . . . 100
. "one bad apple rule" repealed . . . 100

Multiple employer plans—continued
. open MEPs . . . 100
. pooled plans . . . 100
. pooled plan provider MEP
. . required terms . . . 100
. transfer of plan assets and employer liabilities . . . 100

N

Nondiscrimination rules
. closed plans
. . cross-testing . . . 225
. . participation requirements . . . 225
. cross testing
. . aggregation with defined contribution plan on basis of benefits . . . 225
. . closed defined benefit plans . . . 225
. . make-whole contributions . . . 225
. . post-enactment amendments . . . 225
. . testing of defined contribution plan on benefits basis . . . 225

P

PBGC premiums
. Cooperative and Small Employer Charity (CSEC) plans
. . flat rate premium . . . 230
. . variable rate premium . . . 230

Penalties
. failure to file income tax return . . . 305
. failure to file required plan reports . . . 310

Plan amendments
. qualified disaster distributions . . . 175
. remedial amendment period . . . 170
. retroactive application . . . 170

Prohibited transactions
. pharmacy benefit services
. . 5-year exemption . . . 515

R

Reporting requirements
. combined annual report for group of plans . . . 205
. failure to file penalties . . . 305; 310

Required minimum distributions
. distribution date
. . eligible designated beneficiaries . . . 300
. . existing qualified annuity contract . . . 300
. stretch IRA, elimination . . . 300
. ten-year default rule . . . 300
. required beginning date, increased . . . 165

S

Safe harbor 401(k) plans
. nonelective safe harbor plans
. . extended amendment deadline . . . 120
. . notice requirement, repealed . . . 115

T

Tax credits
. plan start-up costs . . . 130
. small employer automatic enrollment credit . . . 135

Termination of plan
. 403(b) plan custodial accounts
. . in-kind distribution of account . . . 185

U

Unrelated business taxable income (UBTI)
. exempt organizations
. . nondeductible fringe benefit expenses . . . 530

V

Volunteer emergency responders
. qualified reimbursement payments
. . federal tax exclusion restored . . . 525